THE RISE AND DEMISE OF BLACK THEOLOGY

Black Theology emerged in the 1960s as a response to black consciousness. In South Africa it is a critique of power; in the UK it is a political theology of black culture. The dominant form of Black Theology has been in the USA, originally influenced by Black Power and the critique of white racism. Since then it claims to have broadened its perspective to include oppression on the grounds of race, gender and class.

In this book Alistair Kee contests this claim, especially by Womanist (black women) Theology. Black and Womanist Theologies present inadequate analyses of race and gender and no account at all of class (economic) oppression. With a few notable exceptions Black Theology in the USA repeats the mantras of the 1970s, the discourse of modernity. Content with American capitalism, it fails to address the source of the impoverishment of black Americans at home. Content with a romantic *imaginaire* of Africa, this 'African-American' movement fails to defend contemporary Africa against predatory American global ambitions.

RECLAIMING LIBERATION THEOLOGY

The Rise and Demise of Black Theology

ALISTAIR KEE
University of Edinburgh

This enlarged edition published in 2008 by SCM Press
13–17 Long Lane,
London EC1A 9PN

First published in the USA in 2006 by Ashgate Publishing Company and in the UK by Ashgate Publishing Limited.

www.scm-canterburypress.co.uk

British Library Cataloguing in Publication data

A catalogue record for this book is available from the British Library

978 0 334 04164 1

Printed in UK by
MPG Books Ltd, Bodmin, Cornwall

Contents

Foreword

I am pleased to write a foreword to this book by Alistair Kee. In *The Rise and Demise of Black Theology* he has managed to put at risk the relative calm and peaceful coexistence which exists between Black liberation theologians and white North American and European theologians. Perhaps not since the early formations of Black theology in the United States in the 1960s and 1970s has a white theologian taken on the audacious task of mounting a full-scale critique of Black theology. This is not to say that Black theology has not been the subject of critical engagement by white theologians. Theologians such as Peter C. Hodgson, Joseph C. Hough, Jr., Frederick Herzog, Benjamin Reist, Paul Lehmann and Rosemary Radford Ruether readily sought to engage in conversation with the nascent theological movement, with James Cone being the leading interlocutor. However, many others appeared to be put off by Cone's militancy and indeed heeded Cone's demand to Whites 'Keep your damn mouth closed.'[1] Criticisms by white theologians were quickly shut down. What resulted was a kind of peace that was based on what might be called a 'sphere of sovereignty'. Under sovereign spheres Black theology was produced and reproduced by black theologians for the black community. White theologians could learn from the discourse and might even enter into solidarity with the causes of Black theology such as those mentioned above (symbolic blackness), but the audacity of criticism properly belongs internally to black theologians themselves and other people of colour. Under sphere sovereignty, the critique of Black theology was protected by 'race privilege.' *The Rise and Demise of Black Theology* has unsettled that privilege.

Alistair Kee is no stranger to the role of the agent provocateur. I encountered his work first with my reading of *Marx and the Failure of Liberation Theology.* There he deployed what I take now to be his signature method of criticism. It is a mode of critique that is paradoxical or ironic, issuing in a critique of Latin American liberation theology similar to that unleashed in *The Rise and Demise of Black Theology.* With the earlier book, the scope of Kee's criticism was full scale. It covered a wide and inclusive list of Latin liberation theologians and movements and rendered an indictment as alarming then as is now his overall assessment of Black theology. It opens with a bold assertion:

> Latin American theology of liberation is widely assumed to be too Marxist: in reality it is not Marxist enough. It is frequently criticized for its unquestioned acceptance of Marx: on closer inspection there are crucial aspects of Marx's work

> which it simply ignores. In its rhetoric liberation theology submits all religion to the scrutiny of Marxist analysis: in fact it preserves its own theology as a no-go area which is beyond examination. It is in good standing with self-styled Marxists throughout the world in its denunciation of European capitalism: with friends like these it is small wonder that Marx once said prophetically, 'As for me, one thing I do know is that I am not a Marxist.' Liberation theology continually declares itself to be on the side of the oppressed: through its resistance to Marx it perpetuates an ideology of alienation.[2]

Throughout Kee maintains a paradoxical and ironic critique.

I have described Kee as an agent provocateur. Still, it is not easy to decide on just what use he makes of this curious subject position in either *Marx and the Failure of Liberation Theology* or *The Rise and Demise of Black Theology.* The image is one of an "inciting agent", which also suggests a rather sinister picture. The provocateur infiltrates a particular group positioning himself as a member of the group – let us say as a liberation theologian – only to instil his own interests on the group by secretly disrupting the group's activities from within. His mission is to directly provoke unrest within the group by producing debate or argument. The image is strained because Kee is neither Latino nor Black, nor is he a self-identified Latin or Black liberation theologian. But he is a European theologian with a great, long-term and passionate stake in liberation theology.

Immediately following his stinging indictment of Latin liberation theology, in an important self disclosure, Kee writes:

> This outburst may come as a surprise to those who think of me as a defender of the theology of liberation . . . I have continually argued for the importance of liberation theology. Its significance has now been long recognized throughout the world and Christians in very different situations have attempted to face up to its challenge. In my own work I have been critical of European theology. In *The Way of Transcendence* I challenged its metaphysical presuppositions, and in *Constantine versus Christ* I exposed its ideological subversion. Liberation theology's criticism of European theology I have therefore found particularly helpful, especially coming as it does from outside our situation. I have nothing but admiration for the moral courage and spiritual insight of liberation theologians individually, and if I criticize their work it is certainly not to protect European theology in its self-congratulatory, triumphalist and alienated forms.[3]

However, in his typically paradoxical mode of criticism, Kee reiterates its failure. Having become establishmentarian and conservative, liberation theology 'has failed the cause of the gospel of Jesus Christ in the modern world and consequently the very people it has attempted to serve.'[4] While Kee's words are alarming, it is the statement of the provocateur who demands of the theologian more analysis, not less; more social change, not complacency; more criticism, less satisfaction with the formation of a theological canon. What is at stake for liberation theology, as I read Kee, is its need to advance a critical political theology of radical engagement on behalf of the poor.

I am not surprised that almost two decades since *Marx and the Failure of Liberation Theology*, this University of Edinburgh professor of religion and political economy, this long-time admirer and critic of liberation theology, brings an equally paradoxical and ironic critique to bear on Black theology. However, if conversation is the goal of this book, such a strong indictment of Black theology is a strange way to begin the discussion. It opens with this assessment:

> Many theologies describe themselves as contextual: they arise within a certain socio-cultural context and respond to it. But frequently they are not contextual enough. Contexts change, but the theologies continue, repeating their original forms. So it is with Black Theology. Its dominant form emerged in the 1960s and 1970s, an important movement which displayed courage and creativity. By the 1990s, the context had entirely changed, but this contextual theology did not reposition itself. Far from exhibiting a new flourishing of creativity, commitment and imagination, it has been content to repeat the mantras of a previous period.[5]

Wow! Given such an opening, I have no difficulty in understanding the reaction of the Black theological academy toward Kee's book and its stinging indictment. In addition, I also imagine that a good number of white North American and European theologians along with Latin American, African, Asian, Feminists and Queer theologians, who have had long-standing interest in and sympathy with Black theology, will be shocked by Kee's overall assessment of its rise, demise, and obituary. I was myself advised by dear friends and colleagues not to contribute this, my own assessment of Kee's book, to the new edition, for fear that I should be accused of aiding and abating the enemy. However, I have resisted their advice. Although I do not share his overall assessment and judgement of where Black theology is, nevertheless I do take very seriously and agree with Kee's urging of Black theology to 'move on for the sake of the black poor.' This commitment is one of radical engagement that, for the sake of the global poor, ought never to recede into the background of our liberation projects. This is exactly what Kee fears has happened to Black theology. And from where I sit, it is a threat that needs to be taken seriously if Black theology is to expand into a global force of religious criticism.

Having followed his work for some time, I find in Kee a persistent, passionate attentiveness to the plight of the world's poor, with an emphasis on the words *world's poor*. For him, nothing is more urgently at stake in his intervention, as a European theologian, than that the black theological enterprise use all of its critical technologies to defend the cause of the wretched of the earth whose lives and deaths are entangled in the non-self-correcting machinery of a global economic capitalism, devoid of any moral directives for the maximising of the economic fulfilment of the world's poorest populations. This is Kee's continual, sustained, passionate, and ultimate concern and commitment throughout his long career. Again, in his initial assessment of Latin liberation theology Kee said:

> I am more concerned in the long term, as I have been throughout my adult life, with the pastoral and evangelical issues. Liberation theology has failed the academic community, but more importantly, it has failed the very people to whom it is committed.[6]

The failing points to all our liberation projects that fall short of adequately attending to the ever-evolving socio-economic conditions of globalisation that poison the world with mass poverty in places where liberation theology once championed God's preferential option for the poor.

Such a warning is brought to bear on Black theology. Kee astutely recognises that the context of race discourse in the 1960s to 1980s was most determinant in the advancement of Black theology. Race was the taken for granted condition for its possibility, its vibrancy, and its reproduction. But where race is greatly mitigated by market forces and the structures of global economic capitalism, Kee contends that Black theology has yet to marshal a rigorous criticism of this global menace, to deploy rigorous analysis of class and caste dynamics that fuel the disenfranchisement of the Third World poor, and to critique the technologies of political economy that keep the poor in Africa, South America, Mexico and Asia trapped in economic terror. I agree with him.

Criticizing what he sees as a stultifying positionality of contemporary Black theology, Kee asks:

> Why is this of concern to a white European male? Because the forces of oppression and exploitation are increasingly taking control of the world through the processes of global capitalism. They cannot be successfully opposed simply by progressive Europeans. It requires an alliance of men and women of good will throughout the world. In this black Americans could play a vital part, if they read the new context and move their agenda forward.[7]

The Rise and Demise of Black Theology positions Alistair Kee, the provocateur himself, within the subject position of 'interventionist.' This book foregrounds Kee's long-standing commitment to incite debate and change by his interventionist strategy. The hope of this intervention is that what will result is not only a challenge filled with frustration, perhaps disappointment, but also a renewal of a critical theology whose future will depend on its perpetual, ultimate concern for the world's poor. Such a theology will require the kind of sustained imagination, creativity, and commitment that marked the best of Black theology, which Kee sadly thinks is passing from contemporary Black theology. I, too, worry that the state of Black theology may be risking its vibrancy, robust criticism and power to intervene in the critique of global capitalism, when race continues to operate in a manner that obscures the demonic power that global economic capitalism deploys on the world's poorest communities.

I am not a self-identified Black theologian of liberation. However, like Alistair Kee, I too have devoted my academic career to reading and engaging this important intellectual movement over the past thirty-odd years. I am an African-American Philosopher of Religion in Religion, Ethics, and Politics. Still, critical engagement with this US theological movement is central to my own reflections, criticisms, and constructive proposals. What was begun by inaugurators of Black theology and sustained by three generations of black male and female theologians is a work of immense global importance. It is important for the future of religious and cultural criticism that targets class, caste, power and economic tyranny wherever they are found. Black theology has an important role to play in this ever ongoing demand of religious criticism. It has shown its creative energies best when it remains focused on its fundamental and ultimate concern for the oppressed not only at home but the world's poor.

To be sure, while many African-Americans in the United States have economically advanced, many still linger far behind. When I continue to speak to black communities about the AIDS pandemic throughout Africa, I hear many saying that: 'We got AIDS at home! We have poverty right here at home!' I hear them saying: 'Take care of home first before you give your resources to somebody else!' However, the reality is that home has changed. And we are connected by an ever-enlarging machinery of global capitalism that has not only blurred national boundaries but has also enlarged the faces at the bottom of the well into a sea of global poverty and devastation. Now is not the time for national, racial or cultural myopia.

Black theology has shown its capacity to enlarge its frames of concern from race and class to gender and now sexuality over the past thirty-odd years. It now faces the global challenge of economic tyranny by global capitalism. To meet this challenge, it will need the resources of its most talented, creative, courageous, and economically privileged members not only to speak truth to power (at home) but also to mobilise its resources in education, ministerial training, religious leadership, and economic power to engage our own nation in a discourse of repentance. Black theology is important for the development of such an African-American political theology. Repentance calls for a sort of realism that acknowledges the complicity, of citizens of the United States in the advancement of world poverty and the devastation of African states by AIDS. Repentance also calls for black theologians, African-American religious critics, philosophers, and critical theorists to use our best energies towards making concrete the demands of liberation in a world of global economic consequences. So great is the challenge; so great the demand; and so great is now the need for the vitality of Black theology. Black theology will be as vital as its interests in the suffering, survival, and resistance of oppressed people expand into global consciousness.

It is my hope that whatever frustrations, disavowals, or perhaps even anger Alistair Kee's book may incite for self-identified black theologians, as well as sympathisers, his moral challenge will not be wasted on reactionary politics but rather that creative energies will be channelled towards partnering with all who demand a critical theology of radical engagement in the critique of world poverty, global economic exploitation and the forms of human misery resulting from the our western centres of power. *The*

Rise and Demise of Black Theology is a reminder to Black liberation theologians and to all of us who make liberation of the oppressed and human fulfilment the soul of our religious criticism that, 'To whom much is given, much is required.'

Victor Anderson
Vanderbilt University

Notes

1 James H. Cone, *Black Theology: a documentary history, 1966–1979*, Orbis Books, Maryknoll, NY, 1979, p. 138.

2 Alistair Kee, *Marx and the Failure of Liberation Theology*, SCM Press, 1990, p. ix.

3 Ibid.

4 Ibid., p. x.

5 Alistair Kee, *The Rise and Demise of Black Theology*, Ashgate, 2006, p. xiii.

6 Kee, *Marx,* p. 266.

7 Kee, *Black Theology*, p. 216.

Introduction: Beyond the Mantras

Many theologies describe themselves as contextual: they arise within a certain socio-cultural context and respond to it. But frequently they are not contextual enough. Contexts change, but the theologies continue, repeating their original forms. So it is with Black theology. Its dominant form emerged in the 1960s and 1970s, an important movement which displayed courage and creativity. By the 1990s the context had entirely changed, but this contextual theology did not reposition itself. Far from exhibiting a new flourishing of creativity, commitment and imagination, it has been content to repeat the mantras of a previous period. Four mantras can be used to illustrate.

Black theology in the USA arose at the same time as Latin American liberation theology and soon adopted the terminology of liberation. Blacks in America, the descendants of slaves, took heart from the ancient Exodus when God freed the Hebrew slaves. Exodus is repeatedly alluded to as if its message is so self-evident that no exegesis is necessary. God frees slaves. But this claim is so patently false that it surely requires some explanation. This contextual theology has not noticed that the Bible is also contextual. God does not liberate slaves. God had a plan for the Hebrews and since they were slaves in Egypt, they had to be liberated. They were freed so that they could become the servants (slaves) of God. Their emancipation was so that they could take possession of the land of Canaan. To do this God commanded them to commit acts of genocide against the local people, massacring men, women and children. God does not liberate slaves. The Chosen people happened to be slaves, but God did not oppose slavery as such. In the Bible the Ten Commandments are set out in Exodus 20. The following chapter provides more detailed legislation governing the conduct of daily life. Surprisingly Exodus 21 begins with God's laws concerning the treatment of slaves. Later, slavery was the economic foundation of the Roman empire. Paul assumes it and never suggests that it is against God's will. Slavery continued in America for 250 years and is carried on in West Africa to this day. To claim that God frees slaves, *tout court*, requires some explanation.

The second mantra is the passing reference to the first sermon of Jesus in which he quotes the prophet Isaiah: 'The Spirit of the Lord is upon me, because he has anointed me to preach good news to the poor, He has sent me to proclaim release to the captives and recovering of sight to the blind, to set at liberty those who are oppressed' (Luke 4: 18). What was the context? The original context was in the sixth century BCE, when the descendants of the Jews taken into captivity in Babylon would be allowed to return to Judaea. In the context of the ministry of Jesus good news was preached to the poor and some blind men were healed. But captives were not released and those who were oppressed were not freed. Within months Jesus himself became a captive and he and his followers were oppressed. If God does not free slaves, neither does he release captives. No Christian contextual theology should make this casual assertion about emancipation. The Gospel is much more realistic and powerful than that false assurance. God condemns evil, but brings good out of that evil. The evil that men do cannot in the end defeat the purposes of God. God condemned the seizing of Jesus, but did not intervene to release the captive. But God was able to take the evil done to Jesus and make of it the corner stone of salvation. What of slavery? The paradigm is not Moses, but Joseph. God condemned the selling of Joseph to the Ishmaelites, but did not prevent him becoming a slave in Egypt (Genesis 37). God did not prevent slavery, nor end it. God does not intervene to release slaves, but God can bring good out of evil. This never justifies the evil, but God can in the end redeem it.

The third mantra is that Black theology addresses oppression caused on the basis of race, gender and class. Original Black theology did address oppression arising from race and gender, although in Chapter 6 we revisit these issues in the light of the present context. However, what is perfectly clear is that Black theology has never faced up to oppression related to the disparity of economic power. Class is a Marxist category and was widely used in Latin American liberation theology because in that subcontinent more than 80 per cent of the population were poor. If liberation theology wished to address the main source of oppression and suffering in its context it had to adopt an analysis and critique of both feudalism and capitalism, the two economic formations characteristic of that area. Black theology has wished to associate itself with liberation theology but has refused to analyse the dominant economic formation of its context, American capitalism. James Cone, the leading Black theologian in America, after writing on the subject for 35 years, has recently made this poignant confession. 'Black suffering is getting worse, not better, and we are more confused than ever about the reasons for it.'[1] What a terrible admission: not that unfortunately suffering amongst blacks is getting worse, but that Black theology has not even yet begun to address the reasons for it.

A fourth mantra is the repetition of the uncontested claim by W.E.B. Du Bois that 'the problem of the Twentieth Century is the problem of the color-line'.[2] Du Bois was writing in 1903, but century-old prophecies have one thing in common, they are disproved by events. The most important line of the twentieth century was the telephone line, which in its metamorphosis into the coaxial cable has become the basis for the development of global capitalism, the most powerful economic – and ideological – system the world has ever known. A few months ago I visited Bangalore, Tamil Nadu, the most rapidly developing commercial centre in the Indian subcontinent (and beyond). The expansion of office blocks and apartment buildings is unrelenting as global capitalism seeks an advantage in moving jobs from (white) Europe and America to the (non-white) third world. Race is not a problem for capitalism: it will not allow such a non-economic factor to hinder its expansion.

This book therefore traces the rise and demise of Black theology. Black theologians are reluctant to criticise each other. One of the few Black theologians who is trying to move the agenda on is Victor Anderson. Black theology, however, is determined not to learn from him, even as it has refused to come to terms with the work of Cornel West, the most sophisticated critical resource available to Black theology. Those who oppose Black theology, for various reasons, religious, cultural or economic, do not necessarily wish to see it come to an end. It would suit their purposes equally well if Black theology simply repeated itself, losing touch with a changing reality. The opponents of Black theology would like to see it become not a theology about race, but a racial theology. They would like to see a theology of the ghetto become a ghetto for theology. However, the issue at the end of the day is not the future of Black theology, but the fate of the black poor in the present context and Black theology is not addressing this gospel call.

My reasons for writing this book are to call on Black theologians to move on, for the sake of the black poor. First of all for the sake of poor blacks in the USA. They are not interested in Black theology, nor are the Black churches. In the present context the issue is the suffering of poor black people which no longer arises predominantly from race but from the inherent inequities of American capitalism. They need not a mantra condemning poverty, but a serious analysis and a programme to counter the injustice. Second, for the sake of the black poor in Africa. Black theology has allowed itself the luxury of idealising an *imaginaire*. Whether in ancient African societies individuals only existed in community, whether women ever had power in the local market, whether children were valued, whether religion was unitary, whether or not these things used to be the case we must look to the present context of Africa, the context which we see every day on TV news programmes and read about in the international press. The context is no longer European racism and colonialism. Contemporary Africa is ravaged by civil wars in which men are being brutalised, women are being raped, children are having limbs amputated, dictators are preventing development, and corruption is the name for the system of local and national government. It is time for those who call themselves African-American to address what Tony Blair has described as 'Africa, the scar on the conscience of the world'. The black poor in America, the black poor in Africa. But third, this is no longer about race, and in any case 'race' cannot be restricted to African-Americans. In the previous context blacks were seen as African captives within America. But the context has changed. First, they are beneficiaries. The rising black middle class have done very well in recent years. Good luck to them, but as far as the third world is concerned they have now become part of the problem. They now assume a commonality of interest with whites when US companies strike deals with corrupt foreign regimes or decimate the environment of desperately poor communities. Blacks in America are no longer the victims. But second, they are friends at court. They are American citizens, voters and consumers who should be able to influence America's relationships with the rest of the world. Is it not possible that 35 million African-Americans could change American policies towards Africa in particular and the third world in general? This book does not argue that black theologians should give up, but that they should move on, for the sake of the black poor of America, Africa and the third world.

Their failure to do so is a cause for concern beyond the circle of practitioners of Black theology and it should not be surprising therefore to learn that the author of this book is what blacks would categorise (essentialise) as a white European. The future or fate of Black theology is a legitimate concern for those outside its guild.

Notes

1 James H. Cone, 'Calling the Oppressors to Account: God and black suffering' in Linda E. Thomas (ed.) *Living Stones in the Household of God: the legacy and future of Black Theology*, Fortress Press, Minneapolis, 2004, p. 10.

2 W.E.B. Du Bois, *The Souls of Black Folk*, Dover Publications, New York, 1944 (1903), p. v.

CHAPTER 1

Assimilation and Alienation: Double Consciousness

Negritude

In 1976 two old friends greeted each other. They had first met in Paris in 1931 as students, one from Senegal in West Africa, the other from the Caribbean island of Martinique. In the meantime Léopold Sédar Senghor had become president of his country, and now he was visiting Aimé Césaire, mayor of Fort-de-France, Martinique. They had both contributed to the revolution in black consciousness which had swept around the world. Césaire recalled their early meeting. 'For us, it was not a question of metaphysics, but of a life to live, an ethic to create, and communities to save. We tried to answer that question. In the end, our answer was Negritude.' [1] In this case the word itself tells a story. It is negritude, not blackness, for they both grew up in French colonies. But it is *nègre*, not *noir*, for they were in dialogue with Americans who called themselves Negroes. The formation of black consciousness has led to a preference for the term black instead of Negro, but all of the early writers on the subject use the term Negro, and we shall do so to avoid anachronism. Negritude was many things, but for Césaire it was a philosophy of life, a system of justice and equity, a cause to which he was committed – the resurrection of black men. (This non-inclusive language is used here because at that time it was used by black men – and black women – and because as we shall see, it was eventually challenged by women.)

The development of negritude as an ideology is associated with Senghor. He was born in Joal, a small coastal town in the French West African territory of Senegal in 1906. As an able student he was subject to the French colonial policy of assimilation. 'Assimilation had both a political and a social and cultural dimension. In essence, it aimed toward a future when the colony would become an integral part of metropolitan France. The African peoples of Senegal were to become as much like Frenchmen as possible, in language, manners, and political orientation.' [2] The policy reflected assumptions which were at once liberal and chauvinist – the equality of all men, and the superiority of French culture. In a predominantly Muslim country Senghor's family were Christian, and he himself wished to become a Catholic priest. However, at the seminary in the capital, Dakar, he encountered the attitude that Africa had no traditions or culture worth preserving. Soon after protesting that Africans had their own civilisation, he was told by Father Lalouse that he would not be allowed to be a priest. Senghor was devastated by this decision, yet reflecting on the outcome some years later he could see that when one career was closed off to him, another opened up that was more significant. As a priest in Senegal he would not have developed the philosophy of negritude. The bitter experience was indeed part of that learning process. 'I owe to him not the word negritude ... but the idea.'[3] He continued to be a devout Catholic, he aspired to be a true Frenchman, but already he was experiencing the tension of living in two worlds. He continued his education in Dakar, and in 1928 was the first black student to receive a scholarship to study in France.

It was in Paris that he began to experience the contradictions of the policy of assimilation. On arrival in France he had answered an immigration question by asserting, of course, that he was French. In reality he discovered in Paris that he was not treated as if he were French. But where did that leave him? An existential rather than a metaphysical question. As he enrolled at the Sorbonne to study literature he met Aimé Césaire. It was in dialogue with him over the next few years that Senghor finally formulated his philosophy of life, negritude. The term was coined by Césaire, appearing for the first time in a journal in which they were both involved, *L'Etudian Noir*. Senghor readily admitted his debt and was always willing 'to render to Césaire what is Césaire's'.[4]

In reality Senghor and Césaire were stimulated by the environment in which they found themselves in the Latin Quarter of the city. There are three sources of negritude: the New Negro, of the Harlem Renaissance; West Indians, especially from Martinique; and a small number of Africans. Black Americans do not have the historical or cultural associations with Europe that white Americans do, especially those from old New England families. But at the end of the nineteenth century there emerged the beginnings of a new Negro culture. Some of these writers converged in Paris, notably W.E.B. Du Bois whose *The Souls of Black Folk*, published in 1903, opens with the analysis of a particular experience. The experience was precisely that which we observed in the young Senghor, but the subtlety of the analysis is beyond anything of which he was then capable.

> It is a peculiar sensation, this double consciousness, this sense of always looking at one's self through the eyes of others, of measuring one's soul by the tape of a world that looks on in amused contempt and pity. One ever feels his two-ness – an American, a Negro; two souls, two thoughts, two unreconciled strivings; two warring ideals in one dark body, whose dogged strength alone keeps it from being torn asunder.[5]

Du Bois attended the first Pan-African Congress in Paris in 1919. In 1921 René Maran, the Martinique writer, published his prize-winning novel *Batouala*, which included a devastating criticism of the French administration in the colonies. Many years later Senghor wrote a memorial essay entitled 'René Maran: precursor of Negritude'. In 1925 there appeared *The New Negro*, an anthology-manifesto. Senghor was particular influenced by the contribution of Alain Locke, a black professor of philosophy at Howard University. Locke was a frequent visitor to the salon of the Martinique writer Paulette Nardal and it was there that Senghor met him, and also at the house of René Maran. Senghor was also impressed by Claude

MacKay, the Jamaican writer and author of *Banjo*, who claimed that 'to plunge to the roots of our race and to build on our own foundations is not returning to a state of savagery'. [6] Senghor was to declare that 'Claude MacKay can be considered ... as the veritable inventor of negritude ... not of the word ... but of the value of negritude.'[7] And so at last count the originators of negritude are Senghor, Lalouse, Césaire, Du Bois, Maran and MacKay.

What is clear is that at this stage the important axis was West Indians and black Americans, a dialogue promoted through the French/English *Revue du Monde Noir*. A significant contribution was the essay by Paulette Nardal which appeared in 1932. Hymans declares that 'this document constitutes tangible evidence of the moment when American Negro ideas first infiltrated to French-speaking Negroes, thus starting the chain of events leading to the theory of negritude'.[8] (Perhaps Paulette Nardal deserves to be added to the list of originators.) Through their contacts in Paris both groups came to recognise that they belonged together. Both had a history in slavery, of being deprived of their own culture, language and identity. But there was also a significant difference. The West Indians had been provided with a French culture, language and identity, while in America blacks had been despised, discriminated against and prevented from entering the mainstream. It is significant that at that time West Indians did not associate themselves with Africa, which they viewed as being primitive. Franz Fanon, whom we shall meet soon, makes some shrewd observations about the relations of Europeans, West Indians and Africans, relations which we shall encounter in other contexts later in this chapter.

> We may say that the West Indian, not satisfied to be superior to the African, despised him, and while the white man could allow himself certain liberties with the native, the West Indian absolutely could not. This is because, between whites and Africans, there was no need of a reminder: the difference stared one in the face. But what a catastrophe if the West Indian should suddenly be taken for an African![9]

Whether Paulette Nardal shared the view, she does not include Africans as she envisages a future for black people which acknowledges a debt to white civilisation.

> We are fully conscious of our debts to the Latin culture and we have no intention of discarding it in order to promote I know not what return to ignorance. Without it, we would have never become conscious of our real selves. But we want to go beyond this culture in order to give our brethren, with the help of white scientists and friends of the Negroes, the pride of being the members of a race which is perhaps the oldest in the world. Once they become aware of their past history, they will no longer despair of the future of their own race, part of which seems, at the present time, to be slow in developing. They will give to their slower brothers a helping hand and try to understand and love them better.[10]

Nardal assures us that this project does not involve a 'return to ignorance', a sentiment which echoes our earlier quotation from Claude MacKay that to return to black foundations 'is not returning to a state of savagery'. Neither exhibits that romantic longing for Africa which has so characterised the writings of black Americans. Senghor saw a deeper significance in this attitude. Afro-American poets, he thought, 'have a completely romantic idea of Africa: it is a refuge from the ugliness and inhumanity of the American world; it is a bath of primitive life cleaning away the sophistication of white culture'.[11] However, Nardal in particular seems to view Africans as at a previous stage, unable to catch up. But if this was a widespread prejudice, it was challenged by the presence in their midst of a small number of Africans living at a very different level of culture and consciousness. To the axis for the future Senghor contributed that which neither of the other two groups possessed, a past. As Vaillant notes, 'the Africans gave West Indians something they had lacked, a sense that it was possible for black men to have a world of their own'.[12] Blacks need not begin with French or English, with European civilisation or the American way of life. They had behind them a very different history, with its own values, its own art, social relations and political structures. Nor was this simply antique, antiquarian voyeurism: influences ran both ways. Jane Nardal was drawn to Surrealism and its disenchantment with the rationality of European life; Picasso, Matisse, Modigliani were influenced by the freshness and power of African art.

The perspectives of the three groupings therefore came together in Senghor's conception of negritude. Its first stirrings were in his defence of African civilisation against the insistence in the Libermann Seminary that only French culture was of value. His horizons were expanded by his encounter with West Indians and then Americans. Negritude is therefore a philosophy for those who return, not for those who have never left home, who have never known anything else. It is a philosophy for those who have been encouraged to betray their heritage. When Senghor first visited the grave of his father, he composed the poem 'The Return of the Prodigal Son'. Here indeed was a young man who had wasted the substance of his inheritance, who had gone into a far country in forgetfulness of his duty towards his ancestors. In 1937 he delivered an important speech in Dakar, advocating an education system which supplemented French with African traditional languages and culture. This developing position was not without its own contradictions. He advocated a return to African culture – in French. His audience were fellow prodigals. Twenty years later he was to address the Black Artists and Writers conference in Rome on 'The Constituent Elements of a Civilization of Black African Inspiration', in which he expounded black personality as it is related to 'environment, psychology, ontology and religion, society, property and work, ethics, and art'.[13] Ironically he was encouraged to write on these themes because of his detailed studies of African ethnology carried out by European scholars such as Delafosse, Frobenius and Delavignette.

As it developed negritude took several different forms: 'the aggressive negritude clamouring for recognition of African values; the conciliatory negritude advocating cultural miscegenation or cross-breeding; and an inventive negritude tending towards a new humanism'.[14] What began as a schoolboy intuition about culture ended as the ideology of a political leader. Vaillant traces the path.

> He defined negritude as the sum total of the qualities possessed by all black men everywhere. As his thinking focussed more and more on this concept, he moved away from the realm of fact and individual experience into the realm of abstraction. By the time he had matured as a politician, he had the concept of negritude ready to serve as the keystone of an ideology, designed to describe a new vision of the black man's place in the world.[15]

It was in the political sphere that the ideology attracted criticism, from whites of course, but also from blacks. It developed during a time when fascism was a potent force in Europe: a black shirt was more than a fashion statement in Germany, France, Spain, Portugal and Italy. Spleth suggests that Senghor's own name as a modification of *senhor* may point to some historical connections with the Portugese. But it was his concentration on race which dismayed his critics, many of them Marxists. Sartre wrote a preface to Senghor's anthology of new black poetry. 'Black Orpheus' was how he described negritude's descent into inner being. More ominously Sartre saw in it 'an anti-racist racism'.[16] But Senghor himself recognised the weakness of his early position (abandoned by 1935).

> Our distrust of European values quickly turned into disdain – why hide it – into racism. We thought – and we said – that we Negroes were the salt of the earth, that we were the bearers of an unheard message – and that no other race could offer it but us. Unconsciously, by osmosis and reaction at the same time, we spoke like Hitler and the Colonialists, we advocated the virtues of the blood.[17]

This is hardly surprising, according to Hymans, because of a common ancestry: 'both negritude and Nazism were part of an anti-rational intellectual tradition'.[18]

There were also Marxist criticisms of Senghor's negritude. Markovitz provides a significantly different list of its manifestations:

> a critique of imperialism; a revolutionary African development distinguished from the proletarian revolt; the birth of a new black civilization; a philosophy of life; an ideology for African unity; a methodology for development; a justification for rule by indigenous elites; a defence of the dignity of cultured blacks.[19]

Negritude on this account reflects the experience of the privileged *asimilados* and seeks to further their interests. It displays no concern for the needs of the poor and exploited. It is a row-over, not a revolution; a domestic tiff between the French and the wanna-be French. From Africa itself came the criticism that negritude was based on race and not class divisions. It therefore disguised the fact that West Indians and American blacks were not in the same situation; it divided blacks from the white proletariat.[20] One of the most strident criticisms came from the South African exile Ezekiel Mphahlele who claimed that the poetry of Senghor falsifies Africa. Its romanticism and antiquarianism leaves the lives of the peasants unchanged. 'An image of Africa that only glorifies our ancestors and celebrates our "purity" and "innocence" is an image of a continent lying in state.'[21] This introduces an important theme to which we shall return in subsequent chapters: there is no way forward which declines to admit that the poor and the exploited are themselves far from perfect. Mphahlele does not fail to make this point, indeed insists upon it in a long passage in which he thrashes about like a man who is far from ready to lie down and be immortalised.

> What I do not accept is the way in which too much of the poetry inspired by it romanticizes Africa – as a symbol of innocence, purity and artless primitiveness. I feel insulted when some people imply that Africa is not also a violent continent. I am a violent person, and proud of it because it is often a healthy human state of mind; someday I'm going to plunder, rape, set things on fire; I'm going to cut someone's throat; I'm going to subvert a government; I'm going to organize a *coup d'état*; yes, I'm going to oppress my own people; I'm going to hunt down the rich, fat black men who bully the small, weak black men and destroy them; I'm going to become a capitalist, and woe to all who cross my path or who want to be my servants or chauffeurs and so on; I'm going to lead a breakaway church – there is money in it; I'm going to attack the black bourgeoisie while I cultivate a garden, rear dogs and parrots; listen to jazz and classics; read 'culture' and so on. Yes, I'm also going to organize a strike. Don't you know that sometimes I kill to the rhythm of drums and cut the sinews of a baby to cure it of paralysis?[22]

This passage focuses attention on violence. Not whether Mphahlele is a violent man; not whether Africa is an inherently violent continent; but the place which violence should occupy in negritude. If an analysis of Africa without violence offers no hope to the poor, what is the connection between violence and liberation? How should negritude include violence, the exercise of violence, the preparedness to use violence, the *right* to violence? This dimension is added to the ideology by the Martiniquans, Aimé Césaire and Franz Fanon.

There is one final point that might be added. Senghor distinguishes two types of society, the African and the European, the black and the white. Vaillant lists the features of both. The black African uses 'all his senses, intuitive reason and empathy to understand the world and to create communities that nurture the development of human personality. The African values the emotional and spiritual aspects of life that bind him to the community, and seeks through poetry and art to enshrine them.'[23] In contrast there is the white European

> who searches restlessly for material power and individual autonomy. The European seeks to develop his individual distinctiveness, and to escape from community and any obligation it might impose on him. His society is bound together only by formal law, regulation, and force, and has become a society in which each person jostles the other in his struggle for private material success. The Europeans have created a civilization of great technical and material power, but it has been bought at the price of an emotional and spiritual impoverishment.[24]

This representation of African life is reminiscent of romantic feminism, as is the characterisation and implied condemnation of European man. In reality it is not a 'return' to innocence, it is a characterisation of life which is independent of gender and race. The contrast lies rather in the economic formation of society. It is the life in turn of pre-industrial and industrial society. Senghor thought it was possible to reconcile these two types of society in what he called a 'new planetary civilization'.[25] He was critical of both the Soviet Union and the USA. 'We stand for a middle course, for a democratic socialism, which goes so far as to integrate spiritual values, a socialism which ties in with the old ethical current of the French socialists.'[26] He rejected Marxism in its scientific form, as can be seen in his ahistorical aspiration to combine primitive African communalism and modern industrial socialism. It is at this point that negritude is exposed in its incoherence. African peasants in pre-industrial societies cannot simply bolt on to the socialism of a post-capitalist society. Alternatively, *déraciné* blacks in America have no way back to the lives or consciousness of their ancestors – nor is this an aspiration. They are Americans, which means that their present culture is formed by capitalism. Blacks throughout the world live in a variety of economic systems and their potential as well as their problems vary accordingly. Senghor's dream of a 'new planetary civilization' lacks historical foundation. However, we must now continue with our examination of the relationship between violence and liberation within negritude, turning first to Senghor's lifelong friend Aimé Césaire.

Césaire was born in 1913 in Martinque. He grew up in poverty. He recalls the house 'in a very narrow street smelling very bad, a tiny house which within its entrails of rotten wood shelters rats by the dozen and the gale of my six brothers and sisters'.[27] His father seems to have been a very troubled man, his mother the provider. Césaire recalls her working far into the night: 'the Singer which my mother pedals, pedals for our hunger night and day'. (When I was a schoolboy I worked each summer in the Singer Sewing Machine factory in Clydebank. Wherever I have lived or visited in the third world I have always been particularly interested in the universal presence of this machine, especially in its treadle form. I should like to encourage some young graduate student to write about its place in the social history of the world.) This was the life which lay ahead of him, until in 1931 he won a scholarship to study in France. But then we already knew that. It was on his arrival in Paris that he met Sédar Senghor. Like Senghor he was a product of assimilation, that process by which he was encouraged to transfer his loyalty from his own people and their culture, to France and its culture. For Césaire the process was never completed and the strain caused a breakdown. The project of developing what eventually became known as negritude was therefore a personal matter. In 1939 he planned to go back to Martinique. A very natural thing to do, indeed exactly what was expected under assimilation.

Return to My Native Land was written in a few weeks prior to making the journey. Indeed the narrative-poem itself traces a journey, the three phases of his life. He is apprehensive about the return. Assimilation had succeeded in alienating him from his home, from 'this disowning town'. How can he return to a land of disease, ignorance, prejudice, stupidity, squalor, poverty, meanness; mix with the crowd which rejects everything 'affirmative or free'; associate with the crowd so unpredictable and inhuman, 'this crowd like a woman whose lyrical walk you have noticed but who suddenly calls upon a hypothetical rain and commands it not to fall; or makes the sign of the cross without visible reason; or assumes the sudden grave animality of a peasant women urinating on her feet, stiff legs apart'. Assimilation has inspired in him feelings of disgust for his own people and the life which would have been his. Life! Such a life is more like death, 'this death without sense or piety, this death where there is no majesty'. And yet the socialisation process was not complete: he was not entirely assimilated to France. And here is the irony, that it was by going to France that he learned what had been done to him. The return is not as the leaving. Something has happened to him which the Bible would called repentance, *metanoia*, a change of mind, a change of consciousness. 'As a result of an unforeseen happy conversion I now respect my repellent ugliness.' That conversion is negritude. The ugliness is there, but it belongs not to his people, but to what has been done to them. 'I have wandered far and I am coming back to the lonely ugliness of your wounds.' What disgusts him is the result of a ferocious attack. He recalls its origins, on the slave ships: the sights, the sounds, the smells. 'For centuries this country repeated that we are brute beasts; that the human heart-beat stops at the gates of the black world.' They were wounded in their minds as well as their bodies: 'for centuries Europe has stuffed us with lies and crammed us with plague'.

It is at this point that Césaire departs from Senghor. They have been stolen from Africa. They have lost their old life and culture, but the new life was no life at all. He cannot follow Senghor and advocate a joining of the native culture to that of France. Senghor's problem was the problem of privilege. Only the *asimilados* suffered from double consciousness. The majority of the population preserved their traditional culture. Césaire cannot recommend that the native population continue as before. No, they must be freed from their inhuman life. Césaire returns to advocate a new life in Martinique. His return is not to the life of his childhood: he would not wish that on anyone. He returns to call the people to something they have never had. 'My mouth shall be the mouth of misfortunes which have no mouth, my voice the freedom of those freedoms which break down in the prison-cell of despair.' Senghor could call for a return to the life of the people. It is this presumption of innocence which others, even in Africa – especially in Africa – found so objectionable. For Césaire something has to be *done*, not said. It is at this point that for the first time he uses the term *negritude*. And more interesting than the term is the new context in which it occurs. He refers to Haiti, 'where negritude rose to its feet for the first time and said it believed in its own humanity'. Why Haiti? I assume it is a historical reference to slavery. Three years after the French Revolution slavery was abolished in the French colonies. But Napoleon reinstated it, or at least attempted to do so. It was restored in Martinique, but not in Haiti where the resistance was led by a black nationalist Toussaint Louverture. Napoleon was later to have him arrested. Césaire recalls this sequence. 'This man is mine/ a man alone, imprisoned by/ whiteness/ a man alone defying the white cries of a white death.' Haiti was free of slavery not because of the French, but because the Haitians acted as free men. And that is negritude. Not the negritude of Senghor, but the negritude of Césaire. This negritude first appeared in Haiti because the people *acted*. They rose up. It was more than rebellion, it was assertion. Haitian negritude 'believed in its own humanity'. Césaire will return to his own people and speak for them, but this must not be a substitute for their own action: 'beware above all of crossing your arms and assuming the sterile attitude of the spectator, because life is not a spectacle, because a sea of sorrows is not a proscenium, because a man who cries out is not a dancing bear'.

From Senghor, Césaire gained knowledge of Africa and its great civilisations. He 'adored the Zambezi' and refers to 'my Bantu ugliness' as if he shared the features of the people of Central Africa. It is one thing for Senghor to look back to Senegal with pride, but that is not the inheritance of Martinique. 'No, we have never been amazons at the court of the King of Dahomey, nor princes of Ghana with eight hundred camels, nor doctors at Timbuctoo when Askia the Great was king, nor architects at Djenné, nor Madhis, nor warriors.' No, they were 'undistinguished dishwashers, small-time shoeshines'. Césaire does not have the history on which to build the new culture, the new society. He is not ready for Senghor's project of 'a new universal civilization'. His people cannot yet make their contribution, since they are 'those who invented neither gunpower nor compass ... those who were domesticated and christianized'. And yet they are those 'without whom the earth would not be the earth'. Their first step is not to bring together two cultures, one unworthy and one problematic, but to act decisively, to free themselves from Europe, 'the castrator of negroes'. 'What can I do?/ I must begin./ Begin what? The only thing in the world that's worth beginning:/The End of the World, no less.'

Senghor was no revolutionary; Césaire's revolution begins where all revolutions must begin, in the mind. He refers disparagingly to the corrupted natives as 'niggers'. What is required is the death of the nigger, the good nigger. 'To be a good nigger he must believe honestly in his unworthiness and never feel any perverse curiosity to check those fateful hieroglyphics.' The new consciousness must lead to decisive action: 'the sitting-down niggers/ unexpectedly on their feet'. Césaire avoids the innocence and the romanticism of Senghor. He also addresses his particular situation, avoiding universal platitudes. But there is one issue he must yet address, and that is the most important of all so far as the outcome is concerned. Decisive action will be met with a powerful reaction. The colonial power, no more than the pharaoh of old, will not let slaves go free on request.

In 1906 a natural disaster overtook Martinique, a disaster of such proportions as to enter into the psyche of the people. Mount Pelé erupted, killing all 6000 inhabitants of Saint-Pierre (except for one man, legend has it – who had been sentenced to death). By the time Césaire was an adult that scene of destruction and devastation had become a fertile land on which new crops could be grown. This was to be a powerful metaphor. When the native rises to his feet and in the exercise of violence destroys the old, inhuman and unworthy world in which he has been forced to exist, then the land is renewed – and so is he. As Césaire contemplated the return to his native land the time had come: 'at the end of the small hours ... the volcanoes will erupt'. For a more extensive analysis of the relationship between liberation and violence we must turn to Césaire's younger contemporary, Franz Fanon. There is, however, one final point which must be mentioned. After such a history of violence, repression, cruelty and humiliation it would be the most natural thing in the world for the native to be motivated by hatred. Natural yes, if the revolution is to be about property, control, displacement. But if he allows hatred to be his guide then he is still the creature of his tormentor. If motivated by hatred he will never be free. When the sitting native stands up it must be for himself, to assert his freedom, his right to act, his human right – his right to be human. Césaire is poised to act: 'the time has come to gird my loins like a man of courage, but at the execution let my heart preserve me from all hate, do not make of me that man of hate for whom I have only hate'. Now when the moment has come he realises that he is not just as good as the European, but better: Europe in its actions has dehumanised the natives, but has degraded itself. 'Listen to the white world, appallingly weary from its immense effort.' What would be the point of hating such a pathetic spent force. 'Pity for our conquerors, all-knowing and naïve!'

It is remarkable that Martinique, a small island with a population of less than 400 000 should produce two such powerful contributors to the development of negritude. Or rather it was France which produced Franz Fanon, for he too was the product of assimilation. Born in 1925, twelve years younger than Césaire, he also was educated first in Martinique and then in France. But his experience was significantly different. In 1944 he volunteered to serve in the French army. Africans served in their own regiments, but 'West Indians were proud to serve in European units.'[28] Thus he demonstrated his commitment to France. After the war he studied medicine in Lyon, going on to qualify in psychiatry in 1951. Indeed assimilation seemed to be complete when in 1953 he married a white woman, the highest aspiration of the mulatto. The culmination of this success story came later that year with his appointment as head of the Psychiatric Department in the hospital in Blida, some 40 kilometres south of Algiers. Algeria at that time was a French colony, but beginning to feel the first stirrings of that wind of change which was soon to sweep away colonialism in Africa. The rebellion began in 1954. Fanon first of all observed it, then participated in it. He did not need to return to his native land to discover what had been done to him, indeed he began to see through assimilation even when he was a medical student.

Like Césaire before him, living in France forced him to confront his situation. 'However painful it may be for me to accept this conclusion, I am obliged to state it: for the black man there is only one destiny. And it is white.'[29] The betrayal, the falsehood, the eventual despair of this situation is summed up in the title of his first book, published in French in 1952 and translated as *Black Skin/White Masks*. In the Antilles the process begins in the cradle, when a mother sings French love songs which include no Negroes. It continues in childhood. 'When I disobey, when I make too much noise, I am told to "stop acting like a nigger".'[30] In the home no middle-class person ever speaks Creole, except to the servants. When contemplating marriage a woman will look to marry the least black of men, a man will aspire to marry a white woman. Fanon knows Negroes of the Antilles 'who are annoyed when they are suspected of being Sengalese'.[31] And with this we come to the heart of the matter, and to a new element in negritude. They are 'suspected of being Sengalese', more generally suspected of being African. Does it not sound like an offence of which they might be accused? Worse than that does it not sound like a disease from which they suffer? Are they not, like lepers, *carriers* of a virus which could spread to the population around them and destroy the very fabric of life itself? Not for the first time we see a psychiatrist offering a medical diagnosis of a social ill. In *Black Skin/White Masks* young Dr Fanon provides us with 'an attempt at a psycho-pathological and philosophical explanation of the *state of being* a Negro.'[32] A telling phrase: 'the state of being a Negro'. Being a Negro is a nervous condition from which he needs to be cured. Of course this depends on using the term 'Negro' in a particular way. It is not a simple designation of race. No, Fanon has in mind the Negro who is the creation of the white man.[33] 'The black man has two dimensions. One with his fellows, the other with the white man. A Negro behaves differently with a white man and with another Negro. That this self-division is a direct result of colonialist subjugation is beyond question.'[34] With all due respect to Fanon, we might say that the situation is much worse than this, for he gives the impression that in the presence of the coloniser the black man acts out the role of the Negro, with the full range of embarrassing ticks and linguistic mistakes. But Dr Fanon knows that this nervous condition reaches into the unconscious: the black man is a Negro even in his solitude, through the ever present judgement of the ever absent master. The self-understanding of what it is to be a Negro is provided by the coloniser: it is like a uniform which goes with the job. 'Willy-nilly, the Negro has to wear the livery that the white man has sewed for him.'[35] It is in this context that being a Negro is a state of being, or in Dr Fanon's view, a nervous condition. 'I believe that the fact of the juxtaposition of the white and black races has created a massive psycho-existential complex. I hope by analysing it to destroy it.'[36] So writes the early Fanon. He has removed his own mask and looks in the mirror with interest and with realism. However, we know that a diagnosis is not a cure: an interpretation of the world changes nothing. This liberal, optimistic position which he developed in France was to be overtaken by the harsh reality of the French–Algerian war.

This liberal view of the early Fanon continued as he took up his appointment and can be seen his in discussions with Muslim friends. 'But we diverged on the question of the "rebellion". For my part, I considered it understandable, like an excess made possible by the excess of colonialism, but I refused to accept the validity of violence.'[37] By the following year he began to accept that nothing could be changed unless Algeria became independent. Interestingly he could see that there were different possible forms of independence. He was to be drawn towards a socialist state, and certainly not 'a theocratic, feudal, Moslem state that frowned on foreigners'.[38] In 1958 he resigned from the hospital and joined the FLN, the revolutionary army. *A Dying Colonialism* was published in 1959 and contains his observations about the effects of the war. If colonialism was dehumanising, it was as nothing compared to the brutality of the war itself. Dr Fanon treated patients from both sides and makes observations about the effects of atrocities committed by the army and acts of terrorism perpetrated by the guerrillas. He clearly sees the war not simply as a means to an end, but as an important process. 'In a war of liberation, the colonized people must win, but they must do so cleanly, without "barbarity".'[39] He understands the feelings of the Algerian *maquis* but will not excuse them: 'we condemn, with pain in our hearts, those brothers'.[40] The war is not only to liberate the country, but to liberate the people. If they mirror the ways and values of the oppressor how are they thereby made free? This theme of the war as a process of liberation is continued in his observation of the social effects of the war. At first sight he seems to involve himself in contradiction.

Although coming from the Antilles, he now writes 'what we Algerians want'.[41] He shows solidarity with them in the struggle. Even so our credibility is stretched when he defends their traditional way of life. He grew up in the Creole culture of the French West Indies: they are Arabs living in a Muslim culture. But more than that, he is the product of a modern medical school, who has bought into the European scientific world view. He defends the traditional institutions and relationships, yet he is a socialist who is therefore committed to the rationalisation and modernisation of social life at all levels. There is a perspective from which these seeming contradictions can be resolved. As already noted, the war is a process and not a means. Liberation could not be achieved by, for example, the employment of foreign mercenaries who would defeat and expel the French. No, the execution of the war is the process by which the people themselves are liberated. Take, for example, relations between fathers and sons. In the struggle the son, who might become the commander of a local unit, must now take responsibility for the people in his area, even if this runs counter to the traditional protocols. The younger brother might be promoted above the older brother. Fanon approves of this rationalising and modernising: it prepares for socialism. It is a subtle but real distinction. Much of the traditional way of life must go, deserves to go – but it must be overcome by the people themselves. They must be involved in a process which liberates them from the restrictions of the past. What must be resisted is the attempt of the colonial power to sweep away the tradition. In that case they would not be liberated by the sweeping away of the tradition. To the contrary, they would only find themselves further subject to foreign control, more dependent on those who manipulate their lives. This distinction is well illustrated in what at first sight seems an unlikely subject, the veil. Fanon defends the wearing of the veil by women in this traditional Muslim society. He rehearses the familiar arguments, but it is still difficult to believe that he shares the patriarchal values which maintain the practice. Come now, Dr Fanon, surely you would be happy to see this whole system dismantled. But what is at stake is not the wearing of the veil, but who decides and for what ends. The French decided that unveiling of women would de-stabilise society and thereby weaken resistance. As early as the 1950s they therefore adopted some feminist arguments (Simone de Beauvoir's *The Second Sex* was published in 1948) so that the policy could be presented not as anti-Algerian but as pro-women.

> The dominant administration solemnly undertook to defend this woman, pictured as humiliated, sequestered, cloistered ... It described the immense possibilities of woman, unfortunately transformed by the Algerian man into an inert, demonetized, indeed dehumanized object.[42]

Ironically, I expect that Fanon actually believed this description to be accurate. In a later work he writes of the danger 'of perpetuating the feudal tradition which holds sacred the superiority of the masculine element over the feminine'.[43] He goes on to describe how young women set aside the veil when they joined in the struggle. They set aside the veil when they carried hand grenades in their handbags into the European quarter of the city. They unveiled themselves when they acted as couriers for the *maquis*. And that is precisely the point. They unveiled themselves. They liberated themselves in the process. They were not unveiled by others to further the interests of the colonial regime. As a socialist Fanon was not committed to the maintenance of the traditional pre-modern structures, but he was committed to the process by which the people liberated themselves from their own past. As Caute observes, 'he rejected the narrow empirical view that a good thing given has the same meaning as a good thing seized and taken'.[44] Liberation is not received, it is taken, asserted, affirmed. This leads us to the most important element which Fanon contributed to the development of negritude, the necessity of violence. It is the prominent theme of the last book which Fanon was to see published. *The Wretched of the Earth* appeared in 1961 a few weeks before he died of leukaemia in a Washington hospital at the age of 36.

Decolonisation sees some strange alliances. Colonisation is driven by economic interest. The native labour force is used in the production of the natural resources which are required by the imperial power. This arrangement requires stability and peace, whether through concession or repression. The modern colonial power attempts to rule through the incorporation of the pre-modern 'feudal leaders', that is the tribal chiefs. But when the nationalist movement threatens the continuity of production there can be an unexpected realignment of interests. Capitalism cares nothing for the traditions of the nation, but neither does it care about the colour of the flag which flies above the state house. It can suddenly bring pressure to bear on the colonial power to graciously grant independence through an orderly transfer of power. The nationalist leaders belong to the elite who have always been in contact with the imperial power. The kind of transfer which takes place guarantees that capitalist interests will be maintained, and the interests of the elite will be taken care of. The threatened violence – which would have been disastrous for capitalist interests – is avoided, and so is any fundamental change in the lot of the population at large.

> In its simplest form this non-violence signifies to the intellectual and economic elite of the colonized country that the bourgeoisie has the same interests as them and that it is therefore urgent and indispensable to come to terms for the public good. Non-violence is an attempt to settle the colonial problem around a green baize table.[45]

Fanon has a very different reading of the problem and therefore a different agenda.

'Decolonization is the veritable creation of new men.'[46] Decolonisation is not about the orderly transfer of the levers of power in such a way that a native elite replaces a colonial elite. Colonialism is about dehumanisation, the invasion of the mind, spreading the message of inferiorisation. It is a process by which the people of a country are turned into natives. It is a tribute to the importance of the analysis of Fanon that Jean-Paul Sartre wrote a Preface to *The Wretched of the Earth*. In it he paraphrases Fanon's diagnosis. 'The status of "native" is a nervous condition introduced and maintained by the settler among colonized people *with their consent*.'[47] The settlers believe that they have a (divine) right to rule. That matters less than the fact that the colonised people also believe it. And this is the strength of the colonial ideology. If they believe that they need to be ruled, either by white foreigners or subsequently by a black elite, then decolonisation has no effect on them. The circumstances of their lives change little: their lives change not at all. In *Black Skin/White Masks* Fanon had illustrated this from an earlier example of the orderly transfer of power.

> *Slavery shall no longer exist on French soil.* The upheaval reached the Negroes from without. The black man was acted upon. Values that had not been created by his actions, values that had not been born of the systolic tide of his blood, danced in a hued whirl round him. The upheaval did not make a difference in the Negro. He went from one way of life to another, but not from one life to another.[48]

It is impossible to read this analysis without reflecting on the situation of blacks in America. One hundred years after the Emancipation Proclamation of 1863 they still were not free: they had done nothing for themselves. 'The white man, in the capacity of master, said to the Negro, "From now on you are free". But the Negro knows nothing of the cost of freedom, for he has not fought for it. From time to time he has fought for Liberty and Justice, but these were always white liberty and white justice; that is, values secreted by his masters.'[49] To this point we shall of course return, but for the moment this is the problem which Fanon addresses. How can the people so participate in the process of liberation that they ensure not simply that the circumstances of life change, but that they themselves are changed? If they cannot be cured by actions taken on them or on their behalf, what action is open to them? Fanon's answer is violence. As Sartre summarises it, 'the native cures himself of colonial neurosis by thrusting out the settler through force of arms. When his rage boils over, he rediscovers his lost innocence and he comes to know himself in that he himself creates his self.'[50] This is quite the opposite of mindless violence: it a violence which is both mindful and mind creating. It is an action which has an effect on the aggressors but also reconstitutes those who undertake it: it 'invests their character with positive and creative qualities'.[51] Fanon was not himself a violent man and as we have seen, he originally 'refused to accept the validity of violence'. But he is insistent on the therapeutic value of violence as a considered action of free and responsible people. 'At the level of individuals, violence is a cleansing force. It frees the native from his inferiority complex and from his despair and inaction; it makes him fearless and restores his self-respect.'[52]

Indeed Fanon concentrates so much on the therapeutic efficacy of violence he writes of it almost as if it had no other object, ignoring the effect of violence on the enemy. The theme becomes hypnotic. 'Violence alone, violence committed by the people, violence organized and educated by its leaders, makes it possible for the masses to understand social truths and gives the key to them.'[53] It is as if the violence takes place in the doctor's consulting room or in the group therapy suite. No thought is given to the unforeseen consequences of this therapy or its side effects. Indeed it is as if it is not after all the violence, but the preparedness to use violence, the capacity to conceive of striking out against those who have hitherto been superior, untouchable, impregnable. It is not the violent act itself but freedom which comes from choosing this option, the sense of taking responsibility for life, for the family, for the community. The addition of violence to the situation changes the former relationships, discloses the fragility of the dominant race. The de-humanisation of the native ends and the re-humanisation of the settler begins. But he has lost interest in the fate of the colonial power.

> Leave this Europe where they are never done talking of Man, yet murder men everywhere they find them, at the corner of every one of their own streets, in all the corners of the globe. For centuries they have stifled almost the whole of humanity in the name of a so-called spiritual experience. Look at them today swaying between atomic and spiritual disintegration.[54]

For all its religiosity Europe is in danger of losing its soul. Not for the first time the apparently irreligious man exhibits a concern for the spiritual dimension of life. 'If it is true that consciousness is a process of transcendence, we have to see too that this transcendence is haunted by the problems of love and understanding. Man is a yes that vibrates to cosmic harmonies.'[55] For Fanon the future of mankind lies elsewhere. It is for the third world to start 'a new history of Man'. Human history has for so long been dominated by Europe, but now its only hope lies with those whom it abused. 'For Europe, for ourselves and for humanity, comrades, we must turn over a new leaf, we must work out new concepts, and try to set afoot a new man.'[56] Within a few weeks of writing these words he was dead. His body was flown back to Algeria, to be interred in a cemetery of the National Liberation Army. He had become a spokesman for the third world, yet has been largely forgotten and ignored in present day Africa. The black elites who came to power were already anticipated and condemned in his writings. Tragically the post-colonial violence which has broken out throughout the continent has been psychotic rather than therapeutic. In Uganda, Rwanda, Sierra Leone and more recently in Sudan we have observed not simply a return to that historical ignorance and savagery identified by Paulette Nardal and Claude MacKay. Through the availability of modern weapons and military technology thuggery, brutality, racism, ethnic cleansing and heartless cruelty have been raised to levels previously inconceivable. Ezekiel Mphahlele need not have worried about a romantic picture of Africa as a continent of 'innocence, purity and artless primitiveness'. Fanon's writings, however, were eagerly taken up in the USA. They came exactly a century after the Emancipation Proclamation and they challenged blacks in that country with his diagnosis and prescription. 'But the Negro knows nothing of the cost of freedom, for he has not fought for it.' The message was received not directly, but in a context in large part created by two further writers from the Caribbean.

Black Consciousness

In the first half of the twentieth century all the major elements of black consciousness were being explored among Francophones, from the Antilles, Harlem and Senegal. Leopold Sédar Senghor is credited with being the leading exponent of negritude. However, towards the end of his life he himself admitted that much of it had already been said. 'Nevertheless, all the themes which were to be developed by the negritude movement were already treated by Blyden in the middle of the 19th century, both the virtues of negritude and the proper modes of illustrating these virtues: through scholarly studies, life styles, and cultural creation.'[57]

Edward Wilmot Blyden (1832–1912) was a most extraordinary man, who from very humble beginnings in the West Indies became a scholar and statesman with an international reputation in Africa, Europe and America. He was born in St Thomas, a Danish colony in the Virgin Islands. An American Presbyterian minister, impressed by his ability, arranged for him to go to the USA to further his education. Blyden lasted only seven months there: he found that his colour prevented him from achieving his goal. In 1851 at the age of 18 he emigrated to Liberia, crossing the ocean, apparently to a strange, dark continent which was foreign to him. In reality he returned home, to Africa from which his forebears had been stolen. Others were to speak of returning: Blyden as a teenager took the decision and acted on it. Towards the end of the eighteenth century plans were formed in Britain to send freed slaves back to Africa. The first arrived in Sierra Leone in 1787. In 1792 over 1000 arrived from Nova Scotia, to which they had escaped from the American South. In 1800 over 500 Maroons arrived from the British colony of Jamaica. (We shall hear of this tribe again.) At the beginning of the nineteenth century the American Colonization Society was established to enable any Negroes who wished, to return to Africa. It is a curious name, and Blyden himself thought it would have been more aptly called the African Repatriation Society. Liberia, in West Africa, had been founded in 1822 as an American colony to receive the returnees. Before that, in 1820 the good ship *Elizabeth* had arrived carrying the earliest immigrants. During the next three decades there was no mass take-up of repatriation, though in the 1850s some 5000 made the journey. With Emancipation few ex-slaves thought it worth emigrating. In a lecture delivered in 1908 Blyden was to make a distinction which was fundamental to his own life and thought.

> And when Abraham Lincoln in 1863, proclaimed freedom for the Negroes throughout the United States, he delivered them from material shackles which hampered and degraded the body. The body was set free, but the soul remained in bondage. Therefore, the intellectual, social and religious freedom of the American ex-slaves has yet to be achieved.[58]

More than 45 years later those who chose the secure, safe and simple option had not achieved freedom.

On arrival in Liberia, Blyden studied at the Alexander High School, an institution supported by the Presbyterian Church, and was ordained to its ministry in 1858. He went on to study at the College of Liberia and in 1862 became its Professor of Classics. His writings and correspondence are peppered with classical quotations. He was a scholar of Latin and Greek, fluent in French, German and Italian. He taught himself Hebrew, but most significantly of all Arabic. Christianity and Islam were the two modern religions of West Africa and he wished to see better relations between them. He spent two years in the Middle East, mainly in Egypt and Syria, becoming fluent in Arabic and studying the Qur'an as well as the history and culture of north Africa. We might note in passing that Blyden did not take sides. He writes of his boyhood in St Thomas, growing up with Jewish friends and going with them to the synagogue to observe the services. He was later to see a parallel between the exile and return of Negroes to Africa and of Jews to Jerusalem.

Blyden's unique abilities were also put to use by political leaders. He became Secretary of State and a close adviser of President Roye. From 1877–78 he was Liberian ambassador to the United Kingdom. During the years 1850–95 he made eight extended visits to the USA and became a world famous figure, lecturing on three continents. His extensive and cordial correspondence with members of the British government reflects his involvement with neighbouring Sierra Leone, where he lived for two years, carrying out various diplomatic missions to the powerful chiefs of the interior. He was the recipient of many international honours and memberships of various associations. By the time of his death in 1912 he was known for his scholarship, his views on education, his concern for native traditions and his advocacy of pan-Africanism. Speaking at the Lagos Training college and Industrial Institute in 1896 he recommended a syllabus that included classics, literature, European languages and a programme which enabled the students 'to study from a scientific standpoint native law, tribal organization, native languages, native religion, native politics, and the effect of all these things upon their life'.[59] His legacy is his contribution to the formation of black consciousness.

Blyden was concerned with race, the black race, the Negro race as he called it. He knew about white racism, from his early experience in America. He had observed the attitude of Europeans towards Africans. But although he could be critical of white racism, he was *passionate* on the subject of the unity of the Negro race. Africa was the Fatherland: indeed he could even refer to it as Negroland. All Negroes living in Africa were of the same race, and long before Senghor, he was fearful of the Balkanisation of Africa which was taking shape. The colonial powers were dividing the continent and obscuring its essential unity. But beyond that, Negroes of the West Indies and the Americas belonged to that same race. (He is one of the few writers on this subject to acknowledge the black population of Central and Latin America. As a teenager he had lived for two years in Venezuela.)

They of the diaspora should be able to return to the home. And if they did not do so physically, then mentally they should know that they had roots in that continent. He was passionate on the subject, but his strongest criticism was reserved not for white racism, but for those blacks who undermined Negro unity. These he described as mulattos, that is of mixed race, usually light brown in colour. In an address to the Maine State branch of the Colonization Society in 1862 he claimed that the generality of Negroes were supportive of the idea of return. 'All bitter and unrelenting opposition comes from a few half-white men, who, glorying in their honourable pedigree, have set themselves up as representatives and leaders of the coloured people of this country, and who have no faith in Negro ability to stand alone.'[60] These mulattos do not believe in Negroes, that is they continue to accept the views of the white community. Why? Because they consider themselves to be half-white, to be almost white. Their interests lie in being accepted by whites. If they only knew! It is significant that this man who reached out to anyone who might further the Negro cause had no dealings with W.E.B. Du Bois, one of the light skinned leaders of American Negroes. A few years later, after Emancipation, he returned to the same theme. 'The friends of the Negro in America must learn to believe that the Negro can exist and prosper without the aid of white blood in his veins.'[61] After Emancipation blacks should no longer think it an honour to be part white. There is no reason for miscegenation. Blyden described himself as being pure Negro: he was a striking figure, very black, with Negro features. His mistrust of mulattos arose from personal experience in Liberia as well as observation of America. So far as Liberia was concerned, as an adviser to President Roye – also a Negro in this sense – he could see policies designed to develop the interests of the Negro community being thwarted by the powerful mulattos of Monrovia. They forced Roye from office, and Blyden fled to Sierra Leone. At a personal level, and not without irony, Blyden's wife was a mulatto. In a letter of 1875, in a private aside he describes his situation. 'As to myself, I have passed through another year in Liberia by the mercy of God but it has been a year of hard work and suffering. I live among an unsympathizing people – and I regret to say an unsympathizing family – *inter nos*. My wife seems entirely unimprovable. She is of the mind and temperament of the people around her.'[62] He passionately believed that Negros could be improved, that their lives could be enriched, their spirits liberated if the circumstances were right. As a scholar, a politician, a social reformer, he dedicated his life to bringing about these circumstances. He felt that the greatest opposition came not from whites but from coloureds.

Blyden's vocation was to the development of a sense of African nationalism. In 1862 he made a speech in New York in which he claimed that Negroes would not be respected unless they had power, economic and intellectual. He went on to advocate a 'pride in race' and 'enlightened patriotism'. He also spoke of the 'African personality', a concept he first used in 1893 in a lecture to the Young Men's Literary Association of Sierra Leone.[63] Each race has its own personality. Negroes must understand themselves in their own terms and cease to view themselves through the eyes of white people. This for their own sake, but also for the sake of mankind as a whole. Each race must makes its complementary contribution to civilisation as a whole. In terms of the Second Great Commandment, we must love our neighbour, but love our neighbour as ourselves. We cannot fulfil this law except we first know how to identify and love ourselves. But what is the character of this African personality? Blyden reflects on this in a letter to the American Negro reformer Booker T. Washington.

> It is a small matter that the 'white man has not yet advanced to the point where he will invite the Negro to his prayer meeting'. Perhaps he will never advance to that point. The Negro is on a different plane, religiously, from the white man. He has a more spiritual nature; and may yet be the teacher of his master in spiritual matters.[64]

The Negro race has something to contribute to other races. Blyden courageously describes the Negro in a way which could be misunderstood and used against him. 'The African spirit is a spirit of service. I do not mean in a degrading sense, but in the highest sense, in which the Son of Man came not to be ministered unto but to minister.' The African personality is a 'supple, yielding, conciliatory, obedient, gentle, patient, musical spirit'.[65]

Blyden can also describe African personality in terms which are more surprising.

> The world needs such a development of the Negro on African soil. He will bring as his contribution the softer aspects of human nature. The harsh and stern fibre of the Caucasian races needs this milder element. The African is the feminine; and we must not suppose that this is of least importance in the ultimate development of humanity.[66]

Those who have lived in Africa, or who have African friends or postgraduate students normally agree that African men practise chauvinism with a natural confidence which leaves all other races struggling behind them. If Africa hosted the World Chauvinist Games they would no doubt make a clean sweep of the medals in all events. The idea that 'the African is the feminine' therefore is a disorienting claim, but there are signs that Blyden himself seems to have been deficient in the chauvinist gene. He became president of Liberia College in 1881, and in his inaugural lecture he makes a proposal which, perhaps not surprisingly for a former Professor of Classics, is reminiscent of an observation by Plato in *The Republic*.

> I trust that arrangements will be made by which girls of our country may be admitted to share in the advantages of this College. I cannot see why our sisters should not receive exactly the same general culture as we do. I think that the progress of the country will be more rapid and permanent when the girls receive the same general training as the boys; and our women, besides being able to appreciate the intellectual labours of their husbands and brothers, will be able also to share in the pleasures of intellectual pursuits.[67]

What the world does not need is a replication of Europe or America. In a lecture to the American Colonization Society in 1883 he seems resigned to the fact that there is not going to be mass emigration to Liberia. However, even the emigration of a certain few might achieve a significant development. Those who return to Africa to participate in this great historic project 'will be among the redeemers of Africa'.[68] And not only Africa. America does not need Negroes to repeat its story, and its mistakes.

> The nation now being reared in Africa by the returning exiles from this country will not be a reproduction of the American. The restoration of the Negro to the land of his fathers will be the restoration of a race to its original integrity, to itself; and working by itself, for itself and from itself, it will discover the methods of its own development, and they will not be the same as the Anglo-Saxon methods.[69]

This last point leads Blyden to make a criticism which is of particular significance for our subject. Emigration to Africa is an idea, an ideal, a metaphor, a symbol – but for Blyden it was a necessity. He believes that the Negro 'can never enjoy this complete emancipation in the United States'.[70] As we shall see, the phrase 'Afro-American' is now used to signify a free black man, a 'wicked' man who has emancipated himself from the swarming clutches of white America. If only that were the case. Edward Blyden knew better and this is reflected in *his* use of the phrase 150 years ago. He defines Afro-Americans as 'Africans with the prejudices and predilections – the bias and aspirations – of white men.'[71] Afro-Americans are first, middle and last, Americans. That is one reason why they did not emigrate. A wise move. If they did emigrate it would only become crystal clear that they are Americans first and Africans not at all. Afro-Americans do things in Africa the American way: 'we have been legislating as Americans in America for Americans'.[72] In Africa they have divided the land to possess it as a commodity in the American way, not the African communal way. Afro-Americans think and behave as Americans, that is, as white Americans: 'the political economy of the white man is not our political economy, his moral philosophy is not our moral philosophy, and far less is his theology our theology: and wherever he has been successful in forcing these upon us there has been atrophy and death.'[73]

Blyden was not inhibited by political correctness. American Negroes arriving in Liberia need to be Africanised. That indeed is the whole point. He does not welcome them as they are; they have to recover from the American experience. There is no sacrilising of returnees. Worse, he claims that those who were taken as slaves in the first place were 'mostly of the lowest orders – of the criminal and servile classes'.[74] Those who return need have no illusions that they were from noble families. This in turn leads to an even more sensitive point. In Liberia there were the Africans who had never left the continent, and the returnees, the descendants of those who had been taken. It was clear to Blyden that the immigrants brought with them skills and knowledge that they could not have otherwise gained. While denouncing the human suffering and degradation of slavery, he did not lack the courage to acknowledge its gains for the Negro. 'His residence in America has conferred upon him numerous advantages.'[75] Africa had its civilisation, but in America the Negro encountered a more sophisticated culture, a more scientific economy and higher religion. No political correctness, no ideological party line will silence his assessment that 'the Negro's residence in America, in spite of all drawbacks, has been of incalculable advantage to him; nor has it been without peculiar benefits to the dominant race'.[76] On this latter point he has in mind that in America slavery became a moral issue, an issue of human rights, human dignity. That might seem inevitable, but in the ancient world slavery was simply a mode of production or a consequence of defeat in war. Nor did Christianity change this view. Jesus was silent about slavery: Paul, as was his way, legitimised it. For a thousand years the ecclesial hierarchy had their own slaves and later serfs.

On this view the whole sad episode of slavery had a positive outcome for Negroes in America, and through them for the Africa to which they should now contribute. That in itself is a courageous position to take, but Blyden was a committed Christian throughout his life and he goes on to draw a conclusion which is as theologically orthodox as it is politically incorrect. The sun never sets on the publication of yet another theological text in which it is claimed that the Christian God is a God of history, guiding history towards the *eschaton* which He has planned for it. But these works have one thing in common. They can trace the divine hand in the history of the Jews up to and including Paul's arrival in Rome. Then silence. They cannot interpret European or world history according to the divine plan. But Blyden can. He too believes that human history is guided by God's hand.

> We believe that the deportation of the Negro to the New World was as much decreed by an all-wise Providence, as the expatriation of the Pilgrims from Europe to America. When we say that Providence decreed the means of Africa's enlightenment, we do not say that He decreed the wickedness of the instruments.[77]

Blyden bites the bullet, or perhaps he hits the nail on the thumb, but Christian claims are surely weakened if it is not possible to provide a religious interpretation of such an important passage in world history. This view was also to be found in the American Colonization Society, which he praises as the first association in America 'to have distinctly recognized the hand of God in the history of the Negro race in America – to have caught something of the meaning of the divine purpose in permitting their exile to and bondage in this land',[78] and he goes on to quote one of its members, Edward Everett.

> Mark the providence of God, educing out of these natural disadvantages, and this colossal moral wrong – the African slave-trade – educing, I say, from these elements, by the blessed alchemy of Christian benevolence, the means of the ultimate regeneration of Africa.[79]

This is an unusual theological view for a Christian to take. Given Blyden's love of the classics, I digress for a moment to draw attention to a similar position by another classical scholar, Adam Smith, writing a century earlier when he was Professor of Moral Philosophy at the University of Glasgow.

> The ancient stoics were of the opinion that as the world was governed by the all-ruling providence of a wise, powerful, and good God, every single event ought to be regarded, as making a necessary part of the plan of the universe, and as tending to promote the general order and happiness of the whole: that the vices and follies of mankind, therefore, made as necessary a part of this plan as their wisdom or their virtue; and by that eternal art which educes good from ill, were made to tend equally to the prosperity and perfection of the great system of nature.[80]

In both passages we have an all-wise Providence, educing good from ill, where the good ends of God could not come about apart from the evil that men do. It is a traditional religious position, if anything more Stoic than Christian, and inevitably Hegel could express it more succinctly. 'God lets men do as they please with their particular passions and interests; but the result is the accomplishment of – not their plans but his, and these differ decidedly from the ends primarily sought by those whom he employs.'[81] Cyrus, King of the Persians, conqueror of Babylon and unwitting servant of God, we know about.[82] But as Sir John Hawkins fearlessly approached the 'mountain of the lion' (Sierra Leone) in 1562 to begin the slave trade with St Domingo, he would have been astonished, but gratified to learn that he was about to effect God's will.

This leads in turn to our final point, the subject of Blyden's major work *Christianity, Islam and the Negro Race.* Blyden could provide a Christian interpretation of the slave trade. He could provide a similar interpretation of the colonisation of Africa. An example of this can be seen in his letter of 1873 to John Wodehouse, the British Colonial Secretary. In it he encourages the Earl of Kimberley to pursue and extend the colonisation of the hinterland of Africa.

> The steamship has taken the place of the sneaking slaver, and is carrying the marvellous powers of commerce, under the English flag, to every accessible point along the coast; and though, to serve the inscrutable purposes of an All-wise Providence, the progress of civilizing agencies must occasionally be checked by such occurrences as those now transpiring on the Gold Coast, yet it is evident that England has been marked out by the Almighty for the future work of the civilization of inner Africa, and that she is fulfilling her appointed mission.[83]

For Blyden an important element in this whole process is the introduction of Christianity to the people of Africa. However, although a committed Christian, he was ambivalent about the form of Christianity which was brought from Europe. The Christianity which Negroes had encountered in America was the religion of slavery and enslavement, a religion which far from protecting them, legitimised their plight. Yet he can contrast the Christianity of Europe and that of America. The latter is 'the religion of a democratic people'.[84] (A century later a very particular kind of American Christianity has entered Liberia.)[85]

The Christianity which was being spread in Africa by missionaries from Europe was shaped by the experiences and conflicts of that continent.

> But it is evident that to make these creeds in all their details authoritative in Africa, the intellectual and spiritual growth of the people must be checked or distorted by the introduction of the bitterness of theological rancour, and the harshness of conflicting sects, which had their origin abroad and must necessarily exist in the African mind only as a fungus.[86]

Blyden would like to see a truly African Church and a form of Christianity which is native but not local, rooted but not tribal. This is not simply an ideal, for Blyden was impressed by the presence of Islam in West Africa. It was spread by traders who lived among the people, who studied the Qur'an and spoke to the people about how to live according to its teaching. For Blyden, Islam had not come to West Africa as an imperial power. It did not destroy the institutions of communities. It represented 'a healthy amalgamation, and not an absorption or an undue repression'.[87] He could see parallels between Islamic and traditional African art and aesthetics. In Islamic literature Negroes are mentioned as a matter of course, frequently as leaders. By comparison Negroes are never mentioned in Christianity in anything but a negative way. The conclusion is clear. 'The gospel, to be successfully carried into Africa, must be carried by Africans.'[88] But then according to Blyden this is also the lesson of history regarding the three churches of Africa. Like the seeds in the parable, the first two sprang up, but have withered and disappeared, the Latin and the Greek.

> The Church of Tertullian and St Augustine was Latin, not Punic; the Church of Origen and St Athanasius was Greek, not Egyptian. The case has been far different with the third African Church – the Abyssinian or Ethiopian. Founded by a native, it took hold of the inhabitants of the country, and struck its roots deep into the soil.[89]

Blyden had very good relations with Muslims both in West Africa and in the Middle East, not least because he had taken the trouble to learn Arabic and study the Qur'an. He admired Islam and was very critical of the dominant forms of Christianity. However, he did not simply recommend that Africans become Muslims. Rather, as we have just seen, he recommended that Christians learn from the methods of Islam in order to devise a truly African form of Christianity. But of his preference for and commitment to Christianity there is no doubt. 'And once brought within the pale of Christianity, these Mohammedans would be a most effective agency for the propagation of the Gospel in remote regions.'[90]

Blyden, this man from humble and limited origins in the West Indies, became a figure of world significance. He did not idealise or sacrilise his people. In a lecture entitled 'Liberia as She is: the Present Duty of her Citizens' he was strongly critical of its materialism and conspicuous consumption. But he did create a form of black consciousness in which Negroes from the West Indies and the Americas could understand themselves in relation to Africa. It was their land, the land of the ancestors. If Negroes of Africa and of the diaspora could unite to form a self-conscious race, a nation, they could be a powerful force in the world and make a significant contribution to the development of a world civilisation. It was left to another West Indian, Marcus Garvey, to develop this thought that a united Africa would supply power to Negroes, the real power without which emancipation would never be complete.

Although today black consciousness is regarded as primarily an American movement, West Indians, both Francophone and Anglophone, have played a surprisingly important part in its formation. In terms of ideas we should look to Blyden and Césaire, in terms of practice, to Fanon, but if we reflect on how black consciousness reached the masses then there is no name more important than that of Marcus Garvey. The least well qualified academically, Garvey spoke directly to the urban poor of black America giving them hope in conditions of despair, and self-esteem in a society which routinely demeaned them.

Garvey was a product of his nature and nurture, but above all of his experience and his capacity to observe, analyse and learn from that experience. He was born in Jamaica in 1887 the eleventh child of Sarah and Marcus Garvey. His mother wanted to call him Moses, and his father agreed to Marcus Mosiah Garvey. He was indeed to be a leader of his people, one who would enable others to enter the promised land, a land on which he was never allowed to set foot. Race was to be the focal point of his work. Two experiences were to prove seminal, one personal and the other more communal. As a boy he grew up playing with the children of local families, both black and white. His mother attended a Wesleyan church and Marcus was friendly with one of the daughters of the white minister. At the age of 14 her parents drew the colour line. They sent her to Edinburgh to continue her education, and told Marcus Garvey not to try to contact her, because, as he recollects 'I was a "nigger".'[91] He had discovered that humanity is divided into races and that they are distinct and separate. The second experience was cumulative. Garvey left school at 14 and became an apprentice printer. At 20 he was a master printer and foreman at the P.A. Benjamin Co. He was an activist and throughout his life founded and used newspapers for his campaigns. Regarded as a leader of a printers' strike he was black-listed [sic!] and eventually moved to Costa Rica where his uncle enabled him to work as a time-keeper in the United Fruit Company. He worked and travelled throughout South and Central America: Ecuador, Guatemala, Panama, Nicaragua, Chile, Peru, returning to Jamaica in 1911. Throughout his travels and work experience he observed the same phenomenon. The poor blacks from Jamaica and other islands were exploited wherever they worked – in mining, fruit growing, canal digging. They were robbed and abused and no one took responsibility for their plight, not the British consulates in these countries, not the local governments and certainly not the companies, often North American, for which they worked. They were exploited by capitalism, which is what capitalism means. They were exploited by whites, which is the order of things. Garvey was angered by these relations, although they were to be expected. What incensed him was that the poor blacks were also exploited by the mulattos. Garvey was a Maroon. We have met this tribe before, courageous Africans who escaped to the mountains, and defied the Spanish and then the British in Jamaica to establish their right to be free. Garvey was very black, as Blyden was a 'pure Negro'. He could see that if Negroes were to enjoy any improvement in their lives it could only come about when they took responsibility for themselves. The poor blacks could not look for help to those of light skin, those of better education, professional people who had some status in white society. For Garvey it was a matter of observation: the lighter the skin the more such people distanced themselves from the blacks. They did not put their training at the service of Negroes. And far from advocating the case of the poor blacks to their white employers, the mulattos disowned any connection between themselves and Negroes. This was an early lesson which Garvey learned and it was to guide him throughout his life. In an article entitled 'A Journey of Self-discovery', published in 1923, he reflected on a choice that had confronted him. 'I had to decide whether to please my friends and be one of the "black-whites" of Jamaica, and be reasonably prosperous, or come out openly and defend and help improve and protect the integrity of the black millions and suffer.'[92] He chose the latter, dedicating his life to helping his people. In this he had some success, and the more he was successful the more he suffered for it.

In 1912 Garvey came to Britain, staying for a time with his sister in London, and working in the docks of London, Liverpool and Cardiff. He met Duse Mohammed Ali, an Egyptian nationalist who published *The African and Orient Review*, the leading voice of the pan-African movement through which the ideas of Blyden were continued. He also read and was much influenced by the autobiography of Booker T. Washington, *Up From Slavery*. At the outbreak of the war in Europe in 1914 he returned to Jamaica and set up UNIA (the Universal Negro Improvement Association). Its motto was 'One God! One Aim! One Destiny!', with the following General Objects:

1. To establish a Universal Confraternity among the race.
2. To promote the spirit of race pride and love.
3. To reclaim the fallen of the race.
4. To administer to and assist the needy.
5. To assist in civilizing the backward tribes of Africa.
6. To strengthen the Imperialism of independent African States.
7. To establish Commissionaries or Agencies in the principal countries of the world for the protection of all Negroes, irrespective of nationality.
8. To promote a conscientious Christian worship among the native tribes of Africa.
9. To establish Universities, College and Secondary Schools for the further education and culture of the boys and girls of the race.
10. To conduct a worldwide commercial and industrial intercourse.[93]

The improvement was to be effected through the establishment of educational and industrial colleges in Jamaica for Negroes, on the pattern of the Tuskegee Institute founded in Alabama by Booker T. Washington. On the other hand, Garvey was too militant to accept the quietism of the *Atlanta Compromise* (1895) in which Washington offered the following advice to Negroes in America. 'Do not antagonize the white majority. Do not ask for the right to vote. Do not fight for civil liberties or against segregation. Go to school. Work hard. Save money. Buy property. Some day, the other things may come.'[94] Garvey was more ambitious, and more realistic. The lot of the Negro people would not be improved until they took responsibility for their own lives, and that meant gaining independence from white control, socially, economically and politically. In confirmation of the early lesson, Garvey's work received some support from liberal whites, but was opposed by the mulattos of Jamaica. He called on them to associate themselves with the Negro's problem.

> You who do not know anything of your ancestry will do well to read the works of Blyden, one of our historians and chroniclers, who has done so much to retrieve the lost prestige of the race and undo the selfishness of alien historians and their history which has said so little and painted us so unfairly.[95]

Washington had invited him to visit Tuskegee, but by the time Garvey left for New York in 1916 the great man had died. He could not expect to attract the liberal white support shown to Washington's project, but he did inherit much of the opposition. It is not difficult to see why.

Fundamental to Garvey's analysis and programme was the distinction between blacks and coloured, Negroes and mulattos. Like Blyden before him he found that mulattos opposed him and tried to undermine his work. And like Blyden he mistrusted and disliked coloureds for that reason. As we have seen, Blyden declined to have anything to do with W.E.B. Du Bois. Du Bois had opposed Booker T. Washington: now for different reasons, he opposed Garvey. Garvey had been one of those who welcomed Du Bois on a visit to Jamaica in 1915, but Du Bois had no sympathy for the recently formed UNIA. He was even less sympathetic to it when the following year Garvey set up his Liberty Hall in Harlem and began to preach the message of Negro Improvement. Soon they moved beyond disagreement on policies to the much more entertaining field of personal abuse. Du Bois, Harvard scholar, participant in the Harlem Renaissance, international literary figure whom we have met before in the salon of Paulette Nardal, used all his sophistication and skills to mock and undermine his uncouth opponent. Garvey, a powerful if less cultured writer, derided Du Bois as a man committed to a cause, the cause of his own self-interest, who had no intention of letting Negroes get in his way. One of Du Bois's criticisms of Garvey was that he had introduced into the USA a division which however apt in Jamaica was a misreading of the American situation, a misreading which was dangerous and destructive. However, a prima facie case could be made for Garvey's analysis simply by looking at their two organisations. Du Bois was one of the leaders of the prestigious NAACP. Precisely: the National Association for the Advancement of Colored People studiously avoided the N-word. UNIA by comparison espoused the cause of Negroes. The NAACP reputedly only employed people of very light skin colour. In New York and Boston light skinned Americans formed the 'Blue Vein Society', while West Indian mulattos had their 'Colonial Club'. Garvey mocked the aristocratic pretentions of Du Bois. Born in Great Barrington, Massachusetts, Du Bois considered himself part of the New England aristocracy. A frequenter of the Parisian salons, Du Bois was of course French. If that were not enough, Burghardt Du Bois was also Dutch. But there was one thing that he never claimed to be, according to Garvey: 'he has been trying to be everything else but a Negro'.[96] We can imagine the ire and frustration of Du Bois at being dragged into this unsavoury public exchange which undermined his ambition to become accepted in polite white society. In anger, as in dreams, we sometimes reveal what we hoped to conceal. In an article Du Bois, in exasperation, described Garvey as a 'little, fat, black man; ugly but with intelligent eyes and a big head'.[97] *The Sun* could have provided the headline – 'It's official: black is ugly, claims Du Bois.' Black is ugly in this case because Du Bois views from the perspective of white society and according to the aesthetic criteria of that race. Garvey describes Du Bois as 'a hater of dark people' and enquires about the meaning of 'advancement' when the NAACP is directed by such a man. 'We can conclude in no other way than that it is in the direction of losing our black identity and becoming, as nearly as possible, the lowest whites by assimilation and miscegenation.'[98]

The first thing the *asimilados* from the Antilles did when they docked in Marseilles was to make for a brothel where they could screw a white woman. Césaire and Fanon both write about black men and black women who aspire to have light skinned partners. For Garvey it is necessary to separate the races, not because one is inferior to the other, but for the sake of the integrity of both. 'We believe that the white race should protect itself against racial contamination, and the Negro should do the same. Nature intended us morally (and may I not say socially?) apart, otherwise there never would have been this difference.'[99] Such words were music to the ears of white racists. In 1922 Garvey had talks with the Imperial Wizard of the Ku Klux Klan. His defenders have admitted that this was probably ill-advised and naïve. It certainly gave a propaganda victory to the Klan. But we should not be too quick to rescue Garvey from the error of his ways. He claimed to prefer the Klan to the NAACP, 'for their honesty of purpose towards the Negro'.[100] The Klan is saying clearly, bluntly, that blacks are never going to be accepted as equals in American society. The NAACP leadership are the ones who are naïve. Or worse, they know that this is the reality for the vast majority of blacks, but they hope that at least at dusk they may be able to slip past the gate-keepers into the promised land. Not until the Klan's message is accepted in all its finality and injustice, not till the gate is locked, bolted, boarded up and electrified, only then will blacks be forced to face the reality that they must make their own way. This is the message of UNIA. It appalled the coloureds, but it was received as good news to the poor blacks who always knew that this was one gate that was too strait for them.

Black citizens had bought government bonds to assist the war effort, but it did not buy them the vote in 1918. Four hundred thousand black troops had the privilege of making the world safe for democracy, but when they returned home oppression increased and the Klan grew more blatant. According to Du Bois 'Marcus Garvey is, without doubt, the most dangerous enemy of the Negro race in America and the world.'[101] I am not able to report on the attitude of Du Bois to gun control, but if shooting yourself in the foot ever became compulsory, that would have been one law with which he would never have any difficulty complying. Given the white supremacists throughout the land he once again gives away his own self-interests by identifying Garvey as 'the most dangerous enemy of the Negro'. Or was Garvey perhaps the saviour of the Negro race, dangerous only to those like Du Bois, or Cyril V. Briggs, publisher of *The Crusader*, whom Garvey described as 'a white man passing as a black'.[102] Were the coloureds not simply fulfilling the role laid down for them in all scenarios of assimilation, never more explicitly set out than in the words of Napoleon (whom Garvey admired) to Le Clerec concerning the governance of Haiti. 'You should give particular attention to the castes of coloured people. Put them in a position to develop their national prejudices on a wide scale and give them the opportunity to rule over the blacks, and by these means you will secure the submission of both.'[103] Historically the Maroons could not be used for such a purpose. And now the Manhattan Maroon exposed the modern equivalent of this collusion. Du Bois was right, in part. There is nothing more dangerous than a man who cannot be bought or used.

The Klan only exposed what was otherwise concealed: America is for the white race, its government acts according to the interests of that race. Where, asked Garvey, is the black man's government, king, kingdom, president, army, navy? Where is the black man's land? The answer is – Africa. 'If Europe is for the white man, if Asia is for brown and yellow men, then surely Africa is for the black man.'[104] The slogan of UNIA was not 'To Africa!', but 'Back to Africa!' Four hundred million black people throughout the world should look to Africa as their homeland.

> The Universal Negro Improvement Association seeks to do for Africa ... what the Pilgrims and, later George Washington sought to do for America. We Negroes want a government of our own in Africa, so that we can be nationally, if not industrially and commercially, removed from competition in race, a condition that will make both races better friends, with malice toward none, but respect and appreciation for each.[105]

There they once had kings, kingdoms, armies, civilisation and culture. Europeans should cease to colonise Africa. It should now be colonised by black people returning home. There is no hatred here and above all no inferiorisation of any race. 'Therefore, the fullest opportunity should be given to both races to develop independently a civilization of their own, meaning not to infer thereby that either race would not, in a limited degree, become a part of the civilization of each without losing their respective racial, cultural, social and political identities.'[106] A very practical illustration of this concerns *The Negro World*, the weekly newspaper and official organ of UNIA. It would not accept advertising for skin-whitening products or hair-straightening compounds.

In 1920 Garvey organised the first International Convention of the Negro People of the World. It opened in Madison Square Garden in New York with 25 000 delegates from the Americas, north and south, from the West Indies and Africa. It began with the singing of the Universal Ethiopian Anthem. Garvey was elected Provisional President of Africa, a development which, if truth be told, was not viewed with total acclaim by African kings and chiefs. However, the office was powerful only as a symbol, as was the creation of peerages and orders of chivalry. Was it all absurd and ridiculous? Well, let us not look too closely at the basis on which the European aristocracy was originally created, or the aristocracy of New England for that matter, to which Du Bois aspired. What was important was that the Negro race could take responsibility for itself, that it could identify its own values, affirm its own leaders and conceive of the manner of its own government. 'The Negro of the world, and America in particular, needs a national homeland with opportunities and privileges like all other peoples.'[107] The homeland, the separation: it all sounds negative and angry, but this is not the case. It is to be a time of rejoicing for blacks who go back: but it is to be a time of possibilities also for whites, who can have their part to play. 'We have found a place; it is Africa, and as black men for three centuries have helped white men build America, surely generous and grateful white men will help black men build Africa.'[108] Above all, separation is espoused without any trace of racial hatred. 'We are not preaching a propaganda of hate against anybody. We love the white man; we love all humanity, because we feel that we cannot live without each other.'[109] Separation is not rejection of white people, nor of the achievements of American society. The General Objects of UNIA include 'civilizing the backward tribes of Africa'. There is also the aim of promoting 'conscientious Christian worship among the native tribes of Africa'. Like Blyden before him Garvey sees Christianity as being a real contribution which American Negroes can make to Africa. However, like Blyden, he could conceive of an appropriate form of Christianity.

> Whilst our God has no color, yet it is human to see everything through one's own spectacles, we have only now started out (late though it be) to see our God through our own spectacles. The God of Isaac and the God of Jacob let Him exist for the race that believes in the God of Isaac and the God of Jacob. We Negroes believe in the God of Ethiopia, the everlasting God – God the Father, God the Son and God the Holy Ghost, the One God of all ages. That is the God in whom we believe, but we shall worship Him through the spectacles of Ethiopia.[110]

The General Objects of UNIA also include aspirations towards moral and social improvement. This is more than welfare, it is 'to reclaim the fallen of the race'. He does not sacrilise Negroes as they are. 'Negroes are divided into two groups, the industrious and adventurous, and the lazy and dependent.'[111] Garvey can present the work of UNIA as a work of redemption.

> May we not say to ourselves that the doctrine Jesus taught – that of redeeming mankind – is the doctrine we ourselves must teach in the redemption of our struggling race? Let us therefore cling fast to the great ideal we have before us. This time it is not the ideal of redeeming the world, such as was the ideal of Jesus, but it is the ideal of redeeming and saving 400 million souls who have suffered for centuries from the persecution of alien races. As Christ by His teachings, His sufferings and His death, triumphed over His foes, through the resurrection, so do we hope that out of our sufferings and persecutions of today we will triumph in the resurrection of our newborn race.[112]

His project is not a plan for economic development, it is 'the cause of African redemption'.

After the Convention in 1920 Garvey began to negotiate with the President of Liberia for the return of western blacks to colonise and develop the country. Over the next four years three delegations were sent to make assessments of what was required for the intended immigrants. Liberia was to be the headquarters for UNIA in Africa. Then without consultation or even communication, the President changed his policy and denied entry to the immigrants. The reason was 'the incendiary policy of the Universal Negro Improvement Association, headed by Marcus Garvey'.[113] What had gone wrong?

At one level UNIA was the opium of the masses. The Provisional President of Africa was driven about in a huge convertible wearing a uniform which must have been the envy of many a circus ringmaster. There were marching bands and street parades for various sections, including the Juveniles, the Black Cross Nurses and the Black Star Line. The Royal African Guards and the African Legion appeared on 125th Street in imperial uniforms as if they had been transported from Nairobi or Lagos. Who would have opposed such an organisation. Indeed any request for support might have been sympathetically entertained by those who wished to perpetuate a stereotype of Negroes as simple and gullible. But behind the outrageous uniforms and titles UNIA had plans for economic development. Grocery stores were set up, laundries, restaurants, hotels and printing plants. All this in the name of justice and the end of exploitation, but also self-confidence that Negroes could look after themselves. What did it matter that each in turn failed almost as soon as it was set up? The most ambitious project was the Black Star Line. Several ships were bought to transport goods and people from America to Africa. What did it matter that the ships were inappropriate, bought at too high a price, incapable of being properly converted for their new purpose? The whole conception caught the imagination of black people, the idea that Negroes could conduct trade on the high seas. Garvey had a Midas deficiency: every asset he touched turned to debt. He would have been well qualified for appointment as Professor of Management at the Alessandro Fiasco School of Business Studies. Du Bois was scathing about Garvey's commercial ineptitude yet was quick to add, 'I have not found the slightest proof that his objects were not sincere or that he was consciously diverting money to his own use.'[114] Yet in 1922 Garvey was arrested on a charge of mail fraud, using federal mail to sell stocks of a company in financial trouble. The evidence seemed inadequate in several fundamental respects, the charges against his co-accused were dropped, fraud was completely out of character (as evidenced even by Du Bois), but he was found guilty and sentenced to five years imprisonment. Garvey was later to reflect that at the same time there were well publicised cases in which white men committed mail fraud – intending to defraud – and either avoided prison sentences altogether or received sentences of one year. Observers at the time concluded that it was a political trial intended to discredit Garvey and with him the UNIA movement. It is not difficult to imagine white interests which would have benefited from this outcome, but as usual the most vociferous of his opponents were the coloureds, who mounted a strident 'Garvey Must Go' campaign. Whatever the truth, the effect was to kill off the movement. In 1927 President Calvin Coolidge acceded to a request for clemency and Garvey was released and deported as an undesirable. Undesirable but certainly not a communist! UNIA's economic aims were only broadly stated. There was certainly no criticism of capitalism as such, though the young Garvey had seen the effects of its unregulated practice. His opposition to communism was not so much economic as racial. 'When you scratch the Communist beneath the surface, you will find him the same vicious Southerner whose political belief will not surmount his racial prejudices and for this, we have always kept Communism at bay.'[115]

Garvey received a hero's welcome from blacks in Jamaica. He was prevented from visiting the countries of South America, and was never permitted to visit a single country in Africa. In 1934 he transferred the headquarters of UNIA to London and attempted to continue his work from there, but he was never able to regain the momentum of the early years. He died in London in 1940.

The legacy of Marcus Garvey was greater than the ideas of the other writers we have considered. He was indeed a world figure, more than he could know at the time. John White claims, with justification, that 'his ignorance of Africa was profound'.[116] Yet Africa was not ignorant of him. Jomo Kenyatta, when President of Kenya, recalls

> how in 1921 Kenya nationalists, unable to read, would gather round a reader of Garvey's newspaper, the *Negro World*, and listen to an article two or three times. Then they would run various ways through the forest, carefully to repeat the whole, which they had memorised, to Africans hungry for some doctrine which lifted them from the servile consciousness in which Africans lived.[117]

Jabez Ayodele Langley has a comparable memory. Even as late as 1933 there were African nationalists in South Africa who, in spite of police surveillance, were receiving copies of Garvey's banned *Negro World*. Jame Stehazu, for example (signing himself, 'Yours Africanly'), wrote to the *Negro World* editor 'to express the feeling of our African brothers towards the American or West Indian brothers'. His observations were frank and sharp: 'The Africans are now wide awake in affairs affecting the black races of the world, and yet the so-called civilized Negroes of the Western Hemisphere are still permitting the white men to deceive them as the Negroes of the old regime, Uncle Tom stool pigeons.'[118] And Kwame Nkrumah, President of Ghana and father of modern pan-Africanism, acknowledged that Garvey's *Philosophy and Opinions* did more to fire his enthusiasm than any other book.[119]

Garvey was opposed not because of his audacious dress sense but because UNIA's policies threatened to make a difference. His defeat was in a real sense confirmation of one of his main convictions. 'The only protection against *injustice* in man is *power* – physical, financial and scientific.'[120] He wished to see a reborn Africa, an Africa for the Negro peoples. They would bring their knowledge and skills to develop the continent culturally but also economically. This was one part of the project, important for those who returned. Equally important was the part that the new Africa would play in world affairs. It would take the part of the Negroes who did not return. It would defend them in the countries where they lived. Garvey was not an admirer of Gandhi, but he was not personally a violent man, nor did he incite his people to violence. However, he was realistic about the prospects for change within America. Negroes had been controlled, exploited and abused by those who cared nothing for justice or right, but who had the power. There was no question of basing hopes for change on an appeal to equity or even the Constitution. It is at this point that a more ominous note enters Garvey's message.

> Power is the only argument that satisfies man. Except the individual, the race or nation has *power* that is exclusive, it means that that individual, race or nation will be bound by the will of the other who possesses this great qualification ... Hence it is advisable for the Negro to get power of every kind. *Power* in education, science, industry, politics and higher government. That kind of power will stand out signally, so that other races and nations can see, and if they will not see, then *feel*.[121]

This steely conclusion might well have been what the President of Liberia had in mind in his reference to 'the incendiary policy' of Marcus Garvey.

In 1965 the Nobel Peace Prize winner Dr Martin Luther King, Jr. visited Kingston, Jamaica to stand beside a bust of the great man in King George VI Park. He praised Marcus Garvey as 'the first man of colour in the history of the United States ... on a mass scale and level to give millions of Negroes a sense of dignity and destiny and make the Negro feel he was somebody'.[122] It was an homage to Garvey but also an appeal for the continued support of the Negro people. But it was already too late. Negritude and black consciousness had overtaken the civil rights movement in America. Black Power grasped the torch – and set fire to Babylon.

Notes

1 Quoted in Janet G. Vaillant, *Black, French and African: a life of Léopold Senghor*, Harvard University Press, Cambridge, Mass., 1990, p. 90.

2 Ibid., p. 37.

3 Quoted ibid., p. 32.

4 Quoted in Jacques Louis Hymans, *Léopold Sédar Senghor: an intellectual biography*, Edinburgh University Press, 1971, p. 23.

5 Du Bois, *The Souls of Black Folk*, p. 2.

6 Quoted in Hymans, *Senghor*, p. 54.

7 Quoted ibid., p. 54.

8 Ibid., p. 278.

9 Franz Fanon, *Toward the African Revolution*, Penguin Books, 1970 (1964), p. 30.

10 Quoted in Hymans, *Senghor*, p. 278.

11 Quoted ibid., p. 57.

12 Vaillant, *Black, French and African,* p. 101.

13 Janice Spleth, *Léopold Sédar Senghor*, Twayne Publishers, Boston, 1985, p. 28.

[14] Hymans, *Senghor*, p. 23.

[15] Vaillant, *Black, French and African*, p. 244.

[16] Quoted in Spleth, *Senghor*, p. 23.

[17] Quoted in Hymans, *Senghor*, p. 71.

[18] Ibid., p. 70.

[19] Irving Leonard Markovitz, *Léopold Sédar Senghor and the Politics of Negritude*, Heinemann, 1969, p. 42.

[20] Hymans, *Senghor*, pp. 125–6.

[21] Quoted ibid., p. 283.

[22] From a paper on 'Remarks on Negritude', presented at the Conference of African Literature in French, University of Dakar, 1963. Quoted in Hymans, *Senghor*, pp. 282–3.

[23] Vaillant, *Black, French and African*, p. 258.

[24] Ibid., p. 259.

[25] Léopold Senghor, *African Socialism: a report on the constitutive congress of the Party of African Federation*, American Society of African Culture, New York, 1959, p. 31.

[26] Ibid., p.29.

[27] This quotation and those that follow are taken from *Return to My Native Land,* Penguin Books, 1970 (1956). It is a mixture of narrative and poetry and since it is only some 50 pages in length it would be too pedantic to provide the page reference to every quotation.

[28] David Caute, *Fanon*, Fontana, 1970, p. 11.

[29] Franz Fanon, *Black Skin/White Masks*, Paladin, 1970 (1952), p. 11.

[30] Ibid., p. 136.

[31] Ibid., p. 19.

[32] Ibid., p. 11.

[33] Franz Fanon, *A Dying Colonialism*, Penguin Books, 1970 (1959), p. 32.

[34] Fanon, *Black Skin/White Masks*, p. 13.

[35] Ibid., p. 26.

[36] Ibid., p. 11.

[37] Fanon, *A Dying Colonialism*, p. 145.

[38] Ibid., p. 148.

[39] Ibid., p. 12.

[40] Ibid., p. 13.

[41] Ibid., p. 20.

[42] Ibid., pp. 23–4.

[43] Franz Fanon, *The Wretched of the Earth*, Penguin Books, 1967 (1961), p. 163.

[44] Caute, *Fanon*, p. 53.

[45] Fanon, *The Wretched of the Earth*, p. 48.

[46] Ibid., p. 28.

[47] Jean-Paul Sartre, ibid., p. 17.

[48] Fanon, *Black Skin/White Masks*, p. 156.

[49] Ibid., p. 157.

[50] Sartre in Fanon, *The Wretched of the Earth*, p. 18.

[51] Ibid., p. 73.

[52] Ibid., p. 74.

[53] Ibid., p. 118.

[54] Ibid., p. 251.

[55] Fanon, *Black Skin/White Masks*, p. 8.

[56] Fanon, *The Wretched of the Earth*, p. 255.

[57] 'Edward Wilmot Blyden, Precursor of Negritude', Léopold Sédar Senghor, President of the Republic of Senegal, in Foreword to Hollis R. Lynch (ed.) *Selected Letters of Edward Wilmot Blyden*, KTO Press, New York, 1978, p. xx.

[58] Hollis R. Lynch (ed.) *Black Spokesman: selected published writings of Edward Wilmot Blyden*, Frank Cass & Co., 1971, p. 120.

[59] Ibid., p. 266.

[60] Ibid., p. 15.

[61] Ibid., p. 189.

[62] Lynch, *Selected Letters of Edward Wilmot Blyden*, p. 183.

[63] Lynch, *Black Spokesman*, pp. 224–5, 201.

[64] Ibid., p. 205.

[65] Ibid., p. 207.

[66] Edward W. Blyden, *Christianity, Islam and the Negro Race*, Edinburgh University Press, 1967 (1887), p. 111.

[67] Ibid., p. 89.

[68] Ibid., p. 109.

[69] Ibid., pp. 109–10.

[70] Ibid., p. 38.

[71] Lynch, *Black Spokesman*, p. 120.

[72] Ibid., p. 121.

[73] Ibid., p. 122.

[74] Blyden, *Christianity, Islam and the Negro Race*, p. 273.

[75] Ibid., p. 338.

[76] Ibid., p. 355.

[77] Ibid., p. 338.

[78] Lynch, *Black Spokesman*, p. 45.

[79] Edward Everett in Blyden, *Christianity, Islam and the Negro Race*, p. 358.

[80] Adam Smith, *The Theory of Moral Sentiments*, Clarendon Press, Oxford, 1976 (1759), p. 36 = I.ii.3.4.

[81] G.W.F. Hegel, *Logic*, Oxford University Press, Oxford, 1975 (1812–16), p. 273 = # 209.

[82] Isaiah 45: 1.

[83] Lynch, *Selected Letters of Edward Wilmot Blyden*, p. 146.

[84] Blyden, *Christianity, Islam and the Negro Race*, p. 372.

[85] Paul Gifford, *Christianity and Politics in Doe's Liberia*, Cambridge University Press, 1993.

[86] Lynch, *Black Spokesman*, p. 227.

[87] Blyden, *Christianity, Islam and the Negro Race*, p. 12.

[88] Ibid., p. 166.

[89] Ibid., p. 165.

[90] Ibid., p. 188.

[91] John Henrik Clarke (ed.) *Marcus Garvey and the Vision of Africa*, Random House, New York, 1974, p. 72.

[92] Ibid., p. 75.

[93] Ibid., p. 60.

[94] Quoted by E.U. Essien-Udom in his introduction to the second edition of *Philosophy and Opinions of Marcus Garvey*, compiled by Amy Jacques Garvey, Frank Cass & Co., 1967 (1923) p. xv.

[95] Clarke, *Marcus Garvey*, pp. 85–6.

[96] Quoted by John White, *Black Leadership in America 1895–1968*, Longman, 1985, p. 91.

[97] Quoted by Garvey in *Philosophy and Opinions of Marcus Garvey*, vol. 2, p. 310.

[98] Ibid., vol. 2, p. 311.

[99] Ibid., vol. 2, p. 234.

[100] Ibid., vol. 2, p. 71.

[101] Clarke, *Marcus Garvey*, p. 226.

[102] Ibid., p. 223.

[103] Quoted ibid., p. 227.

[104] *Philosophy and Opinions of Marcus Garvey*, vol. 1, p. 25.
[105] Ibid., vol. 2, p. 234.
[106] Clarke, *Marcus Garvey*, p. 250.
[107] *Philosophy and Opinions of Marcus Garvey*, vol. 2, p. 10.
[108] Ibid., vol. 2, p. 5.
[109] Ibid., vol. 2, p. 98.
[110] Ibid., vol. 1, p. 34.
[111] Ibid., vol. 2, p. 122.
[112] Ibid., vol. 1, p. 45.
[113] Ibid., vol. 2, p. 389.
[114] Clarke, *Marcus Garvey*, pp. 202–3.
[115] Ibid., p. 319.
[116] White, *Black Leadership in America 1895–1968*, p. 85.
[117] Quoted by William Z. Foster in Clarke, *Marcus Garvey*, p. 426.
[118] Quoted ibid., pp. 403–4.
[119] Kwame Nkrumah, quoted by William Z. Foster, ibid., p. 426.
[120] *Philosophy and Opinions of Marcus Garvey*, vol. 2, p. 5.
[121] Ibid., vol. 2, p. 9.
[122] Essien-Udom, ibid., p. xxvi.

CHAPTER 2

Sickness in Babylon: Black Theology in the USA

Black Power

Social movements have a complex history, but there are sometimes defining, datable moments. In June 1966 Stokely Carmichael, the newly elected chairman of SNCC (the Student Non-Violent Co-ordinating Committee) addressed a crowd in Greenwood, Mississippi in which for the first time he used the term 'Black Power'. (This is the defining moment, even though Adam Clayton Powell might well have coined the term a year earlier in Chicago.) The concept of civil rights never alarmed anyone. To graciously accede to the request – eventually – would not undermine the order of things, indeed it would only confirm White Power and its capacity and legitimacy to grant or withhold. Black Power, by comparison, was an assertion of rights, a declaration of intent to gain and use power, and a preparedness to use whatever means were required along the way. Its symbol was not a cap in hand, but a militant beret. At a stroke the phrase changed the debate into a struggle, the request into a demand. It transformed the short-term single issue movement into a long-term political programme. A concession that would leave America unchanged was now overtaken by a call to revolutionary activity which would recast the foundations of the Republic. The phrase Black Power struck fear into the hearts of whites who heard it. Where would it all end? Yes, indeed. And in a pattern which is already clear, it utterly depressed those liberal blacks who thought that by being reasonable in tone and limited in the extent of their requests, they were just about to be granted entry through the pearly gates into American society.

The immediate context of the Black Power speech was the shooting of James Meredith on the day after he began his Freedom March through Mississippi. Martin Luther King, as Director of SCLC (the Southern Christian Leadership Conference) went to Memphis for a meeting with Stokely Carmichael of SNCC and Floyd McKissick the National Director of CORE (Congress of Racial Equality). They agreed that their three organisations would jointly continue the freedom march. But according to King, the mood of blacks had significantly changed after the shooting. Some were no longer committed to non-violence. 'We Shall Overcome' became 'We Shall Overrun'. Others did not want whites to participate. There was a feeling, especially in SNCC, that northern white students by their enthusiastic participation in integrated marches and projects had overwhelmed the poorer, less well educated black people they had come to help, ironically producing a new field for dependency. When they reached Greenwood Carmichael mounted the platform to tell the people, 'What we need is black power.' Willie Ricks leaped to the platform, converting the conclusion into a slogan. To the call 'What do you want?' came the response from the crowd 'Black Power'. As King observed, 'So Greenwood turned out to be the arena for the birth of the Black Power slogan in the civil rights movement!'[1] He could sense the transition from 'Freedom Now!' to 'Black Power!' 'Immediately, however, I had reservations about its use. I had the deep feeling that it was an unfortunate choice of words for a slogan. Moreover, I saw it bringing about division within the ranks of the marchers.'[2] It marked a change of direction from non-violence and integration under King to a preparedness for violence and a call for separation under Carmichael.

Stokely Carmichael, the most charismatic, admired and – yes, loved – militant leader of American blacks, was also from the Caribbean, born in Port of Spain, Trinidad in 1941. At the age of 11 he followed his parents to Harlem, where they had gone to seek work. His early schooling had a politicising effect on him. He later recalled having to memorise Kipling's 'White Man's Burden', and was also resentful of the idea that his people did not exist until Sir Walter Raleigh 'discovered' them. He was therefore attracted by the model presented by I.F. Stone. 'In an age of decolonization, it may be fruitful to regard the problem of the American Negro as a unique case of colonialism, an instance of internal imperialism, an underdeveloped people in our very midst.'[3] A specific example was the way in which the ghettos, such as Harlem, were controlled. 'The white political bosses could rule the black community in the same fashion that Britain ruled the African colonies – by indirect rule.' Blacks must assert themselves, to control their own lives and communities. 'Black Power seeks to correct the approach to dependency, to remove that dependency, and to establish a viable psychological, political and social base upon which the black community can function to meet its needs.' Integration will not challenge the situation, will not change the basis of relationships. It is 'a subterfuge for the maintenance of white supremacy'. Separation is not a long-term goal, but it is a necessary first step if blacks are to identify their enemies and discover themselves.

> [Black Power] is a call for black people in this country to unite, to recognize their heritage, to build a sense of community. It is a call for black people to begin to define their own goals, to lead their own organizations and to support those organizations. It is a call to reject the racist institutions and values of this society. The concept of Black Power rests on a fundamental premise: *Before a group can enter the open society, it must first close ranks.*

They must separate themselves from whites in order to redefine themselves, for themselves, 'as black people who are in fact energetic, determined, intelligent, beautiful and peace-loving'. They should not assume that the goals of white society are the goals for them, or that the values of white society should be their values. This reorientation will mean, for example, 'an emphasis on the dignity of man, not on the sanctity of property'.

Carmichael came to his views through some hard and unpleasant experiences. He had worked with SNCC after graduating from Howard University in 1964. These young militants, black and white, had worked to set up schools and clinics in black communities in the South, and to register voters. He himself had been arrested more than 30 times. They had borne the brunt of the attacks on the civil rights movement. Although loyal to Martin Luther King, initially, they shared his frustration that even the black churches failed to commit themselves to the struggle. This in turn led to a secularization of SNCC in particular, and a lack of interest within the northern ghettos for Martin Luther King's 'Negro Baptist brand of civil rights evangelism'.[4] As the movement changed from moral righteousness to political and economic revolution, so the issue of means looked very different.

> Those of us who advocate Black Power are quite clear in our own minds that a 'non-violent' approach to civil rights is an approach black people cannot afford and a luxury white people do not deserve. It is crystal clear to us – and it must become so with the white society – *that there can be no social order without social justice*. White people must be made to understand that they must stop messing with black people, or the blacks *will* fight back!

Over the next two years there were indeed riots in the streets of the major cities, but when the flames went out there had been no revolution. In 1969 Carmichael and his first wife, the South African born singer Miriam Makeba, left America to set up home in Guinea. From this time his agenda changed to pan-Africanism. He was later to take the name Kwame Toure, combining the names of two of the main figures in the pan-Africa movement, Kwame Nkrumah the first president of independent Ghana and Sekou Toure, president of Guinea. In the mid-1970s he returned to the American South to preach pan-Africanism.

> Our fight is not as simple as it was before. Our fight is going to take on an international atmosphere. We must fight wherever our people are. We are Africans. We come from Africa. Africa is our home. The white man stole us from Africa ... We must now build a nation in Africa as strong as the United States of America ... We have got to build a power so strong and so powerful that nobody will ever mess with a black man again.[5]

The Jews in New York had enabled the establishment of the state of Israel: the blacks in America could establish a homeland in Africa. Thus Stokely Carmichael returned to the black consciousness of Blyden and Garvey. He died of cancer in Conakry, Guinea in November 1998. None of the militants of his generation was able to keep his eschatological faith as he did. To the end he answered the phone: 'Kwame Toure – Ready for the Revolution.'[6] This was in turn inspiring to those who longed for justice, alarming for those whose interests he threatened – and not a little puzzling for those who were merely cold calling about double glazing.

Christianity has been a powerful element in the history of black America, for good and ill. It has been a good influence. Blyden tells as much; Martin Luther King shows us as much. It has also been an evil influence, or at least has legitimised the evil suffered under slavery and then racial discrimination. The secularisation of the black cause which took place under Stokely Carmichael was something new. For many it took the spiritual heart out of a righteous crusade. Not surprisingly the sentiments of Black Power were to be found in a very different religious movement which came to prominence at this time, the Nation of Islam.

The disturbance several rows back in the audience of the Audubon Ballroom in Harlem was intended to distract attention from the three men who stood up at the front. They had taken their seats early to ensure that with shotgun and handguns they would have a clear sight of their victim. Afterwards one woman said it looked like a firing squad. El-Hajj Malik El-Shabazz, previously known as Malcolm X, originally baptised Malcolm Little, died on the platform as he addressed his audience on the brotherhood of man. A few weeks earlier, in January 1965, he wondered whether in retrospect it might be said that he had helped America to avoid total catastrophe, he and Martin Luther King: Malcolm, the angriest black man in America, and Martin, the proclaimer of reconciliation. 'And in the racial climate of this country today, it is anybody's guess which of the "extremes" in approach to the black man's problems might *personally* meet a fatal catastrophe first – "non-violent" Dr. King, or so-called "violent" me.'[7] Three years almost to the day, in February 1968, Martin Luther King was assassinated. Martin was murdered by a white extremist: Malcolm was executed by his own fellow black Muslims. In 1955 Martin Luther King was drawn into the civil rights movement. By that time Malcolm X had come to a more radical assessment. 'How is the black man going to get "civil rights" before first he wins his *human* rights?'[8] Dr King, for all his personal integrity, moral and physical courage, had no analysis and no programme. For Malcolm X, both were to be found within the Nation of Islam.

Once again we see the Caribbean connection. Malcolm Little was born in 1925 in Omaha, Nebraska. His mother was born in Grenada to a black woman and a white father. She looked like a white woman and Malcolm had a light reddish brown skin. His father was from Reynolds, Georgia, a Baptist minister and an organiser for Marcus Garvey's UNIA who believed that blacks could only be truly independent when they returned to Africa. The family were harassed by the (white) Black Legion and moved to Lansing, Michigan, when their house was burned down around them. Earl Little was brutally murdered by the Legion when Malcolm was 6 years old, and his mother was left to raise eight children. Eventually she was admitted to the State Mental Hospital at Kalamazoo and the family were split up. Although these experiences never left him, Malcolm was not politicised by them. Through his foster parents he attended a white school and achieved very good grades. One of his teachers asked him what he planned to do when he left school. He said he would like to become a lawyer. The teacher shook his head, 'A lawyer – that's no realistic goal for a nigger',[9] and suggested he become a carpenter. Malcolm later demonstrated capacities that would have made him a very successful lawyer: a passion for justice, a quick mind, a retentive memory, a love of argument, a disdain for money. (Well, four out of five is not bad.) Malcolm said it was with this incident that he began to change, inside, drawing away from white people. More to the point he began on a downward path morally and economically, first of all in Boston and then in New York where in Harlem he became a hustler, losing touch with all religion. He had little contact with white people, though he did have a long-term relationship with Sophie, a white married woman in Boston whom he eventually involved in a series of burglaries. It was at this point that he once again experienced the judgement of white society on an uppity nigger. He was caught and found guilty – but of what? The sentence for burglary for first offenders should have been two years. His sentence was ten years, presumably for messing with a white woman. He served seven years in prison, feeling that he had sunk to the very depth of the white man's America. He cursed the white man, God and the Bible. However, it was while in prison that he was converted to the Nation of Islam.

Malcolm describes it as an experience as dramatic as that of Paul on the road to Damascus, like a blinding light. Allah entered his life and re-created him. He became a different person, in a different world, or at least a world which he now understood clearly for the first time. He accepted the teaching of the Honorable Elijah Muhammad, beginning with Yacub's History. The first humans were black, and founded the city of Mecca. One scientist among them became alienated from the others and created the strong black tribe of Shabazz from which American blacks are descended. Six thousand, six hundred years ago a big-headed scientist called Yacub became embittered towards Allah and decided to create a demonic people, the white race. This devil race through its evil influence had a destructive effect on the black race, and they were exiled to Europe. The devil race became strong and ruled the world for 6000 years, until our own time, taking some of the black people to America as slaves. Yacub's History involves many more details, constituting a myth which would be completely incredible to most people. Indeed towards the end of his life, when Malcolm visited Mecca, he was to discover that orthodox Muslims were 'infuriated' at this teaching. On release from prison he was accepted into the Nation of Islam, and given the name Malcolm X, to symbolise that the white devils had taken from the black African people their names, as well as their language, religion and culture. He was eventually to become the first National Minister of the movement. The tremendous impact which he made on American society, however, did not depend on the exotic details of Yacub's History but on a few premises. The white man is the enemy of the black. Blacks must reject both segregation and integration and choose the path of the separation of the races. There must be black power. They must have control of their own businesses and communities. They must address the social problems endemic in a society which has been exploited by white interests. Thus, for example, they devised a very effective programme to get addicts off drugs. The Nation of Islam involved a strictly disciplined life. The members were to provide a moral, spiritual and mental example to all blacks. They were to show respect for each other, and black men were enjoined to show respect for black women. However, 'the true nature of man is to be strong, and a woman's true nature is to be weak, and while a man must at all times respect his woman, at the same time he needs to understand that he must control her if he expects to get her respect.'[10] So, no change there.

The feature of Malcolm X's preaching and teaching is that he has a new perspective from which to understand reality. Thus he sees Christianity as the white man's religion. 'The Holy Bible in the white man's hands and his interpretation of it have been the greatest single ideological weapon for enslaving millions of non-white human beings.'[11] He is not confused by the liberal sentiments of individual whites: the enemy is institutionalised racism which leads all whites into oppression of blacks. He certainly sees all whites as evil. What is more puzzling is his apparent acceptance of the corollary, that blacks are essentially good. His detailed recounting of his life as a hustler uncovers evidence to the contrary. Evil in the black communities can hardly be attributed entirely to the dehumanising influence of whites. To this point we shall return in the next section. What he was not prepared for was the hatred and jealousy which emerged towards him among black Muslims, especially after he had discovered evidence of adultery by the man he 'worshipped', the Honorable Elijah Muhammad.

After he was silenced and marginalised he resigned from the Nation of Islam and announced that he would set up his own organization, the Muslim Mosque, Inc., in New York. He felt free to concentrate on his own agenda. 'It will be the working base for an action program designed to eliminate the political oppression, the economic exploitation, and the social degradation suffered daily by twenty-two million Afro-Americans.'[12] It was at this time that he made the pilgrimage to Mecca, an experience which was to change his life once again. Four features of the *hajj* are of particular importance. The first is that Malcolm X now experienced orthodox Islam for the first time, and the black Muslims suffered by comparison. He knew that Wallace, Elijah Muhammad's son, was in favour of accepting orthodox Islam: now he understood why. Here he was part of the authentic worldwide religious tradition. The second is connected to this. In Saudia Arabia, but also in the visits he then made to various African countries, he saw how important it was to establish international contacts. This is a curiously late discovery for someone whose father was a Garveyite. He set up the Organization of Afro-American Unity. Free of the constraints imposed by Elijah Muhammad he could embark on a more active social and political programme. A speech in Harlem in December 1964 broke new ground.

> Almost every one of the countries that has gotten independence has devised some kind of socialistic system, and this is no accident ... You can't operate a capitalistic system unless you are vulturistic; you have to have someone's blood to suck to be a capitalist. You show me a capitalist, and I'll show you a blood sucker.[13]

He never espoused Marxism, which he viewed as another white man's ideology. The third feature was the experience of brotherhood and acceptance which he met from the moment he became a pilgrim. And fourth, and connected to this, was perhaps the most important experience of all. Yes, he found himself part of a great international brotherhood of orthodox Muslims representing virtually every race on earth – including the white race. From his earliest days he had always tried to face the facts, to begin from the reality around him. Now that reality included white men who treated him as if they were colour blind. It was within orthodox Islam that all men could be brothers. He still did not believe that by secular means, such as legislation, this could be brought about.

And so as he returned to America he knew that he had been changed once again.

> In the past, yes, I have made sweeping indictments of *all* white people. I never will be guilty of that again – as I know now that some white people *are* truly sincere, that some truly are capable of being brotherly toward a black man. The true Islam has shown me that a blanket indictment of all white people is as wrong as when whites make blanket indictments against blacks.[14]

The white man is not inherently evil. We might surmise from this that his contact with Mecca had led him to set aside the myth of Yacub's History. And now, as he moved towards the stage of the Audubon Ballroom in Harlem on that fateful night, he could speak in more conciliatory tones about Martin Luther King. But as he did so he became even more of a threat to the black Muslims. Thus the most charismatic black leader of his day was poised to raise black consciousness to a new level, when a disturbance broke out a few rows back and three men in dark suits rose to their feet. Malcolm X on several occasions expressed admiration for a young leader of the Nation of Islam, one who had taken over his work in Boston, the 'outstanding young Minister Louis X', 'our talented Louis X'.[15] It was widely believed that Louis Haleem Abdul Farrakhan was implicated in his assassination. What is clear is that Farrakhan has steered the Nation of Islam away on a very different course from that charted by Malcolm X in his final days.

Louis Eugene Walcott was born in 1933 in the Bronx. We should not be surprised by this time that his roots lay in the Caribbean. His mother, Sarah Mae Manning, was born in St Kitts and his father, Percival Clarke, had immigrated from Jamaica. Sarah Mae Manning arrived in New York in the mid-1920s and was a strong supporter of UNIA. Her son recalls visiting an uncle in New York and observing a picture of Marcus Garvey on the mantel. On being told that this man 'was the greatest leader our people ever had', he wept that he had come too late to support his work.[16] However, he inherited some of Garvey's ideas. Gene Walcott grew up in the West Indian neighbourhood of Roxbury, in Boston. Although the family was poor he had some middle-class experiences. He was an Episcopalian. He learned to play the violin, an instrument which became a consuming passion. He attended the historic and elite Boston Latin school and then the English High. After college in North Carolina, and to the dismay of his mother, he became a nightclub entertainer appearing with his calypso band under the title of 'The Charmer'. It was while on tour in Chicago in 1955 that he heard Elijah Muhammad speak, and became a convert to the Nation of Islam. He returned to Boston, to work as captain of the Fruit of Islam in the temple which Malcolm X had left the previous year. In 1957 he was appointed minister of the Temple No. 11, and impressed everyone, including Malcolm X, with the increase in membership, and the discipline and control he exercised over the members, although there were complaints about his violent methods. However, when the split came in 1964 with Malcolm's dismissal, he continued to support Elijah Muhammad. The Boston Temple lost over half of its members and Louis X began to attack his former friend and patron, denouncing Malcolm as having made friends with Jews, Christians and white men. 'Only those who wish to be led to hell, or to their doom, will follow Malcolm. The die is set, and Malcolm shall not escape ... Such a man as Malcolm is worthy of death.'[17] He was not one of the three black Muslims convicted for the murder, but at the very least he contributed to the climate in which the assassination was seen as a religious duty. He was transferred to the prestigious Temple No. 7 in Harlem. In the early 1970s there was internecine war, Elijah Muhammad had lost control and Louis X was legitimising the executions of dissidents with passages from the Qur'an.

On his father's death in 1975, Wallace Deen Muhammad took over leadership of the movement. He was determined to bring it within orthodox Islam, to turn it from its political activities to emphasise the spiritual life, to end the culture of violence and confrontation, indeed to end the separation from and hatred of white people and to welcome them as members. In other words, Wallace was intent on directing the movement along the path which Malcolm X had prophetically identified at the end of his life. Louis X, now given the name Abdul Haleem Farrakhan, was brought to Chicago to receive a higher title, but a restricted office. By 1977 he was forced to make a choice between the path of the son or the heritage of the father. Wallace had closed down the Nation of Islam. Farrakhan decided to resurrect and lead it. During the last 25 years he has continued the attack on racism, but it is his anti-Semitism which has frequently brought him to public attention.

Growing up in Boston the young Gene Walcott seems to have had little experience of racism. The examples he gives are of attacks by Irish gangs on black youths. Many of his young friends were Jewish, as was his violin teacher. His contacts with Judaism within the Nation of Islam are not without irony. His first experience of Muslim worship was at the Chicago Temple. It was situated in a district on the south side which was changing from predominantly Jewish to predominantly black. 'One talisman of the change was the stone replica of the Ten Commandments that remained on top of the front façade of the Nation of Islam's Temple No. 2, a former synagogue.'[18] Similarly, when he wanted to establish a proper temple in Boston, as distinct from the various apartments which had been used by Malcolm X, he bought a building which had been until recently an orthodox rabbinic seminary. But now he turned from the Yacub account of white racial oppression to identify the Jews as being the devils behind the suffering of his people. In 1984 he supported the presidential candidacy of the Rev Jesse Jackson, regarded by many as pro-Palestinian and by some as anti-Semitic. Farrakhan warned those who sought to harm Jackson. 'We are not making idle threats.'[19] In particular he claimed that Israeli hit squads had been sent to America to kill Jackson. Nathan Perlmutter, in an image which recalled Hitler in Munich in 1923, deplored this 'beerhall demagoguery'.[20] No doubt in the spirit of the enemy of my enemy,

Farrakhan said that if there was a parallel, both he and Hitler were attempting to raise their people up from the depths to which others had consigned them, a worthy project which made Hitler 'a very great man'.[21] Asked at a Washington press conference a month later if he still thought Hitler truly great Farrakhan made his now famous response. 'I don't think you would be talking about Adolf Hitler forty years after the fact if he was some minuscule crackpot that jumped up on the European continent. He was ... a great man, but also wicked – wickedly great.'[22] It seems clear that Hitler was of no interest to Farrakhan. It was not he who had brought up the subject. In the original remark he was praising a leader who addressed the suffering of his people. In the later comment he is saying that Hitler was a man of great ability, who eventually used it for evil. 'Wicked' is a strangely dated term in the modern world: it represents moral condemnation in an age of relativism, scolding in an age when leaders decline to take responsibility for condemning evil. Hitler, for Farrakhan was 'wicked'. It is of some interest that the wildest spokesman for the Nation of Islam, Khallid Abdul Muhammad, uses precisely the same term. 'Now, he was an arrogant, no-good, devil bastard, Hitler, no question about it ... He used his greatness for evil and wickedness.'[23] Both Khallid and Farrakhan are openly anti-Semitic, but this can be established clearly without attempting to prove that they were supporters of Hitler. When the then mayor of New York, Ed Koch, described Farrakhan as a 'Nazi in clerical garb'[24] he sets his anti-Semitism in the wrong context. Farrakhan has no sympathy for National Socialism, indeed for any kind of socialism. It was a strategic mistake for the NAACP to seek to associate Marcus Garvey with the Klan: that only gave a certain standing to white supremacists. There is a history of white supremacists seeking to associate with the separatist policies of the Nation of Islam. Thus in 1962 George Lincoln Rockwell, leader of the American Nazi Party, attended the annual convention of the Nation of Islam in Chicago and claimed that 'Elijah Muhammad is the Adolf Hitler of the black man.'[25] In 1985 Thomas Metzger, leader of the white supremacist White American Political Association and former leader of the Klan in California, attended a Farrakhan rally in Los Angeles and made a very public (though modest) contribution to the collection taken at the meeting. Those who attack Farrakhan should perhaps pause before making claims about him which can only further the interests of neo-Nazi and white supremacist groups.

Others have attacked Farrakhan because of his essential religious and political conservatism. A veteran civil rights activist, Julian Bond, described him as 'a black Pat Buchanan' claiming that he is 'notoriously and unapologetically anti-Semitic, anti-Catholic, anti-white, misogynist and anti-gay'.[26] Farrakhan's position has developed over the years, leading one commentator to observe that 'like a bad bottle of wine, Farrakhan seems to immature with age'.[27] However, in other respects the ethos of the Nation of Islam has been compared to the Protestant work ethic. 'While Farrakhan never presented himself as a Republican or a Democrat, many of his values – discipline, self-reliance, economic self-betterment, even an abhorrence of welfare – were bedrock, country-club Republicanism.'[28] In this context we could mention the Million Man March, of 16 October 1995, for which Farrakhan urged black men to repent of their sins, and to march with self-dignity and self-respect. We shall discuss the Pledge taken on that occasion in the Conclusion.

Farrakhan, this friend of Kwame Toure, therefore represents a particular reception of Black Power in a religious context. Yes, it is the religion of the black Muslims, and yet it has not broken its links with that form of Christianity which has been at the heart of the black communities. When Louis X returned to his home city of Boston, he visited the Reverend Nathan Wright, the minister who had married him and Betsy Ross in St Cyprian's Church. He called on his friend to tell him that he had followed him 'into the ministry'.[29] As Arthur Magida observes,

> Louis may have been a Muslim, but he had not forgotten his Christian roots. If anything, his visit to Wright made it clear that Louis did not think he had abandoned the faith of his youth by joining the Nation of Islam. Rather, he was spearheading a parallel church, a 'protest' church, a reform movement that would purge Christianity of its hypocrisy and spiritual sterility.[30]

There were also Christians who attempted this project, and to them we now turn.

Black Theology

The 1950s were decisive years for race relations in America. In Washington in 1954 the Supreme Court outlawed segregated education. In the following year in Montgomery, Alabama, Mrs Rosa Parks refused to give up her seat on a bus to a white man. In 1952 Malcolm Little became a member of the Nation of Islam receiving the name Malcolm X. But in 1953, also in the city of Detroit, there took place a little publicised event, namely the dedication of a church by Rev Albert B. Cleage Jr. as *The Shrine of the Black Madonna*. At the dedication of the chancel mural on Easter Sunday, Cleage declared 'our unveiling of the Black Madonna is a statement of faith'.[31] But the object of faith was not that aristocratic white woman so beloved of medieval European art, balancing on her lap a child who has turned his back on her. Revealed to the congregation was the tall and striking figure of a black woman, cradling a child in her arms. She stands with steady gaze looking out upon the world, her face at once witness to generations of slave women who had their children taken from them, and also to her simple dignity and pride at having borne this child and her determination to love and protect him. She is not the mother of that 'fairest Lord Jesus' who looks as if he would not say boo to a goose. The faith which Cleage confesses is in a Black Messiah, 'a powerful black man supplanting the weak little mamby-pamby white Jesus'.[32] Thirteen years before Stokely Carmichael began to speak about black power, Albert Cleage displayed black consciousness. Sixteen years before James Cone published the first book on Black theology, Albert Cleage was presenting a new black perspective on Christian faith. Albert Cleage has never received the recognition due to him. Why should that be so? In a book dedicated to the analysis of ideology and religion one answer immediately suggests itself. The forces which control society – white society but also black society – could cope with others, such as Carmichael and Cone, could come to terms with them and finally use them, but not so in the case of Cleage. His analysis was more subtle than theirs, his programme more comprehensive: he could not be incorporated.

It is surely no coincidence that living and working in Detroit, the headquarters of the Nation of Islam, the most central concept in Cleage's position is the Nation. He did not believe that the black Muslims could be anything but a minority in the black community, nevertheless their focus on the Nation was a challenge to the Christian church. From the founding of the Republic till the present time, the Christian church – regardless of the much vaunted separation of church and state – has been the single most important influence in the development of the American way of life. While this might be a matter of congratulation in white suburbia and small town America, it looks like a serious accusation to the denizens of the black ghettos. Cleage could not ignore the concept of the *black* Nation, and yet his treatment of the subject is entirely different from that of Elijah Muhammad.

To understand Cleage's position we must understand his rejection of integration. He does not stop to declare himself on miscegenation. The matter is in the mind rather than the loins. Regardless of the constitution, blacks have historically been excluded from the American way of life. Cleage does not hesitate to uncover the feet of clay of the Great Liberator. Abraham Lincoln 'freed all the slaves only because it was necessary to preserve the dominant power and supremacy of the white group of which he was leader'.[33] Ironically, America, founded ostensibly by a revolution to end injustice, has seen the white man 'willing to sacrifice the Constitution, the courts and the law, to preserve what he held sacred, the status quo'.[34] Blacks have been forced to live separately from the white mainstream. They have been in America, but not of America. The right to life, liberty and the pursuit of happiness, the right to vote and even the right to bear arms was never intended to apply to blacks. In a phrase which Cleage uses frequently the separation is founded on 'the white man's *declaration of black inferiority*'.[35] It is therefore more than ironic that black radicals should be described as separatists, should be *accused* of being separatists. The separation has always been there. How to respond to it? Integration is unacceptable to Cleage because it requires blacks to accept 'the white man's declaration of black inferiority'. Integration does not describe a coming together such as might be seen in the merging of two companies in which each contributes from its strength, each sets aside elements which do not enhance the new reality. In the case of integration there is no new reality. The old reality continues, except that a door is opened fractionally, grudgingly, to permit a few selected blacks to pass into white society. In passing through this door 'into Uncle Tom Land',[36] they must first agree to black inferiority. Integration means giving up being black insofar as this is humanly possible, and accepting white values and the white way of life as the ultimate goal. Of course it cannot be achieved. The requirement cannot be met. But this only confirms the premise concerning black inferiority. 'Self-hatred was a part of the Black man's desire for integration.'[37]

Those who have been brought up to believe that white is right and white is best are devastated by this exclusion. But this act of exclusion, this enforced separatism can also be experienced in a positive way. What if blacks decide that they do not want to enter that door marked 'self-castration'? They are being told to stay where they are, but what if they *decide* to stay where they are? Once the decision has been made to stay outside everything changes. Instead of being excluded from the American nation it is now possible to conceive of blacks forming their own nation. No, they need not travel one mile to do so: this is not a matter of geography. They can be a Nation within the nation. They can be a Black Nation living within America, no longer begging at the door of the white nation. 'We are not Americans. We are an African people who against our will were brought to America.'[38] They can begin to affirm themselves and reject inferiority; they can look to themselves instead of turning to whites; they can unite as friends instead of being divided by their enemies.

We can sense here a dynamic, but it must have a direction. Black, yes, but being black, affirming blackness is not enough. 'Being black is a condition, not a program.'[39] Black people have suffered from separation: now they must learn from it. 'Black people must remain separate using the separateness that already exists as a basis for political power, for economic power, and for the transmission of cultural values.'[40] The affirmation of blackness must issue in black power, the power to be able to control black neighbourhoods, schools, shops, businesses. It is with the taking of power that the black Nation will be united and enriched. It is on this reading of the situation that Cleage is so scathing of Roy Wilkins and the NAACP, but also critical of Dr Martin Luther King and the SCLC.

'Genuine black leadership cannot lead in the direction of integration.'[41] The old reality was separation, the new reality is pan-Africanism, 'the bringing together of Black people across artificial national boundaries as one people'.[42]

In all this we see some common themes with the broad spectrum of black consciousness in the USA. Cleage displays originality: he is not simply repeating other people's slogans. However, the decisive difference in his position arises from the fact that he is not simply a black nationalist, but what he specifically calls a Black Christian Nationalist, a movement established in 1967. The specifically Christian dimension of his nationalism forms his Black theology, to which we now turn.

The problem for Cleage is that it is Christianity itself which has been the single most important factor in legitimising 'the white man's declaration of black inferiority'. Deprived of their own traditional religions of Africa, the slaves were drawn into the white man's religion: not Christianity, but that European form of Christianity which developed to suit the white man's needs and interests. 'A black church which is a copy of the white church cannot meet any of our needs.'[43] But how should the Black church serve the needs and interests of black people? It is at this point that Cleage takes a step which is at once so astonishing, brilliant, creative, original and bold that he should have immediately been appointed to the chair of boldness at Harvard University. At a stroke he wrests Christianity from the control of the white community, and delivers it to its rightful heirs, the black nation.

Anyone familiar with modern western theology will know that it is now written within the university rather than the church: its dialogue partner is the academic community rather than the community of faith. The attraction is obvious, but the cost has been high. In the secular university theology has undertaken its task on the same basis as other humanities disciplines: neither faith nor belief is required. The results correspond. The most striking feature of Cleage's theology therefore is that it is set out not in lectures but in sermons. They do not end with a hurry bell but with a prayer. His concern is not to justify the ways of God to men, but to teach, encourage, inspire and edify the faithful. His first book, *The Black Messiah*, is a series of sermons in which he preaches the good news to black Christians. Cumulatively he develops a Black theology. There are no footnotes, no pedantic digressions to display scholarship; assertions replace tentative hypotheses. Some of the conclusions would require more argument and evidence, but there is no doubt about the impact. Cleage reconstructs Christianity to serve the needs and interests of black people. Before scholars weigh in with their objections to this approach, perhaps they would first care to apply their criticisms to generations of white preachers who have justified every evil known to man and beast if they served the needs and interests of the white community.

Separatists have divided the world into two camps, the white race and the others. As we have seen, Cleage begins with the reality of separation. Christianity begins among the Semitic peoples, who for millennia had mixed with peoples from north Africa. If there is but one division permitted, then Christianity belongs to the blacks. In the Christian era Europe has dominated the known world. It has colonised all in its path and has forced everything to serve its needs and interests: so with the Christian religion. Cleage therefore sets up a parallel of ancient and modern. The white Roman empire conquered the coloured Semitic world: Christianity was transformed into a religion suitable for white people. In the modern world the white race dominates all others. White Christianity has been conveyed to all subject peoples, where it has furthered at an unconscious level the self-hatred which is the outcome of 'the white man's declaration of black inferiority'. For Cleage the only way to break this cycle is to insist that Christianity was originally a religion of black people. He must indicate what was the nature of that black religion, its main features which distinguish it from its white appropriation and distortion. Only then can the Black church preach good news to black people today, in Detroit. It is a daring project. To attempt to preach to blacks from a Christianity constructed to serve whites seems radical, but it is destined to fail the people it intends to serve. It is integration by religious means, which is to say it is the perpetuation of inferiority and self-hatred in sonorous tones. The alternative is to reach back behind the origins of white Christianity and find in history an authentic black Christianity which across the centuries speaks strangely to the black nation: the true word of God always comes strangely in a world of injustice and oppression.

Where could an authentic Christianity begin except with a new (or old) understanding of Jesus Christ? Cleage tells his people that 'Jesus was the non-white leader of a non-white people struggling for national liberation against the rule of a white nation, Rome.'[44] Here is the parallel between the life and times of Jesus and the conditions of blacks in America. Jesus' project must be their project. 'Jesus was a revolutionary black leader, a Zealot, seeking to lead a Black Nation to freedom, so the Black Church must carefully define the nature of the revolution.' [45] This statement might be offensive, alarming or absurd to white people, but its most important feature is the responsibility given to the Black church. Jesus came to liberate his people: they must be involved in the contemporary liberation movement. Yes, but it is not simply a religious legitimation of a protest movement. The Black church must have its own interpretation of events, a Christian interpretation. It must be able to see the hand of God in this historic moment, follow the Black Messiah in the course of events unfolding. Above all, the Black church must participate in God's revolution and proclaim it as such to the black nation: 'the revolution becomes part of our Christian faith'.[46] As evidence of the extent to which Christian faith is now black, the prayers with which the sermons end are 'in the name of the Black Messiah, Jesus Christ'.[47] This is not a religious legitimation, he is calling for Christian initiatives. If the revolution is to be more than a riot, more than criminality, then it must be a historical movement which incarnates human values. No other group is in a position to ensure that this is so. 'The church is the soul of the Nation.'[48]

The revolution is something that is happening to blacks, but also to whites. Why then is it the responsibility of blacks only? For reasons of separation, as we have seen, but also because God has so determined it. 'We are God's chosen people, God is with us in our struggle. Our freedom struggle, our movement, our Black Revolution is in the hands of God.'[49] This is an immensely fruitful line of thought for Cleage. It enables him to draw parallels between the experience of ancient Israel and modern black Americans – and of course to see white America as the heir of ancient Rome. 'We have now reclaimed our covenant as God's Chosen People and our revolutionary black Messiah Jesus.'[50] Separation is a central theme in the Old Testament. Abraham is called to found a Nation. The Promised Land refers to life with God rather than the ownership of territory.

Cleage develops an extensive Black theology: he is not guilty of selecting a few proof texts with which to legitimise a secular black revolution. One theme sees him make a distinction which is already familiar to us, the distinction between the teaching of Jesus and that of Paul. How did we get from the religion of Jesus to the religion of oppression? All liberation movements follow the same line: Paul is the villain, who departed from the teaching of Jesus. Cleage does this, but in a way which has – unlike the case of feminism – theological and not merely sociological significance. He presents black people as standing in the tradition of Israel, inheritors of a religion which is fundamentally concerned with the Nation: chosen people, Abrahamic covenant, Promised Land. Jesus is hailed as son of David, that is as the king and defender of the Nation, his message is about the Kingdom of God – the life of the Nation faithful to the covenant. This is the context in which Cleage presents the message and ministry of Jesus.

> I am reminded of the last days of Jesus, the black Messiah who came to a Black Nation of people who were divided and didn't know which way to turn, just as we don't. He came to bring them together to teach them that unity, love for each other, sacrifice, commitment and discipline were essential if they were to be free. His whole ministry was going about among a Black Nation preaching to them about the things that had to be done if they were to find freedom from oppression by a white nation, Rome. Everything he did was trying to bring a people together.[51]

When a Gentile woman asked him to heal her daughter, addressing him as son of David, Jesus simply ignored her, and told his disciples, 'I was sent only to the lost sheep of the house of Israel' (Matt. 15: 21–28). His mission is to the Nation, not to the Gentiles.

The charge against Jesus was that he aspired to be King of the Jews (like his father David). He and his followers lived a communal life, and after his death they re-organised themselves into a community of 'primitive socialism'[52] in Jerusalem. If this presentation of Jesus seems alien to us, then according to Cleage it is because it was overtaken by the teaching of Paul. Paul departed from the traditions of Jesus and the early church. He conceived of himself as the apostle to the Gentiles, that is the white people. Those living in the Hellenistic culture of the Roman empire knew nothing about Israel, about the Nation, the son of David and the Kingdom. Paul could not preach the gospel to them in these terms. 'The New Testament reflects the primitive pagan distortions that the Apostle Paul foisted upon the early church as a self-appointed apostle to the white Gentile world.'[53] Good news to the Gentiles was very different from the message of Jesus. They needed a religion of personal salvation, of personal conversion. Paul was able to provide this, in the light of what Cleage rather disparagingly calls 'his little experience on the Damascus Road'.[54] This is the religion of individual self-interest. It is not the religion of Jesus. Paul, instead of repeating the message which Jesus proclaimed, initiated a theology of the significance of Jesus, thus 'changing the religion *of* Jesus to a religion *about* Jesus'.[55] For Cleage Christianity then becomes the white man's religion, a religion that caters for the needs of the white man. The most pressing of these needs is forgiveness of sin, but the sins are the petty personal sins of morality.

> We, as black Christians suffering oppression in a white man's land, do not need the individualistic and otherworldly doctrines of Paul and the white man. We need to recapture the faith in our power as a people and the concept of Nation, which are the foundation of the Old Testament and the prophets, and upon which Jesus built all of his teachings 2,000 years ago.[56]

(White) Christianity is slave religion: it is used to control people, to deflect their aspirations for the Nation and raise their eyes to heaven where a white God and a white Jesus will at the last forgive them of their greatest sin, being black.

Thus did Paul betray Jesus more fundamentally than Judas – this 'Apostle Paul, who was an Uncle Tom who wanted to identify with his white gentile oppressors. Paul was proud of his Roman citizenship, even though he was an oppressed Black Jew.'[57] In Cleage's terms Paul was an integrationist who betrayed his Nation in order to ingratiate himself to the enemy. But his betrayal of Jesus must be seen in theological and not simply sociological terms. It redefines and distorts the very doctrine of salvation. According to Cleage's Black theology, Paul transforms the significance of Jesus from that of revolutionary leader who was prepared to die for the Nation, into a sacrificial victim whose death itself – and without context – atones for individual sins. 'It was not enough to say that Paul lost the meaning of the life and death of Jesus, the Black Messiah, by making him a pagan atonement symbol.'[58]

> But if God does not save individuals one by one – and obviously He does not – then how does God save? If we are not saved by the healing blood of Jesus on Calvary – and obviously we are not – then how does the Black Messiah save? The impotence of the traditional church lies in its inability to understand the process of salvation.[59]

For Cleage the Black church cannot continue to preach the white gospel: the needs of the black Nation are not addressed in this medium, indeed they are deliberately set aside. He claims that the basic problem of the Black church is theological. Cleage's Black theology does not stop at a few proof texts: it enters into the substance of Christian doctrine. 'Black Christian Nationalism redefines salvation, calls men to a rejection of individualism, and offers a process of transformation by which the individual may divest himself of individualism and submerge himself in the community life of the group.'[60] Cleage therefore makes a very significant distinction between 'a gospel of liberation and the gospel of salvation'.[61] The theological basis of the gospel of liberation is the life and teaching of Jesus – not his death, except for his preparedness to die for the Nation. The gospel of salvation, as he calls it, is the gospel of Paul, which totally ignores the life and teaching of Jesus in favour of a white (Hellenistic) pagan doctrine of the metaphysical significance of the death, *qua* death, of Jesus as victim. 'Our development of a Black theology separates us from Christians who do not accept a theology of liberation.'[62]

The distinction between these two gospels is not simply doctrinal, but has very practical consequences. We might illustrate the point at issue by two contrasting episodes in the Old Testament. In the first God arranged for the exodus of the Hebrew slaves from Egypt without their participation. In the second the tribes of Israel carried out the conquest of Canaan by a campaign of genocide at the explicit command of God. In the one case God's will is done by God alone. In the other Israel cooperates with God in the achievement of His will. According to Cleage white Christianity has had the effect of making black people passive and accepting of their lot. 'It is hard to lead a people whose basic orientation to struggle is not in terms of what they can do or must do but rather in terms of God's intervention to do for them that which must be done.'[63] The Black church has taught that God will come as righteous judge to deal with oppression and injustice. That is His responsibility, not theirs. There have of course been notable exceptions, black leaders of the nineteenth century such as Gabriel Prosser, Denmark Vesey and Nat Turner who led militant campaigns against slavery, but they have been just that – notable exceptions. It is regarded as a properly pious attitude to await the return of the Son of Man, but this exodus confidence drains away the militancy of the conquest. 'You can't lead a people who are sitting around waiting for Jesus to come back on clouds of glory. All you can do is prepare a landing field for him.'[64]

Cleage sees the Black revolution as the activity of God in contemporary events, and on the conquest model, the Black church is called upon to participate in the liberation struggle. 'The Black Church must offer leadership in the Black Revolution.'[65] However, the actual events in the late 1960s in Watts, Newark, Chicago, New York and Detroit were much more ambiguous and this leads to an important moral dilemma. What should the Black church say about the rioters whose contribution to the struggle seemed to be to liberate TV sets and washing machines from vandalised stores? Insofar as the Black church is but an arm of white Christianity, reinforcing social control and bourgeois values, then of course the white church expected the Black church to do its duty and condemn offences against property. Cleage preferred to take the longer view. The founding fathers were revolutionaries, criminals guilty of treason. But as with the revolutionaries of France and then Russia, success legitimises the crimes. The rightness of the cause cannot be evaluated on the basis of the breaking of laws imposed from elsewhere. Just as the government could act like criminals in Vietnam, so the police could act like thugs in the ghettos. In a troubled period Cleage ends one sermon with a prayer of thanksgiving for the continued existence of the church building. 'We thank thee for protecting it during the week from the defenders of the law.'[66] For Cleage there is but one line to be drawn, and those who take to the streets are part of the revolution. 'You ought to love the looters because they are part of the black Nation.'[67] And if this did not raise sufficiently the blood pressure of church leaders, black and white alike, he can even detect the presence of God in the heat of the action. We have indicated that Cleage covers a broad theological spectrum in his reflections on the liberation struggle. He can even speak of 'the revolutionary Holy Spirit'.[68] As the cities of America were turned upside down he viewed the revolution as a new Pentecost. 'It was as though the cities were filled with a rush of a mighty wind and tongues of fire rested over each Black head.'[69]

Wonderful rhetoric, but at the same time depressing. Cleage has accused the white church of legitimising naked power. He seems to be offering a licence to every mindless act so long as it is committed by a black man. But no, Albert Cleage is more courageous than that. He has already told us that there must be a Christian view of the revolution. He does not follow along ingratiating himself to black radicals by saying Amen to every black excess. He is confident in his own Christian Black Nationalism, from which standpoint he can say some brave and salutary things about the rioters. He derides the self-styled radical blacks, who announce that they go to the ghettos to learn from the ordinary people. This is an idealising of the victims which can only arise from a false reading of the situation, and a total lack of critical perspective. 'Black people are not good because they are poor and powerless.'[70] We were careful to point out that Blyden and Garvey refused to sacrilise Negroes. Cleage has committed his life to working with poor blacks. That experience does not lead him to a romantic idealising of them, but rather to a clear view of why the revolution is necessary. 'Basically, oppressed masses are sick.'[71] The ideology of black inferiority has impoverished their lives, but only after it has contaminated their minds. 'Masses of people who have been oppressed, discriminated against, who have lacked opportunity, who have in every way been shut out of the mainstream of life are sick because of their oppression.'[72] It is in this context that we can understand his support for the looters. At least they are beginning to act, to fight back. Here is the affirmation of Césaire and Fanon. But there is a long road to travel to health and fulfilment. Anyone who has been involved in political struggle knows that you cannot be too purist about those with whom you must work. As Cleage observes 'Samson wasn't any hero kind of person in normal circumstances.'[73] Only the Lord God would choose a violent, mindless skirt-chaser to save Israel. Cleage knows very well what is going on in the streets. His response is neither to condemn nor to condone – but to propose a solution.

> So we are developing a generation of monsters, little vicious individualists concerned only about themselves. You can idealize them, you can say, 'They are the vanguard of the revolution.' But they are the vanguard of no revolution. They are the vanguard of chaos. They are mad, they are evil, and they are lonesome. They are by themselves, and nobody offers them anything to believe in and to become a part of. This, then is a basic task of the Black Nation.[74]

This is the good news that Black Christian Nationalism offers to the rioters and looters. Cleage sets out in detail the 'Programming for Liberation', an education and discipline training which we might say begins with seven steps towards 'deprogramming'. Black people must recognise that white society has made them sick, has taught them self-hatred, has mis-educated them and has led them to betray their own. This last point of course is a favourite theme for Cleage, since he is able to draw a parallel with those who betrayed Jesus as he sought to unite the black Nation. The white nation, the Romans, could count on the Jews to betray their own people, whether John the Baptist or Jesus of Nazareth. One of the features of life for those of us who worked for majority rule in African colonies in that same period was that the security forces had an endless supply of black informants. The deprogramming in Black Christian Nationalism releases blacks from their former lives as Uncle Tom and Aunt Jemima, blacks whose first loyalty was to their white masters.

The programme is a resource to help people change their lives. Indeed they must change their minds, which is what *metanoia*, conversion, originally meant. One of the most striking features of the Black theology of Albert Cleage is that it takes place not only within the church, but in the context of worship. Others are content to discuss ideas: he revises doctrine, music, liturgy in the light of his Black theology.

So it is that the Eucharist and baptism come to be understood no longer in the light of the religious needs of individualistic salvation, but as resources in the building of the black Nation. Thus baptism is not a washing away of petty indiscretions, but the incorporation of the individual into a greater whole. 'We baptize into the Nation in the Name of the Father, the Son and the Holy Spirit. This baptism is meaningful because you die to your old Uncle Tom ways, the slave ways you used to have. And you are born again, you are resurrected in the newness of life into the black Nation.'[75] The Eucharist is a sacrament, not to satisfy individual religious needs, but to be part of the body of the Black Messiah. And we are saying in our participation in the sacrament of Holy Communion, 'I am a part of the nation. I accept this sacrifice which the Black Messiah made as the symbolic sacrifice which I'm willing to make that the Nation may be built, that it may grow, that it may have power.'[76] It is an open table, or at least open to those who in addition to loving the Lord, share one commitment. 'Any Christian who commits himself to the freedom struggle, to the Black Revolution, and to the Black Messiah, is invited to share it with us.'[77]

The revolution then is God's revolution, and the struggle is the project of the Black Messiah, to which the Black church must be committed. But what is impressive is that Cleage is able to distinguish this work from that of Black Power in some general or secular sense. He has very clear views on the significance of other black leaders, but his racing instructions come from a higher authority. This is nowhere better illustrated than in his appreciation of Malcolm X. There are several factors to be taken into account, especially in Detroit. As a black activist Cleage can express his admiration for Malcolm X, but as a Christian he is critical of the black Muslims. We find him therefore concentrating on that phase in Malcolm's life in which he was emerging from the shadow of Elijah Muhammad and developing his own position. He begins by criticising not Elijah Muhammad, but the Yakub myth, the myth that a black scientist Yakub created the white beast who was permitted by Allah to reign for 6000 years, a period which ended in 1914. He attacks the myth not so much as a construct which has no basis in history, a scenario which must be incredible to any reasonable person who hears of it, but as a dangerous misreading of the real situation, an analysis which fails to identify the nature of the problem. It is bad psychology, bad sociology and bad anthropology.[78] He might also have said it is bad theology. 'In reality we are dealing with a man with a human nature just like our own, but with power. We ought to realize that this is what power does to human nature. This is reality. The white man is not a beast. He's not a devil. He's just a human being with power.'[79] Given the popularity of Malcolm X's presentation of the white man as the devil, this criticism is very courageous. 'As black men get little bits of power they become a little bestial.'[80] Once again Cleage refuses to idealise the black victims. It is not that the white man is evil and the black man is good: the white man has power which abuses and also corrupts, and this pattern will be repeated if the black man is fortunate enough ever to have power. Cleage therefore presents another aspect of his Black theology. The way forward is not to replace one abuser and corrupter with his mirror image, but to find a new way of creating a community, a Nation, in which the gaining of power will not destroy. This of course is the programme of Black Christian Nationalism. Indeed his vision is wider than black communities within America. 'No concept of power short of a worldwide Pan-Africanism can protect Black people from the dehumanizing effects of white individualism.'[81] His starting point is not a black Muslim myth, but the Christian doctrine of sin. 'We have two beasts to fight: the beast within and the beast without ... We reject the Yakub myth because it obscures an understanding of our own inner nature, and makes it difficult to comprehend the motivation and strategy of our enemy.'[82] This is a very nuanced argument which demonstrates Black theology's capacity to focus on reality more comprehensively than white Christianity or black Muslim teaching. Cleage is therefore able to praise Malcolm X while at the same time criticising the black Muslim analysis. Malcolm, he claims was moving beyond the Yakub myth. Had he lived, although still a black Muslim, his position would have been the same as Cleage's. As he sees it, Malcolm was moving from the schematic reading of the myth to a more realistic view of the issue. 'We are oppressed by a white institutionalized power establishment from which we are excluded.'[83] The autobiography of Malcom X presents a rather romantic picture of race relations within Islam because he was reflecting on his experience of individual behaviour. But this is not an adequate basis for analysis. Cleage regrets that Malcolm was not able to edit this part of the story. 'No white individual can escape involvement in white racist society, not in Mecca or anywhere else. But the white individual is not the entity with which we must deal.'[84] His admiration for Malcolm does not prevent him from identifying a weakness found also among Christians, not least in the wrist-slapping moralism of much feminist theology. 'This was the basic weakness in the philosophy of Brother Malcolm when he broke free of the Muslim mythology – which escaped the confusion of human morality by attributing the immorality of vengeance and punishment to God.'[85] Entrenched racism cannot be addressed in its particular instances. 'The white man's conscience has nothing to do with his institutional power struggle. Touching his conscience is a waste of time. Malcolm never completely escaped from Black morality.'[86] Black Power, even Black Christian Power has nothing to do with moralism, and certainly nothing to do with the idea of divine intervention in the pursuit of justice. 'Malcolm never entirely escaped the Black man's naïve faith that God would somehow intervene on the side of right. Up until the very end Malcolm was a moralist, thinking in terms of people being good and bad.'[87] But he was moving, and he would have ended up close to the analysis of Black Christian Nationalism.

Nevertheless the black movement cannot afford to allow the white community to drive a wedge between Malcolm the Muslim and Martin the Christian. On one Sunday in the year *The Shrine of the Black Madonna* paid tribute to Brother Malcolm, and Cleage could not 'resist the temptation to compare Brother Malcolm to Jesus, the Jesus whom we worship, the Black Messiah'.[88] They both identified the white enemy, worked for the unification and liberation of the black Nation. And both were betrayed by Uncle Toms. The service ends with the prayer: 'Keep bright our remembrance of Brother Malcolm.'[89] This is a living Black theology, a theology of the heart.

The other black leader whom Cleage admired was Stokely Carmichael. As we have seen, Cleage does not simply say me-too to Black Power. The Black church is the soul of the nation and the revolution can only proceed as far as the Black church can be transformed. Stokely Carmichael 'was wonderful all the way',[90] but Cleage wished to go beyond adulation of a secular leader. He therefore addresses 'An Epistle to Stokely' and SNICC: the movement is going to fail unless these young black radicals end their alienation from the real Black church. In terms not unlike Rahner's proposition about anonymous Christians, he is going to show that the young blacks, committed to the movement, must see that the movement and the Black church are one and the same. 'So then, I would say to you, you are Christian, and the things you believe are the teachings of a Black Messiah named Jesus, and the things you do are the will of a black God call Jehovah; and almost everything you have heard about Christianity is essentially a lie.'[91] It is slave/white Christianity they have quite properly rejected: but this has nothing to do with the Black Messiah.

By comparison, Cleage's response to Martin Luther King is more ambiguous. Of his personal integrity there is no question. In a tribute to Dr Martin Luther King a few days after his assassination, he claims that no one would have listened to Malcolm if Martin had not created the confrontation situations which unmasked white oppression for all the world to see. However, he considers that Dr King had no programme: God would intervene. 'It was a fantasy.'[92] His entire approach was 'as a mystical kind of idealism which had no roots in objective reality'.[93] King believed in redemptive suffering, but Cleage believes that the reality was of black people being beaten up in front of the TV cameras of the world. Malcolm X was accused of preaching hatred of the whites, but in face of such violence 'not to hate people like that was a sign of mental illness'.[94] This in turn leads into the question of violence, which has been an important ethical issue for Black theology. However, Cleage's wider position enables him to resolve the matter swiftly. The admonition to love your neighbour applies only within the Nation. The murder of Martin Luther King 'only proved that non-violence can never work in white racist society'.[95]

Non-violence is not the criterion by which Cleage operates, but he does have a very clear understanding of the criterion. There are many things going on – rioting, marching, protesting – but to assess their value Cleage keeps his eye on the goal. 'If these things lead to power, then they are good. If they do not lead to power, then they are a waste of time.'[96] How things serve the cause of the Black revolution is the criterion of their value in the long term. 'By the yardstick of that struggle all things must be judged, evaluated, maintained, or discarded.'[97] The logic is simple: whatever supports the liberation struggle is the will of God.

As we have seen, Marcus Garvey was a dangerous man: he could not be incorporated. Neither could Cleage be incorporated. He proclaimed his Black theology week by week from the pulpit, developing it in that dialectic of the Bible and the experience of the street. Black theology as we know it, however, was soon to be produced in the very different context of the university and the seminary. It gained status from this development: it lost infinitely more than it gained. Black theology begins with the Black church. In the early 1960s clergy were behind the formation of the National Committee of Negro Churchmen, which in 1968 reconstituted itself as the National Conference of Black Churchmen. Albert Cleage belongs in this constituency: *The Black Messiah* was published in the same year. It could not have been otherwise, since the black clergy had been trained for the most part in white seminaries, or at least in seminaries in which white theology was the norm. For Cleage it was all part of the same process of incorporation, by which the leaders of the Black church would serve the interests of the white church. And the further blacks went in this process the closer was the bond. 'When you step out with a doctor's degree, they have guaranteed that there is nothing real left in you.'[98] Black theology as an academic discipline was to come later, and the first to publish a full length work under this title was James H. Cone, with his *Black Theology and Black Power*, which appeared early in 1969. Cone and his contemporaries were in double jeopardy. On the one hand, Black Power activists saw them as house niggers, since they still adhered to the white man's religion, the slave's religion of Christianity. On the other hand, they were the products of a white education system. They had proved themselves to their white instructors, had been given fancy costumes to wear, and had eagerly agreed to act as token blacks in liberal institutions. Previously middle-class blacks had identified themselves uncritically with the white ideology: the American dream. What could this new generation of black academics do but attempt to prove themselves more angry, righteous, out of control and offensive than any other adherent of the ideology of Black Power: the American nightmare. James Cone was the leading figure in Black theology in its academic mode. When I taught Black theology in Georgia some years ago white people were exasperated by Cone's work: fit to be tied. And yet let me say at the outset that I believe the work of Albert Cleage is far more radical and much more credible.

Cleage had black consciousness, but as noted earlier his racing instructions came from a higher power. Cone lacks the vision of Cleage: he constantly relates Black theology to Black Power. The critical distance between the two is lost. 'Black Power is the most important development in American life in this century.'[99] In a century which at that time had seen women enfranchised, two world wars, the great depression, the development of flight, the control of nuclear energy and the promise of space exploration – the greatest development is Black Power. Here is myopia or me-tooism. How should Christians respond to these developments? Is there a Christian view of the jet engine or the universal franchise? Why should there be a specifically Christian view of the Black Power movement? *A fortiori*, why should Black Power be 'Christ's central message to the twentieth-century America'? [100] Is it more important to the quality of human life than the women's movement, television, the telephone or birth control? We do not see God in goretex or Christ in the condom. Why should we seek to see the divine in the dynamo? 'Christianity is not alien to Black Power; it is Black Power.'[101] What an extraordinary claim. Not that Black Power is simply another social movement of the mid-twentieth century. Not that, as an apparently secular movement, it is irreligious. Not that as a movement critical of the practice of the churches it is against the Christian faith. Not that Black Power is something that might be understood in the light of Christianity. No, none of these things: quite the reverse. Christianity is to be understood in terms of Black Power. And this means that the critical distance between Christianity and Black Power is given up. Whatever Black Power is, Christianity is just that: Black Power is neither challenged nor changed by it. Whatever Christianity is or has been or promises to be – if it is not what Black Power presently is, then that is not Christian. This is the religious legitimation of the ideology of Black Power. No gossamer membrane exists separating the two, no cigarette paper divides historic, global Christianity from this lately come social movement which affects the lives of a number of Americans approximating to the size of an average Chinese city. Christianity we know; Black Power at that time was a new phenomenon. Therefore the question might reasonably be asked: is Black Power compatible with Christianity, or is it alien to Christianity? But Cone panics and puts the question exactly the wrong way around. Black Power apparently is known and the question is whether Christianity is compatible with it, or alien to it? Black Power is the norm by which Christianity is to be judged. Is Christianity to be set aside now that Black Power has appeared? But no, Christianity may be permitted to continue with this assurance – it *is* Black Power. What a comfort in troubled times. Cleage offered a form of Christianity equivalent to Black Power, one which stood over against the ideology and which could enrich and purify it. By contrast from the outset Cone gives up this confident assertion of the value and independence of Christianity, black Christianity, and settles for the role of house chaplain to black radicalism.

What we have is not simply Christianity but white Christianity, not simply theology but white theology. 'There is, then, a desperate need for a black theology, a theology whose sole purpose is to apply the freeing power of the gospel to black people under white oppression.'[102] Now this is quite different. Here is the confident assertion of Cleage that Christianity has power to liberate, in this case Christianity understood from a black perspective has the power to liberate black people from white oppression. The source of liberation is properly faith in the black Christ. Cone introduces Luke 4 at this point, the litany of every liberation movement: 'to set at liberty those who are oppressed'. Black consciousness enables them to know the will of God: Black Power puts its faith elsewhere. He quotes Galatians 5: 1 'For freedom Christ has set us free.' Christian faith is about freedom – and the goal of Black Power is freedom. Ergo. 'It would seem that Black Power and Christianity have this in common: the liberation of man.'[103] In fact the 'yoke of slavery' to which Paul refers is that of the Law, symbolised in circumcision. It never occurred to Paul that God frees slaves. In fact Cone falls into a rather disturbing pattern of quoting rather obscure proof texts about Christ defeating the devil and putting evil under his feet (1 John 3: 8; 2 Timothy 1: 10; Hebrews 2: 8) It does not at all clarify how this has been borne out in the last 2000 years of world history, or even in the history of the Christian church, especially in view of Cone's criticism of the oppression caused by whites, including the white churches. But it does enable him to present a Manichaean view of the present struggle. Black Power is exorcising the white demons. But that echoes the black Muslim teaching that whites are devils. Is it the work of God or of Black Power? But then Cone cannot tell the difference. 'Black rebellion is a manifestation of God himself actively involved in the present day affairs of men for the purpose of liberating a people.'[104]

Whilst Cleage claimed that love should be limited to the Nation, Cone simply claims that love has no place until justice and power are established. We might wonder if love would be necessary then. As we shall see, this is a criticism which has been raised against Cone from South Africa: it shows a lack of faith in the power of love. For Cone it is possible to love the neighbour, but that neighbour is the oppressed, not the oppressor. Love 'is revolutionary in that it seeks to meet the needs of the neighbour amid the crumbling structures of society. It is revolutionary because love may mean joining a violent rebellion.'[105] Cleage recognised why the looters were on the streets, but he did not sacrilise them. He was still confident enough to make Christian judgements about them. Cone has no critical distance and therefore can only applaud them. The Black church 'cannot condemn the rioters. It must make an unqualified identification with the "looters" and "rioters" recognising that this stance leads to condemnation by the state as law-breakers.'[106] The Black church provides 'the necessary soul' in the revolution. Is this simply what Marx elsewhere calls 'the spiritual aroma', 'the halo'? Black Power makes the running and the Black church provides the religious justification for whatever is done. We saw that Cleage had a criterion for truth, but Cone makes the truth of theology, even Black theology, subservient to the demands of Black Power.

> To put it simply, Black Theology knows no authority more binding than the experience of oppression itself. This alone must be the ultimate authority in religious matters. Concretely, this means that Black Theology is not prepared to accept any doctrine of God, man, Christ, or Scripture which contradicts the black demand for freedom now. It believes that any religious idea which exalts black dignity and creates a restless drive for freedom must be affirmed. All ideas which are opposed to the struggle for black self-determination or are irrelevant to it must be rejected as the work of the Antichrist.[107]

Cleage claimed that the movement could never connect with the people unless it took into account their religiosity. It could not be simply a secular movement. But in saying this he was calling on black activists to come to terms with his Black theology, his understanding of faith in the Black Messiah. When Cone claims that the movement must be religious he has left no critical dimension to the faith.

Black Power and black religion are inseparable. Both seek to free black people from white racism. It is impossible for Black Power to be effective without taking into consideration man's religious nature. It is impossible for black religion to be truly related to the condition of black people and to the message of Jesus Christ without emphasising the basic tenets of Black Power. Therefore, Black theology seeks to make black religion a religion of Black Power.

The final effect is to make Christian faith totally subservient to Black Power. What is to be gained by this? It guarantees a certain status for James Cone in the eyes of his contemporaries. He is no Uncle Tom. But is he an Uncle Jude? Is there anything in the Christian faith that he would not betray if Black Power tells him to set it aside? Apparently not. Does it really guarantee status? The Black Power radicals were men of faith who had principles for which they were prepared to suffer and perhaps die. Surely they would not be impressed by someone who is prepared to surrender the foundations and principles of his faith. It is all very unedifying, but that is not the worst of it. It is a missed opportunity. Black theology owes it to Black Power to make a critical evaluation of the movement. Black Power is not one thing. It represents several possible ways forward. It would benefit from fraternal criticism: it does not need religious legitimation.

There is little theology in this Black *theology*: it is a triumph of style over substance. 'My style of doing theology was influenced more by Malcolm X than by Martin Luther King, Jr.'[108] What could this mean, since Dr King had a genuine Christian theology and Malcolm X believed in the Yacub myth? The reference can only be to the anti-white character of Cone's position. His characterisation of 'satanic whiteness'[109] is an echo of that angriest black man in America, and his belief in the Yacub myth. Cone has a good deal to say about whiteness and blackness. There is of course the white God, created by racists. The appropriate response is iconoclasm and 'the destruction of *everything* white'.[110] While Cleage proclaims that God was originally black, Cone speaks curiously in kenotic tones of 'God's willingness to become black'.[111] What colour was he previously? Becoming black has its own significance, since 'black theology refuses to accept a God who is not identified totally with the goals of the black community'.[112] Once again we have the loss of all critical distance. The black community is now the basic reality, and its goals the norm. In the Christian tradition (would that be white?) God reconciles the world to himself, but here in the best ideological tradition God reconciles himself to the goals of the black community by becoming black.

In a parenthesis we raised the question whether the Christian tradition is white. Cleage was perfectly clear on this. For him 'white' is not that which is done by white people, but that which serves the needs and interests of white people, especially against the interests of blacks. Cone has no such analytical base. Because of Cleage's advocacy of separation he can happily envisage white folks doing white things, so long as they do not oppress blacks. If we took this further we might say that blacks can borrow from whites a whole range of ideas, practices and products in mathematics, management and medicine – where these have not been developed through oppression and do not oppress in their acceptance. But Cone has no basis for such a common-sense distinction. 'In order to be Christian theology, white theology must cease to be white theology and become black theology by denying whiteness as an acceptable form of human existence and affirming blackness as

God's intention for humanity.'[113] To make sense of this we should have to say with Cleage that 'white' here does not refer to that which is done by white folks, but that which is done for their interests and which oppresses blacks. To cease to be 'white' then would mean to cease to oppress blacks. But this begs the question, what does 'black' mean? Cone does not provide any guidance here but we should begin by noting that the terms represent a value judgement. 'White' means bad and 'black' means good. 'White' refers to attitudes and behaviour which dehumanise blacks, but also dehumanise whites. Hence the term 'white' means less than human (as the Yacub myth claims) while 'black' means being fully human: 'affirming blackness as God's intention for humanity'. Thus being black need not be identical with being 'black'. Many black people, because of oppression, are not yet 'black'. (Cleage was clear on the need for therapy.) Could it be that some white people are not 'white', but already 'black'? Blackness, Cone tells us is 'an ontological category'.[114] The terminology can be made to make sense, though it is suspiciously convoluted. Beware a philosophy which requires quotation marks. The high water mark of this line of thinking comes when Cone claims that 'there will be no peace in America until whites begin to hate their whiteness, asking from the depths of their being: "How can we become black?"'[115] Indeed the question itself, as Cone observes, seems to echo that poignant question of the Philippian jailer to Paul and Silas, 'What must I do to be saved?' (Acts 16: 30). But there was nothing he could do: he must believe in the grace of God. The question is almost worthy of Nicodemus himself (John 3: 4). How can a man who is born white, become black? 'But the misunderstanding here is the failure to see that blackness or salvation (the two are synonymous) is the work of God, not a human work.'[116] How eagerly does the oppressed adopt the role of the oppressor. Blackness could become a new imperialism if somehow it came to oppress others, if it came to silence their protests, if it insisted in speaking for them. And this is indeed what happens in Cone's early work. Blackness becomes a universal category, it 'stands for all victims of oppression who realize that the survival of their humanity is bound up with liberation from whiteness'.[117] But as soon as we are confronted by 'all victims of oppression' we begin to reflect on other sources of oppression beyond racism. For the victims of the third world, racial discrimination is the least of their problems. For them 'white' means Europe and the USA, and the oppression is through unequal economic power. And for the purpose of this analysis black Americans are also 'white'. Or again, Cone quotes Jesus' sermon at Nazareth, in Luke 4. 'In view of the biblical emphasis on liberation, it seems not only appropriate but necessary to define the Christian community as the community of the oppressed which joins Jesus Christ in his fight for the liberation of humankind.'[118] And when we look around the 'community of the oppressed' whom do we find? Yes, we find poor men of the third world suffering economic oppression. But poor women too, suffering other forms of oppression in addition to the economic. And we find women who are not necessarily poor economically, but who suffer oppression, some of it at the hands of black men.

This leads to a final point. 'Black theology does not deny that all persons are sinners.'[119] But what are the sins of black people? 'According to black theology, the sin of the oppressed is not that they are responsible for their own enslavement – far from it. Their sin is that of trying to "understand" enslavers, to "love" them on their own terms.'[120] Cleage saw this as a sickness brought about by enslavement. It does not deserve to be called 'sin'. But more than that, by restricting sin in this way it excludes the more profound issue of the real evil of which black people are capable – when they have power over others. Cleage was clear and honest on this matter. Cone avoids it. It therefore weakens his position when we adopt a global perspective. Racism is but the large scale form of ethnic and tribal discrimination. There has been ethnic cleansing in Bosnia and Kosovo: white on white. There has been black on black tribal violence in Rwanda. There has been black on black mutilation of children in Sierra Leone. To say that sin for blacks is simply the 'desire to be white'[121] is to remain at a superficial level, a superficiality which inevitably follows on from a refusal to adopt any critical distance between Christian values and the black community. This is symptomatic of the triumph of ideology, where inconvenient facts are pushed aside. For me this is illustrated in the following example. 'White missionaries have always encouraged blacks to forget about present injustices and look forward to heavenly justice.'[122] In the early 1960s, the decade in which Cone began to write, there was a popular movement for independence in Nyasaland, Central Africa. Prominent and active in the struggle for justice were Scottish missionaries, several of them members of the Iona Community. In our previous terms they were more black than 'white' and took risks to serve the interests of the African population. When independence came Dr Hastings Banda became the first president of Malawi, as it was renamed. The Scottish missionaries were not committed to personalities, and they continued to be active against injustice and oppression – now carried out by blacks on blacks. They did not adopt that liberal position of ignoring the sin when carried out by Africans. For this one by one they were deported from the country. But the love of justice continued, and eventually Banda was removed. This is reality, but it does not fit the ideology of Black Power. Hence Cone's sweeping statement about 'white missionaries'.

The position we have described is that of the early James Cone. This is the work of a radical, filled with righteous anger. Here is a position which is completely unbalanced and overstated. And why not. What should we have thought of him if he had *not* carried his point too far, if he had *not* been offensive in his unqualified assertion of his case. What passion, what commitment: how will society ever change if such witnesses to the truth die out. But they do get older. Their fame does lead them to new places to meet people with different experiences. And they become – reasonable: they become statesmen-like, and balanced. They, who *should apologise for nothing*, begin to confess their sins. They did not pay attention to feminist consciousness, thinking it 'a white thing'.[123] They had no global awareness, and certainly no understanding of their complicity within America. They had no social analysis of the links between racism and capitalism. They failed to suspect that the enemy of their enemy might be their friend: as good Americans they refused to consider socialism or make use of Marxist analysis. How true. And yet how much more exciting and dangerous was the young lion. Black theology 'maintains that all acts which participate in the destruction of white racism are Christian, the liberation deeds of God'.[124] Here is Black Power ascending the pulpit, but there are other types of Black theology.

Critics of Cleage and Cone might claim that they have been unduly influenced by the ideology of Black Power. Of J. Deotis Roberts it might well be asked whether he has been influenced by it at all. When Black theology began to appear Roberts was already an established scholar, having taught at Howard University for the previous decade. His field was philosophy of religion and his first book, *Faith and Reason*, arose from his PhD at the University of Edinburgh, a comparative study of Pascal and Bergson. It was unusual at that time for black scholars to study in Europe, but throughout his publications he has continued to dialogue with European writers, especially of the Reformed tradition: John Baillie, Donald Baillie, H.H. Farmer, Barth and of course Schleiermacher. Indeed dialogue has been a feature of his life's work. He has increasingly engaged with worldwide Christianity, notably in Latin America, India, Korea and Japan. His ecumenical interests have extended to encounters with scholars of other world religions. When in 1993 he returned to Edinburgh to be awarded the higher degree of DLitt, it was in recognition of his work as a leader in Black theology, but this *corpus* has a world setting.

Because Roberts has been one of the most prominent exponents of Black theology we might assume that he too has been influenced by Black Power. On closer inspection it is not formative in his work. When it is mentioned it is in a very different context from that of Cone. Paul wrote to the church in Corinth about the inevitable limitations of human perception: 'for now we see through a glass darkly' (1 Cor. 13: 12). We might consider that our inability to see clearly can also be due to the intervention of some ideology. In this life we shall not see 'face to face' but anything which removes false consciousness is to be welcomed. Roberts claims that this is the contribution of Black Power. 'Black power has enabled black people who once saw through "a glass whitely" to be deculturated to the extent that they now see through "a glass blackly".'[125] In this context Roberts sees Black Power as a form of critical consciousness. (We could compare it to feminist consciousness in this respect.) Thus he claims that Black Power plays a similar role in the formation of Black theology that conscientisation plays in the liberation theology of Latin America. It supplies a necessary component for Black theology, which 'requires a decolonization of the mind'.[126]

By restricting Black Power in this way Roberts, by intuition or by intention, avoids the polarisation associated with Black Power as an ideological movement. He realises that the contestation of Cleage and the confrontation of Cone are much more exciting and attractive to young militants. Black versus white. By comparison his position although commendable makes rather sombre reading. 'In the long run, gray is more honest and realistic.'[127] We might reflect that no one ever mounted the barricades to risk all and inspire the oppressed by waving a grey flag. (The exception to this rule might be the taking of a stand by the last able-bodied man at a free bus-pass rally of the Grey Panthers: in the land of the zimmers, the walking-stick man is king.) However, this is not a matter of shades and hues, for Roberts it is a matter of fundamental Christian conviction. As a Christian and as a Christian theologian he must be guided by revelation and not by ideology. His motto is Paul's great affirmation: 'God was in Christ reconciling the world to himself' (2 Cor. 5: 19). Yes, he is opposed to 'integration as a goal'.[128] Yes, to begin the process of change it is necessary to separate those who have become alienated from each other, but neither can that be the goal for Christians. 'Separation must give way to *reconciliation*. The gospel is a reconciling as well as a liberating gospel and Christ is at once Liberator and Reconciler.'[129]

As we have seen it is possible to accuse Cone of providing no more than a religious legitimation of Black Power. Worse than that, a legitimation of whatever goes on in the streets. It is as if he cannot bring himself to criticise the brothers. Cleage knew better, and so does Roberts. It cannot have been pleasant for Roberts to criticise a brother who had succeeded in getting the race issue onto the agenda of seminaries and churches, but it had to be done. 'Can an apostle of love turn, all of a sudden, to being an apostle of hate and sprinkle "holy water" upon the most inauthentic, racist, pathological, irresponsible and violent approaches to racial change?'[130] The Black theologian cannot afford the luxury of being chaplain to such movement of polarisation. 'While Cone confesses an indifference toward whites, I *care*.'[131] Is this further confirmation of Cone's own claim, mentioned earlier, that he was more influenced by Malcolm than by Martin? Roberts exposes and rejects Cone's position. 'A Christian theologian is not an interpreter of the religion of black power.'[132] The Christian theologian must have another place on which to take his stand. (Inclusive thinkers need not be alarmed. I am using male language here, to reflect common premises of all of these Black theologians. Towards the end of the chapter we shall see them challenged, even denounced. Courage.) Condemning white prejudice is not a basis for theology.

> Black theology must not be a simple reaction to white oppression. It is rightly interested in the misinterpretations and the omissions of 'white theology', which have often provided justification for the oppression of blacks, but it is considerably more than this.[133]

Black theology must be based on Christ, Christ the Liberator and Reconciler, not Christ the Legitimator. 'Liberation and reconciliation are the two main poles of Black Theology.'[134] Roberts refuses to begin with a secular ideology. There is Black Power, but there is also another power and it is to that power he testifies and commits himself. 'There is a point where our Christian faith can lead us beyond the most robust humanism, for we are heirs of a grace that *enables* as well as sanctifies.'[135] Unlike Cone he does not put his faith in the power of a movement to force change on a reluctant enemy, least of all by using the same means as the enemy. In sentiments that are closer to Martin Luther King, Roberts confesses his faith in a mystery which looks to the world like the foolishness of God (1 Cor. 1: 25).

> There can be no liberation without reconciliation and no reconciliation without liberation. The only Christian way in race relations is a liberating experience of reconciliation for the white oppressor as well as for the black oppressed.[136]

Almost 30 years after these words were written we see throughout the world that even quite secular people recognise the truth of this model – in El Salvador, Bosnia, Northern Ireland, South Africa: 'the *liberated* man is also the *reconciled* man'.[137] In one of his later books, *The Roots of a Black Future*, Roberts revisits this theme, now as an agenda for the churches. Liberation and reconciliation are set in parallel to the prophetic and priestly functions of the churches.[138]

Grey theology will not sell: militancy is more sexy. Superficially militancy is in solidarity. And yet, as we have seen, militants do not need a chaplain. They do not need a pious echo of their own analysis. Along with encouragement the militants need to be pointed beyond the cul de sac of violence. Roberts is harsh in his criticism of Cone's legitimation, that blacks could win their freedom 'by any means necessary'. It is not true, it is not realistic: the militants deserved better.

> The statement appears to be an ethic of no ethic. This was a reckless and irresponsible statement in the midst of a tense and explosive situation. Young angry militants were seeking guidance. They asked for bread: he cast them a stone. A moral paralysis remains inherent in Cone's theological method.[139]

It might be assumed that Roberts would have much in common with Cone. On closer inspection he has more in common with Cleage, although he finds some of Cleage's premises quite incredible. The reason is, I believe, that Roberts has not been sufficiently influenced by the ideology of Black Power. He sees two of the main influences on Cleage to be Marcus Garvey and S.G.F. Brandon. The latter is of course the source of Cleage's description of Jesus as a Zealot and militant Messiah. Loyal to his own original training Roberts finds this whole presentation of Jesus lacking historical confirmation, although the impact of the image is not lost on him. 'I do not take the figure of a black Messiah in a literal historical sense. It is rather a symbol or a myth with profound meaning for black people.'[140] I believe that this is an indication that Roberts has not been influenced enough by Black Power and is still functioning within a European environment. He has not taken seriously Cleage's point that the 'historical' sources are themselves ideological constructs.

The same might be said about a second criticism, concerning the idea of a chosen people. Once again, it is an offence against historical evidence to see black Americans as God's chosen people, in continuity with the children of Israel. I believe this leads Roberts to miss the plot. What makes incredible the idea that blacks in America are God's chosen people is the assumption at the foundations of the nation that whites are His chosen people. White people assume it and blacks have been taught it more thoroughly than whites themselves. Once again, it is not a matter of history but ideology. Roberts warns against the 'perils' of the idea of a chosen people.[141] Of course there is a danger of Manichaeism, of demonising whites. But if this is a danger for black Muslims, it plays no part in Cleage's theology. Roberts warns that 'black men must face their sins and white men must face theirs'.[142] But whereas Cone cannot bring himself to criticise the looters, Cleage is quite clear that they are 'a generation of monsters, little vicious individualists concerned only about themselves'. Related to this Roberts can criticise another of Cleage's themes, describing black nationalism as 'a fantasy more akin to rhetoric than to reality'.[143] And yet for most of its history the USA has denied that blacks (*qua* blacks) were Americans. As Cleage observes: 'We are not Americans. We are an African people who against our will were brought to America.'

In these examples I believe Roberts has not been sufficiently influenced by the ideology of Black Power. There are two further criticisms which are more surprising, and which seem ill-founded. 'Cleage does not indicate the positive value of worship and its relation to the prophetic as well as the priestly ministry of the church.'[144] As we saw, one of the features of Cleage's theology is that he relates it directly to worship in a way which is as creative and imaginative as it is unique. There is a second surprising criticism. 'He does not give proper attention to the need to make individuals healthy and whole in order that they may fulfill their life and purpose within the black community.'[145] Nothing could be further from the truth. We have just re-quoted Cleage's view that the looters are sick. 'Masses of people who have been oppressed, discriminated against, who have lacked opportunity, who have in every way been shut out of the mainstream of life are sick because of their oppression.' Cleage is one of the few Black theologians prepared to say just how bad the situation is and what programmes need to be mounted if these young blacks are to be healed, resurrected as members of the black community, the nation.

As noted at the outset, one of the features of the writings of Deotis Roberts is his engagement with others: whites within America, Christians of the third world, adherents of other world faiths. Admirable though this undoubtedly is, yet precisely when he turns to Africa his work is disappointing. In *Black Theology in Dialogue*[146] he discusses the work of several African theologians, but he does this within the terms of a debate set out by European scholarship. There is more than one kind of theology in Africa. His dialogue is with those who write without black consciousness. The book was published in 1987, but the previous year a historic conference had taken place in New York between American Black theologians, and Black theologians from South Africa. The Americans were subjected to devastating criticisms for their ideological naivety. 'Afro-American is my version of blackness', declared Roberts. This confrontation was to demonstrate how little American 'Afro' had to do with contemporary African thought and experience. We have heard a great deal about Africa from non-Africans. It is high time we listened to Africans themselves and it is to Africa that we now proceed in the next chapter.

Notes

[1] Martin Luther King Jr, *Where do We Go from Here: chaos or community*, Harper & Row, 1967, p. 34.

[2] Ibid.

[3] Quoted in Stokely Carmichael and Charles V. Hamilton, *Black Power: the politics of liberation in America*, Penguin Books, 1969 (1967), p. 19. Other quotes from Carmichael come from this short book.

[4] Gayraud S. Wilmore, *Black Religion and Black Radicalism*, Doubleday & Co., New York, 1972, p. 249.

[5] *The Times* (London), 29 July 1974.

[6] *Independent*, 17 Nov. 1998.

[7] *The Autobiography of Malcolm X, with the assistance of Alex Haley*, Penguin Books, 1968 (1965), p. 496.

[8] Ibid., p. 274.

[9] Ibid., p. 118.

[10] Ibid., p. 326.

[11] Ibid., p. 343.

[12] Ibid., p. 428.

[13] John White, *Black Leadership in America 1895–1968*, Longman, 1985, p. 113.

[14] *The Autobiography of Malcolm X*, p. 479.

[15] Ibid., pp. 352–3.

[16] Arthur J. Magida, *Prophet of Rage: a life of Louis Farrakhan and his nation*, Basic Books, New York, 1996, p. 16.

[17] Ibid., p. 83.

[18] Ibid., p. 31.

[19] Ibid., p. 146.

[20] Ibid.

[21] Ibid.

[22] Ibid., p. 148.

[23] Ibid., p. 175.

[24] Ibid., p. 2.

[25] Ibid., p. 155.

[26] Robert Singh, *The Farrakhan Phenomenon: race, reaction and the paranoid style in American politics*, Georgetown University Press, Washington, DC, 1997 p. 14.

[27] Ibid., p. 71.

[28] Magida, *Prophet of Rage*, p. 180.

[29] Ibid., p. 60.

[30] Ibid.

[31] Albert Cleage, *The Black Messiah*, Sheed & Ward, 1968, p. 85.

[32] Ibid., p. 86.

[33] Albert Cleage, *Black Christian Nationalism*, William Morrow & Co., New York, 1972, p. 163.

[34] Cleage, *The Black Messiah*, p. 17.

[35] Cleage, *Black Christian Nationalism*, p. xxvi.

[36] Cleage, *The Black Messiah*, p. 154.

[37] Cleage, *Black Christian Nationalism*, p. 24.

[38] Ibid., p. xxx.

[39] Ibid., p. 197.

[40] Ibid., xxxvii.

[41] Ibid., p. 13.

[42] Ibid., p. 198.

[43] Cleage, *The Black Messiah*, p. 108.

[44] Ibid., p. 3.

[45] Ibid., p. 4. Without tedious reference Cleage adopts the scholarly conclusions of S.G.F. Brandon, *Jesus and the Zealots:a study of the political factor in primitive Christianity*, Manchester University Press, 1967, published only a few months before *The Black Messiah*.

[46] Cleage, *The Black Messiah*, p. 7.

[47] Ibid., p. 21.

[48] Ibid., p. 32.

[49] Ibid., p. 133.

[50] Cleage, *Black Christian Nationalism*, p. 175.

[51] Cleage, *The Black Messiah*, p. 24.

[52] Ibid., p. 91.

[53] Cleage, *Black Christian Nationalism*, p. 3.

[54] Cleage, *The Black Messiah*, p. 91.

[55] Ibid., p. 91.

[56] Ibid., p. 4.

[57] Cleage, *Black Christian Nationalism*, p. 35.

[58] Ibid., p. 68.

[59] Ibid.

[60] Ibid., p. 73.

[61] Ibid., p. 188.

[62] Ibid., p. 52.

[63] Cleage, *The Black Messiah*, p. 171.

[64] Ibid., p. 173.

[65] Ibid., p. 183.

[66] Ibid., p. 142.

[67] Ibid., p. 19.

[68] Cleage, *Black Christian Nationalism*, p. xiii.

[69] Ibid., p. 252.

[70] Ibid., p. 139.

[71] Cleage, *The Black Messiah*, p. 179.

[72] Ibid.

[73] Ibid., p. 118.

[74] Ibid., p. 234.

[75] Ibid., p. 33.

[76] Ibid.

[77] Ibid., p. 264.

[78] Cleage, *Black Christian Nationalism*, pp. 97–8.

[79] Ibid., p. 101.

[80] Ibid.

[81] Ibid., p. 103.

[82] Ibid.

[83] Ibid., p. 112.

[84] Ibid., p. 113.

[85] Ibid., p. 116.

[86] Ibid., p. 117.

[87] Ibid., p. 118.

[88] Cleage, *The Black Messiah*, p. 186.

[89] Ibid., p. 200.

[90] Ibid., p. 252.

[91] Ibid., p. 37.

[92] Cleage, *Black Christian Nationalism*, p. 194.

93 Ibid., p. 106.

94 Ibid., p. 190.

95 Cleage, *The Black Messiah*, p. 208.

96 Ibid., p. 198.

97 Cleage, *Black Christian Nationalism*, p. xviii.

98 Cleage, *The Black Messiah*, p. 165.

99 James H. Cone, *Black Theology and Black Power*, Seabury Press, New York, 1969, p. 1.

100 Ibid.

101 Ibid., p. 38.

102 Ibid., p. 31.

103 Ibid., p. 39.

104 Ibid., p. 38.

105 Ibid., p. 113.

106 Ibid.

107 Ibid., p. 120.

108 James H. Cone, *A Black Theology of Liberation*, Orbis Books, Maryknoll, NY, 1986 (1970), p. xvi.

109 Ibid., p. 64.

110 Ibid., p. 62.

111 Ibid., p. 73.

112 Ibid., p. 27.

113 Ibid., p. 9.

114 Ibid., p. 7.

115 Ibid., p. vii.

116 Ibid., p. 66.

117 Ibid., p. 7.

118 Ibid., p. 3.

119 Ibid., p. 51.

120 Ibid.

121 Ibid., p. 108.

122 Ibid., p. 137.

123 James H. Cone, *For My People: Black theology and the Black church*, Orbis Books, Maryknoll, NY, 1984, p. 97.

124 Cone, *A Black Theology of Liberation*, p. 10.

125 J. Deotis Roberts, *Black Theology Today: liberation and contextualization*, Edwin Mellon Press, New York, 1983, p. 153.

126 J. Deotis Roberts, *A Black Political Theology*, Westminster Press, Philadelphia, Pa., 1974, p. 70.

127 J. Deotis Roberts, *Liberation and Reconciliation: a black theology*, Westminster Press, Philadelphia, Pa., 1971, p. 14.

128 Ibid., p. 177.

129 Ibid., p. 10.

130 Ibid., p. 17.

131 Ibid., p. 20.

132 Ibid., p. 21.

133 Roberts, *A Black Political Theology*, p. 40.

134 Roberts, *Liberation and Reconciliation*, p. 26.

135 Ibid., p. 119.

136 Roberts, *A Black Political Theology*, p. 222.

137 Roberts, *Liberation and Reconciliation*, p. 107.

138 J. Deotis Roberts, *The Roots of a Black Future: family and church*, Westminster Press, Philadelphia, Pa., 1980, p. 110.

[139] Roberts, *Black Theology Today*, p. 39.
[140] Roberts, *Liberation and Reconciliation*, p. 130.
[141] Ibid., p. 49.
[142] Ibid., p. 109.
[143] Ibid., p. 27.
[144] Roberts, *Black Theology Today,* p. 173.
[145] Ibid.
[146] J. Deotis Roberts, *Black Theology in Dialogue*, Westminster Press, Philadelphia, Pa., 1987.

CHAPTER 3

The Redemption of the Poor: Black Theology in South Africa

The Black Consciousness Movement

The black consciousness movement began in South Africa about 1970. Contrary to what might be assumed, it did not arise because of influences from the USA. Rather its sources, political, theoretical and economic, lay entirely within Africa. First, at a political level, there was the example of decolonisation throughout black Africa, the consequence of the 'wind of change' to which British Prime Minister Harold Macmillan alluded as early as 1956 when he visited South Africa. Through examples in East and West Africa, South Africans could at last conceive of their country under black majority rule. Second, at an analytical level this Anglo-Dutch country was influenced by Francophone negritude. South Africans were equipped to reflect on the nature of decolonisation. Black consciousness appeared in South Africa – but not elsewhere. This was due to the third element, the economic. In *The Communist Manifesto* Marx wrote of the effect – and achievement – of capitalism. 'The bourgeoisie has subjected the country to the rule of the town. It has created enormous cities, has greatly increased the urban population as compared with the rural, and has thus rescued a considerable part of the population from the idiocy of the rural life.'[1] Capitalism and its associated industrialisation and urbanisation transforms consciousness to a higher level, even as it exploits. It is hardly surprising that the most significant if unintended product of this system is 'its own grave-diggers'. Black consciousness arose in a society which was being transformed by capitalism: the largest industrial centre south of Milan is Johannesburg.

The administrative separation of the races, apartheid, was introduced into South Africa in 1948 by the National Party, under the leadership of Dr D.F. Malan. Opposition to the policy and its implementation was not based on political or economic grounds: apartheid was condemned on moral grounds. It was denounced outside South Africa by many diverse groups and individuals, some of whom made it their life's work, wilfully ignoring elsewhere discrimination on grounds of gender or genocide on grounds of religion. It was condemned by governments throughout the world, thus enabling them to occupy the moral high ground. Some of them could at least claim that their repression of their own people was carried out day and daily without a hint of racism. Their corruption and greed was pursued with a single-mindedness of which Afrikaners were constitutionally incapable. More impressively however, apartheid was opposed within South Africa by blacks, by coloureds and by some whites. They were intimidated, but remained resolute; they suffered but were not broken; they were killed – but even then their lives served the cause to which they had committed themselves. In the providence of God when the exponents of the Lie attempt to silence the witnesses to the Truth, their violence is counter-productive. One of these witnesses to the truth, perhaps the most widely admired man of the twentieth century, is Nelson Mandela. Throughout his 25 years of incarceration on Robben Island his silence sent out a message, his being hidden away illuminated oppression, his sentence convicted his accusers, his restriction made him a world figure, his integrity denied legitimacy to the state, his common humanity eroded the credibility of successive defenders of apartheid. Some men have given their lives for their people: by their willingness to die when their lives had only just begun they have given up the lives which they would otherwise have enjoyed. Others have given up their lives to imprisonment and have lost the lives which they could have enjoyed with their wives, children and friends. Nelson Mandela is such a man and his capacity to survive and overcome such a long and harsh imprisonment is awesome. But when that is said, gladly, he is not a source of black consciousness.

I was living in New York in 1964 and obtained from the United Nations a copy of a document which I have kept beside me and treasured through the years. It is 'The Statement by Mr Nelson Mandela at his trial in Pretoria on 20 April, 1964'. I have never ceased to be inspired and touched by its concluding paragraph.

> During my lifetime I have dedicated myself to this struggle of the African people. I have fought against White domination, and I have fought against Black domination. I have cherished the ideal of a democratic and free society in which all persons live together in harmony and with equal opportunities. It is an ideal which I hope to live for and to achieve. But if needs be, it is an ideal for which I am prepared to die.[2]

Read in an armchair or by a desk we are struck by the rhetoric, but when this statement was read from the dock in the Supreme Court of Pretoria Mandela was facing four charges under security legislation which carried the death penalty. If found guilty, which was certain, it was likely that he would be executed. The preparedness to die did not refer to a peaceful end many decades later in Umtata. But having said that, what strikes me now as I read through the whole document is its links with other liberation movements of the time and its lack of any element of black consciousness. It presents an analysis and a programme which was flawed, and which failed. The demise of apartheid is attributable to the rise of black consciousness. Its architect was not Nelson Mandela, but Bantu Stephen Biko. South Africa after apartheid is governed by the heirs of Mandela. It is a land of confusion and uncertainty, frustration and a sense of betrayal. This is manifest in levels of lawlessness and crime never seen in the days of apartheid. The days of promise have turned into nights of casual murder and the threat of anarchy. South Africa will not fulfil its destiny until it comes to terms with Steve Biko. Mandela, the man who turned reluctantly to violence, was prepared to die, but survived to see the end of apartheid. Biko, who could see no hope in violence, was beaten to death in a police cell by the defenders of apartheid. They represent two very different views of liberation and therefore of the future.

Leaders of revolutionary movements seldom come from poor families. Mandela was born in 1918 the son of a Transkei chief, and his guardian was Paramount Chief David Dalindyebo. On the other hand, he was related to Kaizer Matanzima who collaborated with the Nationalist Government in setting up the Transkei Bantustan. Leaders of revolutions are frequently professional men. Fidel Castro and Ernesto (Che) Guevara were both medical doctors in their youth. Like Marx and Lenin, Mandela was trained in law. He chose law under the influence of Walter Sisulu, and practised in Johannesburg with Oliver Tambo. In 1944 he joined the ANC (African National Congress, formed in 1912), and with the institutionalisation of apartheid in 1948 he was one of those who advocated a more militant policy of direct action and mass protest by Africans. In 1956 he and others were arrested and charged with conspiring with international communist elements to overthrow the state by force. At the Treason Trial, which continued for four years, Mandela spoke of the policies and objectives of the ANC. The campaigns of direct action were to secure adult franchise. What a revolutionary demand! His hope was the overthrow not of government, but of the racism institutionalised by this government. 'We are not anti-white, we are against white supremacy.' The reason is obvious. 'White supremacy implies Black inferiority.'[3] Mandela has never been a communist: indeed when he helped to form the ANC Youth League, he wished communists to be expelled. His vision has been essentially moral and liberal.

> We were inspired by the idea of bringing into being a democratic republic where all South Africans will enjoy human rights without the slightest discrimination; where Africans and non-Africans would be able to live together in peace, sharing a common nationality and a common loyalty to this country, which is our homeland.[4]

In face of peaceful demonstrations the Government refused to countenance constitutional change. Indeed it was during the Treason Trial that at Sharpeville 69 Africans were killed and 178 wounded when the police opened fire on an unarmed crowd. It was clear to the authorities who was to blame: the ANC was declared an unlawful organisation. The following year, 1961, Mandela declared: 'The struggle is my life. I will continue fighting for freedom until the end of my days.'[5] But in face of such intransigence and brutality, could the struggle be continued by non-violent means?

In his speech during the Rivonia trial Mandela quotes a fomer President of the ANC, Chief Albert Luthuli, a Nobel Peace Prize laureate. 'Who will deny that thirty years of my life have been spent knocking in vain, patiently, moderately and modestly at a closed and barred door?' When all attempts at dialogue through peaceful means had been exhausted, when every peaceful organisation was declared illegal, when every advocate of non-violent protest had been charged under the Suppression of Communism Act, the state itself seemed to force Africans to draw only one conclusion. 'A government which uses force to maintain its rule teaches the oppressed to use force to oppose it.'[6] It was therefore with reluctance that Mandela and others formed Umkonto We Sizwe (The Spear of the Nation). Its manifesto was briefer than the Declaration of the US Congress of 1776, but expresses a similar sentiment towards oppression by unrepresentative government. 'The time comes in the life of any nation when there remain only two choices: submit or fight.'[7] The reasons for turning at last to violence were twofold. The first was that the government had closed every other door. The second was more complicated. Violence was already breaking out, sporadic and unplanned. The danger was that it would become anti-white, that it would descend into racism. They wished to avoid a civil war. There was also the danger that ordinary people would be drawn into it and suffer retribution. Umkhonto was therefore formed as a separate organisation, which meant that membership of ANC did not automatically mean guilt by association. Umkhonto targeted buildings and installations which were symbolic of apartheid. It avoided racism. On 16 December 1961 explosives were set off in the main industrial centres of South Africa, at selected buildings and without loss of life. The hope was that such a demonstration would bring the government to the negotiating table. But these were the descendents of the Voortrekk[8]: they immediately formed a *laager*. The following month Mandela was sent to attend the Conference of Pan-African Feedom Movements held in Addis Ababa, Ethiopia to represent the ANC on the world stage. Thereafter he toured African countries to make contacts, arrange scholarships and also military training. He was welcomed by the presidents of independent former territories throughout Africa, including Leopold Senghor who had no experience of such matters. There is no indication that Mandela learned anything from the father of negritude. He acted as one of the leaders of a liberation movement, acting on behalf of the people.

In August 1962 Mandela was arrested in those circumstances which were so familiar to those of us living in Africa during that decade. He, the man who gave his life for his people, was betrayed by a (black) police informer. He was sentenced to five years with hard labour for inciting a strike and leaving the country illegally. A year later the police raided a farm at Rivonia, near Johannesburg and arrested ten members of the Congress Alliance. Mandela was brought from prison and the eleven were charged with sabotage and attempting to overthrow the government by violent revolution. With the arrest and conviction of the leadership of the ANC, the movement came to an end. Gandhi had learnt his non-violence when he lived in South Africa. It worked in India against the British: against a very different regime in South Africa it failed. The movement then turned to armed struggle: as a liberation movement it also failed.

In 1976 S.R. Maharaj was released from Robben Island after serving 12 years for sabotage. He makes some interesting observations about Mandela as a leader of the prisoners. There was no doubt about the general admiration and acceptance of Mandela, but it is clear that on Robben Island the prisoners were still conscious of their identity as members of different organisations. He tells us that 'no black group which claims to be standing for the rights of the black man and the ending of national oppression, however much they may differ even on tactics and theory and strategy, fails to mention Nelson Mandela when it talks of a future South Africa'.[9] What would be an example of such division on tactics, theory and strategy? According to Maharaj 'Nelson's view as he put it to me in conversation is that the armed struggle is central to our liberation.'[10] But was that the view of the next generation? All groups accepted Mandela's position 'as a spokesman of the prisoners. This was true too of the "younger generation" of prisoners, those who began to come in from the so-called "black-consciousness" groups from 1973 and the young people imprisoned after Soweto.'[11] To describe them as 'so-called "black-consciousness" groups' indicates that the leadership might be – with justification – somewhat out of touch. Although constantly harassed and frequently banned Mandela's second wife, Nomzamo Winnie Madikizela – at that time 'Mother of the Nation' – was certainly not out of touch. 'Winnie Mandela had already lent her support to the various Black Consciousness organisations which, with the liberation movement banned, had come into existence to express black demands and solidarity.'[12] In South Africa there was a constant recycling process. When movements were banned, they were reconstituted under different names, until they too were banned. This last comment, not by Maharaj, but perhaps by an editor in London, implies that black consciousness was simply the ANC renamed. This would quite misleading. Donald Woods was editor of the East London *Daily Despatch* at that time, a white liberal later himself to be banned and then deported. He makes a more nuanced assessment of the situation. 'With Mandela (ANC) imprisoned and Sobukwe (PAC) [= Pan-Africanist Congress] banned, there was for some years a leadership vacuum in South African black politics. It was filled toward the close of the 1960s by Bantu Stephen Biko.'[13] I believe that this vacuum was not of personalities but of policies.

Steve Biko was 20 when in 1966 he entered UNNE (University of Natal Non-European) as a medical student. Nelson Mandela was already in prison and the main organisations banned. Biko became active in NUSAS (National Union of South African Students), the multiracial body founded some 50 years before. Inevitably NUSAS was strongest on white campuses and was dominated by white concerns. At the annual conference of the University Christian Movement (South Africa's SCM) in 1968 Biko and others decided to break with NUSAS and set up their own union. SASO (South African Students' Organization) was formed the next year and Biko was elected as its first president. In 1970 he became chairman of the SASO Newsletter and began to produce a series of articles under the general title of *I Write What I Like*. In the best student tradition he adopted the nom de plume of Frank Talk. Not surprisingly he was expelled from the university in 1972, on the grounds that he was not devoting enough time to his studies. He was in fact devoting himself to something very different, which he was later to call black consciousness, and went to work for BCP (Black Community Programmes) in Durban. Before we are swamped by all these initials, there is a final set which must be mentioned. In 1972 the BPC (Black People's Convention) was formed. It is to be distinguished from the

BCP and functioned as a political party, in the absence of the ANC and PAC. In 1973 Biko was banned and restricted to his family home in Kingwilliamstown. Banning meant that he could not associate with others, nor could he publish anything. It was from this unlikely setting that his reputation was to extend throughout the country, the continent and indeed the politically conscious world: Steve Biko, the leader of the black consciousness movement.

In August 1976 Biko was arrested under the Terrorism Act and held for 101 days before being released without being charged. A year later he was arrested and taken to Port Elizabeth where on 6 September he was subjected to almost 24 hours of interrogation. During the torture he sustained several blows to the head which caused fatal brain damage. He lapsed into a coma and died six days later. He was the acknowledged and unrivalled leader of the movement. If it had been a political party, then his death could have marked its demise. His friend, the Anglican priest Aelred Stubbs, indicates why this did not happen.

> Given the circumstances he faced of a strongly entrenched, powerfully armed minority on the one hand and a divided, defeated majority on the other, perhaps the political genius of Steve lay in concentrating on the creation and diffusion of *a new consciousness* rather than in the formation of a rigid *organization*.[14]

His death was indeed seed, more like a mustard seed which to begin with can hardly be seen. Organisation after organisation had been identified and banned. It was Biko's genius to see that the revolution begins in the mind and that its growth cannot be contained. The new consciousness was more insidious than the old parties: it could not be banned. It was more dangerous than insurgents bearing arms: its supply lines could not be cut and its participants were not a few young men but a whole population.

Steve Biko was only 30 years old when he was murdered, but already he had formulated a critique of the alternatives on offer and an outline of his way forward. Of course he was against apartheid. The enemy was not white people but white supremacy. But he was also critical of the option represented by liberal whites. One of the reasons for setting up SASO was the feeling that it was no longer appropriate for liberal whites to be the leaders of opposition to apartheid. In practice it was easier for whites to organise groups: they were often more articulate. But somehow their social status, their racial security which were so useful to opposition groups, only perpetuated the stereotypes of black and white. Without a hint of racism, blacks had to take responsibility for the struggle against apartheid and the vision of a new South Africa. Naturally this was misunderstood. 'The idea of everything being done for blacks is an old one and all liberals take pride in it; but once the black students want to do things for themselves suddenly they are regarded as becoming "militant".' No hint of racism: individual white people could be accepted, but more importantly the liberal white *analysis* was rejected. On the liberal view the enemy is apartheid and the solution is non-racialism. On Biko's view the enemy is white supremacy. This must be countered by a new black consciousness. Only then can society proceed to 'a true humanity where power politics will have no place'. Blacks have been damaged by racism and they cannot simply proceed to a non-racial society. 'Hence what is necessary as a prelude to anything else that may come is a very strong grass-roots build-up of black consciousness such that blacks can learn to assert themselves and stake their rightful claim.' This is clearly a criticism of the liberal white analysis, but I believe in reality it is also a criticism of the analysis – or rather the lack of analysis – of the ANC. This is also implied by Donald Woods. 'The idea behind black consciousness was to break away almost entirely from past black attitudes to the liberation struggle and to set a new style of self-reliance and dignity for blacks as a psychological attitude leading to new initiatives.'[15] Biko's language is similar to that of the ANC, but the analysis and the implications are very different. 'Liberation therefore, is of paramount importance in the concept of Black Consciousness, for we cannot be conscious of ourselves and yet remain in bondage.' Che Guevara reflected on the guerrilla campaign in Bolivia. 'We spoke to the people about their lives, and *that* was the revolution.'[16] I believe that this is also the insight of Steve Biko. The revolution must begin with the consciousness of the black majority, with their self-affirmation and the re-evaluation of their relations with whites. Without that the armed struggle is about the exchange of power, as we see continually in post-colonial Africa.

> The first step therefore is to make the black man come to himself; to pump back life into his empty shell; to infuse him with pride and dignity, to remind him of his complicity in the crime of allowing himself to be misused and therefore letting evil reign supreme in the country of his birth. This is what we mean by an inward-looking process. This is the definition of 'Black consciousness'.

Non-racism does not describe the goal, for it does not address the problem. White control will continue regardless: 'the most potent weapon in the hands of the oppressor is the mind of the oppressed'. This is the premise of all ideologies, including apartheid: he who controls the mind creates and therefore controls the world.

The goal of a new and renewed humanity which Biko envisages cannot be brought about by supplication to the white oppressors: this invites contempt. But neither can it come about by moral hectoring. It is interesting to observe the wider context in which he places current problems. From 1652 and Van Riebeeck's arrival in the country there has been a progressive detribalisation and destruction of traditional African life, community and custom. This has had consequences which cannot be simply subsumed under the goal of non-racialism. In the townships 'we see a situation of absolute want in which black will kill black to be able to survive. This is the basis of the vandalism, murder, rape and plunder that goes on while the real sources of the evil – white society – are sun-tanning on exclusive beaches or relaxing in their bourgeois homes.' Writing at the same time as Albert Cleage, Biko refuses to sacrilise the people of the townships: they have been damaged by racism and no exchange of power will heal them. It is disappointing but not surprising that the end of white racist control has ushered in an era of indiscriminate violence.

Not surprisingly Biko is ambivalent towards integration. 'If by integration you understand a breakthrough into white society by blacks, an assimilation and acceptance of blacks into an already established set of norms and code of behaviour set up by and maintained by whites, then YES I am against it.' This he describes as 'the myth of integration' propounded under the banner of liberal ideology. It is the opium of the gullible blacks and the absolution of guilt-stricken liberal whites: 'black souls wrapped up in white skins'. If there is to be an integration it must come about by a more complex process which begins with an element of separation. 'Each group must be able to attain its style of existence without encroaching on or being thwarted by another. Out of this mutual respect for each other and complete freedom of self-determination there will obviously arise a genuine fusion of the life-styles of the various groups. This is true integration.' Just as non-racialism is an insufficient goal, so Biko declares himself on pigmentation. In South Africa being non-white is not the same as being black. Being black is a mental attitude. Non-white refers to someone whose aspirations are to be white, but who is prevented from achieving this because of pigmentation. 'Any man who calls a white man "Baas", any man who serves in the police force or Security Branch is *ipso facto* a non-white. Black people – real black people – are those who can manage to hold their heads high in defiance rather than willingly surrender their souls to the white man.' Black is not an aberration from the white norm.

It is of interest that Biko never refers to American sources, but frequently quotes Aimé Césaire, and to a lesser extend Franz Fanon. His black consciousness arises from within the African experience. This is true also on his reflection on the implications for a Black theology. Steve Biko was an Anglican and the inspiration to form SASO came at a meeting of the University Christian Movement. His friend Stanley Ntwasa, an Anglican priest, took a year out in 1971 as a travelling secretary for UCM to promote Black theology. Biko was drawn into reflecting on this subject. The Christianity which replaced traditional African religion has been a religion focusing on individual sin and guilt. Little has been said about the God who is concerned about the suffering of his people. Biko sees other, neglected themes. 'It must rather preach that it is a sin to allow oneself to be oppressed. The bible must continually be shown to have something to say to the black man to keep him going in his long journey towards realisation of the self. This is the message implicit in "black theology".' This traditional Christianity has moulded African consciousness towards compliance with law rather than seeking after justice.

> Black theology therefore is a situational interpretation of Christianity. It seeks to relate the present-day black man to God within the given context of the black man's suffering and his attempts to get out of it. It shifts the emphasis of man's moral obligations from avoiding wronging false authorities by not losing his Reference Book, not stealing food when hungry and not cheating the police when he is caught, to being committed to eradicating all cause for suffering as presented in the death of children from starvation, outbreaks of epidemics in poor areas, or the existence of thuggery and vandalism in townships.

Black theology, like black consciousness, requires people to take responsibility for their lives: 'God is not in the habit of coming down from heaven to solve people's problems on earth.' God is a militant God who contests such evils as oppression by white supremacy. 'It is the duty therefore of all black priests and ministers of religion to save Christianity by adopting Black Theology's approach and thereby once more uniting the black man with his God.' There is no rejection of Christianity in all this, but there is a distinction between the spiritual heart of Christianity and the purely cultural western mores with which it has become associated. Young blacks are asking 'whether the necessary decolonization of Africa requires the de-Christianization of Africa. The most positive facet of this questioning is the development of "black" theology in the context of Black Consciousness. For black theology does not challenge Christianity itself but its Western package, in order to discover what the Christian faith means for our continent.'[17] As we shall see, Black theology in South Africa arises from Biko's black consciousness. It is not simply imported from America.

Black Theology, Class and Power

The outcome of Stanley Ntwasa's year out to promote Black theology was the publication in 1972 of an edited collection of *Essays in Black Theology*, published by the Black Theology Project of the University Christian Movement. It was immediately banned. This was the predictable response of a censorship regime which had already banned *Black Beauty*, and perhaps in this case also their fears were unfounded. The banning of Ntwasa's collection leads us to anticipate that it will be radical, even dangerous. For the most part it is disappointing. The government might well have taken the view that if this is the best that Black theology can come up with, then bring it on: it shows how vacuous is the movement. The book is yet another example of a collection gathered around a concept which goes beyond the capacity of the contributors to develop it. Once again we have essays in which writers deal with topics with which they feel comfortable and show no capacity to reflect radically, creatively, originally on a new and exciting agenda. They demonstrate how well trained they are in the European theology they purport to criticise. Far from building on the foundations laid by Steve Biko for the most part they do not even connect with his programmatic remarks on the subject. There is one exception, to which we shall return, but this the first 'wave' of Black theology was hardly engulfing.

The second wave of Black theology in South Africa is best represented in the work of Allan Boesak. The black consciousness movement insisted on including Indians and Coloureds. 'Coloured' refers to those of mixed race. It is commonly said that one drop of black blood makes a person black. This is true, but not absolutely true. Anyone who has lived in southern Africa will be aware of a very curious ambiguity in this matter. There are certain very old white families who are conservative but not racist. They have been there a long time and from generation to generation there is sometimes a trace in the hair or the complexion which hints at inter-racial liaisons in the early days. These families are so secure in themselves that they are not concerned to strenuously deny such lineage. Indeed when in colonial clubs it is noted that one of the members (not present) has a touch of the tar brush it is said with humour and not malice. But these families are the exception. Coloureds are the product of two races and liable to be rejected by both. It was the strength of black consciousness to insist that they be included. Such a one is Allan Boesak. He was one of several church leaders of the 1970s and 1980s prominent in their active opposition to apartheid. This was the more ironic – or tragic – in the case of Boesak who was a minister of the Dutch Reformed Mission Church, a body created in 1881 when the Dutch Reformed Church set up separate institutions for blacks and whites. In 1982 he was elected president of the World Alliance of Reformed Churches and in the name of the Reformed churches throughout the world was able to lead the condemnation of the role which the Dutch Reformed Church played in legitimising apartheid. Boesak was able to place South African Black theology in a world, ecumenical context. There are three elements in his theology: the context in South Africa, a dialogue with Black theology in the USA and the influence of the liberation theology of Latin America.

Boesak's most important book, *Farewell to Innocence: a socio-ethical study on Black Theology and Black Power*, was originally published in 1976. It was dedicated 'in memory of Steve Biko with respect' and is indebted to black consciousness in South Africa. The book is an attempt 'to interpret honestly and authentically a black experience within the complexity of the meaning of blackness in South Africa'.[18] It is to the credit of the inclusiveness of black consciousness that this coloured man is able to claim to express the black experience. To have written of the 'coloured' experience would have been to accept the validity of the categorisation of the population under apartheid legislation. Although Biko is not mentioned in the book, his influence is clear at several places, not least in the title itself, *Farewell to Innocence*. Boesak does not trouble to describe the black experience of humiliation and oppression. Instead he draws the line at which the fight back must begin. We recall that Biko began by addressing the black man, 'to remind him of his complicity in the crime of allowing himself to be misused and therefore letting evil reign supreme in the country of his birth'. The architects of apartheid are guilty of oppression, but the oppressed are not entirely innocent. They are guilty in another way, by complicity, by accepting the situation both in its reality and the theory which justifies it. There is nothing they can do: they are the innocent victims in this matter. Boesak declares this to be a 'pseudo-innocence'. 'When people face issues too horrendous to contemplate, they close their eyes to reality and make a virtue out of powerlessness, weakness and helplessness.'[19] This pseudo-innocence enables them to accept and live with their plight. (Boesak might have added here the opportunity presented to religion in restraining black people from retaliation.) But the pseudo-innocence has another function. 'It effectively blocks off all awareness and therefore the sense of responsibility necessary to confront the other as a human being. This leads to an inability to repent which in turn makes genuine reconciliation impossible.'[20] Blacks fail to take responsibility for themselves and what has become of them. This in turn prevents whites from being confronted with the enormity of their crime. There must be a farewell to innocence among whites as well as blacks: among whites, when they come to appreciate blacks as human beings with normal feelings and aspirations, but also among blacks. Apartheid is maintained not simply by force of arms, but through its acceptance by blacks. As Biko pointed out, 'the most potent weapon in the hands of the oppressor is the mind of the oppressed'. So Boesak concludes that 'the greatest ally of the oppressor is the mind of the oppressed'.[21] Biko had accused pseudo-innocent blacks of being 'non-white', of accepting the aspiration to become white. So Boesak sees the need for a further break, a 'farewell to the non-white mentality'.[22] Likewise Black theology must be negative and positive. Negatively it must be 'a theology of refusal: a theology that refuses to accept that God is just another word for the status quo'.[23] This view must be rejected because '*apartheid* is more than an ideology ... *Apartheid* is also a pseudo-gospel.'[24] Pseudo-innocence and now a pseudo-gospel. It is often said that the Dutch Reformed Church legitimised apartheid as the will of God. Boesak claims that it was 'the brainchild of the Dutch Reformed churches'.[25] I believe that the situation is if anything more convoluted. The principal architect of apartheid was D.F. Milan, but the terms in which he described it were not simply political or ideological. They were theological, reflecting the fact that Milan had taken his doctorate in theology at the University of Utrecht before entering politics. Thus he described apartheid as more than a political programme. 'Afrikanerdom is not the work of man but the creation of God.' 'Our history is the highest work of art of the Architect of the centuries.'[26] This represented a new hard-line Afrikanerdom, greatly suspect to the older Boer tradition represented by General J.B.M. Hertzog. As W.A. de Klerk notes, 'what Hertzog vaguely felt about Milan, was the first indication of a reaction to the theologizing of Afrikaner politics'.[27] However this may be, Black theology has to expose apartheid in its role as a pseudo word of God. Little wonder that so much has been written on the parallel between the church struggle in Germany in the 1930s and in South Africa in the apartheid era. The great danger is that Black theology falls under the sway of an anti-apartheid ideology. Boesak assures us that 'black theology itself falls under the judgement of the word'.[28]

Two further points might be added in this context. The first is important, but can be mentioned briefly at this stage. Black consciousness left the violent response to apartheid to the ANC, or at least to Umkhonto. When Steve Biko was banned he was removed from the dilemma which faced Allan Boesak, which he illustrates as follows. 'The man from Samaria, however, first appeared in the parable after the injured man's struggle was ended, when everything was over ... What will happen if love is expressed during the struggle, not after the struggle?'[29] Boesak espoused non-violence, but as we shall see, the issue was a matter of Christian conviction and not simply strategy. The second point concerns realism about human nature, black and white. Black is in turn a colour, a condition, but it is never simply synonymous with good. At that time Africa was a battle ground of the Cold War, with countries being coerced to line up on the side of one ideology or the other. But Boesak is realistic about the behaviour of Africans who came to power. 'But it is also true that Africa knows too many iron-fisted rulers who have no respect for human rights. The colonial governor's mansion is now occupied by the representatives of new power elites that have as little concern for the people as did the colonialists.'[30] This was written in 1981. If anything it is more true today. 'Black' does not mean innocent. Nor does Boesak admire the behaviour of the appointed rulers of the Bantustans within South Africa. 'These homelands are places where the signs and tokens of *apartheid* have been replaced by the relentless grip of black dictatorship.'[31] The transfer of (some) power changes nothing. The black consciousness revolution must proceed, and Black theology has its part to play in this process.

Allan Boesak is at his best, his most credible and authentic when he writes from the perspective of black consciousness about the agenda for Black theology in South Africa. However, his *Farewell to Innocence* was renamed to make it comprehensible and therefore more attractive to a wider market. The sub-title *Black Theology and Black Power* was substituted, thus focusing on the second element of Boesak's work, the dialogue with American Black theology. Its foundations in black consciousness and its South African roots were ignored and it seemed as if Black theology in South Africa was merely imported from the USA. Boesak was influenced by American Black theology but he retains a South African perspective which makes him deeply critical of the assumptions, values and aspirations of the American form.

It is not difficult for Boesak to repeat with approval some of the rhetoric of James Cone, but that is what it remains. Black theologians are never done describing their work as contextual. Frankly, the contexts could hardly be more different. In South Africa blacks live in their own country, they are the majority. It is the land of their ancestors, the very land to which the spirits of their ancestors are attached. They have their own names, languages, culture and in some cases religion. There has been no colonial policy of assimilation. Even if they had heard of the concept blacks in South Africa could not aspire to become part of white society. Controlled, yes, but they have never been enslaved. They have a history which they can remember and a hope to which they can aspire. When Boesak echoes the words of Cone they are rhetoric because there is no single common black experience to unite them. When Boesak writes of the oppression of South African blacks, he might easily have added that black Americans inadvertently contribute to that suffering. Here would be another innocence to which they should bid farewell. Boesak's fraternal criticism of Cone therefore focuses on two points. The first is indeed a theological issue, related to his insistence that 'black theology itself falls under the judgement of the word'. We noted earlier that Cone loses any critical distance between Black theology and Black Power. God may reveal Himself in the black experience but that is not at all the same as saying that God can be identified with black experience.

> Cone, we have noted, speaks of reflection 'in the light of the black situation'. This formulation calls for caution. The black situation is the situation within which reflection and action take place, but it is the Word of God which illuminates the reflection and guides the action. We fear that Cone attaches too much theological import to the black experience and the black situation as if these *realities within themselves* have revelational value on a par with Scripture. God, it seems to us, reveals himself *in* the situation. The black experience provides the framework within which blacks understand the revelation of God in Jesus Christ. No more, no less.[32]

The second criticism of Cone arises out of an observation he makes about J. Deotis Roberts, another black American theologian whose contribution we have already discussed. Perhaps we could say that on this view Roberts's position is closer to the liberal white analysis exposed and condemned by Biko. That is to say, the analysis is about ending racialism, but does not reach to the deeper level of criticising the fundamental values on which a non-racial society would be based. 'Once more, we see a black theologian ask for nothing more than to get "into" the existing American structure. Roberts sees no need to criticize the system in depth.'[33] It is here that once again we see exposed the essential conservatism of American Black theology.

> A solution cannot be sought by imitating the American white capitalist system, or by creating a 'better' kind of capitalism in the black community. What Roberts should ponder is a way in which blacks could really make a significant and fundamental contribution to the transformation of the system instead of a way of strengthening it by 'getting in'.[34]

Boesak therefore criticises American Black theology for failing in its analysis of its own situation. It is contextual theology which has only a shallow understanding of that context and consequently only a limited vision of its task. Boesak's second criticism is that American Black theologians have the audacity to generalise their analysis about their situation, as if it were the norm for all blacks throughout the world. He is also very critical of Cleage's Black Christian Nationalism. For Boesak it is all too reminiscent of the ideology of apartheid and the white Christian nationalism of Afrikanerdom. However, in fairness, Cleage is not absolutising his position as normative for others.

> We fear that in this respect Cone's theology is particularly vulnerable. Cone claims, so we saw, God *solely* for the black experience. We submit that to make *black* as such *the* symbol of oppression and liberation in the world is to absolutize one's own situation. Black Theology, says C. Eric Lincoln in a critique of Cone, 'is bound to the situation in this sense, that God's confrontation with white racism is but *one* aspect of God's action in a multi-dimensional complex of interaction between man and man, and God and man'. Cone's mistake is that he has taken Black Theology out of the framework of the theology of liberation, thereby making his own situation (being black in America) and his own movement (liberation from white racism) the ultimate criterion for all theology.[35]

In this quotation we are already presented with the third element in Boesak's theology. The USA is like a large island. Most of its inhabitants never leave it even for a vacation. It is notoriously difficult to get news about events happening in other countries unless they are linked to some ethnic group (for example in Israel or Poland). The early James Cone writes as if the interests of black Americans is a criterion of twentieth-century world history. Boesak by comparison writes as someone aware of events throughout Africa and movements throughout the world. In particular he is influenced by the liberation theology of Latin America and quotes with approval from the works of Gutiérrez and even Assmann. He writes of the 'gospel of the poor', pursues the theme of Exodus, and believes that 'God has taken sides in the South African situation'.[36] He can even echo a distinction found in Sobrino and Boff. 'Indeed the church in Africa itself is in need of liberation. The church in Africa is still plagued by a colonial mentality; we have not truly become a *church for Africa*.'[37] All of these are recurring themes in Latin America. However, their context is significantly different from his and he concentrates on the theme of liberation theology as such. Thus Black theology is set in the wider context of the worldwide struggle for liberation. 'Black Theology is not the *only* theological expression in the world, but in my opinion it is the only authentic way for blacks to pursue their Christian faith.'[38] However, 'Black Theology is a liberation theology.'[39] This means that he can advocate Black theology in a context in which race is the dominant issue, without making imperialistic claims which would downgrade other theologies of liberation in contexts in which class or gender were the dominant issues. This opens the door to dialogue with other liberation theologies throughout the world, but also paves the way for the development of other liberation themes within South Africa itself.

There is one final point to which we must return, namely the place of violence in Black theology. When we see footage of Allan Boesak and Desmond Tutu linking arms and striding along at the head of a protest demonstration we cannot but be reminded of the great civil rights marches lead by Martin Luther King, Jr. Indeed Boesak has made a study of the American alternatives, entitled *Coming in Out of the Wilderness: a comparative interpretation of the ethics of Martin Luther King and Malcolm X*.[40] His most sustained criticism of American Black theology is that it has fallen in behind the violence of Black Power and has failed to display the truly Christian insights of Martin Luther King. Allan Boesak takes the side of Martin Luther King not simply for strategic reasons, but out of the profound truth within Christianity of the relationship of love and power. Cone could see nothing profound: he simply followed Black Power at this point. King claimed that 'one of the greatest problems of history is that the concepts of love and power are usually contrasted as polar opposites. Love is identified with a resignation of power and power with a denial of love.'[41] It is for this reason that he rejected Black Power's analysis: as a secular movement it had no faith in love. 'Beneath all the satisfaction of a gratifying slogan, Black Power is a nihilistic philosophy born out of the conviction that the Negro cannot win. It is, at bottom, the view that American society is so hopelessly corrupt and enmeshed in evil that there is no possibility of salvation from within.'[42] As with other prophetic figures King faced the challenge of being unrealistic and impractical, and faced it with his own counter-challenge.

> My only answer is that mankind has followed the so-called practical way for a long time now, and it has led inexorably to deeper confusion and chaos. Time is cluttered with the wreckage of individuals and communities that surrendered to hatred and violence. For the salvation of our nation and the salvation of mankind, we must follow another way.[43]

King might be right or wrong, wise or foolish, but at least his position arises from a spiritual insight about the redemptive power of suffering love. He acknowledges that the young black militants are now reading Fanon's *The Wretched of the Earth* and in consequence are advocating that violence which has been such a feature of European history in the twentieth century.

> Humanity is waiting for something other than blind imitation of the past. If we want truly to advance a step further, if we want to turn over a new leaf and really set a new man afoot, we must begin to turn mankind away from the long desolate night of violence.[44]

Boesak quotes this passage from King, and prefers it to the more blatant American Black theologians, such as Joseph Washington whose understanding of power was that it came from the barrel of a gun. 'We submit that this argument carries a lot more weight than Washington's short-sighted violent ethic.'[45] Black consciousness in South Africa knew better than a simple exchange of power. 'All in all, Washington's thinking is so strongly reminiscent of the ideology of the ruling class that we cannot but reject it outright.'[46] Boesak in turn might be right or wrong, wise or foolish, but in Christian faith he seeks to go beyond that liberal analysis which seeks peace without laying new Christian foundations. 'Behind these questions lies the deeply disturbing theological question for any Christian, namely this: Is it not the essence of discipleship that the Christian is required to react on a completely different level in order to create and keep open the possibilities for reconciliation, redemption, and community.'[47] Twenty years later this insight would be taken up in its secular form as the Truth and Reconciliation Commission, chaired by Archbishop Desmond Tutu. The anti-apartheid movement had triumphed and happily did itself out of a job. The armed struggle was over. But what of black consciousness and Black theology? If they had been simply about apartheid then they would have come to an end. But if Allan Boesak was right, and Black theology was part of a larger and on-going movement of liberation, then it must turn its attention to any persisting or emerging forces which cause human alienation. This is the agenda of the third wave of Black theology.

The third wave is of the 1980s, and yet its agenda had been set by the only essay of significance to be included in the Ntwasa collection of 1972. 'Black Theology and Authority' was contributed by Mokgethi Motlhabi, originally a candidate for the Catholic priesthood, who became acting director of the Black Theology Project when Ntwasa was banned. All opposition groups agreed that there must be an end to racism, but Motlhabi claims that this is seldom illuminated by an analysis of racism. 'It should be clear that a frontal attack on racism, even if it were to succeed, would change society very little.'[48] Racism is evil, but it is symptomatic of other evils. Racism is easily identified, but it is an expression of other factors in society which are not so obvious. Racism constructs myths and these myths cannot simply be scoffed at and set aside. Their appeal and their persistence arises from a deeper, ideological level: they maintain interests through certain social structures. The institutions of apartheid were not brought about simply by racism, but in order to further and perpetuate inequalities of power. 'This racial prejudice gets blown up into the huge racism myth in order to internalise the values which place and keep the whites at the tip of the power structure and the blacks at the bottom.' It would be superficial to think that the end of racism would radically alter relations of power and advantage: 'no radical social change will be brought about by attacking the myth without attacking the causes of the myth'. Racism is the narrative which explains why things are 'just so'. Its removal would not in itself change the 'just so', the status quo. Racism is the legitimation of unequal power relations, and religion plays its part. 'It is not surprising, therefore, that religion has been one of the major bastions and creators of the race myth of the inferiority and labour – or "Ham" – quality of the blacks.'

Motlhabi's essay stands out from the others in the Ntwasa collection. It provides an analysis of racism, and with its sophisticated consciousness of racism as an ideology, identifies its true nature and its real roots. It therefore sets a new agenda for Black theology, which goes beyond race or colour, placing it firmly in the wider context of liberation theology. Beneath the surface level of racism lies the privilege of power, the control of the many in the interests of the few. 'Racism as such is not the real poison in inter-personal relations. It is that for which racism exists, i.e. vast discrepancies in the distribution of power.' This has implications in two directions.

The first is the churches themselves. They are structured in a patriarchal and hierarchical way, to ensure that the male prevails over the female and the clergy over the laity. This is taken to be a matter of religious values and not simply of social management. 'It is the social structure in which some people are regarded as having the right to exercise control over the lives of others by virtue of the position they hold within the social structure.' Below the surface of racism lies the acceptance of authoritarianism. The ending of racism will not alter such social relations. The language of religion is inherently authoritarian: the titles of God are feudal – Lord, King, Master. Submission is a religious virtue. Ecclesial structures must liberate rather than control. 'We cannot have the authoritarians who try to tell us what we believe or what to believe and who have the power to reward or punish us. We need a Church which is authentically a Church of the people for their liberation.' This is a conclusion which Motlhabi draws concerning the churches, but it is also applicable to society at large.

> To reject racism and leave the authoritarianism basically unchanged may be to change the names of the people in 'office' but is unlikely to change the names or the lot of the people at the bottom of the power pile. And one of the main reasons for Black Theology is that black people are the oppressed end of society. If all that is achieved is that black rulers replace white rulers but those at the 'bottom'

> experience very little change in their freedom and recognition, then there will still be a need for a Black Theology, or a theology of the oppressed.

Those who identify racism as the enemy find that with the end of apartheid their work is ended. To criticise the new black leadership would be politically incorrect, and yet in their liberal souls they are disappointed that things have changed so slowly, or not at all. Twenty years before the end of apartheid Motlhabi offered a more subtle analysis of the roots of oppression. No one who takes this view could be surprised that the new South Africa is so much like the old. Indeed it has followed a pattern in the region. Forty years ago Malawi became independent, but for the sake of the economy the white tea planters were allowed to stay on. The race line lost its colour. The black elite simply crossed the line to join those who held power and privilege. Twenty years ago Zimbabwe became independent, but for the sake of the economy the tobacco farmers and cattle ranchers were allowed to stay on. The land issue was not addressed. The race line lost its colour. The new black elite crossed the line to join those who held power and privilege. (The present chaotic circumstances in Zimbabwe have been caused by Robert Mugabe's desperate measures to cling on to power in the country.) Ten years ago majority rule came to South Africa. The race line was declared illegal, but the black elite crossed the line to join those who held power and privilege. The land issue was not addressed. In a curious, but tragic way, liberals who were anti-apartheid were in fundamental agreement with their opponents that race was the problem in South Africa. Hence their disillusionment with post-apartheid South Africa. They have yet to draw the appropriate conclusion: their analysis was superficial and inadequate. If racism is the agenda then Black theology becomes redundant with the end of apartheid. If the roots of oppression are thought to lie deeper, then the end of apartheid is a welcome development along the way, but Black theology as a theology of liberation still has much to do.

The third wave of Black theology in South Africa can continue beyond the end of apartheid because its analysis of oppression is more profound than opposition to racism. It also includes an ideological edge which comes from a reading of Marx in addition to black consciousness. This is appropriate to a theology which is part of the wider genre of liberation theology, which is highly critically, even disdainful of the narrow, blinkered and self-obsessed project of American Black theology. In tracing the origins of oppression back to interest and relations of power Black theology roots oppression in the economic base of society. In espousing materialism it avoids the idealist trap of analysing social ills at the level of moral behaviour. The leading exponent of this third wave is Itumeleng Mosala.

Black theology is not an end in itself – although it has brought tenure and security to some – but rather a means to a greater end, namely the establishment of communities of equity and justice. As theory it can achieve nothing, but as Marx notes, it can become a 'weapon' in the struggle when it is made available to the most oppressed classes. For Mosala, Black theology in South Africa has not performed this function, because it has not been developed in association with 'black working-class people, the most exploited of the black community'.[49] This may seem unfair and unjustified when we consider the personal involvement of black leaders both in the USA and in South Africa with the most poor and vulnerable groups in society. This is to miss the point. Black theology cannot be an instrument of liberation until it is fit for purpose, and that means until it has freed itself of common assumptions and basic presuppositions which it shares with the ruling classes, those who (white or black – or any other colour) benefit from the present order of things. This is nowhere better illustrated than in biblical hermeneutics, the interpretation of the Word of God. Black scholars, at least as far as their postgraduate studies are concerned, have normally been trained in white universities and seminaries. Such is the prestige of these institutions that black colleges consider it of the utmost importance to be seen to maintain the same traditions of objective, historical-critical analysis. There is biblical literalism and there is historical criticism: these are the choices. Not so. In one important respect these opposing traditions are agreed: the Bible is the Word of God and as such is ideologically neutral. But this is precisely the ahistorical idealism which is such a feature of class interest. It is the assertion that these ideas, these texts, these narratives derive from elsewhere, either from heaven or from an archaic world quite unlike our own. It is for this reason that Mosala chooses historical-materialist analysis over historical-idealist analysis. The Bible will be an instrument of liberation for the oppressed classes only when it is acknowledged that the class struggle of the contemporary world is already present in the Bible, present in the very production of the Bible itself. It is the assumption of 'a false notion of the bible as non-ideological, which can cause political paralysis in the oppressed who read it'.[50] Mosala is critical of Black theologians such as James Cone and Cornel West. They claim to be alive to ideological manipulation: white people have (mis)interpreted the Bible to suit their interests. For them the Bible as the Word of God is on the side of the oppressed. What they do not see is that the ideological interests of the ruling class are already there in the Bible itself. To begin with a non-ideological view of the Bible is to unwittingly accept the premises of the ruling classes and therefore to take their side against the poor. To describe the Bible as the 'Word of God' *tout court* is an ideological act. To accept the 'authority of scripture' without qualification is to ensure that the Bible can never speak to the condition of the oppressed. Only when such a qualification is made are we free to acknowledge what is perfectly clear, that 'not every God of every biblical text is on the side of the poor'.[51] Liberation theologians frequently quote the prophet Amos who denounces those who 'sell the righteous for silver, and the needy for a pair of shoes' (Amos 2: 6). But whose interests are being served by the narrative of the Conquest of Canaan, in which God orders ethnic cleansing of the inhabitants and the genocide of men, women and children? It is clear that 'not all of the bible is on the side of human rights or of oppressed and exploited people'.[52] Liberation theologians claim that God takes the side of the poor, but this can be said only in relation to a very few, scattered texts. In a collection produced by the ruling classes, how could it be otherwise? We might pause to consider an example which Mosala only mentions in passing, namely the famous passage in Romans 13. It was written only a few years after the Jewish leaders and the Roman imperial administration had conspired to execute Jesus. 'For rulers are not a terror to good conduct, but to bad.' It is one of the most scandalous texts in the Bible, yet far from being offended by it, generations of the ruling classes have brandished it as a weapon in defence and promotion of their own interests. From what perspective is this written? Jesus was a subject of the Roman empire: he was tortured to death although innocent. Paul was a citizen of the Roman empire, one of the elite in whose interests the enslavement of the world took place. Does God take sides in the Bible, or is it the writers who take sides and claim God as their authority? And what of those who now read the Bible? 'What one can do is take sides in a struggle representing different positions and groups in the society behind the text. That provokes different appropriations of those texts, depending on one's class, gender, culture, race, or ideological position and attitude.'[53] If Black theology is to become a weapon for the oppressed it has to progress beyond two distracting alternatives: (a) an ahistorical (non-ideological) reading whose aim is simply to recover the meaning of the text, and (b) an existential (spiritual) privatised internalising of it. 'The social, cultural, political, and economic world of the black working class and peasantry constitutes the only valid hermeneutical starting point for a black theology of liberation.'[54]

To digress for a moment, what might strike us about this last sentence is not that it slavishly follows Marx, but that it actually departs from Marx in one significant respect – the reference to 'the black working class *and peasantry*'. At the beginning of this chapter we claimed that the third source of Black theology was the presence, uniquely in South Africa, of a significant industrial working class. For Marx the proletariat was that oppressed class which would liberate itself from oppression – and liberate all other classes at the same time. He did not expect emancipation to come from the peasantry. Indeed, as we noted, capitalism had 'rescued a considerable part of the population from the idiocy of the rural life'. However, the proportions are different in South Africa today and Europe a century and a half ago. It is interesting therefore that Mosala adds 'and peasantry' – realistically or grudgingly, but certainly departing from historical materialism. To this point we shall return when we consider Black theology's relations with African traditional religion.

From a historical-materialist perspective it is necessary to co-relate the context in which the biblical texts were composed, and the context in which they are now read by the working classes. The context will be provided by a reconstruction of the sequence of modes of production, thus avoiding both selective romanticism about the African past and its dismissal as inconsequential. The parallel could work, and might even be illuminating, but it seems to me that Mosala does not treat the matter with sufficient precision. The idea of a sequence of modes of production of course goes back to the famous Preface which Marx wrote to *A Contribution to the Critique of Political Economy*. The work itself is little studied, since it is often regarded as a first draft of *Capital*, but the Preface is of fundamental importance in the development of historical materialism. In it Marx indicates how the history of the world could be rewritten. Or rather he indicates how it could be correctly conceived of for the first time. Instead of the usual romantic and idealistic categories used to characterise different periods he proposes that the great turning-points in history have each been ushered in by a change in the mode of production which comes to characterise the new age. 'In broad outline, the Asiatic, ancient, feudal, and modern bourgeois modes of production may be designated as epochs marking progress in the economic development of society.'[55] This revolutionary view of history, of breathtaking originality and – if true – of such fundamental importance for the understanding of history in its macro and micro forms, is presented in one sentence. Could we not have at least a paragraph! It would need an entire library of empirical research to test out. Mosala proposes a materialist account of African history under three headings which are somewhat related to Marx's categories: the communal mode of production, the tributary mode of production and the capitalist mode of production. The categories are not well developed. The parallel between the materialist history of Israel and African materialist history might have been conceived of as primitive communalism (up to and including the alliance of tribes) and the tributary (including the establishment of the monarchy). It is surprising that Mosala does not use the category of feudalism to draw the parallel between Israel under the foreign powers and colonialism in Africa.

However that may be, he now turns to illustrate his hermeneutical method with two specific studies. The first is 'A Materialist Reading of Micah'. The two sections of the book are taken to reflect two modes of production, the early communalism and the tributary. The relevance of this reflects the base and superstructure model which Marx outlined in the Preface which we have just discussed. Mosala follows Marx here, claiming that ideas and institutions are part of what the mode of production produces. 'How a society produces and reproduces its life is fundamentally conditioned by its mode of production. The legal, religious, political, and philosophical spheres of society develop on the basis of the production mode and refer back to it.'[56] Chapters 4–7 express the ideology of early communalism, including 'themes such as justice, solidarity, struggle, and vigilance'.[57] The opening chapters express the ideology of the tributary mode: the monarchical ideology is concerned with 'stability, grace, restoration, creation, universal peace, compassion and salvation'. The African peasantry should be able to appropriate the later part of Micah as a Word of God to them. They too are involved in a struggle to recover their land, to restore equity and justice in their communities. The early chapters, however, reflect the concerns of those who have taken control of the land, those who rule the nation rather than those who are ruled. The God of these chapters is not concerned with the plight of the poor. I am not sure that Micah can be fitted so neatly into two sections expressing contrasting ideologies, but the study is illustrative of Mosala's method. There must be a dialectical relationship between the experience of the oppressed in Micah and that of the oppressed in South Africa.

> The task now facing a black theology of liberation is to enable black people to use the bible to get the land back and to get the land back without losing the bible. In order for this to happen, black theology must employ the progressive aspects of black history and culture to liberate the bible so that the bible may liberate black people. That is the hermeneutical dialectic.[58]

The second specific study which Mosala provides to illustrate his hermeneutical method is 'A Materialist Reading of Luke 1 and 2'. He uses the same categories to describe society even though they are separated by the best part of a millennium. Perhaps more could have been made of the colonialism of the Roman empire. Marx's early categories are vague, but I believe what he calls 'ancient' could include slavery. The mode of production of the Roman empire was slavery and I believe that this is the main reason why Paul does not condemn the practice: he could not conceive of an economy based on any other mode of production. This is another indication why he as a citizen found the superstructural arrangements of the empire suited him very well and why he therefore legitimised them: all authorities 'have been instituted by God' (Rom. 13: 1).

Once again we find liberation theologians reading Luke's gospel as the Word of God. It is here that the liberationist mantra is found, the first sermon of Jesus in Nazareth, in which he turns to Isaiah for his text. 'The Spirit of the Lord is upon me, because he has anointed me to preach good news to the poor.' (Luke 4: 18, cf. Isaiah 61: 1–2) Luke has been hailed as the champion of the poor, blacks, captives and any category of people who are oppressed. New Testament scholars assume that the Acts of the Apostles was written by the same author (whom for convenience we shall describe as Luke). Mosala's purpose would have been better served if he began with the intention of the author. 'In the first book, O Theophilus, I have dealt with all that Jesus began to do and teach' (Acts 1: 1). Luke is presenting an early history of the Christian church which is surprisingly selective. It is increasingly about the apostle Paul, about his conversion, but more importantly how he as a citizen was taken under imperial protection to appear before Caesar. Paul's testimony was that the empire afforded him the opportunity to preach the gospel, an experience which lies behind his legitimation of the authorities. The intention of the author is not to write a history of the early church, but to make clear its relations to the state. Acts begins in Jerusalem and finishes at the heart of the empire. 'And so we came to Rome' (Acts 28: 14) It is a narrative intended to present the Jews on the one hand as the real trouble makers, guilty of bad faith, and the Christians on the other as law-abiding victims who pose no threat to the empire. We should be aware therefore that when we read Luke-Acts the author is set on assuring the colonial ruling classes that the friends of Jesus are the friends of Rome. Whatever Jesus may or may not have said, Luke assures the authorities that Christians are not going to make waves or attempt to overthrow the order of things. 'When scholars use these ethnic divisions of Jew and Roman they collude in Luke's obscuring of the class basis of exploitation, in which the Romans were as much the enemy of the poor as the rich and powerful Jews.'[59]

This is the context in which Luke's gospel was produced. In ancient Israel there were two centres of power, the monarchy and the priesthood. Jesus of Nazareth was an artisan and his closest friends were fishermen. Not simple fishermen, but belonging to families who owned their own boats and who employed others to assist in the business. This could have been of interest to the industrial working class of South Africa. But Luke has intervened to prevent this. Jesus is presented not in relation to labour within the conditions of colonialism. Instead we are introduced to him through his family connections. Crown and temple. Through his father he is of the ruling house of David. Through his mother he is related to the Jerusalem priesthood. Luke is assuring the authorities that Jesus of Nazareth comes from a good family.

> Luke's ideological production of the story of Jesus within the historical context of first-century Palestine has made available a gospel that is acceptable to the rich and the poor of Luke's community, but in which the struggles and contradictions of the lives of the poor and exploited are conspicuous by their absence. By turning the experiences of the poor into the moral virtues of the rich, Luke has effectively eliminated the poor from his Gospel.[60]

If Jesus the artisan is set aside in favour of the well-born itinerant, a parallel fate has befallen his mother. Mary of Nazareth could have been the inspiration of third world women who give birth every year. (The evidence suggests she had perhaps nine children.) She could have been a comfort to every young woman who has become pregnant outside of marriage in a society in which insecure women condemn their own. Mary could have been an encouragement to every one-parent family whose eldest son got into trouble with the law. But no, her real life, the life of the poor in third world shanty-towns, has been exchanged for a myth of purity and innocence. 'The hope that Mary might have inspired the hearts of millions of single mothers under conditions of monopoly capitalism was first dashed by Luke in his Gospel.'[61] As with Micah, Mosala could argue that within Luke-Acts there is material which could have been a weapon for the poor and the exploited, but that it has been neutralised by the intention of the author to present the tradition in terms acceptable to the ideology of the ruling classes – both Jewish and Roman. 'From the point of view of the oppressed and exploited people of the world today, Luke's ideological co-optation of Jesus in the interests of the ruling class is an act of political war against the liberation struggle.'[62]

Black theology in South Africa can therefore be a weapon in the liberation struggle, but only if it is developed from the perspective of the working class. Apartheid was legitimised by a very detailed use of the Bible. The Bible can play an equally important role in the liberation of South Africa, but it cannot be done by employing the same hermeneutical method as the Broederbond.

> The theoretical tragedy in South Africa has been that black theologians, in opposing the theology of the dominant white groups, have appealed to the same hermeneutical framework in order to demonstrate a contrary truth. The contrary truth black theologians wish to assert is that God is on the side of the oppressed

> and not of the oppressors. This study has tried to show, however, that black liberation theology needs an ideologically, epistemologically, and theoretically different biblical hermeneutics.[63]

Mosala has been praised for his efforts in grounding Black theology in the life context of the African working class. Takatso Mofokeng sees this approach also in the work of Buti Tlhagale.

> By identifying black people as workers these theologians have lifted our struggle beyond civil rights to human rights, from an exclusive struggle against racism to a social and national revolution. This deepening by the identifying of the black interlocutors as the black worker is very important for black theology. It introduces theology into the area of the material basis of theology which has been somewhat neglected by Euro-American theologians in favour of spiritualization.[64]

There have been criticisms of this approach for concentrating too narrowly on class analysis to the exclusion of race. Lebamang Sebidi claims that South Africa needs both race and class analysis.[65] Bonganjalo Goba claims that 'we need a much more comprehensive analysis of our own situation, one which avoids ideological reductionism current in some of the vulgar materialistically oriented approaches to our situation'.[66] Indeed Mofokeng himself in the same article accepts the American view that Marxist analysis has to be expanded to include culture and race.[67] After all, Marx dealt only with class analysis and failed to consider race. Really? That claim is made frequently, routinely, casually by black activists and scholars alike. It is repeated confidently on the sure and certain grounds that – well, everyone else repeats it. It reflects that carelessness about sources which is regarded as acceptable among those who are promoting a righteous cause rather than making a sound case. The fact that it is not true is of little consequence. In the grand scheme of things misrepresenting a nineteenth-century moral philosopher is hardly a hanging offence. However, the misrepresentation is itself evidence of racism, and that is more important and altogether more interesting. Prominent in the life experience and consequently in the early writings of Marx is a concern for anti-Semitism, racism against the Jews. Do I hear groans of anguish: 'Oh yes, I forgot about the Jews?' Precisely. Marx constantly had in mind racism, the only form of racism which was an issue in the Europe of his day. He not only observed it, he experienced it. He came from a very distinguished Jewish family which had been forced to 'convert' to Christianity because of anti-Semitic Prussian laws. Far from ignoring racial discrimination, he suffered from it. Why is the misrepresentation of Marx important and interesting? Because it is another example of blacks (normally American) who think that the racism they experience is the only form of racism and that their experience can be normative for the rest of the world. We should be quite justified in identifying this kind of myopia as itself a form of racism. However, the point of this apparent digression is that as so often with Marx, when he turned to a matter of current concern, he treated it in a fresh and insightful way. His essay 'On the Jewish Question' was a response to the approach to the subject adopted by

Bruno Bauer. The latter had turned the question of Jewish emancipation (from discrimination) into a purely religious question. Marx, as usual, sees in this a reversal of consciousness. 'We do not turn secular questions into theological questions ... The question of the relation of political emancipation to religion becomes for us the question of the relation of political emancipation to human emancipation.'[68] Any black theologian who wishes to follow the method of historical materialism should deal with race as a political issue, and hence as part of the class struggle for emancipation from oppression and injustice. But this has already been made clear by Motlhabi: race analysis is an inadequate way of approaching the underlying sources of human alienation. As Lebamang Sebidi notes, race analysis is incapable or unwilling to distinguish between the exploited black working class and black capitalists who exploit them. It encourages the dangerous fiction that they are part of the same struggle. 'Such a movement cannot but be bourgeois – and somehow reactionary.'[69]

This division between South African and American Black theologians could be observed at a conference held at Union Theological Seminary, New York, in 1986. The intention was to bring both groups together for the first time, and to demonstrate their essential unity. The papers were published under the title *We Are One Voice*. They were not. In a juxtaposition reminiscent of Marx's derisory representation of Proudhon, we might say that in America the so-called African-Americans look very African (especially to those who have never ventured further towards the dark continent than the East River Drive), but in Africa itself African-Americans are always and emphatically Americans. Sibidi had already rejected the race paradigm for Black theology as found in America as 'inadequate, shallow and misdirected. Talk about something as being only skin-deep! You are talking about the insights of Black Theology.'[70]

The refusal to accept race analysis as the basis of Black theology does not mean ignoring race, but rather understanding it in a context which is neither idealist nor moralistic. Earlier in discussing Mosala we saw that his application of the categories of historical materialism to the African context lacked precision. Africans are not to be regarded as united simply by virtue of race. Throughout the independent countries of Africa I believe that tribalism is the new form of racism. Divisions which were suppressed by colonialism have re-emerged but now armed with cut-price Kalashnikovs. Within South Africa the most depressing and dangerous example of political tribalism is the Zulu Inkatha. However, I believe a more fundamental and extensive division in South Africa is between the proletariat and the peasantry – an issue touched on earlier in discussing Mosala. Then he referred to 'the social, cultural, political, and economic world of the black working class and peasantry'. As we noted at the time this is not historical materialism. The proletariat and the peasantry live in different worlds, characterised in turn by capitalism and feudalism. The end of apartheid has been irrelevant to this fundamental division. It is inevitable that the black urban, industrial elite will rule South Africa in their own interests. In the countryside the revival in the status of tribal chiefs reasserts feudal interests. Black theology must address these issues, but they cannot be addressed now by race analysis. It is against this background that we must understand the disillusionment caused by the remit and activities of the Truth and Reconciliation Commission. Under the chairmanship of Archbishop Desmond Tutu it combined the therapy of confession with a faith in reconciliation of which Deotis Roberts might have been proud. But representing the interests of the new South Africa elite – black and white – it refused to address the issue, that one issue which is of fundamental concern to peasants throughout the world who live in feudal conditions. The Commission sought reconciliation without justice. It did not address the question of land.

Black theology of the third wave did not fall into the acceptance of a superficial race analysis. It can therefore continue after the end of apartheid, in a situation in which race is no longer the main issue. Within class analysis the problem is as ever the distribution of power, the quest for equity and justice. But within this class analysis there is an issue of fundamental importance, the reconciliation of the proletariat and the peasantry. This of course was an issue which the USSR was never able to resolve. The enforced sovietisation of the peasantry never unified society. At least in South Africa the Black theologians are attempting to take it on board in their own context and this includes African traditional religion.

Mokgethi Motlhabi addresses the issue in a suitably dialectical manner. On the one hand, there are beliefs and practices from the past which should be set aside. Ambiguous though it is, western culture has liberated Africans from many elements of their past which were, looking back, constraining, even dehumanising. Black theology must also be against 'enslavement to the cultural past and outmoded traditions'.[71] No romanticism here: we have met this realism before in Blyden and Césaire. On the other hand, the roots and resources of Black theology cannot be simply or solely European. African traditional religions preserve elements of anthropology and ecology which should be sifted and re-evaluated. Motlhabi also suggests that another source for Black theology might be the African Independent Churches, combining as they do Christian and traditional features. They may be considered as protest movements which took what they could approve from this western religion, but which remained loyal to some fundamental beliefs and practices of the older tradition. We might say that European Christianity is itself an eclectic amalgam of Sectarian Judaism and European folk religion. Indeed when we consider festivals, vestments, architecture, statues and even beliefs and spirituality perhaps 95% of Christianity as we know it has its origins in pre-Christian European and Egyptian folk religions. What conclusions should Black theology draw about its own roots? Indeed J.B. Ngubane makes an important point about those aspects of the African tradition which were condemned by missionaries as unChristian.

> Strangely enough, most of these values and needs were recognized and sanctioned by either the Old or New Testament, e.g. in the Old Testament: revelation through dreams and visions, complex rituals, purification, polygamy, the descent of God's spirit on the prophets etc.; in the New Testament: healing,

> expulsion of evil spirits, apocalyptic and eschatological doctrines, denunciation of the pharisees, etc.[72]

All this is very interesting at a cultural level but it seems to assume that ideas can be appropriated independently of the stage of economic formation. Mosala seeks to address the issue in an essay on 'The Relevance of African Independent Churches and their Challenge to Black Theology'. He restates the premise of historical materialism. 'Man's understanding and positing of divine reality must of necessity correspond in some important ways with the level of development of historical society.'[73] African traditional religion reflected the economic formation of society at a particular stage in its development, but Mosala goes on to make a further claim. 'African traditional religions reflect the point at which the historical development of the Africans was arrested and halted.'[74] This seems unlikely. Their world was invaded by economic, religious and cultural productions which grasped their minds as well as their lands. Mosala ends with a rallying cry intended to prevent alienation between the new and the old South Africas.

> The point must be made unequivocally, therefore, without creating the impression that all elements of African traditional culture and religion are progressive and relevant for contemporary society, that without a creative reappropriation of traditional African religions and societies both African and black theologies will build their houses on sand. A Black Theology of liberation must draw its cultural hermeneutics of struggle from a critical reappropriation of black culture, just as an African theology must arm itself with the political hermeneutics that arise from the contemporary social struggles of black people under apartheid capitalism.[75]

As strategy it is understandable, but as analysis it falls back into romantic idealism. *Hic Rhodus, hic saltus*. While it is possible for the urban proletariat to look back to the religion of a former epoch with sympathy, imagination and expressions of solidarity, those still actually living in that epoch cannot reciprocate. Black theology cannot be handed to them as a weapon in their liberation. As we have seen, Mosala inadvertently uncovered the fundamental problem at an early stage in referring to the 'social, cultural, political, and economic world of the black working class *and peasantry*' (my emphasis). They are not one voice, neither are they one world. Mosala has departed from his historical materialist reading of the situation. When Marx first introduces us to the new class, the proletariat, he describes its character and mission. It is

> a sphere, finally, which cannot emancipate itself without emancipating itself from all the other spheres of society, without, therefore, emancipating all these other spheres, which is, in short a total loss of humanity and which can only redeem itself by a total redemption of humanity. This dissolution of society, as a particular class, is the proletariat.[76]

If Mosala is indeed to follow the analysis of historical materialism, then the responsibility of the urban blacks towards the rural blacks is not that they join them, but that they liberate them, that they *redeem* them. The first step in this process is to address the issue of land. This then is the obligation of the third wave of Black theology in South Africa, the redemption of the peasantry. Unfortunately this wave has fallen on the shore of post-apartheid South Africa and has dissipated. Itumeleng Mosala is working in the government Ministry of Culture. Buti Tlhagale has become bishop of the Catholic Church of Bloemfontein. Under apartheid creative black leaders were silenced by banning orders. Now they are silenced by administrative duties.

Notes

1 Karl Marx and Frederick Engels, *Collected Works*, Lawrence & Wishart, 1976, 5.488.

2 The whole speech is reprinted in Nelson Mandela, *The Struggle is My Life*, International Defence and Aid Fund for Southern Africa, 1978, pp. 155–75.

3 Ibid., pp. 93, 174.

4 Ibid., p. 145.

5 Ibid., p. 115.

6 Ibid., pp. 159–60.

7 Ibid., p. 153.

8 Brian Lapping, *Apartheid: a history*, Grafton Books, 1986, p. 63.

9 Mandela, *The Struggle is My Life*, p. 187.

10 Ibid., p. 198.

11 Ibid., pp. 196–7.

12 Ibid., p. 205.

13 Donald Woods, *Biko*, Paddington Press, 1978, p. 30.

14 Steve Biko, *I Write What I Like*, The Bowerdean Press, 1978, p. 182. All of the following quotations from Biko are taken from this book.

15 Woods, *Biko*, p. 30.

16 Che Guevara, *The Complete Bolivian Diaries*, Allen & Unwin, 1968, p. 124.

17 Steve Biko in an interview by Bernard Zylstra of the Canadian Institute for Christian Studies, included in Woods, *Biko*, pp. 96–7.

18 Allan Aubrey Boesak, *Farewell to Innocence: a socio-ethical study on Black Theology and Black Power*, 1976, published as *Black Theology Black Power*, Mowbrays, 1978, p. xi.

19 Ibid., p. 3.

20 Ibid., p. 4.

21 Ibid., p. 6.

22 Ibid., p. 28.

23 Allan Boesak, *Black and Reformed: apartheid, liberation and the Calvinist tradition*, ed. Leonard Sweetman, Orbis Books, Maryknoll, NY, 1986 (1984), p. 26.

24 Ibid., p. 48.

25 Ibid., p. 85.

26 Quoted in 'An Open Letter Concerning Nationalism, National Socialism and Christianity', in Supplement to *Pro Veritate* (July 1971), p. 3.

27 W.A. de Klerk, *The Puritans in Africa: a history of Afrikanerdom*, Penguin Books, 1976, p. 114.

28 Boesak, *Black and Reformed*, p. 56.

29 Ibid., p. 18.

30 Ibid., pp. 70–71.

31 Ibid., p. 112.

32 Boesak, *Black Theology Black Power*, p. 12.

[33] Ibid., p. 133.

[34] Ibid.

[35] Ibid., p. 143.

[36] Boesak, *Black and Reformed*, p. 55.

[37] Ibid., p. 75.

[38] Ibid., p. 56.

[39] Boesak, *Black Theology Black Power*, p. 9.

[40] Allan Boesak, *Coming in Out of the Wilderness: a comparative interpretation of the ethics of Martin Luther King and Malcolm X*, Kamper Cahier No. 28, Kampen, 1976.

[41] King, *Where do We Go From Here?*, p. 43.

[42] Ibid., p. 51.

[43] Ibid., p. 75.

[44] Ibid., p. 76.

[45] Boesak, *Black Theology Black Power*, p. 70.

[46] Ibid., p. 70.

[47] Ibid.

[48] Mokgethi Motlhabi, 'Black Theology and Authority' in Basil Moore (ed.) *Black Theology: the South African voice*, C. Hurst & Co., 1973, p. 119. All quotations from Motlhabi are taken from this essay.

[49] Itumeleng J. Mosala, *Biblical Hermeneutics and Black Theology in South Africa*, William B. Eerdmans Publishing Co., Grand Rapids, Mich., 1989, p. 2.

[50] Ibid., p. 6.

[51] Ibid., p. 8.

[52] Ibid., p. 30.

[53] Ibid., p. 27.

[54] Ibid., p. 21.

[55] Marx/Engels, *Collected Works*, 29.263.

[56] Mosala, *Biblical Hermeneutics*, p. 103.

[57] Ibid., p. 120.

[58] Ibid., p. 153.

[59] Ibid., p. 178.

[60] Ibid., p. 166.

[61] Ibid., p. 169.

[62] Ibid., p. 171.

[63] Ibid., p. 192.

[64] Takatso Mofokeng, 'Black Theological Perspectives, Past and Present' in Simon S. Maimela and Dwight N. Hopkins (eds) *We Are One Voice*, Skotaville, Braamfontein, SA, 1989, p. 109.

[65] Lebamang Sebidi, 'The Dynamics of the Black Struggle and its Implications for Black Theology' in Itumeleng J. Mosala and Buti Tlhagale (eds) *The Unquestionable Right to be Free: essays in black theology*, Skotaville Publishers, Johannesburg, 1986, p. 31.

[66] Bonganjalo Goba, 'The Black Consciousness Movement: its impact on black theology' in Mosala and Tlhagale, *The Unquestionable Right to be Free*, p. 69.

[67] Mofokeng, 'Black Theological Perspectives', p. 110.

[68] Marx/Engels, *Collected Works*, 3.151.

[69] Sebidi, 'The Dynamics of the Black Struggle', p. 19.

[70] Ibid., p. 22.

[71] Mokgethi Motlhabi, 'The Historical Origins of Black Theology' in Mosala and Tlhagale, *The Unquestionable Right to be Free*, p. 53.

[72] J.B. Ngubane, 'Theological Roots of the African Independent Church and their Challenge to Black Theology' in Mosala and Tlhagale, *The Unquestionable Right to be Free*, p. 76.

[73] Itumeleng J. Mosala, 'The Relevance of African Independent Churches and their Challenge to Black Theology' in Mosala and Tlhagale, *The Unquestionable Right to be Free,* p. 94.

[74] Ibid., p. 98.

[75] Ibid., p. 99.

[76] Karl Marx, 'The Critique of Hegel's Philosophy of Right: introduction' in *Karl Marx: early writings*, trans. and ed. by T.B. Bottomore, C.A. Watts & Co., 1963, p. 58.

CHAPTER 4

As Purple is to Lavender: Womanist Theology

Womanist Consciousness

Black consciousness has entered into the field of religion, but influences have run in both directions. There has been a powerful tradition of preaching in the black churches and this in turn has entered into the black consciousness movement. Its leaders have not simply advocated political change; they have not simply brought forward programmes of social reform. They have gathered strength for the movement by proclaiming it as a great moral crusade: they have used the language and the body language of the pulpit to characterise it as a righteous cause to expose and condemn oppression, in this case the oppression of black people in a society in which for too long they were treated without consideration or respect. It is not difficult to recreate in the imagination a scene embodying these features. It is a dance hall, or a church hall; we can hear the echo of these words as the speaker ends his address to the faithful, see the indignation and anger on his now perspiring face – and yes, detect some quiet satisfaction at the effect he has had on the people before him. The adrenaline high continues for some time after the meeting ends. It is gratifying to meet sympathisers who have travelled some distance to hear him. In an act of spontaneous generosity he invites some to come home with him to share a simple meal. He has been out contesting the world all day. How fortunate that he can assume that in his absence his children have been well cared for, fed, clothed, loved and protected. How fortunate that his home will be clean and welcoming for any invited or unexpected guests who might be brought there at any time of night or day. How fortunate that he has a Martha in the kitchen while his entourage sits round him and hangs on his every word in another room. Our crusader refers to the history of oppression when black people were treated without consideration or respect, oblivious to the fact that this public tragedy is reproduced as domestic farce by his treatment of his own wife. (The juxtaposition of tragedy and farce comes from Marx, in the opening sentence of *The Eighteenth Brumaire of Louis Bonaparte*: 'Hegel remarks somewhere that all facts and personages of great importance in world history occur, as it were, twice. He forgot to add: the first time as tragedy, the second as farce.')[1]

The 1960s saw the rise of two parallel movements in the USA, black consciousness and feminist consciousness. Far from working together for social and political reform they viewed each other with suspicion. Black people saw feminism as a movement amongst white women: feminists considered black men to exhibit the worst aspects of those values and forms of behaviour to which they most objected in white men. But as they formed two lines shouting abuse and displaying contempt at each other neither side seemed to be aware of the spectators on the sidelines. Black women experienced it as in turn tragedy and farce. The slanging match was between women and blacks. Neither side seemed to notice that some present were both. And yet if both sides were alienated from the other, black women bridged the gap between them – and were sometimes alienated from both. Black women were loyal to their men and yet they could not help but see the force of much feminist criticism. They understood very well the critique of sexism and yet they felt no sisterhood with white feminists.

Historically black women were bonded to black men by marriage and by misery In the nineteenth century their common cause was emancipation and black women were persuaded that it could be achieved only through solidarity. They therefore focused on this one goal on the assumption that all black people would benefit equally. They supported the aspirations of black men in the expectation that they would also inherit the gains of social and political advancement. They did indeed benefit from emancipation in 1863, but three years later the 14th Amendment granted the vote only to black men. The following year, 1867, marked the fortieth anniversary of the emancipation of Isabelle Bumfree, who took the name Sojourner Truth as she toured the country speaking out against slavery. She had advocated total emancipation, sadly compromised in the new legislation.

> There is a great stir about colored men getting their rights, but not a word about the colored women; and if colored men get their rights and not colored women theirs, you see the colored men will be masters over women, and it will be just as bad as it was before.[2]

In reality black men did not get their rights and throughout the first half of the twentieth century racism enforced a regime which did not even pretend to South Africa's system of apartheid. Black women once again displayed solidarity in face of discrimination.

One of the most important texts in the articulation of modern feminist consciousness was *The Second Sex*. In it Simone de Beauvoir comments on such solidarity. '[Women] live dispersed among the males, attached through residence, housework, economic condition, and social standing to certain men – fathers or husbands – more firmly than they are to other women.'[3] And if this is less true now than when it was written over 50 years ago, that is testimony to the influence and effect of de Beauvoir's perceptive analysis. The identity of black women was constructed in relation to black men, not white women.

An additional source of separation was that the feminist movement was from the beginning and inevitably a movement of white women. We can see this in the continuation of the quotation from de Beauvoir. 'If they belong to the bourgeoisie, they feel solidarity with men of that class, not with proletarian women; if they are white, their allegiance is to white men, not to Negro women.' The feminists of the nineteenth century who were active in the emancipation movement, women such as

Elizabeth Cady Stanton, Lucretia Mott and Susan B. Anthony, were devastated at the 14th Amendment. Emancipation was one thing, but giving the franchise to black men but not to white women was another. However, this did not produce solidarity with black women. They were still regarded as socially inferior. It was considered that their presence at meetings of the (white) women's conventions would have been very damaging. We see this in the reaction to the appearance of Sojourner Truth at a meeting in Akron, Ohio. The organisers were not happy to see her there and there was opposition to her being allowed to speak. But speak she did when she heard a man argue that women should not be given the vote on account of the fact that they were incompetent and effete. Sojourner Truth famously intervened.

> That man over there says that women need to be helped into carriages, and lifted over ditches, and to have the best place everywhere. Nobody ever helps me into carriages, or over mud-puddles, or gives me any best place! And ain't I a woman? Look at me! Look at my arm! I have ploughed and planted, and gathered into barns, and no man could head me! And ain't I a woman? I could work as much and eat as much as a man – when I could get it – and bear the lash as well! And ain't I a woman? I have borne thirteen children and seen most all sold off to slavery, and when I cried out with my mother's grief, none but Jesus heard me! And ain't I a woman.[4]

The social construction of being a women, the image of what it was to be a woman totally excluded black women from the movement. And so it was a century later. When Betty Friedan described the ideal of the 'happy housewife' of suburbia as the 'feminine mystique' she encouraged women to question and reject a lifestyle which was available to black women neither as a reality nor even as a fantasy.[5] Like Herbert Marcuse's 'great refusal'[6] it was a form of 'oppression' which black women could only dream of – indeed a form of exploitation to which poor women of whatever colour would have happily submitted with unending praise to God the Father.

It is hardly surprising that black feminism arose to insist on a realignment of loyalties in face of the double betrayal of black women, by black men and white women. Audre Lorde explained that sexism was not discussed in the black community. It was identified as a white women's issue.[7] To pursue it would have been to weaken the united front against racism. To focus on anti-sexism was seen as being anti-black. Black women were coerced into remaining silent about sexism, but there was a cost. Sexual oppression within the black community was not identified and challenged. This gave the impression that it did not exist, was not a problem: existing patterns of male behaviour instead of being confronted were confirmed. As bell hooks[8] noted, concentration on the white man as the oppressor of the black community deflected attention from black male exploitation of black females in the same communities.[9] Black men were certainly victims, but their role as oppressors was obscured. Just as 'woman' meant 'white woman', so 'blacks' meant 'black men'. Thus black liberation referred to the aspiration of black men to live as white men. The convert is more stereotypical than one born to a position. Black men sought to become real men: patriarchy, privilege, chauvinism, sexism – the full monty.[10] Black women could not afford pride or image: they had to work at menial jobs in order to take care of their children. Black men by contrast were treated with respect when they refused to submit to the white boss. They preserved their dignity while avoiding their responsibilities.[11] As we saw in Chapter 2, nothing could be more calculated to preserve racism than black men aspiring uncritically to the lifestyle of white men. The refusal to address sexism until racism had been defeated was not only wrong but was a strategy which got these issues exactly the wrong way round, as bell hooks observed. 'Fighting against sexist oppression is important for black liberation, for as long as sexism divides black women and men we cannot concentrate our energies on resisting racism.'[12]

In fact there is a close parallel between the criticisms of black men by these black feminists and their criticisms of white feminism. Black women were absent from critiques of both racism and sexism. As Alice Walker commented, 'white women feminists revealed themselves as incapable as white and black men of comprehending blackness and feminism in the same body, not to mention within the same imagination'.[13] Audre Lorde called for a more holistic account of the suffering experienced by women. 'By and large within the women's movement today, white women focus upon their oppression as women and ignore differences of race, sexual preference, class and age.'[14] It is not simply that one form of oppression is prioritised at the expense of others, but that it is made normative. This is the reality which provided the title for Lorde's book *Sister Outsider*. 'As white women ignore their built-in privilege of whiteness and define *woman* in terms of their own experience alone, then women of color become "other", the outsider whose experience and tradition is too "alien" to comprehend.'[15] This attitude gives the lie to the romantic concept of 'sisterhood': the outsider is not a sister. Alternatively if there is to be a sisterhood, if it is a reality to be acknowledged or a goal to be achieved, then it must be on a recognition and affirmation of difference. Lorde could even address an open letter to Mary Daly, perhaps the most famous feminist writer of her generation. To undertake doctoral studies in Switzerland, to hold a full-time research and teaching post in Boston, to travel the world attending and addressing conferences: what a burden! But above all to live, work and travel without let or hindrance on grounds of colour so that the occasional reference to race can be inserted for effect.

> Mary, I ask that you be aware of how this serves the destructive forces of racism and separation between women – the assumption that the herstory and myth of white women is the legitimate and sole herstory and myth of all women to call upon for power and background, and that nonwhite women and our herstories are noteworthy only as decorations, or examples of female victimization.[16]

Feminism in this context appears as an ideology. An ideology serves the interests of minority groups against the interests of the majority. The minority here is represented by well-educated professional women. They experience oppression because they are not being treated like men. According to bell hooks such feminists therefore compare themselves to men, mainly white but on occasion black. Black women do not enter the equation. Even the occasional call for black women to join them represents self-concern: they have no intention of addressing experiences of race or poverty. The fact that these professional women see their salvation in work confirms the absence of any critique of capitalism and any understanding of the oppressive experience of employment (not to mention unemployment) amongst the poor. 'This emphasis on work was yet another indication of the extent to which the white female liberationists' perception of reality was totally narcissistic, classist and racist.'[17] We should also note in the midst of these criticisms of white middle-class feminism there is no kind of romanticising of poor blacks. Alice Walker specifically claims that she is not romanticising the lives of blacks in the South and as a writer her short stories contain references to harrowing incidents of promiscuity, betrayal, domestic violence, incest and rape, greed, superstition.[18] As we noted in the work of Albert Cleage in Chapter 2, there is no sacrilising the black community.

Earlier we imagined the homecoming of the black crusader. It would not be difficult to construct an *imaginaire* of the homecoming of the feminist crusader. Dr Susan, a single-parent psychiatrist, returns to her apartment off Fifth Avenue after speaking at a conference on the oppression of women by traditional male social structures. She gives a glowing account of the enthusiastic reception with which her talk was received by the guild of professional women. Gertrude, the maid, is very impressed. She reports that the children, Granville and Tatiana, have been watching a DVD which she hired (omitting to mention that it was on the life of Amy Jacques Garvey). As soon as she has put the children to bed and served Dr Susan's dinner she is free to set off on that great adventure which is called taking the midnight bus to the Bronx. Hegel, Hegel: tragedy and farce. In fact it was inevitable that feminism should make the experience of white women normative. According to bell hooks emancipation saw black women aspire to be like white women. 'Modesty, sexual purity, innocence and a submissive manner were the qualities associated with womanhood and femininity.'[19] As we have already noted, such aspirations guaranteed the perpetuation of racial attitudes. The women's movement had no intention of challenging the privileges of race or class. Alice Walker has made the salutary point that 'white "feminists" are very often indistinguishable in their behaviour from any other white persons in America'.[20]

As critical as these writers are of black men, they are still part of the black movement. As critical as they are of white women they are still feminists. There are two possibilities. The first is to attempt to redefine feminism. Audre Lorde took this route. 'Black feminism is not white feminism in blackface.'[21] Black feminism must incorporate the experience of race. The setting aside of race in earlier feminism was not an innocent matter. It was an ideological decision brought about by 'the intransigent racism that white women too often fail to, or cannot address in themselves'.[22] This first route, redefining feminism, is attractive and apparently available, but it is not without its difficulties. In so far as feminism was an ideological movement it is necessary to sift through it to uncover those assumptions so characteristic of ideologies, assumptions which continue to be taken for granted because they seem so obvious and unobjectionable. This is Audre Lorde's continuing contribution to black feminism, the critical examination of feminist method.

Feminism might be a single issue movement but is that issue sexism or should it be more broadly based on the experience of women? This distinction was brought home to Lorde when in 1979 she attended the Second Sex Conference in New York. She felt an outsider to the discussions. Sexism was the sole category for consideration: no mention was made of the other categories with which she could identify – poor, lesbian, black and older women.[23] The contrast is greatest if we go back to the agenda of early modern feminism when professional women campaigned to be treated like men. They too wanted to be masters of the world. But there is no point in being masters of the world if that world is becoming more equitable, just and fair. Feminism might have seemed radical, even revolutionary, but in reality it was conservative and counter-revolutionary. The whole premise of aspiring to become one of the masters was that the edifice erected by men of power and privilege should be preserved. It is in the interests of successful, thrusting professional women that the executive washroom remains locked. There is no point in being rewarded with the key to the door if on that day keys are also given to black men and poor men – not to mention poor black women. But we have seen all this before in earlier chapters. To humbly request the key to the master's house is not the way to liberation. To accept a key from the master is to become complicit. He is no fool: his rewarding of the few will preserve his house against the many. And this is the message of Audre Lorde. 'For the master's tools will never dismantle the master's house.'[24] It is no coincidence that feminism as an ideology confines its agenda to sexism: white professional women have a stake in preserving the social, political and economic foundations upon which the master's house is built and from which they benefit enormously. 'What is the theory', asks Lorde, 'behind racist feminism?'[25] Is feminism to be concerned solely with sexism rather than with women's experience more broadly? But even if restricted to sexism, is this not also conceived within the master's house? 'What does it mean when the tools of a racist patriarchy are used to examine the fruits of that same patriarchy?'[26] bell hooks has drawn attention to the importance of Lorde's insights here for feminist theory, calling for 'a process of visionary thinking that transcends the ways of knowing privileged by the oppressive powerful if we are to truly make revolutionary change'.[27] She also emphasised Lorde's warning 'that it is easy for women and any exploited or oppressed group to become complicit in structures of domination, using power in ways that reinforce rather than challenge or change'.[28] hooks considered that it was inevitable that black feminist groups were established in the light of this danger, but such separation was not ideal for it prevented necessary dialogue. Feminism, for hooks, is more than a struggle to end male chauvinism. She expands it into something of a manifesto:

> It is a commitment to eradicating the ideology of domination that permeates Western culture on various levels – sex, race, and class, to name a few – and a

> commitment to reorganizing U.S. society so that the self-development of people can take precedence over imperialism, economic expansion, and material desires.[29]

Earlier we indicated that in face of the inadequacy of white feminism there were two possibilities. One we have examined, black feminism. It has made important criticisms and includes illuminating insights, but at the end of the day has it escaped from the master's house? Or is it comfortably installed in the chattel house next door thoughtfully provided by the master? The same thought, less charmingly conceived, is expressed by the white feminist Emily Erwin Culpepper, as she seeks to learn from black women writers. 'I would like us to ask ourselves whether our work is aiming toward dismantling the master's house and transforming the territory – or just building one inadequate extra room or section on the back.'[30] It is a familiar problem. Should you attempt to answer another person's question? Are you thereby drawn into the system in which that issue arises? Should you seek other premises from which you can address the underlying problem and thereby resolve the question in very different terms? Since I have earlier quoted Marx on tragedy and farce, let me draw attention to his observations on precisely this conceptual problem.

> The traditions of all the dead generations weigh like a nightmare on the brain of the living. And just when they seem engaged in revolutionising themselves and things, in creating something that has never yet existed, precisely in such periods of revolutionary crisis they anxiously conjure up the spirits of the past to their service and borrow from them names, battle-cries and costumes in order to present the new scene of world history in this time-honoured disguise.[31]

The manifesto of bell hooks suggests that feminism is not the answer, but rather part of the problem. The well-being of women must be considered in a wider context which includes sexism without isolating it from other material factors which determine women's lives. On my reading, this is the contribution of Alice Walker.

In the 1960s women's liberation was an audacious movement, much beloved of the media, which sought to expose and challenge the patriarchal assumptions which provided the licence by which women existed in (especially western) society. Illustrative of the excessiveness of the movement was Dorothy Solanas, founder of S.C.U.M., the Society for Cutting Up Men. Few women identified with women's liberation. The feminist movement seemed more hopeful. However, the term 'feminist' came with ideological baggage. 'Feminine' has connotations of behaviour which is decent and appropriate. It refers to appearance, image, comportment, fragrance, that which is attractive to men, or rather to gentlemen. This is entirely in keeping with the values and aspirations of early feminists. My copy of Marilyn French's first book has a cartoon of a door. The neatly printed sign *Ladies' Room* has been scored out to be over-scrawled by the words *Women's Room*. A lady is a male construct: the life of a woman by comparison is like an iceberg. Most of it takes place beyond the observation and control of men. This was doubly so for black women in the southern USA. White folks hardly appear in Alice Walker's novel *The*

Color Purple, although they have set the parameters of life. Black women have their own lives to live, or endure, with no possibility of being ladylike. Two, of different generations, are of particular interest in that book. One is Sofia who is described standing by an ironing board with an iron in her hand. 'Sofia the kind of women no matter what she have in her hand it look like a weapon.'[32] The other is Shug Avery, described by Albert, her former lover and Celie's husband. 'Shug act more manly than most men. I mean she upright, honest. Speak her mind and the devil take the hindmost, he say. You know Shug will fight, he say. Just like Sofia. She bound to live her life and be herself no matter what.'[33] But Harpo, Sofia's husband thinks these features belong not just to men. 'What Shug got is womanly it seem like to me. Specially since she and Sofia the ones got it. Sofia and Shug not like men, he say, but they not like women either.'[34] Alice Walker was later to develop this theme of what Harpo describes as 'womanly'. She recalls Easter Sunday when she was 6 years old: she spoke her words well in church The people were impressed by her appearance. 'I can tell they admire my dress, but it is my spirit, bordering on sassiness (womanishness), they secretly applaud.'[35] As she grew up she had to learn the facts of life. Her mother took the view that fathers should teach boys and mothers should teach girls. In their rural community fathers took the boys to observe a bull servicing the cows. Her mother would not allow her to go, disapproved of girls having an interest in these things. 'They were "womanish" (a very bad way to be in those days) if they asked.'[36] If feminine is a term of dependence, of *puerización*, womanist describes a spirit of independence, of self-determination to the point of danger. Alice Walkers offers four contexts in which the meaning of the term womanist is gradually clarified.[37] It marks that transition from female child to adult, but it refers specifically to a girl whose inquisitiveness takes her beyond the bounds set by society. She is outrageous and courageous. She is warned about wanting to know more than is good for her. Calling her behaviour womanist is a warning, but a warning which contains thinly disguised approval and admiration. The term womanist is applied also to adult women. They are at peace with themselves and quietly confident. Such a person is concerned for the well-being of the family, the community and beyond. She may love individual men and women sexually and/or non-sexually. While she is not a separatist, she 'appreciates and prefers women's culture, women's emotional flexibility (values tears as natural counter-balance of laughter), and women's strength'. Alice Walker's third use of the term seems more particular, as if she is describing with gratitude the character of, perhaps, her own mother. 'Loves music. Loves dance. Loves the moon. Loves the Spirit. Loves love and food and roundness. Loves struggle. Loves the Folk. Loves herself. *Regardless*.' This then is the second possible route, an alternative to the ideologically compromised term 'black feminist'. She can include one within the other. A womanist is 'a black feminist or feminist of color'. However, it is clear that womanist is the more comprehensive term. This emerged in the late 1980s when Audre Lorde criticised Alice Walker for introducing the term womanist. Walker seemed to be distancing herself from the being a feminist. In reply Walker explained that the term womanist was broader, more comprehensive. 'More reflective of black women's culture, especially Southern culture.'[38] bell hooks also entered the debate.

She began with a frank admission. 'Even though there are a few black women (I am one) who assert that we empower ourselves by using the term feminism, by addressing our concerns as black women as well as our concern with the welfare of the human community globally, we have had little impact.'[39] She was particularly concerned with the rejection of the term black feminism in the academic context.

> Often in these settings the word 'feminism' is evoked in negative terms, even though sexism and gender issues are discussed. I hear black women academics laying claim to the term 'womanist' while rejecting 'feminist'. I do not think Alice Walker intended this term to deflect from feminist commitment yet this is often how it is evoked. Walker defines womanist as black feminist or feminist of color. When I hear black woman using the term womanist, it is in opposition to the term feminist: it is viewed as constituting something separate from feminist politics shaped by white women.[40]

As we have seen, Walker does not set womanist and black feminist over against each other, but neither are they synonyms. Womanist is the more comprehensive term, which includes black feminist. However, there is more to it than that and it is this point which bell hooks chooses to ignore. As we have noted, feminist is an ideological term and black feminism cannot fail to be drawn into the service of the sexism which lies behind it. hooks goes on to claim that 'black women must continue to insist on our right to participate in shaping feminist theory and practice that addresses our racial concerns as well as our feminist issues'.[41] And it is because the wider concerns cannot be accommodated in a feminist theory which is inherently racist and sexist that Alice Walker has turned to the term womanist. She contrasts the two in the fourth definition of the term, in a beautifully crafted simile which is as aesthetically suggestive as it is politically powerful. 'Womanist is to feminist as purple is to lavender.'

Purple symbolises both beauty and strength. Shug Avery (whom we have identified as the embodiment of womanism) tells Celie 'I think it pisses God off if you walk by the color purple in a field somewhere and don't notice it.'[42] By comparison lavender is effete and ineffectual: it is so lacking in life that it has to be helped into carriages and revived with smelling salts. Or as Walker says, disarmingly, 'a womanist is a feminist, only more common'.[43] The usefulness of the term womanist is that it functions as a neologism: it has no ideological pre-history. It is a liberating term. It exerts no procrustean constraints on the women's movement: it can describe women as they are in all shapes and sizes, all social and economic classes, all colours and creeds: it can encompass women as they aspire to be according to their own values, dreams and fantasies. Escaping from the entailments of black feminism it can more comprehensively address the agenda of bell hook's manifesto. It is a platform from which to address issues of sex, yes, but also, as hooks recommends, self-development, race, class, imperialism, economic expansion and material desires – the full ideology of domination.

Beauty and strength, but as we have noted the term womanist is politically powerful. Not surprisingly the manifesto of bell hooks concentrates on 'a commitment to re-organizing U.S. society'. If black women were suspicious of (white) feminism, women of the third world are suspicious of feminism as an American movement constructed to benefit American women both white and black. It is salutary to reflect on the fact that while feminists are a tiny minority in third world countries, in each country women constitute the majority of the population. Even Audre Lorde in her criticism of the Second Sex conference concentrated on the issues which were important for American women: race, sexuality, class and age. This forgetfulness of third world women and, for example, the experience of colonialism is the more surprising in the case of a woman whose parents came from Grenada. One of the most impressive features of the work of Alice Walker is her awareness of women in the third world – and the effect upon them of American policies and western culture. As we noted earlier, womanist includes concern for the family, the community and *beyond*: it is as Alice Walker says, 'universalist'. An example of this womanist perspective is seen in her visits to Cuba. Here was a third world country with high quality health care and education available to all, regardless. It is tempting to say, regardless of race. But why make that point? Walker reflects on a visit to a school where her group were entertained by the pupils, representing a wide range of race and colour. But when they introduced themselves as *black* Americans the pupils were confused. They understood themselves as Cubans. Walker through 'perverted categorization'[44] had assumed that an issue which had been important in her history was universally applicable. A second example was when she realised that Cuban women saw themselves as part of the Cuban revolution, not the feminist revolution. However, she clearly thought they could have benefited from both when she observed that they aspired to the appearance of European women. (But since they had inherited traditions of elegance and courtesy from Spanish women why should Walker assume they would be better served by looking to Africa?) Visiting the USSR about the same time, Audre Lorde seemed to lack appreciation for the concerns of women in another country. When she visited Moscow she recalled New York; when she visited Uzbekistan she thought of Ghana.[45] However, by 1980 she had re-described herself as 'a forty-nine year old black lesbian, feminist socialist mother of two'.[46] On her first visit to Grenada she was very positive about the advances in education, health care and employment brought about by the People's Revolutionary government. Following her second visit she was very critical of the CIA inspired invasion of socialist Grenada by the USA.

Were there foremothers of womanism? There were certainly outstanding individuals who exemplified, at least in some respects, what it was to be womanist. Sojourner Truth was one such. Marcus Garvey claimed that 'Sojourner Truth is worthy of the place of sainthood alongside Joan of Arc.'[47] (She probably deserves more than that.) For an example of a womanist he might have looked closer to home ('twas ever so), to Amy Jacques (born in Jamaica) whom Garvey married in 1922. She respected his creative genius: he admired her considerable intellectual powers.

> Amy Jacques Garvey's contributions to Garveyism went far beyond assisting her husband. Her woman's page in the *Negro World* called on every woman to use her mind to its fullest capacity; news of cocktail parties and bridge games was conspicuously lacking.[48]

However, we have been considering the emergence of womanism as a theory in the 1970s and 1980s. Even at that time Alice Walker was disappointed at dissolution of the early ideals of both the black movement and feminism.

> I think Medgar Evers and Martin Luther King, Jr., would be dismayed by the lack of radicalism in the new black middle class, and discouraged to know that a majority of the black people helped by the Movement of the sixties has abandoned itself to the pursuit of cars, expensive furniture, large houses, and the finest Scotch.[49]

There was already a lack of concern for blacks who were poor. At the same time bell hooks was disillusioned about feminism.

> Whether it was women university professors crying sexist oppression (rather than sexist discrimination) to attract attention to their efforts to gain promotion, or women using feminism to mask their sexist attitudes, or women writers superficially exploring feminist themes to advance their own careers, it was evident that eliminating sexist oppression was not the primary concern.[50]

Feminism spoke the language of resistance, rebellion and revolution, but this illusion 'masked the fact that feminism was in no way a challenge or a threat to capitalist patriarchy'.[51] To this extent feminism represented 'a regression'.[52]

Womanist Theology

In the 1980s several young black women were training for the ministry in various churches in the USA. In addition to courses familiar to any theological student, they were introduced to perspectives on feminist theology and Black theology. Those who had read the emerging womanist literature found themselves in that situation already described. They could appreciate much of feminist theology, but it did not ring true to their experience. They accepted much of Black theology, but there was something missing. It was time for womanist theology, a distinctive theology which applied womanist perspectives to Christian theology. Womanist theology therefore repeats previous patterns. Christian women came to be influenced by secular feminist consciousness, producing feminist theology. Black Christian men came to be influenced by black consciousness and produced Black theology. Now black Christian women adopted the perspective of secular womanist writers, to produce womanist theology. Thus womanist theology when it emerged in the 1980s benefitted from those liberation theologies which preceded it. From feminist theology it has taken the criticism of oppression on the basis of sexual discrimination. From Black theology it has taken the criticism of oppression on the basis of racial discrimination. From Latin American theology of liberation it has taken the criticism of oppression on the basis of class discrimination. (We shall later question this claim.) In the sometimes acrimonious tripartite discussions which took place in the 1970s a new holistic consensus appeared. Theology has to be concerned not with one form of oppression but with all forms: sex, race and class. When womanist theology appeared it simply inherited this consensus, although it often presents this holistic approach as if it were its own unique perspective and its own gracious gift to more benighted theologies.

The books on womanist theology which appeared in the 1980s and 1990s have certain recurring features. They (1) rehearse the main themes of womanist theory; (2) are strong in some areas in which womanist theory is strong; (3) are weak in those areas in which womanist theory is weak; (4) lack the capacity to criticise secular womanist theory; and (5) contain little or no theology. As a writer I long ago decided to follow the example of Alfred Hitchcock who in his films gives the plot away as soon as possible. Let me therefore add a further point, (6) that for the most part the books on womanist theology are not womanist at all. Most of what proudly proclaims itself womanist theology is neither theology nor womanist. How can this be? First, it largely cuts itself off from the sources of Christian theology. Historically Christianity has been a European religion. (If the early church had not spread west into Europe, but turned east instead, to Mesopotamia, to India and China, Christianity would have become a religion entirely different in spirituality, structure, ethos, aesthetics and ethics, unrecognisable to us today.) However, 'European' has become a term of abuse in womanist theology (frequently applied to white American culture and intellectual traditions). For historical and cultural reasons Christianity has been developed by men, but 'male' is another cuss word in womanist theology. Womanist theology has therefore left itself little scope to propose serious reforms in Christian theology. Second, because it has borrowed from feminist theology and Black theology, womanist theology's base is inevitably black feminism which as we discussed earlier is certainly not womanism. Rather confusingly, what is called womanist theology is in fact black feminist theology. For the moment we shall continue to call it womanist theology, but at the end we shall raise questions about its relationship to Alice Walker's definition of the term.

Books purporting to be on womanist theology are largely taken up with repeating the themes from secular womanism. When they finally reach the theology section they have an ambivalent relationship with the two historic sources of Christian theology, the tradition and the Bible. Womanist theology, finding that both of these two universally respected sources of Christianity have lost their authority, must now find its own, distinctive source. That source is the experience of black women. For Marcia Y. Riggs 'one of the tasks of a womanist ethicist is to retrieve Black women's history as a source of ethical reflection'.[53] For this reason books on womanist theology contain little theology but extensive accounts of the lives of black women such as Zora Neale Hurston.[54] Kelly Brown Douglas in *The Black Christ* promotes this source above others.

> Are womanists doing christology? Yes, in the sense that we are attempting to discern, from the perspective of Black women in the struggle, what it means for Jesus to be Christ. No, if doing christology means that the Nicene/Chalcedonian tradition must provide a norm or even a significant source for what we say about Jesus as Christ.[55]

Of course it is easy to be dismissive of the ancient creeds, reflecting as they do metaphysical differences which seem remote to our contemporary thought forms, reflecting concerns which no longer stir us. Yet these matters were of concern to ordinary people, as shown in this weary if ironic observation of life in Constantinople in 380 made by Gregory of Nyssa.

> Everything in the city is full of these people – alleys, marketplaces, streets, crossroads, clothes stalls, banks, take-away food counters. If you ask about small change, they philosophize to you about the generate and the ingenerate. If you inquire about the price of bread, they answer, 'The Father is greater, and the Son subordinate.' And if you say, 'The bath is just right', they affirm that the Son comes out of nothing.[56]

What will people make of our concerns, after 1500 years? It is a populist move to dismiss formulae which take time and effort to understand. But even in the Fourth Gospel we are presented with the cosmic significance of Jesus Christ. Christian faith is trinitarian and requires creation, incarnation and Pentecost. Chalcedon is the culmination of one way of reflecting on that reality. It is not our way today, but to set it aside as 'a norm or even a significant source' is to impoverish ourselves as we seek a contemporary form of expression. 'What Jesus did becomes the basis for what it means for him to be Christ.'[57] The Christian religion may be right or wrong, but if that had been its basis it would never have survived the lives of those who observed Jesus and would never have become a universal faith spreading throughout the world. More briefly Katie Cannon makes a play on her own name as she writes on a 'Womanist Perspectival Discourse and Canon Formation'. Her dialogue partner in this discourse is not the Christian tradition but the novels and short stories of secular womanist writers. In the same populist move as Douglas she is prepared to set aside the traditional themes of 'sin, salvation, grace and forgiveness'.[58] This is the more ironic since secular writers often pursue these realities, if on their own terms. They are not well served when theologians leave the field. As Luce Irigaray observes, 'Sociology quickly bores me when I am expecting the divine.'[59] Womanist theologians have not inherited this position from Black theology. It is interesting to reflect that male Black theologians are less alienated from the European intellectual tradition. The young James Cone, for example, was criticised for being too much indebted to the Swiss theologian Karl Barth. Deotis Roberts gained his PhD from the University of Edinburgh with a dissertation on the Cambridge Platonists.

On the other hand, the ambiguous attitude to the Bible exhibited by womanist theologians *is* inherited from feminist theology. Its authority as a source of revelation is much reduced when it is regarded as a collection of texts written by males, serving male interests, characterised by patriarchy and chauvinism, initiating and legitimising oppression of women. If there is a tendency to dismiss the historic tradition as irrelevant to black women, womanist theologians follow the feminist lead in their alienation from the Bible with its 'texts of terror' and patriarchy. However, there is a very careful distinction which needs to be made here. Womanist theologians cannot afford to carry over to the Bible the dismissive judgement of Douglas on doctrine, denying it its place as 'a norm or even a significant source'. Delores Williams provides a much more nuanced approach to the issue.

> I think we womanist theologians want to be ever conscious of the way we are doing things in theology so that we do not lose our intention for black woman's experience to provide the lens through which we view sources, to provide the issues that form the content of our theology and to help us formulate the questions we ask about God's relation to black American life and to the world in general.[60]

I take this to mean that the Bible is the source of revelation, but womanist theologians will read that source differently from other groups. This is a very important hermeneutical principle to which we shall return to consider in some detail in a specific example, namely Williams's reading of the biblical references to Hagar. The distinction between black women's experience as a source and as a perspective replicates the criticism of James Cone made by Allan Boesak in Chapter 3. This issue is one which womanist theology has inherited from Black theology. However, it is an example of a much wider problem which womanist theology has inherited from feminist theology – and one which feminist theologians have consistently ignored. During a Roundtable discussion of her book *Daughters of Jefferson, Daughters of Bootblacks*, Barbara Hilkert Andolsen formulates this hermeneutical problem. 'A central and difficult question is what criteria justify rejecting a massive body of patriarchal, and even misogynist, biblical teachings in order to lift up as authoritative those strands which are consistent with full human development for women?'[61] The question awaits an answer, but it can only be a problem for those who accept the Bible as 'a norm or even a significant source' of revelation for Christians. To present the experience of black women as *the* religious source rather than traditional 'European' sources or even the Bible itself, womanist theologians present the experience of black women as a separate and parallel historical tradition. The justification of this secular material is that it will in the end be shown to be a source of a new theology. That remains to be seen.

Womanist theology therefore presents the experience of black women as its own tradition. There are frequent references to features of African culture which are preserved, perhaps unconsciously and which contrast with European (and white American) culture. These references to world views, community structures, family life and religious beliefs and practices are asserted or alluded to, but seldom supported by studies in anthropology or ethnography. All this is in contrast to the very detailed historical accounts of the period of slavery. The same harrowing descriptions are repeated in books and articles, with special reference to the women slaves. The emergence of literary fragments even under chattel conditions leads with emancipation to the expanding corpus of black women writers in the nineteenth and early twentieth centuries. The historical sweep concludes with the participation of women in the civil rights movement. We are then on more familiar ground, with the locating of black women in relationship to both (white) feminism and black (male) consciousness.

It is right that this tradition, too long suppressed for sexist as well as racist reasons, should be told. And told it has been by secular historians both social and cultural as well as poets and novelists. That needs no justification. What needs justification is the rehearsal of this material in books which purport to be producing a new kind of theology, womanist theology. Not how this material leads to a better understanding of the hopes and fears of black women today, the limitations imposed on their lives, their capabilities and aspirations. But how this material constitutes a source (or is it *the* source) for a new and reformed Christian theology.

Concentration on the experience of black women of course has a certain attraction, but it is not without dangers. It is attractive because it gives a voice to a significant part of society which was previously ignored, dismissed, silenced. It explores the possibility that these experiences were not at all as they were assumed to be. For example, slave owners (or their chaplains) selected biblical texts to instil acceptance of their lot amongst slaves and a humble obedience to the will of God. But as Shawn Copeland considers the spirituality of the slaves themselves, a different picture emerges. 'The slaves understood God as the author of freedom, of emancipation, certainly.'[62] However, the focusing on the experience of black women is not without attendant dangers. First, it appears to offer material over which womanist theologians have proprietary rights. No one else has the right to present it, or evaluate it. Any criticisms (such as the fraternal criticism offered by this writer) can be dismissed with righteous anger, especially if they come from a white, male, European. Second, all experience is socially constructed, for the person having the experience as well as her account of it. For experience to become usable, as in womanist theology, it must be deconstructed and presented in forms defensible to the wider academic community. Third, experience is not as such a source of revelation. Revelation is not the internal replication of the self. That is psychiatry. Revelation is not the expression of what we know but the disclosure of what we need to hear. Fourth, and in consequence, the focusing on experience runs the danger of sacrilising black women as victims, as discussed in Chapter 2 above. Black women have suffered enough without being subject to this. Fifth, there is the danger of taking over from feminism the narcissistic practice of 'telling our stories'. If authors have no shame at least readers should not be subjected to autobiographical accounts of the early years. It now seems that all feminists have wise mothers. The reader has no opportunity to raise the simplest question. 'Since as a teenager you thought your mother knew nothing, is this conversion or feminist ideology?' 'Did she really make quilts in a Manhattan apartment or did they come from Bloomingdale's?' But last and underlying all this, the position is reminiscent of fideism. There is the danger that womanist theologians might withdraw from interaction with the wider traditions of intellectual life. The most obvious deficiency in womanist theology is its lack of theory. More seriously: not a lack of theory by default, but a suspicion of theory in case it spoil pure experience and open the way for outsiders to evaluate the material. The example of Delores Williams is instructive not only because she is against theory, but because the case for rejecting it is based on, yes, autobiography. Williams taught a course jointly with Beverly Harrison at Union Theological Seminary, New York on 'Emerging Issues in Feminist-Womanist Theology'. The first generation of feminist theologians were trained in the western intellectual tradition before they became feminists. Rosemary Radford Ruether, for example, was a fine patristics scholar before applying her scholarship to the new feminist agenda. Beverly Wildung was a sensitive scholar in the field of ethics. However, that tradition is now, as we have observed, under attack by womanist theology. Williams provides an example. 'But white feminist preoccupation with theory had primarily served to perpetuate white supremacy in the academy because this theory (even though it is critical of white male culture) is in response to the thought, values and intellectual categories white Western patriarchal culture created and fosters.'[63] Is that all that need be said about western theory, especially in its theological context? In its European form it opposed National Socialism in Germany and in South Africa. In its American form, at least at UTS in the persons of Reinhold Niebuhr and John Bennett, it supported the civil rights movement and opposed the war in Vietnam. Is an interest in theory all of the same? And would that assertion not be in itself a form of theory, even if ill-considered and misguided? How could any academic hold such a view – and take pride in proclaiming it? The answer, autobiography. Prepare yourself. You are about to be presented with more autobiographical details than you wished to hear. More than that: the autobiography of one person is worth more than the collective experience of many academic communities throughout the world and over several centuries of intellectual history. For Williams 'theory is a difficult word'. In her youth white university researchers came to study black communities. They developed theories which changed nothing in the lives of the people. 'I resented the theory-makers because they never did anything about the poverty and suffering they witnessed.'[64] For Williams theory is an escape which avoids '"the nitty-gritty-nuts-and-bolts-dirty-work" of organizing attack on oppression (especially racial oppression)'. Such theory uses the master's tools and has no interest in dismantling the master's house. 'Current feminist fascination with theory and epistemology indicates the serious degree to which white feminists want to be in relation and dialogue with white males and the patriarchal culture they have created.'[65] Autobiography is clearly an inadequate basis for understanding the nature and function of theory. How could a womanist theologian believe that it is possible, let alone right, to reject theory when womanists themselves have embraced it as absolutely necessary for their work? I am thinking, for example, of bell hooks's *Feminist Theory: from margin to center*.[66] Social theory is indebted to Marx. It is not difficult to indicate how a more sophisticated consideration of the subject might be presented. Did these young researchers come into the community to construct theories which changed nothing. But all that was described 160 years ago. Marx's *XIth Thesis on Feuerbach* says as much. 'The philosophers have only interpreted the world in various ways, the point is to change it.' Marx is describing theory which is not innocently inadequate, but theory which serves the ideological interests of those who have a stake in the status quo. His critical theory exposes the nature and function of such interpretations of the world. Theory is not all of a piece. There is another kind of theory which unmasks the ideological assumptions of the age, to disclose interests and liberate from false consciousness. Such theory does not save the world, but it presents the oppressed with a clear picture of social reality, delegitimising customs, practices and institutions of injustice. This theory is given to the oppressed as an instrument of change. All revolutions begin with conscientisation. 'The weapon of criticism cannot, of course, replace the criticism of weapons, material force must be overthrown by material force, but *theory also becomes a material force as soon as it has gripped the masses*.'[67] And do the masses, in this case poor, oppressed black women, not deserve more from their champions? Should they not expect that womanist theologians will engage with the best critical minds, regardless of race and gender? With all the confidant prejudice of parochialism Nathaniel asked: 'Can anything good come out of Nazareth?' The more pragmatic Philip invited him, 'Come and see.' Could we not have a little more pragmatism? Womanist theologians need neither invent nor reject the wheel. There is usable material in the European intellectual tradition, as can be seen in these quotations from Marx. With the death of the author it is for individuals to evaluate the material, enquiring whether it is usable or not, all things considered – including (in the case of Marx) whether the author was a man, a married man who loved his wife, a Jewish man educated in a Christian school who experienced racial discrimination, a European so dark skinned that his daughter nevertheless called him 'the Moor', a socialist who married into the aristocracy and always wore a monocle. The experience of black women must be taken into account, but not *tout court*. It is the beginning of a complex and sophisticated process, not its only ingredient. Many of the black women who are the subject of womanist theology live in ghettos of various kinds. There is a danger that womanist theology condemns them to yet another ghetto by refusing to bring to bear on their behalf the intellectual and cultural resources of the wider western traditions – to which they also belong. Some aspects of that culture have abused them, but other aspects might yet enrich and liberate them. Having read so much of womanist theology I find it refreshing to be able to engage with it by referring to writers such as Luce Irigaray and Karl Marx. There is a danger that womanist theology itself becomes simply an interpretation of the world of poor black women, which changes nothing. One of the few examples of womanist theology using European theory to better understand its subject is to be found in Kelly Brown Douglas's *Sexuality and the Black Church: a womanist perspective*. In a section on 'Sexuality in Culture' she refers to the work of Michel Foucault, taking care of course to note that although 'Foucault's analyses sometimes reflect a self-serving androcentric perspective (as many feminist scholars have noted) they provide an "insider's" view of White patriarchal culture'.[68] She explores the relationship between power and sexual characterisation. From Foucault she learns that 'there is no better way to impugn the character and humanity of a people than by maligning their sexuality'.[69] It may be that poor black women are less likely to read Foucault than to recite the Nicene creed but those who purport to be their champions owe it to them to make use of the best social theory available – regardless.

As already indicated, womanist theology repeats as a mantra that it is holistic, dealing with oppression by sex, race and class. Its dialogue partners should therefore be those theologies which have led the way in analysing the three forms of oppression. Unfortunately it has not followed their examples in one important respect: they have all maintained a dialectical relationship with the western critical tradition for purposes of deconstruction and reconstruction.

We have observed the relationship between secular womanism and secular feminism. This is repeated in books and articles on womanist theology, but there is little theology. Indeed there is little dialogue with feminist *theology*. We can see this in the 'Roundtable: racism in the women's movement'. Since this was published in the *Journal of Feminist Studies in Religion* readers might be forgiven for expecting a substantial contribution to womanist theology, especially since *Religion* in the JFSR is routinely restricted to the Christian religion. The Roundtable consists of responses by two white and two black feminist scholars to Barbara Hilkert Andolsen's *Daughters of Jefferson, Daughters of Bootblacks*, a study of racism amongst many of the white women abolitionists of the nineteenth century.[70] In the introduction to her book Andolsen claims that 'this book is a work of feminist ethics written from a theological perspective'. The scene is therefore set for a theological response. One of the white scholars, Linda Mercadante, comments on the white feminist criticism of language about God. Instead of God the Father, they attempt to establish 'feminine imagery' for the divine: the focus is 'on birthing, suckling, nurturance, or maternal travail and patience, or other characteristics our culture has determined are related to immanence'.[71] It might be assumed that black feminists would take over this position, but 'immanental images may alienate blacks, including black women', for several reasons. The first is that this language recalls racial stereotypes of black women – in the words of Andolsen, 'a romantic caricature of the strong, nurturing black mammy who will carry us to freedom'.[72] Or again, the limited imagery 'neglects the very attributes of God that comprise a crucial part of black spirituality'. The transcendence of God is necessary if there is to be hope that the powerful forces of evil will be overcome. Thus Mercadante sees the challenge to white theology from the experience of women in the Black church. But why does this come from the white feminist and not from the black? Andolsen sees her book as a theological project. Mercadante formulates a theological response. But Marcia Riggs ignores the theological dimension in Andolsen, while Renita Weems ignores the reflexive criticism offered by Mercadante. Not so much a Roundtable as separate dining facilities: a missed opportunity so far as womanist theology is concerned.

Jacquelyn Grant demonstrates a good grasp of Christian doctrine in her study *White Women's Christ and Black Women's Jesus: feminist Christology and womanist response*. 'The feminist theologies which I examine regard human experience in general and women's experience in particular as primary sources for doing theology.'[73] This approach 'has enabled White liberationist feminists to forge a new theological agenda'.[74] Grant takes the time and trouble to understand writers such as Letty Russell and Rosemary Radford Ruether. She repeats the secular womanist criticism. For example, Ruether 'incorrectly locates the tension between Black churches and the women's movement at the point of the sexism of Black men. One could argue that Black men's responses to the women's movement are due equally to the racism of the women's movement as to the sexism in the Black movement.'[75] Would this be true of the work of Ruether? Rosemary Radford Ruether is now considered one of the founders of feminist theology. However, long before she taught feminist theology she was active in the civil rights and anti-war movements of the 1960s. She was a volunteer for the Delta Ministry in Mississippi when appointed to the faculty of Howard University in Washington, DC. When finally she began to teach feminist theology it was already in the context of race, class and third world awareness, especially of developments in Latin America. One of the reasons for the delay in formally teaching feminist theology was the resistance to the subject by the predominantly black faculty at Howard. To describe her by the stereotype of white feminists as racist, classist and colonialist is gratuitously insulting at a personal level, but at an academic level it is symptomatic of a lack of rigour and accuracy.[76] Turning to a specifically religious theme Grant criticises Ruether for suggesting 'that perhaps a better model for women would be Mary Magdalene rather than Jesus'. Her point is that 'there is little reason to believe that a White woman salvific model would be any more liberating of Black women than a White male model'. So there you have it. It's official: Mary Magdalene was a white woman. So much for Albert Cleage and the wonderful Black Madonna. Grant does not mention Ruether's much more interesting suggestion that Mary Magdalene would be a more appropriate role model (not saviour) for women than Mary of Nazareth. Here is the true woman of faith and initiative, who chose to follow Jesus. Here is the first witness to the resurrection, the woman whom Jesus preferred over the disciples (according to John), the 'apostle to the apostles' the one woman whom tradition tells us Jesus kissed on the mouth.[77] And is this, the most powerful and faithful woman of the early Christian church, to be set aside on the basis of what seems to be a piece of racist prejudice, namely that any model who is recommended by a white woman (Ruether) cannot be appropriate for black women? Why not introduce the Magdalene to black women and let them decide for themselves. Perhaps they would warm to her when they learned that the reputation of this spiritual and entirely innocent women was destroyed by the false claim that she was a prostitute, deliberately maligned by the male supporters of the safe figure of the Virgin Mother. Perhaps they could identify with a vivacious woman who was vulnerable to the misogynism of a black man: Augustine was an African. All this material was brought into the public domain by (white) feminist scholars engaging with western scholarship. Where is the dialogue?

Another issue discussed by secular womanists is sexuality, an important theme in (white) feminist theology. As we saw earlier, secular womanists have given a good deal of thought to homophobia in the black community and some, including Audre Lorde, have paid particular attention to heterosexism and the rejection of black lesbianism. These issues are all rehearsed again in works by womanist theologians. Our interest is in whether they go on to make a theological contribution to the secular discussions. Kelly Brown Douglas has addressed the issue in *Sexuality and the Black Church: a womanist perspective*. In the introduction she explains that she undertook the work to address the following question.

> Why were we womanist theologians, who so aptly criticize Black and feminist theologians for their failure to comprehend the complexity of black women's oppression, so disinclined to confront the oppression of lesbians or broadly the presence of homophobia/heterosexism within the Black community?

Unfortunately this question receives no answer. Instead there is a rehearsal of the secular womanist criticism of black sexuality as a pawn of white culture, the white assault on black sexuality. This is followed by criticism of black men as they accept white stereotypes of female beauty in addition to the stereotypes of black women as in turn Mammy and Jezebel. (A reference to Jezebel does not make it theology.) Also repeated are the secular womanist criticisms of homophobia and heterosexism in the black community.

> Yet, regardless of the pain inflicted upon black people, many persons alleging commitment to the life and freedom of the Black community continue to relinquish responsibility for their life-negating homophobic attitudes and practices with the easy excuse that homosexuality is a White thing.[78]

Right at the end of this chapter there is a reference to the Bible. She complains that biblical texts are interpreted in a homophobic way. But why should this be a source of complaint? Probably a majority of the Black church (and a significant proportion of white Christians in America) believe homosexuality to be wrong, not because it is 'a white thing', but because it is condemned in the Bible. (As I write this section the Episcopal (Anglican) Church is divided by the consecration of a gay priest as bishop of New Hampshire. The most vociferous opposition comes from Anglicans in Africa, notably Nigeria. Yet African-Americans, who cannot wait to contrast and condemn white values over against African values, do not take the side of Africans in this matter. Silence reigns.) If womanist theology were in dialogue with the best western biblical scholarship it might seek to persuade the Black church that the Bible does not in fact condemn homosexuality in the terms in which it is understood today. But that is not the approach adopted by Douglas. We have encountered this issue before: on what grounds are biblical texts set aside? 'To reiterate, the authority of scripture is in large measure determined by whether or not a text supports the life and freedom of the Black community.'[79] An interesting (secular) criterion for selecting biblical texts, which merely poses the inevitable question: what are the criteria by which 'the life and freedom of the Black community' are judged to be Christian? But if the source of womanist theology is the experience of black women the argument becomes circular. 'The very distinctiveness of a womanist theological perspective dictates engagement in a sexual discourse of resistance.'[80] By this Douglas means resistance to the evils of the white community. 'That White culture is sinful is evident.'[81] Indeed it contains much evil, but the majority of black American and African Christians would include homosexuality in the inventory. Douglas is therefore in the position of blaming heterosexism found in the Black church on the heterosexism found in the white community – that community which the Black church condemns for its homosexuality. Clear? Perhaps I should clarify my own position here. I take a liberal view in these matters. I have no problem with homosexual relationships, homosexual Christians, gay bishops – or a lesbian pope for that matter. My point is that those who call themselves womanist theologians must offer *theological* grounds in addition to the secular grounds offered by womanists. Perhaps the least sophisticated way of attempting to make a position theological is to drag Jesus into it. 'To choose Jesus as the center of one's life and faith is to choose one whose very being and way of be-ing in the world compel an appreciation for the sanctity of human sexuality.'[82] Unfortunately for proof-texting Jesus spoke on very few of the matters which concern us today. As noted he was silent on slavery. He was also silent about sexuality, surprisingly so some might think for a man who spent three years of his life in the continual company of 12 men. In some desperation Douglas ends her book with an appeal to the authority of the teaching of Jesus. But as we have seen, this authority has been seriously undermined by womanist theologians. What did Jesus know of the experience of black women?

> Finally, the Great Commandment makes the need for redeeming the sacredness of sexuality clear. It resolves, 'You shall love the Lord your God with all your heart, all your soul, and all your mind. You shall love your neighbour as yourself.'[83]

Is this conclusion the answer to the question posed at the outset: the reluctance to face 'the oppression of lesbians or more broadly the presence of homophobia/heterosexism within the Black community'? Love, says Jesus, with all your heart, soul and mind. Body is not mentioned. It is possible to construct a theology of sexuality (more properly sexualities) but it requires a more sophisticated dialogue with Christian resources, especially the considerable literature available on the subject among (white) feminist theologians. It also requires a more naunced reading of the scriptures, beyond proof texts.[84]

Before leaving this subject we should refer to another Roundtable discussion, this time on 'Lesbian and Feminist Theology'.[85] The main participants were white feminists, some of them lesbians, but with the contribution of Delores Williams it became also an interesting dialogue of white feminist and womanist theologians. The Roundtable began with a joint position paper by two white lesbian theologians, Carter Heyward and Mary Hunt. Williams attempts to be positive about what can be taken from their paper. 'For instance, what can a focus on female erotica, female friendship, female sex and knowledge of our female bodies tell us about the ways individuals and communities are religious?'[86] She is gracious about what she has learned from it. 'And the critique of civil and religious institutions from the perspective of lesbianism can show all of our communities how we have excluded lesbian women who have vital, brilliant and necessary skills to bring to our struggle for liberation, love and real human community.' However, there are three assertions in the paper which attract her criticism. She is sceptical of its exaggerated claims. Heyward and Hunt claim that 'lesbianism is the enemy of the dominant social order, for it embodies the potential collapse of power relations structured to secure men's control of women's bodies, and thereby, women's lives'. But surely 'the dominant social order' is constructed and maintained by a more complex mix of interests. Related to this is their claim that 'as white women are attempting to understand and expunge racism, heterosexual women need to pay critical attention to their heterosexual privilege'. For Williams this does not reflect the real basis of 'the dominant social order'. White women (lesbian and heterosexual) are more privileged than black women (lesbian and heterosexual). Lesbianism cannot perform the destruction of 'the dominant social order'. (She may even imply that its destruction is the last thing white lesbian women would welcome.) Williams has two further objections to the position paper. The first is the claim by Heyward and Hunt that 'in sexual love between women, the feminist word becomes flesh'. Reading this recalled to mind an interview with Germaine Greer, one of the leaders of the women's liberation movement in the 1970s, given just two years before the Roundtable.

> Greer rejected those lesbians who insist that their idea of sexuality is part of the feminist movement. She said: 'It's like the sort of blackmail one got from men who'd say "If you don't sleep with me, then...etc. etc." And I remember lesbians who would say to me, "If you don't sleep with me, you're not really a feminist!"'[87]

This is the imperialistic claim made by some lesbians that lesbianism is the next and final phase in the development of feminism. I see a parallel between this and the proposition that 'in sexual love between women, the feminist word becomes flesh'. Williams rejects its exclusivism. The lesbian experience must be respected, but it has to take its place alongside other experiences. 'Therefore the feminist word must also become flesh through women's experience of heterosexual love and celibacy.' Her final criticism concerns the claim that lesbians are best able to love men, 'since such female-male relations often are marked more by friendship and less by power-games and sex objectification than is customary between women and men in a heterosexist society'. More scepticism on the part of Williams.

> Does this statement mean to suggest that 'sexless' love is a firmer foundation for friendship than sexual love? Or that power games in relationships have only to do with sexuality? Or is the implication that friendship between lesbians is totally lacking in power games and sex-objectification?

She might have mentioned also the incidence of domestic abuse and violence in lesbian relationships.

Womanist theology is confident that it has something to say to (white) feminist theology, but dialogue requires hearing as well as speaking. It could benefit from using more of the resources available within that tradition, critically.

Womanist theology has borrowed a great deal from (male) Black theology, as it should. It has also inherited the secular womanist criticism of the chauvinism which is such a feature of black male thought and behaviour. In *The Black Christ* Kelly Brown Douglas makes use of the work of James Cone, Albert Cleage and Deotis Roberts in tracing the development of the concept. However, she identifies certain deficiencies in their presentation.

> They did not sufficiently specify what it was that Christ affirmed, in affirming Blackness. Not everything that is Black is sustaining or liberating for the Black community. There are aspects of Black culture and religion that do not necessarily foster self-esteem nor do they empower Black people to fight for their freedom.[88]

While this might well be true of the early James Cone, it is certainly not true of Albert Cleage. Cone found it impossible to criticise the actions of black youths on the streets. His disclaimer 'by whatever means' is as famous as Alice Walker's last word on womanism – 'regardless'. But Cleage, as we saw in Chapter 2, refuses to sacrilise the black community. Douglas claims that the black churches have failed to confront the challenges of drugs, sex and insecurity. But Cleage, in the name of the Black Christ, not only preached on these matters, but initiated a programme to redeem lives ravaged by poverty and crime. (Why has Cleage had so little influence on Black theologians?)

The second deficiency which Douglas identifies in Black theology concerns violence within the black community.

> The various versions of the Black Christ do not confront the reality of oppression within the Black community. The Black Christ does not point to the reality of Black on Black oppression. Black people are victimized not only by White people, but also by each other.[89]

As we saw in the critique of Black theology from South Africa, the identification of the problem as one of colour eliminates the distinction between economic exploiters and victims. But womanist theologians do not learn from South African (male) theologians.

A third deficiency extends this theme. Beginning with the civil rights movements, there was little concern beyond racism. 'The Black Christ signalled a one-dimensional understanding of social oppression.'[90] The three culprits did not consider the place of women and their experience of oppression. By the time

Douglas was writing Cone and Roberts had certainly acknowledged that this had been the case in their early works. They had been writing before feminist consciousness influenced the Black church.

There is little (womanist) theology in the book. It is perhaps ironic that when Douglas later returns to the theme of the Black Christ the prophetic figure who extends the theme beyond the works of the three named theologians is another male theologian and activist, Martin Luther King, Jr. The book ends with an acknowledgement of the need for 'a womanist Black Christ'. But is that not what the book promised at the outset? For those who would love to read and learn from womanist theology it is disappointing that there is so little new, creative and critical theology, beyond the secular womanist analysis.

It is therefore a great pleasure to end this discussion, the dialogue with Black theology, with a genuine example of womanist theology. In *Sisters in the Wilderness: the challenge of womanist God-talk*, Delores Williams locates herself in relation to (male) Black theology, but goes beyond it with a positive criticism of its limitations. Earlier we commended her hermeneutical approach to the Bible. Here is a practical example of a womanist theologian who acknowledges the authority of the Bible, but reads it through the experience of black women. This is no religious legitimation or sacrilisation of black women. It is a sensitive, honest and insightful appropriation of the Bible in which there is a dialectical relationship between text and experience. To set the scene we should recall that all liberation theologies quote the first sermon of Jesus, *à la rigueur*. In the synagogue of Nazareth (Luke 4: 18–19) Jesus not only read from the scroll of the prophet, but claimed that its promises were fulfilled in his ministry.

> The Spirit of the Lord is upon me, because he has anointed me to preach good news to the poor. He has sent me to proclaim release to the captives and recovering of sight to the blind, to set at liberty those who are oppressed, to proclaim the acceptable year of the Lord.

This is repeated so frequently, especially in Black theology, that no one now notices that it is not true. Yes, Isaiah prophesied the liberation from Babylonian captivity. Yes, Jesus preached to the poor and healed a few blind people. But from the sixth century BCE, through the time of Jesus, slavery continued. It was the mode of production of the Seleucid empire, the Hellenistic empire of Alexander, the Roman empire. Jesus did not mention it: Paul, if anything condoned it. As it came to an end in European history it was replaced by another kind of slavery, the feudalism of the serfs. And as that came to an end in Europe, traditional African slavery was developed into an international trade with slavery to Brazil, the Caribbean and the USA. What possible sense does it make to claim that the Christian God sends his prophet 'to proclaim release to the captives'? And what slave would be impressed by metaphor, liberation 'in a sense'? But it would take courage and integrity to blow the whistle on the persistent recalling of Luke 4: 18–19 and the claim that God is a God who liberates captives, who frees slaves. How much more courageous when the whistleblower is a black woman. Such a one is Delores Williams.

Elsewhere I have advised against the uncritical reference to Exodus by Christians.[91] Does the God of Jesus Christ kill the Egyptian firstborn, the slaughter of the innocents? Does this God indiscriminately murder the first born not only of the oppressors, but of the enemies of the oppressors, who languish in the dungeons of Pharaoh? And if God on this occasion liberated Hebrew slaves, does this mean that God is always a liberator of slaves? Clearly not. It is at this point that we return to Delores Williams and her exposition of the narrative of the non-Hebrew woman slave Hagar. It is recorded in two episodes, Genesis 16 and 21. In the first Sarah, Abraham's wife, has no children. She gives her Egyptian slave Hagar to her husband. Hagar conceives, but shows contempt for her mistress. Sarah treats her so harshly that pregnant though she is, she flees into the wilderness. The angel of the Lord appears to her and commands her to return to her mistress 'and submit to her'. Williams observes that 'God's response to Hagar's story in the Hebrew testament is not liberation.'[92] In the second episode Sarah bears Isaac and tells Abraham to get rid of Hagar and Ishmael her son. Abraham is reluctant to do so, but God takes the side of Sarah, the mistress against the slave woman. Abraham therefore provides food and water for Hagar and her son and sends them off into the wilderness. (Confusingly for feminist stereotypes, God takes the side of one woman in her oppression of another, while the patriarch shows kindness to the slave woman.) God rescues the pair in the wilderness, leading them to water. In the first narrative God returns the slave to captivity, while in the second he leads her through the wilderness to safety and an independent life with her son. Williams wishes to read the narratives through the perspective of (poor) black women. They may not recognise the God who always liberates but there are many ingredients in these stories which correspond to their experience. Slavery, oppression not least at the hands of the mistress, the giving over sexually to the master, surrogacy, enmity and rejection, responsibility in the single-parent family. Williams looks to 'black women's experience to provide the lens through which we view sources, to provide the issues that form the content of our theology and to help us formulate the questions we ask about God's relation to black American life and to the world in general'.[93] She explores the black women's sense of wilderness, both in the alienation of slavery and in the economic insecurity of post-bellum life. 'Apparently Hagar in the wilderness as an image of womanhood – poor, hardworking, strong, self-reliant, autonomous, committed to her family, communicating with God – continues to live and thrive in the African-American world.'[94]

Although this perspective gets its start in Black theology, it is highly critical of Cone's triumphalist claim that God is a God of liberation. No so fast. God is presented as being biased in favour of Sarah and of returning a runaway slave to submit to her mistress. It all depends on how events play in the providence of God. Slavery can further the divine plan or interfere with it. Slavery as such is not condemned. As Williams observes, 'one quickly discerns a non-liberative thread running through the Bible'.[95] She discusses the regulations concerning slavery in Exodus and Leviticus. 'The fact remains: slavery in the Bible is a natural and unprotested institution in the social and economic life of ancient society – except on occasion when the Jews are themselves enslaved.'[96] Since black women identify with Hagar, they are on the wrong side. Although, as we have seen, womanist theologians would like to work without engagement with the western dogmatic tradition, yet at this point the doctrine of election becomes important. Jesus charges his disciples, 'Go nowhere among the Gentiles, and enter no town of the Samaritans, but go rather to the lost sheep of the house of Israel' (Matt. 10: 5–6). The Gentiles have done no wrong, but they are not of the elect, the people of the Covenant. Linked to this is Paul's reference to the son of Hagar. The other most quoted text by liberation theologians, alongside the first sermon of Jesus, is the claim by Paul in Galatians. 'There is neither Jew nor Greek, there is neither slave nor free, there is neither male nor female; for you are all one in Christ Jesus' (Gal. 3: 28). Never quoted is the following verse. 'And if you are Christ's then you are Abraham's offspring, heirs according to promise.' Paul therefore goes on to contrast two communities, both from Abraham, but from two different mothers. One is from Sarah, the heirs of the promise and freedom. The other is from the slave woman, Hagar, heirs not of the promise but of bondage. The whole discussion ends with another liberation talisman. 'For freedom Christ has set us free; stand fast therefore, and do not submit again to a yoke of slavery' (Gal. 5: 1). It is for this reason that black women, identifying with Hagar rather than Sarah, are on the wrong side of the election line. Black theologians – not least the Barthian James Cone – have too easily read the Bible from the perspective of liberation, election and promise. For Williams, this has made them blind to 'the awful reality of victims making victims in the Bible'.[97] In their own time they ignore black women. This has led them in turn to ignore 'the figures in the Bible whose experience is analogous to that of black women'.[98] To regard Exodus as paradigmatic is to accept uncritically the consequences of that event, namely the ethnic cleansing and genocide of the Canaanite people, men, women and children. Reading the Bible from the perspective of Hagar, Jesus is saviour because he offers black women strategies of survival, not because he died on the cross as a surrogate. Williams therefore concludes that 'Black liberation theology's understanding of incarnation, of revelation, Jesus Christ and reconciliation holds very little promise for black women.'[99]

Similarly, Jesus as surrogate is not an attractive model of redemption among black women. The last thing that the innocent victims of suffering want to be assured of is that there is in heaven a God who for their sake is willing to create yet another innocent victim. Womanist theologians 'must show that redemption of humans can have nothing to do with any kind of surrogate or substitute role Jesus was reputed to have played in a bloody act that supposedly gained victory over sin and evil'.[100] In a parallel discussion Shawn Copeland calls for a fresh evaluation of the virtues of patience, long-suffering forebearance, love, faith and hope. 'Thus, to distance itself from any form of masochism, even Christian masochism, a theology of suffering in womanist perspective must re-evaluate those virtues in light of Black women's experience.'[101] Williams's treatment of this theme is a paradigm of womanist theology. It uses the resources of western biblical scholarship and Black theology but it reads both the Bible and Christian doctrine from the perspective of the experience of black women. It does not sacrilise black women but it refuses to silence their voices for the sake of conformity to classist or sexist interests.

One final point. We saw Jacquelyn Grant rejecting Mary Magdalene as a model for women's spirituality. Not surprisingly Williams declares that for black women in America Hagar is 'a model of full womanhood'.[102] The Virgin Mary proves to be too white, too expressive of the acceptable image of women. But more than that. At the Annunciation Mary is simply told that she is going to be made pregnant. Or as Williams puts it, 'the Spirit mounted Mary'.[103] For black women this is too reminiscent of the situation of the slave woman who cannot refuse the sexual designs of her master. Mary acknowledges that this is her relationship to God. 'Behold, I am *the handmaiden of the Lord*; let it be to me according to your word' (Luke 1: 38). 'Handmaiden' translates *he doule*, which in classical Greek was not just a female slave, but the slave of a despot. No doubt still thinking of her fiancé, the young girl is resigned to her fate and less than enthusiastic about the angel's 'good news'. Before leaving this point we might note the claim of Diana Hayes that it is 'in their reinterpretation of the role and presence of Mary, the Mother of God, that Black Catholic women can make the most significant contribution'.[104] Throughout the book she cannot bring herself to apply womanist criticism to the white, male, European leadership of the Roman Catholic Church. And now, against the evidence of the text she cannot apply a womanist perspective to Mary. In loyalty to traditions which feminists associate with misogyny she represents Mary as yes-saying, as 'courageous and outrageous'. 'She is a role model, not for passivity, but for strong, righteous, "womanish" women who spend their lives giving birth to the future.'[105] The Blessed Virgin Mary is womanish! At the end of this chapter we shall raise the question whether the term womanist retains any of its meaning as set out by Alice Walker.

We noted at the outset that womanist theology inherits a holistic position from the tripartite discussions which preceded its inception. Its main dialogue partners have been feminist theology and Black theology. Although reference is occasionally made to Latin American liberation theology it has not been a significant dialogue partner. Thus although class is included in the mantra of 'sex, race and class' little is said about it. Katie Cannon deals with social class, referring to Benjamin DeMott's *The Imperial Middle Way: why Americans can't think about class.*[106] We might rephrase the question, why can't womanist theologians deal with class in view of the fact that it is continually mentioned along with sex and race? Although Cannon refers to the 'consequences of power in our deindustrialized, capitalist, sociopolitical class system',[107] her article reduces the discussion of economic class to merely social class. This enables her to deal with class as an expression of racism. She considers 'white-skin privileges' as 'sociopolitical mechanisms used by the materially privileged to maintain white supremacist, androcentric, patriarchal elitism'.[108] There is no theology in the article and in the conclusion she claims to have been analysing 'the cultural disposition of class'. As we have just seen in her book *Sisters in the Wilderness* Delores Williams examines the Old Testament regulations concerning slavery. In this context she can refer to the experience of alienation felt by some African-Americans at their 'economic enslavement by the capitalistic American economy'.[109] But this hardly constitutes class analysis. Emilie Townes presents a detailed description of the New Jerusalem.

> The horizon a womanist ethic works toward is a society that respects the rights and humanity of all peoples and nature. It is a society that provides adequate education, health care, and income opportunities. The society that is part of the new Jerusalem respects and cares for the young and the elderly. It is a society that is rich in diversity through its cultural, racial, and ethnic groups. It is a society in which women and men learn to build healthy relationships with one another. It is a society that does not dwell on sexual orientation or life-style. It is a society that addresses the roots of its problems instead of building prison after prison as a vain panacea. It is a society that is uncompromisingly rooted in justice and fuelled by people who use their hope to construct and enact meaningful and significant social change.[110]

But what is the point of such romantic rhetoric if it is not supported by economic analysis? Where is the critique of American society? What are the implications of these liberal, humane values which she is attempting to appropriate for womanist ethics? Why are these liberal values specifically rejected by the neo-liberalism of American capitalism? Why is her New Jerusalem more like Cuba than the Land of the Free (enterprise)? Once again we find that womanist theologians refuse to engage in dialogue with the wider intellectual tradition, decline to use critical resources which could serve them and the poor black women they claim to represent. One of the most creative strands in that western critical tradition is Marxist analysis. There is a particular frisson for Americans when they associate themselves with Marx even as they quickly make it clear that they are not Marxists and are not taken in by him. Kelly Brown Douglas claims that womanist theology involves socio-political analysis.

> It may, for instance, be informed by Marxist thought as it endeavors to understand the class issues within the black community. But it also goes beyond Marxist analysis in an effort to comprehend the multidimensionality of Black oppression. Moreover, unlike Marxist analysis, a social-political analysis of wholeness takes seriously the particularities of race, gender, and culture that shape the nature of Black people's oppression.[111]

The reality, however, is otherwise. Womanist theology does not go beyond Marx's class analysis: it does not appropriate it at all. Far from attempting to illuminate the oppression of poor black women through an analysis of ideological class interests it reduces the description of oppression to the limited categories of sex and race. Jacquelyn Grant hits the nail on the thumb. 'For black women doing theology to ignore classism would mean that their theology is no different from any other bourgeois theology.'[112] Quite so. Womanist theology does indeed ignore class analysis and for that reason it is 'no different from any other bourgeois theology'. We might recall the words of Lebamang Sebidi (a real African) quoted in Chapter 3 concerning a theology which concentrates on race and ignores class. 'Such a movement cannot but be bourgeois – and somehow reactionary.'

A rare example of womanist theologians entering the economic sphere is provided by Katie Cannon in her essay on 'Racism and Economics: the perspective of Oliver C. Cox'. She provides a summary of the critique of capitalism mounted by Oliver Cox (1901–74), a Trinidadian economist who taught at various colleges in the USA including the Tuskegee Institute in Alabama. Although she mentions that Cox was a Marxist she seems to be unaware that the main themes which she identifies arise naturally from Marxist analysis. For example, Cox's study of the relationship of economics to forms of government, religion and legal systems is simply Marx's famous model of the relationship between base and superstructure. His discussion of the relationship between religion and the ruling class is exposed in Marx's theory of ideology. The enforcing of monopoly conditions on the third world by threat or force is an expression of the interests of the so-called military-industrial complex. Cannon is particularly interested in Cox because he introduces race into this presentation, for example in *Caste, Class and Race*.[113] She concludes that 'the insights at the heart of Cox's social theory is that an ideology of White supremacy bolsters and reinforces America's leadership of the world capitalist system'.[114] This is in fact the most problematic aspect of his work. Racism can be linked to slavery as a mode or production, but not to capitalism. It could be argued that the principal cause of the American Civil War was that northern capitalism wished to destroy southern slavery because of its inefficiency. Capitalism does not allow racism to interfere with profitability. The anti-apartheid movement continued ineffectually for 30 years until international capitalism decided apartheid was bad for trade and told the South African government to end it. Or again today, jobs are being exported from Europe and the USA to Bangalore, India, inadvertently bringing (relative) poverty to white workers and (relative) prosperity to coloured workers. However that may be, what is disappointing is that Cannon reduces the class analysis of Marx and Cox once again to the single issue of race. At the end of the essay she draws no conclusions whatsoever about American capitalism and its production of an impoverished and excluded class of black women. So much for the mantra that womanist theology is holistic, dealing with sex, race and class.

It is disappointing that womanist theologians have not paid more attention to class. They could have been inspired by the example of bell hooks and her manifesto *Where We Stand: class matters*. Ironically, by continually relating her subject to Christian ethical values hooks, a secular writer, makes a greater contribution to womanist theology than most womanist theologians. In the opening words of her book hooks acknowledges that class is a neglected subject. 'Nowadays it is fashionable to talk about race or gender; the uncool subject is class.'[115] With the appearance of the 'black bourgoisie' and black gated communities 'our nation is in fact becoming a class-segregated society'[116] in which a new black generation 'is willing to forgo allegiance to race or gender to promote their class interests'.[117] Class allegiance supersedes race loyalty.[118] She notes a fundamental change in the ethos of America. Its Christian traditions fostered a suspicion of wealth and a questioning of the rich. For hooks this reflected the teaching of Jesus and Paul on the dangers of riches in the pursuit of the spiritual life. Now there is a culture of greed and a willingness to blame the poor for their poverty. Christians see wealth as a goal and possession as a divine blessing. In addition to the economic reference hooks includes a political dimension. In dealing with 'the politics of greed' she frequently refers to fascism. Those who use the term 'fascism' seldom attempt a definition: it functions as a sophisticated term of abuse. It might have been interesting if hooks had pursued this issue further. For example, in discussing drug dealers she characterises them as functioning only 'as a fascist force that brings violence and devastation into what were once stable communities'.[119] Fascism historically is associated with racial persecution, but in essence it is a view of society *unified* by race. As we have already observed, there are some black nationalist groups which promote myths of racial solidarity which might well qualify as fascist. hooks addresses that other myth, the myth that America is a classless society. It is a dangerous myth if it allows society (and Christians within it) to eschew responsibility for poverty and deprivation. But hooks makes the point that America is becoming classless in another sense, as the poor are encouraged to share the materialist aspirations and greed of the consuming society. As the poor internalise the values of society at large they become complicit in their own exploitation.[120] And what is to be done? One issue is 'education for critical consciousness.'[121] Although she claims to have learned nothing from Marx she identifies with 'democratic socialism, with a vision of participatory economics within capitalism that aims to challenge and change class hierarchy'.[122] However, there is no indication of how to raise critical consciousness, justify socialism or reconcile it with capitalism. Perhaps surprisingly hooks warns that feminist studies may not be part of this progressive agenda. 'Ironically, focus on race and racism was one of the new directions in feminist thought that deflected attention away from issues of class.'[123] Feminists focusing on race – is this a criticism of some womanists? It is a salutary warning to womanist theologians.

It will be recalled that bell hooks defended the term black feminism. We end this study by raising the question whether what is called womanist theology is in fact better described simply as black feminist theology. As we have seen, with notable exceptions such as Delores Williams's study of Hagar, there is little theology in womanist theology. Now we must ask whether womanist theology, if it is not theological, is even womanist? As has been well rehearsed in the literature, the term womanist was coined, or at least inserted into the literary tradition of black women, by Alice Walker. She presents us with four rather different definitions of its meaning, in the style of an entry in a dictionary of current usage. It would seem entirely reasonable therefore to measure womanist theology against Walker's definition of womanism. This has been done by Cheryl Sanders. Her findings constitute the position paper discussed by yet another *JFSR* Roundtable.

The main concern of Sanders is that the term 'womanist', as defined by Walker, may not be 'an appropriate frame of reference for the ethical and theological statements now being generated by black women'.[124] Sanders does not reject all womanist ethics and theology. Her concern is that an *uncritical* appropriation of the concept of womanist might lead to a distortion of Christian ethics and theology constructed from that perspective. This is an entirely reasonable and important question to raise. If we refer back to Chapter 2 we can see that it forms a precise parallel to the question whether an *uncritical* acceptance of the perspective of Black Power leads to a distortion of Christian ethics and theology. The hostility of some of the responses to her legitimate question indicates that some womanist theologians may indeed have fallen into this trap. Denial is masked by righteous anger. Anger is no substitute for a reasoned argument, though it might indicate a need for professional help. By comparison Sanders treats her subject logically and analytically, not because she does not care about womanist theology, but because the issue is so important that it deserves nothing less than our full attention.

> In our efforts to tailor Walker's definition to suit our own purposes, have we misconstrued the womanist concept and its meaning? Is the word womanist being co-opted because of its popular appeal and used as a mere title or postscript for whatever black women scholars want to celebrate, criticize or construct? Are we committing a gross conceptual error when we use Walker's descriptive cultural nomenclature as a foundation for the normative discourse of theology and ethics?

Which is more important, to defend womanist theology or to write good Christian theology which takes account fully of the experience of black women? And what if the two are not the same? This question can only be answered by attending to Walker's own perspective and definition.

> Walker's definition comprises an implicit ethics of moral autonomy, liberation, sexuality and love that is not contingent upon the idea of God or revelation. In any case, to be authentically 'womanist', a theological or ethical statement should embrace the full complement of womanist criteria without omissions or additions intended to sanctify, de-feminize or otherwise alter the perspective Walker intended the word *womanist* to convey.

Walker's primary claim is the right of black women to name their own experience, a right which includes choosing their own lovers. Sanders describes womanist as 'a secular category'. I do not believe this is entirely accurate, but she means that a womanist displays autonomy in the formation of identity and her choice of lovers. Rebellion against Christian mores is one of the characteristics of a womanist. This in itself raises the question of the coherence of womanism/theology. Sanders warns that 'it would be a mistake to recognize anything that any black woman writes with a womanist title or reference as womanist discourse simply because the author is black and female'. But this is what has happened. Womanist has come to mean – black woman. If Walker's definition is to retain its point, power and potential her criteria have to be observed.

In fact womanist theologians have paid little attention to the setting of the definition of womanist. It arises from an intergenerational conflict. There is the precociousness of the daughter and the acquiescence of the mother, rebellion and resignation.

> Thus, the context of womanist self-assertion includes two apparently inseparable dimensions: the personal struggle for sexual freedom, and the collective struggle for freedom in the political-social sense. Yet, in the theological-ethical statements womanist is used to affirm the faith of our mothers principally in the collective sense of struggle, that is, for freedom from racist or sexist oppression.

Sanders begins her paper by pointing out that Walker's first use of the term womanist occurred in her review of *Gifts of Power: the writings of Rebecca Jackson*, a book edited by Jean McMahon Humez about the legendary nineteenth-century black Shaker. The review is reprinted in *In Search of Our Mothers' Gardens*. Walker objects to the fact that Humez describes Jackson as a lesbian although Jackson described herself as celibate. At this point in the review Walker uses the word womanist in preference to lesbian to describe more appropriately black women's sexual inclusiveness. (In this Walker is reacting against the imposition of a white woman's term to describe a black woman.)[125] Thus a black Christian woman who has chosen celibacy because of her faith is not a womanist. Nor was Sojourner Truth a womanist, since she did not assert sexual freedom in her Christian responsibility to free slaves. Sanders therefore concludes that to 'designate a historic figure as womanist solely on the basis of political-social engagement without addressing the person-sexual dimension is a contextual error typical of womanist theological-ethical discourse'. Sanders's paper appeared at the same time as Jacquelyn Grant's book in which Grant lists the foremothers. 'Womanists were Sojourner Truth, Jarena Lee, Amanda Berry Smith, Ida B. Wells, Mary Church Terrell, Mary McLeod Bethune, Fannie Lou Hamer and countless others not remembered in any historical study. A womanist then is a strong Black woman who has sometimes been mislabeled as a domineering castrating matriarch.'[126] Womanist surely must mean something much more specific than 'a strong Black woman'.

One of the elements of Walker's definition most dear to womanist theologians is her claim that a womanist 'loves the Spirit'. Sanders is concerned that there is little attention to the sacred in Walker's definition. She would have strengthened her case if she had sought the meaning of 'the Spirit' in Walker's other writings. Immediately after the definition of womanist Walker goes on to say that while at college she had rejected Christianity, the 'white man's palliative'[127] she observed in her parents. Thus we see the intergenerational nature of womanism as the daughter rejects the mother's religion. Later she claimed that she was always involved in religious questions, but could not believe in a God beyond nature. 'The world is God. Man is God. So is a leaf or a snake.'[128] This anti-Christian pantheism is later expanded into 'reverence to the Earth' as she comes to call herself a pagan.[129] Alice Walker's four definitions of womanism are continually quoted by womanist theologians. In enquiring into the meaning and appropriateness of the use of the term we must surely pay close attention to Alice Walker herself. An important aspect of being a womanist, according to Walker, is the rejection of the religion of the mother, the Christian religion. Sanders describes Walker's position as secular. As indicated, I do not think this is correct, but it is significant that Walker was named '1997 Humanist of the Year' by the American Humanist Association. In her speech accepting this accolade Walker reiterated her claim to be a pagan. 'In day-to-day life, I worship the Earth as God – representing everything – and Nature as its spirit.'[130] Alice Walker will no doubt take responsibility for being a pagan. What is disappointing is the romantic vacuousness of her brand of paganism. 'We begin to see that we must be loved very much by whatever Creation is, to find ourselves on this wonderful Earth. We begin to recognize our sweet, generously appointed place in the makeup of the Cosmos.'[131] Readers will have noted my admiration for Alice Walker's work up till now, but her thoughts on religion are perhaps her weakest subject. For example, the lecture which she delivered at Auburn Theological Seminary, New York City on her own spiritual quest is simply pretentious ramblings lacking insight or creativity. We saw that Steve Biko's thoughts on black consciousness provided a creative and appropriate basis for Black theology in South Africa. Alice Walker's thoughts on religion provide no basis for womanist theology. However, to return to Cheryl Sanders, the point she is making is that the term womanist theology is 'a forced hybridization of two disparate concepts'. This in turn recalls for her that familiar hybrid, the mule. Zora Neale Hurston called black women 'the mule of the world', but black women looked to the Lord when their burdens were too heavy to bear. 'Not only does this scant attention to the sacred render the womanist perspective of dubious value as a context for theological discourse, but it ultimately subverts any effort to mine the spiritual traditions and resources of black women.' 'The Spirit' in Alice Walker is certainly not the Holy Spirit. Poor black women as slaves or simply as the most oppressed section of society found strength in the Spirit of Jesus. Walker's womanist specifically rebels against this resource and turns to pagan pantheism. For Sanders audacious, courageous black women of the past were inspired by their Christian faith and not by womanist autonomy.

In a final point Sanders adopts a rather conservative but defensible position on womanist sexual ethics. How are wholeness and well-being to be promoted in the black community in a period marked by the normalisation of the single-parent family and its consequences of poverty, welfare dependence, insecurity for women and vulnerability for children? 'The womanist nomenclature, however, conveys a sexual ethics that is ambivalent at best with respect to the value of heterosexual monogamy within the black community.' The Roundtable responses are very disappointing indeed. The positions the respondents advocate could be defended perfectly well under the title of black feminism. Indeed bell hooks seems to acknowledge as much, as we might expect. The paper by Sanders provided the opportunity for womanist theologians to face the question why is there so little theology in womanist theology. Could it be because the term itself is incoherent?

Notes

[1] Karl Marx and Frederick Engels, *Collected Works*, Lawrence & Wishart, 1979 (1852), vol. 11, p. 103.

[2] Mariam Schnier, *Feminism: the essential historical writings, edited with an introduction and commentaries*, Vintage Books, New York, 1972, p. 129.

[3] Simone de Beauvoir, *The Second Sex*, trans. and ed. H.M. Pashley, Penguin Books, 1983, p. 19.

[4] Schnier, *Feminism*, pp. 94–5.

[5] Betty Friedan, *The Feminine Mystique*, Penguin Books, 1971, chapter 2.

[6] Herbert Marcuse, *One Dimensional Man*, Sphere Books, 1970, p. 68.

[7] Audre Lorde, *Sister Outsider: essays and speeches*, The Cross Press, Trumansburg, NY, 1984, p. 120.

[8] Gloria Watkins, who took the nom de plume of her great grandmother. *Talking Back: thinking feminist, thinking black*, South End Press, Boston, 1989, p. 163.

[9] bell hooks, *Ain't I a Woman: black women and feminism*, Pluto Press, 1982, p. 68.

[10] hooks, *Talking Back*, p. 178.

[11] hooks, *Ain't I a Woman*, p. 81.

[12] Ibid., p. 116.

[13] Alice Walker, *In Search of Our Mothers' Gardens*, The Women's Press, London, 1994, p. 374.

[14] Lorde, *Sister Outsider*, p. 117.

[15] Ibid., p. 117; cf. hooks, *Ain't I a Woman*, p. 121.

[16] Ibid., p. 69.

[17] hooks, *Ain't I a Woman*, p. 145; cf. p. 191.

[18] Walker, *In Search of Our Mothers' Gardens*, p. 21. See also Alice Walker, *The Complete Stories*, The Women's Press, London, 1994, *passim*.

[19] hooks, *Ain't I a Woman*, p. 49.

[20] Walker, *In Search of Our Mothers' Gardens*, p. 378.

[21] Lorde, *Sister Outsider*, p. 60.

[22] Ibid., p. 51.

[23] Ibid., p. 110.

[24] Ibid., p. 112.

[25] Ibid.

[26] Ibid., pp. 110–11.

[27] hooks, *Talking Back*, p. 36.

[28] Ibid., pp. 36–7.

[29] hooks, *Ain't I a Woman*, pp. 194–5.

[30] Emily Erwin Culpepper, 'New Tools for Theology: writings by women of color', *Journal of Feminist Studies in Religion*, 4.2 (1988), p. 40.

[31] Marx/Engels, *Collected Works*, vol. 11, pp. 103–4.

[32] Alice Walker, *The Color Purple*, The Women's Press, London, 1983, p. 224.

[33] Ibid., p. 228.

[34] Ibid.

[35] Walker, *In Search of Our Mothers' Gardens*, p. 385.

[36] Ibid., p. 327.

[37] Ibid., pp. xi–xii.

[38] Alice Walker, *Anything We Love Can Be Saved: a writer's activism*, The Women's Press, London, 1997, p. 76.

[39] hooks, *Talking Back*, p. 180.

[40] Ibid., p. 182.

[41] Ibid.

[42] Walker, *The Color Purple*, p. 167.

[43] Walker, *The Complete Stories*, p. 175.

[44] Walker, *In Search of Our Mothers' Gardens*, p. 212.

[45] Lorde, *Sister Outsider*, 'Notes from a Trip to Russia'.

[46] Ibid., p. 114.

[47] John Henrik Clarke (ed.) *Marcus Garvey and the Vision of Africa*, Random House, New York, 1974, p. 156.

[48] Theodore G. Vincent, *Black Power and the Garvey Movement*, The Ramparts Press, New York, 1975, p. 132.

[49] Walker, *In Search of Our Mothers' Gardens*, p. 168.

[50] hooks, *Ain't I a Woman*, p. 189.

[51] Ibid., p. 191.

[52] hooks, *Talking Back*, p. 172.

[53] Marcia Y. Riggs, 'A Clarion Call to Awake! Arise! Act!' in Emilie M. Townes (ed.) *A Troubling in my Soul: womanist perspectives on evil and suffering*, Orbis Books, Maryknoll, NY, 1996 (1993), p. 67.

[54] Katie G. Cannon, *Black Womanist Ethics*, Scholars Press, Atlanta, Ga., 1988. Similarly Ida B. Wells-Barnett in Emilie M. Townes, *Womanist Justice, Womanist Hope,* Scholars Press, Atlanta Ga., 1993.

[55] Kelly Brown Douglas, *The Black Christ*, Orbis Books, Maryknoll, NY, 1998 (1994), p. 111.

[56] Gregory of Nyssa, *On the Divinity of the Father and the Son*, PG 46, 557 C.

[57] Douglas, *The Black Christ*, p. 113.

[58] Katie Cannon, 'Womanist Perspectival Discourse and Canon Formation', *Journal of Feminist Studies in Religion*, 9.1 (1993), p. 30.

[59] Luce Irigaray, 'Equal to Whom?' in Graham Ward (ed.) *The Postmodern God: a theological reader*, Blackwell, 1997, p. 212.

[60] Delores S. Williams, *Sisters in the Wilderness: the challenge of womanist God-talk*, Orbis Books, Maryknoll, NY, 1994 (1993), p. 12.

[61] Barbara Hilkert Andolsen, 'Roundtable: racism in the women's movement', *Journal of Feminist Studies in Religion*, 4.1 (1988), p. 110.

[62] Shawn Copeland, 'Wading through Many Sorrows' in Townes, *A Troubling in My Soul*, p. 120.

[63] Delores Williams, 'Womanist/Feminist Dialogue: problems and possibilities', *Journal of Feminist Studies in Religion*, 9.1–2 (1993), p. 69.

[64] Ibid., p. 68.

[65] Ibid., p. 72.

[66] bell hooks, *Feminist Theory: from margin to center*, South End Press, Boston, 1984.

[67] Marx/Engels, *Collected Works*, vol. 5, p. 5 and vol. 3, p. 182; my emphasis.

[68] Kelly Brown Douglas, *Sexuality and the Black Church: a womanist perspective*, Orbis Books, Maryknoll, NY, 1999, p. 19.

[69] Ibid., p. 23.

[70] Barbara Hilkert Andolsen, *Daughters of Jefferson, Daughters of Bootblacks*, Mercer University Press, Macon, Ga., 1986.

[71] Linda Mercadante, 'Roundtable: racism in the women's movement', *Journal of Feminist Studies in Religion*, 4.1 (1988), pp. 95–6.

[72] Andolsen, *Daughters of Jefferson*, p. 124.

[73] Jacquelyn Grant, *White Women's Christ and Black Women's Jesus: feminist Christology and womanist response*, Scholars Press, Atlanta, Ga., 1989, p. 3.

[74] Ibid., p. 145.

[75] Ibid., pp. 145–6.

[76] See Rosemary Radford Ruether, 'A White Feminist Response to Black and Womanist Theologies' in Linda E. Thomas (ed.) *Living Stones in the Household of God: the legacy and future of Black Theology*, Fortress Press, Minneapolis, 2004.

[77] 'The Gospel of Philip', in J.M. Robinson (ed.) *The Nag Hammadi Library in English*, E.J. Brill, 1984, p. 63. See also Elaine Pagels, *The Gnostic Gospels*, Penguin Books, 1986.

[78] Douglas, *Sexuality and the Black Church*, p. 99.

[79] Ibid., p. 107.

[80] Ibid., p. 127.

[81] Ibid., p. 124.

[82] Ibid., p. 142.

[83] Ibid., p. 143.

[84] See, for example, the journal *Theology and Sexuality* and the works of Elizabeth Stuart, Robert Goss and Marcella Althaus-Reid.

[85] *Journal of Feminist Studies in Religion*, 2.2 (1986).

[86] Ibid., pp. 103–4.

[87] *Sunday Times* (London), 4 March 1984.

[88] Douglas, *Sexuality and the Black Church*, p. 84.

[89] Ibid., p. 85.

[90] Ibid., p. 86.

[91] Alistair Kee, *Marx and the Failure of Liberation Theology*, SCM Press, 1999, pp. 172–3.

[92] Williams, *Sisters in the Wilderness*, p. 5.

[93] Ibid., p. 12.

[94] Ibid., p. 129.

[95] Ibid., p. 144.

[96] Ibid., p. 146.

[97] Williams, *Sisters in the Wilderness*, p. 149.

[98] Ibid.

[99] Ibid., p. 169.

[100] Ibid., p. 165.

[101] Copeland, 'Wading through Many Sorrows', p. 122.

[102] Williams, *Sisters in the Wilderness*, p. 182.

[103] Ibid., p. 168.

[104] Diana Hayes, *And Still We Rise: an introduction to black liberation theology*, Paulist Press, New York, 1996, p. 178.

[105] Ibid., pp. 173, 178.

[106] Benjamin DeMott, *The Imperial Middle Way: why Americans can't think about class*, William Morrow, New York, 1990.

[107] Katie Cannon, 'Unearthing Ethical Treasure: the intrusive markers of social class', *Union Theological Seminary Quarterly Review*, 53.3–4 (1999), p. 59.

[108] Ibid.

[109] Williams, *Sisters in the Wilderness*, p. 146.

[110] Townes, *A Troubling in My Soul*, p. 89.

[111] Douglas, *The Black Christ*, p. 98.

[112] Grant, *White Women's Christ and Black Women's Jesus*, p. 210.

[113] Oliver C. Cox, *Caste, Class and Race*, Doubleday, Garden City, NY, 1948.

[114] Katie Geneva Cannon, *Katie's Canon: womanism and the soul of the black community*, Continuum, New York, 1995, p. 158.

[115] bell hooks, *Where We Stand: class matters*, Routledge, 2000.

[116] Ibid., p. vii.

[117] Ibid., pp. 64–5.

[118] Ibid., p. 96.

[119] Ibid., p. 67.

[120] Ibid., p. 47.

[121] Ibid., p. 88.

[122] Ibid., p. 156.

[123] Ibid., p. 105. Traci West in dealing with violence against women, 'intimate violence', concentrates on contexts of race and gender, although 'these categories are by no means adequate or primary for describing the range of societal problems that black women confront'. She acknowledges the importantance of economics, but declines to deal with it. Traci C. West, *Wounds of the Spirit: black women, violence and resistance ethics*, New York University Press, 1999, p. 6. See also Stephanie Mitchem whose first chapter of *Introducing Womanist Theology* (Orbis Books, Maryknoll, NY 2002) is entitled 'Black Women: race, gender and class'. Race and gender are analysed, but there is no economic analysis of class relations or power in society.

[124] Cheryl Sanders, 'Roundtable: Christian ethics and theology in womanist perspective', *Journal of Feminist Studies in Religion*, 5.2 (1989), pp. 83–90. The following quotations are taken from this text.

[125] Walker, *In Search of Our Mothers' Gardens*, p. 80.

[126] Grant, *White Women's Christ and Black Women's Jesus*, p. 205.

[127] Walker, *In Search of Our Mothers' Gardens*, p. 18.

[128] Ibid., p. 265.

[129] Walker, *Anything We Love Can be Saved*, p. 4.

[130] Alice Walker, 'The Only Reason you Wanting to go to Heaven is that you have been Driven out of your Mind' in Anthony B. Pinn, *By These Hands: a documentary history of African American humanism*, New York University Press, 2001, p. 290.

[131] Ibid., p. 298.

CHAPTER 5

The Concept of Dread: Black Theology in the UK

To the Motherland

The black community in the UK represents a third tradition, very different from the two we have previously considered. We should clarify at the outset that our subject is UK blacks of African descent. Attempts have been made, on ideological grounds or for reasons of political organisation and strategic alliances, to include those from the Indian subcontinent in the category 'black'. There have been organisations such as the Institute of Race Relations, the Black People's Alliance and OWAAD (Organization of Women of Asian and African Descent) in which Asians such as A. Sivanandan and Jagmohan Joshi have taken the initiative. For the most part the Asians, coming from India and Pakistan, have formed communities distinguished by their histories, cultures, religions and economic activities. But beyond cooperation in dealing with common problems, for example in education, there has been a suspicion that the umbrella term of 'black' was an imposition on the Asian communities. Tariq Modood argued in the 1980s that the term could not serve Asians because it was rooted in pan-Africanist movements.[1] We shall still make use of the writings of Asian activists who identify with the black movement. However this may be, Black theology in the UK arises from the Afro-Caribbean community and it is to this community that we turn in this chapter.

References to individual blacks in Britain have been traced back to Roman times and for centuries there have been small groups of blacks in sea ports such as Bristol, but our story begins in 1948 with the docking of the *Empire Windrush*, bringing just over 400 Jamaican immigrants to the UK.[2] They and those who were to follow form a third tradition very different from those we have already considered. Although they are the descendents of Africans taken to the West Indies as slaves, their ancestors were never slaves in the UK. They came of their own volition, as citizens of countries which were for the most part already self-governing, in the process of becoming independent of the UK, the former imperial power. They came of their own free will and with high hopes. They came to the Motherland, an almost mythical country they had learned of at school and about which they had idealised images. Thus when they disembarked at Tilbury and found white porters offering to carry their luggage they must have thought they had got off in the wrong country. Sadly they came to their Mother, but their Mother showed little maternal regard for them. Nevertheless anyone who has spent time on the islands of the Caribbean cannot fail to be struck by the demeanour of the people. In each case it is their island and they are confident of their identity and at peace with themselves. They brought this self-confidence with them to the UK. In a series of cameo interviews in February 2004 for the Channel 4 TV series *When I Came to Britain*, original immigrants recalled their reception with dignity, attention to detail and invariably with ironic humour at the absurdities of life. Arguably the black community in the USA has never had this experience of ownership and responsibility for their country of birth.

When they arrived in the UK they came with their heads up, but their confidence in their identity was challenged in two respects. The first concerns race. It would appear that those who came to the UK during the period 1948–62, from the British Nationality Act to the Commonwealth Immigration Act, coming from self-governing former colonies, experienced racial discrimination for the first time. But this was not entirely true. There had been a great deal of racial mixing in the Caribbean, far more than in the USA, but this miscegenation was codified in great detail, classifying individuals according to the proportion of white 'blood' bequeathed from their parents. Thus a quadroon would have one black grandparent. This detailed categorisation in the Spanish territories was recorded by the anthropologist J.F. Blumenbach in the eighteenth century, extending to fourteen successive categories.[3] The experience of moving to the UK was not without a certain irony. Blacks in the Caribbean were very conscious of their place on this colour spectrum, which they recognised and maintained. Many were therefore disappointed, even distressed, to find that such fine distinctions were not observed in the UK. All cats are black at night: they found themselves classified as black alongside those to whom till recently they had been able to affect superiority.

The second challenge to their identities was the use of the term 'West Indies'. Most of the immigrants came from Jamaica but they brought with them and maintained their attitudes towards those from other islands such as Barbados, Trinidad, Antigua. That first generation, like most diasporic communities in history, fully intended to return home and it did not occur to them to set aside the suspicion even hostility arising from island stereotypes. That was done for them. In the UK they were all classified as West Indian. This name, redolent of the voyages of Christoph Colon, preserving the nomenclature of the empire, they neither used nor recognised. With surprise and incredulity they discovered that they all came from the same place, the West Indies.

How the Afro-Caribbean community came to settle in the UK is therefore very different from the circumstances of Afro-Americans in the USA. Different too from Africans in South Africa. There are disagreements about which tribes were living where when the White Tribe arrived in Kapstad, but blacks in that region were not brought from anywhere and have not gone anywhere. They lost much of their land, but they did not lose their tribal names and identities, languages and narratives, traditions of music and dance. They did not lose their ancestors, many of whom still complain that they have not been taken home. This is not the life of the Afro-Caribbean community in the UK. They have settled in large urban centres, mainly in inner city areas of London and Birmingham.

In each chapter, before turning to Black theology we have considered the features of black consciousness characteristic of that community, American (male), South African and womanist. There is nothing comparable to examine in the case of Afro-Caribbeans in the UK. In the early 1960s there was interest in the civil rights movement but the situation in the UK was not considered to be parallel. Following the visits of Malcolm X in 1965 and of Stokely Carmichael in 1967 there were attempts to set up a militant black organisation but no unified position was established. There were even abortive attempts to set up a Black Panther Movement.[4] During the anti-apartheid movement they expressed sympathy for black South Africans. More recently there has been minimal interest in womanist theory, as we shall see. In one respect it is not surprising that no black consciousness position has been developed. The community forms only 1 per cent of the UK population. It may lack that critical mass which might generate a new movement in black consciousness. And yet in earlier chapters we noted what a disproportionate contribution individuals from the Caribbean had made to negritude, black consciousness and the history of the black movement in the USA. If size does not matter, neither it seems did numbers. Martinique with a population of 300 000 produced in the same generation Aimé Césaire and Franz Fanon. There seems to be little awareness in the Afro-Caribbean community in the UK of the extraordinary tradition in which they stand. If it is at least a distant memory for some it has not generated a creative response. We shall discuss the empirical work of Claire Alexander later but her informants, second generation blacks, did not seem to locate themselves in a history of black consciousness. 'Those I spoke to rarely related their sense of identity in any pan-African sense to Africa as a whole, or the experiences of black people in the United States.'[5] We have noted earlier that sophisticated blacks in the USA could risk political correctness and refer to blacks of whom they disapproved as 'niggers'. With the same disregard for political correctness Claire Alexander's informants could use the term 'African' as a term of abuse for those who were African, but not considered to be Black British:

> you silly African used to be a good phrase to describe someone who was stupid or had done something stupid; even if they weren't an African you'd still say 'you silly African', which is saying that all Africans were silly.[6]

It is always sad to see the thought and energy which people can invest in finding ways to abuse others, especially those who in almost all respects share common problems. That said, it is refreshing to hear what Afro-Caribbeans really think of Africa today, especially in view of the romantic idealisation of a never-existent African past which we encountered continually in womanist literature. In *The Heart of the Race: black women's lives in Britain* one informant describes attitudes amongst the two sides of her family, that of her Nigerian father on the one hand and of her Jamaican mother on the other. No hint of political correctness or romantic idealism here – not even civility.

> My father's family accused him of going to Britain and marrying the descendent of slaves. My mother's family didn't want anything to do with her marrying a Black African. She had 'spoiled' herself. It had all to do with status. A beautiful brown-skin girl wasted.[7]

It is the experience of the USA that if the first generation of migrants retain (increasingly idealised) recollections of the old country, the next generation cannot wait to be absorbed into the mainline culture. This is true of the Afro-Caribbean community in the UK. The first generation were prepared to put up with much of the discrimination and racism because they assumed they were only here for a few years. Men came on their own, or both parents came to work, leaving the children with relatives. They expected that when they had made some decent money they would return to the island of their birth, to buy that prominent house they admired while growing up, to start a little business which would give them a comfortable life. Of course they were not able to make sufficient money to fulfil these dreams.

Eventually, without recognising or admitting it, they became more settled in the UK. If they could afford a visit 'home' they discovered they were treated like tourists and ripped off. Worse still is the more recent 'stigmatising of returnees' as *nouveau riche* drug-dealers.[8] That generation was not well placed to generate a distinctive movement in black consciousness. Nor it seems was the next generation. Most generations find some reason to despise and reject their parents' generation, at least until about the age they themselves become parents. The second generation despised that generation which had accepted discrimination and racism. (In many cases this was unfair, but then who ever accused the young of judicious judgement?)[9] This situation, however, has significantly changed. The second generation were born in the UK. Their belonging in the UK was brought home to them harshly when they were treated badly on their (sometimes one and only) visits to the islands. By language, dress, gesture and values they declared themselves, unconsciously and unintentionally, to be from the UK. One of Claire Alexander's informants reported that when he visited Jamaica he was called 'English white'.[10] They were in danger of being rejected by both islands. Being born in the UK apparently was not enough, at least not according to Enoch Powell. 'The West Indian does not by being born in England, become an Englishman. In law, he becomes a United Kingdom citizen by birth; in fact he is a West Indian or an Asian still.' This is quoted in Paul Gilroy's famously titled work, *There Ain't No Black in the Union Jack*.[11] White racism defined what it was to be English – and they were not English. In an interesting and nuanced distinction second generation Afro-Caribbeans describe themselves as 'Black British'. Why this is so would bear careful investigation. Within the UK the English, the majority, routinely disparage, deride and discriminate against the Scots, Welsh and Northern Irish. These minorities also identify themselves as being British. However that may be, this second generation is now an ethnic group *within* UK society and it is unlikely that they will generate a new black consciousness.

An important feature distinguishing UK and US blacks is the relative balance of race consciousness and class consciousness. As we have seen in earlier chapters, class consciousness is little mentioned in the USA and when it is it is reduced to social class. It was different with those arriving from the Caribbean. 'We arrived in Britain ready-politicised.'[12] Many of the first generation of blacks who came to the UK already stood in a socialist tradition. They were familiar with democratic, egalitarian movements which produced relatively classless societies. Blacks in the USA could not look back to the American Revolution with any sense of participation. The events of 1776 saw the establishment of civil society in which white, male, bourgeois interests were privileged. The first generation of Afro-Caribbeans entered a society which was dominated not by race but by class. They located themselves within that society by identifying with the working class, joining their trade unions and supporting the Labour Party. Needless to say they found racism within each. Although there is working-class solidarity, regardless of race, there is also working-class racism, a complex mixture of the fear that immigrants will steal their jobs and the psychological satisfaction of being able to treat someone else below them as badly as they are treated by those directly above them. Within the trade union movement they found it difficult to become delegates or officers and thus were not able to place their concerns on the agenda. Although there were several highly publicised riots and street confrontations with the police in the 1960s, 1970s and 1980s, increasingly there was a recognition that the cause of black people could only be furthered by constitutional means. This meant by working within the Labour Party to achieve office in local and general elections. At the same time that Audre Lorde was issuing her warning about cooperation A. Sivanandan was using almost identical language to recommend it. 'We don't have the tools, brothers and sisters; we've got to get the tools from the system itself and hope that in the process five out of ten of us don't become corrupt.'[13]

Although black people had consistently voted for the Labour Party, their needs and concerns were not priorities for the party policies or leadership. In 1983 the Labour Party Black Section was set up, followed a decade later by the Black Socialist Society. The institutionalisation of black politics arose from a declining faith in extra-parliamentary action and at the same time furthered that decline. It was not that the radical agenda was carried into the Labour Party, but rather that black politics was now carried out in an institutional form, as Shukra observes.

> The emphasis on organisational matters had the effect of making political debates secondary to organisational questions and tied activists into a mesh of Labour Party bureaucratic structures.[14]

The reward was that in the elections of 1987 hundreds of black local councillors were elected and, 40 years after *Windrush*, the first black MPs were finally elected to parliament. The cost was 'black representation, rather than real mobilisation'. As one unnamed activist commented, 'We do not have black MPs. We have Labour MPs who happen to be black.'[15] With the landslide New Labour victory of 1997 one more black MP was elected and three blacks entered the House of Lords: a small price to pay for getting blacks off the streets. Small wonder that black activists such as Kalbir Shukra believe that the elected radicals are now state representatives, their priorities implementing government policies. She makes the dramatic claim that 'Radical black politics in Britain is dead.'[16]

It would not be surprising therefore if there were no dynamic, new development of black consciousness in the UK. From the time of the *Empire Windrush* there has been a commitment to the political cause, even to the class struggle, but the outcome has been absorption. As one unattributed source notes, 'My impression was always that the left was genuinely concerned to mobilise the black community, but into *their* political battles.'[17] They arrived with British passports but that was not enough.

> All of us ended up being disillusioned with the kind of integration that was on offer; some became disillusioned too with the organised left in British politics. What united many of us then, and continues to do so, is a commitment to socialism which is indivisible from the commitment to race equality.[18]

On balance class was a greater determinant of life than race. Race analysis would not solve the fundamental problems of urban life. In Stuart Hall's famous phrase, 'race is the modality in which class is lived'.[19] For some two dogmatic positions offered themselves at the same time. The Communist Party displayed 'the stubborn class-before-race position'[20] while Black Power displayed the opposite. At this point there is an interesting parallel not with the USA but with South Africa. We recall Motlhabi's focus on power rather than race. Trevor Carter makes something of the same point. 'The interests of the working class movement and the black movement do coincide, given that both lay claim to their fair share of material power and wealth, which would entail a massive redistribution of both.'[21] The experience of blacks in the UK was that this unity was threatened whenever the white working class was required to begin this process of sharing. 'The relationship between the left and black people is like the relationship between parent and child. They always know what's best for us.'[22] The struggle was not about race in isolation, but about democracy. Small wonder that anyone reading the US womanist litany of gender, race and class in the UK context should find the element of class analysis so weak and undeveloped.

The immigrants of the 1940s and 1950s therefore looked to politics to deal with discrimination. It seems now as if the arrival of the *Windrush* was like the opening of the flood gates. Yet it brought fewer than 500 Jamaicans. By 1962 there were 500 000.[23] Some came on contract, for example to work for London Transport. They disappeared into poor housing areas mainly in London. The 1948 British Nationalities Act was not intended to restrict immigration. It was to address the fact that countries in the British empire were becoming independent and developing their own citizenship laws. In order to head off further moves towards independence the Act declared that all citizens of colonies and former colonies were British subjects. It was not anticipated that large numbers from these colonies would take up their right to live in the UK.[24] However, in 1967, during Kenya's Africanisation policy, increasing numbers of African-Asians took up this right. The 1968 Commonwealth Immigrants Act was rushed through parliament within a week. Even passport holders did not have the right to come to the UK unless there was a family connection, such as a parent or grandparent. This discriminated against black Africans in favour of white settlers and those from the Old (white) Commonwealth. The legislation was a response to public apprehension at the lack of control on black immigration. Throughout the twentieth century the UK had generously received immigrants from a variety of European countries, including the Republic of Ireland. Non-white immigration became a political issue, because it had become a racial issue. The year 1967 saw the appearance of the National Front, unifying various fascist groups including the British National Party and the League of Empire Loyalists. In 1968 Enoch Powell, the former Conservative cabinet minister, played the race card and exhibited his credentials as a former classics don at Cambridge. 'As I look ahead, I am filled with foreboding. Like the Roman, I seem to see "the River Tiber foaming with much blood".'[25] The aquatic metaphor was recalled by Margaret Thatcher in a speech delivered a decade later. Powell had called for repatriation of immigrants, she referred to the fear of 'swamping' felt by some whites because of the growing black communities concentrated in some urban areas of the UK. In 1992 the Conservative MP Sir Nicholas Fairbairn expanded on the image by claiming that under a Labour government Britain would be 'swamped with immigrants of every race and, on any excuse, of asylum or bogus marriage or just plain deception'.[26] This introduced the association of immigration with wrongdoing. By implication legal immigrants and British born blacks were all part of the same 'problem'. By a curious reversal those who suffered racial discrimination were somehow responsible for its disruption of society. John Solomos summarises the counter-attack, the view that 'the greatest threat to the development of racial harmony lies in the politicisation of racial issues by black activists and politicians and by race relations professions'.[27] This exonerated both white racism and government legislation at a stroke. As legislation covering immigration became more racial, other legislation outlawed discrimination based on race. The 1965 Race Relations Act set up the Race Relations Board to receive complaints of discrimination. It was followed by further acts in 1968 and 1976. But the legislation on equal opportunities was compromised by the racist elements in immigration legislation. As John Solomos observes, while immigration control is enforced by a government department, the Home Office, the enforcement of race relations legislation was delegated to agencies such as the Commission for Racial Equality. Consequently, 'instead of equal opportunity impinging upon every aspect of every department's business, the issue has, by virtue of the creation of the CRE, been successfully compartmentalised, isolated and marginalised'.[28] As Andrew Pilkington concludes, 'it is scarcely revealing to discover that immigration policy has proved more effective than race relations legislation'.[29]

Up to this point it has been convenient to speak of 'the Afro-Caribbean community' but this essentialism must be viewed with suspicion. It is now of limited usefulness and may serve the purposes of those who wish to create and maintain stereotypes, a crude example of which is given by Harry Goulbourne.

> Thus, when individuals commit a crime, if they are white people they are portrayed as individuals who assume responsibility for their actions; if however, they are Afro-Caribbeans, this is not only trumpeted by the media but their individual actions become the collective responsibility of all who are designated Afro-Caribbean.[30]

It would be interesting to consider our three categories of race, class and gender in relation to stereotypes. This can be most effectively done through considering empirical studies which undermine the stereotypes.

The first is *The Art of Being Black: the creation of Black British youth identities*. It arose from studies of groups of young Afro-Caribbean males in three areas of London. Academically the project was well conceived and professionally carried out. Beyond that it is itself a work of art, beautifully crafted and made possible in no small part by the perceptiveness, sensitivity and humour of the author, Claire Alexander. For example, the whole project seems unlikely: a young woman being allowed access to the lives of a small group of black men. It was made possible only because she was Asian and therefore neither black nor white. When they went out to clubs they would certainly not take their black girlfriends with them. She was allowed to accompany them – on condition that she dressed as instructed – and seems faintly amused that they saw her as a trophy. (Some feminists might be appalled but I should be prepared to trust Claire Alexander's instincts on this one. Feminism and humour need not be strangers.)

As might be expected the study deals with home, work, social life, masculinity (the peer group) and masculinity (attitudes to women). The picture which emerges is not informed or delineated by race, but rather culture. And 'picture' it is, for this is indeed 'the art of being black'. The young men are in process of creating their identities, in part through the surrounding culture, in part in spite of it, in part against it. As Andrew Pilkington observes elsewhere, 'individuals are cultural products as well as cultural producers'.[31] Thus he avoids essentialism and that is also Alexander's point.

> By failing to deal adequately with the idea of black culture, and retreating to theoretical notions of 'race', research on Black British youth has largely consigned them to the margins, cast and miscast as a series of folk devils and policy problems.[32]

To begin with race as the point of departure is what Martin Barker has described as 'pseudo-biological culturalism'.[33] These young men can be understood as Black British, where 'black' refers to culture not to race. Race tells us nothing about them. However, the application by others to them of this 'pseudo-biological' category has disastrous consequences.

> Black youth in particular have been typecast into a role of almost pathological dislocation – culturally confused, alienated from both their parents and society at large, and implacably hostile.[34]

Alexander, writing as an Asian, is well aware that Asians living in Britain are considered to have their own distinctive and distinguishing cultures. Yes, there may well be stereotypes of accent, dress, custom, gesture, diet, familial relations, but identity is not determined by race even though they are clearly not Anglo-Saxon. By contrast black youths, born in Britain, are routinely distinguished by race even though their actual lives are entirely produced through a dialectical relationship with mainline youth culture. They are defined by race not because it is so, but because the dominant culture says so. Culture is fluid, allowing for flexibility, reflexivity, agency, action and reaction. But race is fixed, determined, increasingly irrelevant, given to serving stereotypical misrepresentation and ideological interests. Claire Alexander chooses culture above race.

> My study, then, is of 'culture'; not essentialized, fixed, and traditional heritage but a continually created and 'invented' tradition, which reimagines itself in each mind and life.[35]

The lives of her informants are sympathetically presented: she constantly forgives their absurd pretentiousness. But absent from the picture are such matters as politics, religion and sport, the three no-go areas of drinks parties. Was their lack of interest in sport really a reflection on the fact that Alexander found continual arguments about football boring? Did she censor anything else? Her informants were very conventional in their views that for long-term relationships the races should remain separate. How does that square with Pilkington's (frankly incredible) claim that for Afro-Caribbeans born in the UK, 50 per cent of men have a white partner and 33 per cent of black women have a white partner?[36]

Pilkington provides a convenient point of entry into our second empirical study, this time of class. He has written extensively on the same essentialism that Alexander challenges, exemplified in education. Afro-Caribbean boys fall behind in secondary school. Pilkington observes 'that the concept of underachievement implicitly blames the group deemed to be underachieving' and thereby absolves the education system.[37] Shukra sees a similar agenda with the introduction of 'black history' weeks in the 1990s.

> [This] may have originated as a protest against the exclusion of African experiences but it developed into reinforcing the idea that the individual's lack of identity rather than racism is the source of particular social problems.[38]

This reinforces the double 'cultural essentialism' (Rattansi)[39] that all Afro-Caribbean boys are less able when compared to the normative cultural essentialism of white boys. This is a particular instance of stereotyping and the assumption that all Afro-Caribbeans can be presented as 'ethnically homogenous'.[40] The convenient myth that all Afro-Caribbeans by virtue of being just and only that can be understood as members of the one community does not take account of other factors – educational, economic, political – which attach individual black people to other communities in the wider society. Sharon Daye takes up this issue in her empirical study *Middle-Class Blacks in Britain*. She refers to the strategy of 'co-optation' which avoids assimilation of the whole black population by granting privileges to the black bourgoisie to keep them from becoming leaders of black dissent. We met this strategy in Chapter 1 in dealing with the French, as opposed to British, colonial policy. Daye claims that empirical study reveals this to be the case only in a very few instances. First generation middle-class blacks have emerged from the working-class majority and are but a bachelor's degree away from poverty and welfare. They are not entrenched in the middle class and probably rely on the wife's employment to prevent them falling back. (Does this simple point mean that a higher proportion of the black middle class live in a two-by-two nuclear family? Indeed is such a nuclear family a necessary though not sufficient economic condition to be middle class?) Even so Daye suggests that this means that middle-class blacks do not automatically conform to white middle-class norms. They retain a race consciousness at odds with their new class.

> Of the 120 men and women who took part in this study a significant proportion were unable to reconcile the issue of 'race' and class and perceived themselves within the British context primarily as being Black, and as a consequence *external to the British class structure*.[41]

Since being English is one of the conditions for being middle class (in England), it is by definition impossible for the black middle class to be accepted as middle class. They are indeed 'external to the British class structure'. By objective indicators they could be deemed to be middle class, 'but they were not accepted as such by the class of arrival'.[42] In the last chapter we noted Alice Walker observe that middle-class blacks felt no responsibility for poor blacks. In 2003 *Beyond the Color Line* was screened, a TV documentary series in which Louis Gates visited various black communities in the USA. The last one was an entirely black middle-class gated-community in Atlanta. Daye draws an interesting conclusion about the future of the black middle class in the UK. The small gap between the black middle class and the black majority could grow wider.

> If this situation does emerge it is likely that we would begin to see a situation where the majority of those black people who have managed to secure a relatively stable economic future for themselves and their children will become more insular and seek to protect their own positions rather than being concerned about the lot of the majority of black workers at the bottom of the labour market. The black middle class would come to represent a class fraction of a 'racial' group as opposed to a 'racial' fraction of the British middle class.[43]

If there is no creative critical consciousness emerging from the new Black British working class, it seems even less likely that it will emerge from the new black middle class.

Race, class and now gender. In the best traditions of sisterhood *The Heart of the Race: black women's lives in Britain* was written jointly by Beverley Bryan, Stella Dadzie and Suzanne Scafe. Appropriately it was published by Virago Press. In medieval times a 'virago' was a manlike (*vir*) woman, a bold, quarrelsome shrew or scold. 'Virago' recalls us to a critical but carping period of women's liberation.

'Womanish' by comparison points us to a much more positive, subtle, nuanced, self-confidant exploration of black women's lives and their open-heartedness. It must be said that ironically *The Heart of the Race* exhibits little warm-heartedness, affection or celebration. The issues are real and serious, but it does tend to fall into the stereotype of the scold. *The Heart of the Race* contains many passages in which (anonymous) black women have their say. However, black women in the UK have little interest in womanism, as we shall see later. Their lives have been characterised by organising for the struggle and in this they have formed strategic alliances, with Asian women and with black men. OWAAD (the Organization of Women of Asian and African Descent) was relatively short-lived (1978–83) but articulated the thinking behind these alliances even before womanist writers appeared in the USA.

> We're not feminists – we reject that label because we feel that it represents a white ideology. In our culture the term is associated with an ideology and practice which is anti-men. Our group is not anti-men at all ... When we discuss, organise, campaign ... we are placing our oppression in the context of racism and imperialism. We're not just addressing women or black women ... We don't alienate men because they put down black women, because we recognise that the source of that is white imperialist culture.[44]

It is a matter of priorities and perspectives, as another informant indicates. Sexual preferences and even male violence she describes as 'luxury issues'.

> What's the point of taking on male violence if you haven't dealt with State violence? Or rape, when you can see black people's bodies and lands being raped everyday by the system? If women want to sit around discussing who they go to bed with, that must be because it's the most important thing in their lives and that's all they want to deal with. In my mind, that's a privilege most of us don't have.[45]

She is not against the women's movement but it is seldom concerned with race and when it is then it is only a matter for discussion. 'If you're talking about racism, you're talking about survival issues.'[46] Or again the women's peace movement declares itself against violence, because violence might disrupt their lives. But 'seeing your child slowly starve to death is violence'.[47]

In *The Empire Strikes Back* Hazel Carby points out that when white women researchers go to African villages their questions reflect their own feminist agenda rather than the priorities of the local women.

> In some instances, when the women would like to have piped water in the village, they may be at the same time faced with a researcher interested in investigating power and powerlessness in the household. In yet another situation, when women are asking for access to agricultural credit, a researcher on the scene may be conducting a study on female circumcision.[48]

Priorities and perspectives: the women were perfectly aware of what was going on. *The Heart of the Race* includes interviews which deal with sexism amongst young black men. What could be more hurtful for young women joining a group to dedicate themselves in time and effort to dealing with a matter affecting the black community, than to find themselves 'regarded as sexual prey'.

> So you had the thing where every new woman member was regarded as easy prey. Some of the brothers were called 'flesh heads' because people knew what they were about. It didn't mean that they weren't serious about their work but it just meant that they had a 'leisure-time sporting activity which was chasing women ... Brothers were hauled up and disciplined when what they needed was political education – to read, study and discuss that woman question and to confront their own sexism. No attempt was made to seriously take up women's issues, they just weren't considered immediately pressing.[49]

Solidarity was always being undermined, as illustrated in Iyamide Hazeley's poem *Political Union*. 'You call me "Sister" Brother/ yet I know/ that it is simply a psychological lever to prise apart my legs.'[50]

When we listen to the voices of black individuals and groups we are less likely to fall into the easy acceptance of racial stereotypes and cultural essentialism. As already noted, Hazel Carby finds both present in feminist theory. The familiar categories look very different from a black perspective. They presuppose the cultural normativity of white experience.

> The model of the white nuclear family, which rarely applies to black women's situation, is the measure by which they are pathologized and stands as a more progressive structure to the one in which they live.[51]

The white family is discussed in terms of internal relations: it is assumed that its security is guaranteed. By contrast, 'the black family has been a site of political and cultural resistance to racism'.[52] But in these internal relations Carby points out black men have not held the same patriarchal power established for white men. The term 'patriarchy' is now taken to be a synonym for 'male dominance'. In this situation the concept of 'dependency' looks very different. White women might suffer from dependency. For black women the chance would be a fine thing. These counter-stereotypical relationships are uncovered by Claire Alexander's study, *The Art of Being Black*, to which we have already referred. Her group of young black men are very sensitive to the balance of power with their partners. The context, however, is not simply domestic, but reflects wider socio-political dimensions. Alexander illustrates this by quoting the writer Dona Kogbara.

> If you go out with a nice white window cleaner, you are really slapping black men in the face for preferring 'white trash'. But if you opt for a white man who is Somebody, you are allying yourself with a descendent of supremacist forces that colonised, enslaved and raped us.[53]

The young black men felt the need to own their women. They themselves might be playing away from home but they insisted on fidelity from their women. As much as anything this was because otherwise they would have lost face before the rest of the group. They would also be subject to ridicule if their partner was a 'tyrant'. 'This acknowledged the primacy of the women within the domestic sphere, both socially and often economically.'[54] Alexander makes a subtle distinction concerning stereotypes.

> The women involved in these relationships were always regarded as individuals; they were never approached as representatives of other categories. The same cannot be said of the public sphere, in which women were important primarily as representatives of other groups and other interests.[55]

Perhaps the most surprising counter-stereotype material concerns the respect the black men had for their women. The stereotype is well served by their exploitative view of white women when they went clubbing in the West End of London or when they indulged in opportunist sex with black 'bitches'. However, their attitude was very different to partners and possible partners. 'When the boys met Angelina and Eleanor on two separate occasions, the women were treated with a respect and deference I had rarely witnessed before.'[56] They also disapproved of one of their number who had begun a new relationship but had not ended the old one. 'Indeed, all of the boys felt that the domestic environment should be maintained at all costs, especially if there were children involved.'[57] Alexander observed very respectful behaviour towards women in the family environment, extending to gesture and language.

> Black women were thus associated with notions of family and the community. Integral to this association was the concept of 'respect'; that black women were to be revered in their roles as mothers and culture-bearers.[58]

I can imagine a few raised eyebrows among some black women: which planet is this? It does, however, indicate the complexity of black culture: nothing can be deduced from the term 'race', certainly nothing to do with the production of identity and the transmission of values.

Reality and race. What we are seeing here is a counter-stereotypical exploration of a non-essentialised Black Reality. It is more sophisticated and nuanced than essentialised Race Analysis. The Reality is defined by the parameters of urban, industrial more often commercial life. I believe this is why there is little interest in womanism among black women in the UK. 'In search of our mothers' gardens' says it all. Womanism arises from a romantic *imaginaire* which owes a great deal to the nostalgia of the US black middle class. The mama is as much a stereotype in black literature as in white. She loves roundness because she is round. She has green fingers and can get anything to grow – flower, shrub or vegetable – because she worked on the land. She is strong enough to solve everyone's problems: no weeping head is turned away from that ample bosom. This woman does not exist for black women in the UK, except in the public library. But when did she still exist in the USA? In the early 1960s, before Black Power and before feminism, I was a graduate student in New York and worked as a volunteer in the East Harlem Protestant Parish. The senior pastor at the Church of the Ascension was Letty Russell. She was the complete leader: brilliant mind, Yale trained scholar, insightful biblical preacher, tough as old boots when she needed to be, but without a shred of romanticism she was dedicated to black kids around East 106th Street. (I never saw Letty Russell bettered by any man. She was a feminist *avant le mot*. I admired her more for who she was before she adopted some of the feminist traits.) Letty organised the kids to be bussed up-state to a farm. It must have seemed like the planet Zanussi to them. In their world the only glimpse of grass and trees was the north end of Central Park, recreation area of choice for mugging and cruising. In search of our mothers' gardens indeed, and that was 40 years ago. In the USA blacks came north two, three, four generations ago to inhabit brownstone walk-ups and concrete high rises. The nearest garden was the 24-hour corner store. Blacks came to the UK from the islands and made straight for the centre of the largest cities. No bucolic *pastorale* for them. It is Black Reality that makes them suspicious of womanist archaeology.

The same rejection of white feminism is to be found in the UK as in the USA. The movement among feminists to 'reclaim the night' sought to mobilise women to march through predominantly black communities, calling for better policing to make the streets safe for women. There was resentment by black women at the implication that it was only in black areas that women were unsafe. More than that, given the perceived harassment of women by the police, the proposal to have more police on the streets was not well received. The concept of 'womanism' was seen to include some of the concerns of black women in the UK, but there was a reluctance to substitute it for 'black feminist', as indicated by the Camden and Islington Black Sisters Group.

> Black womynism: [*sic*] is it goodbye to black feminism? Many of us never even said 'hello' ... we can develop our own philosophy and ideology to suit ourselves and to guide our practice, black womynism is about living in dignity. It is about equal responsibility and our right and ability to determine our destiny. Black womynism has to be about the daily lives of ordinary black women as opposed to the static nature of feminism which does not seem to be going anywhere constructively.[59]

The implication is that they can do their own thing without taking on the baggage of other people's concepts. The factors impacting on 'the daily lives of ordinary black women' are more extensive than those indicated by womanism.

> Such factors have to be examined not in isolation, but in relation to the whole oppressive capitalist system. The struggle for women's liberation has to be part of the concrete struggle against class oppression. As women, we cannot consider our oppression and exploitation separately from either the international oppression and exploitation perpetrated by international capital in our countries of origin or from our experiences here in Britain. *Womynism does not embrace the totality of our struggle.*[60]

The third of Walker's fourfold definition of womanist is 'universalist'. One woman's universalist is another's self-concern.

A more sustained reflection on the issue has been undertaken by Helen (charles)'s 'The Language of Womanism: re-thinking difference'. The plantation name (charles) is placed in brackets. Why not (helen)? (Far from being a Bantu or Yoruba name Helen associates the bearer with Helena, mother of the Emperor Constantine, one of the first Christian tourists to Palestine.) She begins with doubts about feminism, a concept or even a movement going out of fashion by the end of the 1980s. It became fashionable to preface it with reference to some group previously not envisaged in the original formulation: black feminism, disabled feminism. Charles is not hopeful about such hybrids. Feminism does not provide a sufficiently agreed common platform from which to hear other voices. Another agreed platform was required. 'When Alice Walker came up with the idea of a special name for black women, her term "womanist" provided an equivalent to "feminist".'[61] Perhaps there was too close a parallel. If feminist was restricted to US white women, is womanist going to be any more 'universalist'? 'It is important to consider at which point womanism as a North American experience departs from the experience of black feminists globally.'[62] While Walker seeks to be sexually inclusive, there is no reference to class and no international dimension. Does 'universalist' refer simply to a reaching out to a broader sexual agenda? And does this kind of universalism serve 'to encourage an essentialist notion based solely on instinct, and in "nature", rather than in combination with activism or socio-political consciousness'?[63] Charles is therefore suspicious of the usefulness of the term 'womanist', not least because she believes its undermining of feminism leads towards another ghetto.

> How easy it would be to assume that the advent of womanism had absolutely nothing to do with anyone but black women, so that within a presumed homogeneous group of women it should stay.[64]

She therefore muses on 'the possibility of a post-black feminist ideology'.[65] Her reading of Walker's fourth definition takes an ominous turn.

> Womanism might be to feminism what purple is to lavender, but it must be remembered that when lavender wanes annually from mid to late summer, the first task of the western gardener is to lop off its purple flowers so as to benefit the lavender as a plant.[66]

Jesus in Dreadlocks

Such is the secularity of academic life in the UK that religion is not regarded as an important research topic amongst those concerned with the majority community. However, as we have already noted, this is true also of research within the black community. Martin Baumann makes a relevant point in his study of the diasporic community of Hindus in Trinidad.

> However, in most studies of migrant groups that explore the retention of their peculiarity, the factor of religion goes unmentioned. Instead, the academically invented concept of ethnicity is given priority as the key factor responsible for a migrant group's persistence and survival in the new, socio-culturally different environment ... Religion is no longer conceptualized as a possible variable ... Other than in studies of contemporary terrorism, the possibility that religion can have any relevance for present-day, modern societies is not taken seriously, by most social scientists. Religion is thought of as a private affair only, not as a

> driving force for entire groups and a significant symbol system of identification, demarcation and support.[67]

Counter-intuitively there is evidence that amongst diasporic communities religion becomes more not less important, but is also subject to transformation in response to the new context. Insofar as the black community in the UK stems originally from the Caribbean diaspora the agenda for Black theology in the UK is twofold. It has to demonstrate that religion is an important factor in the life and identity of that community but also that as a contextual theology it is a progressive force with regard to the well-being of the community. No one has addressed these issues more consistently, vigorously, creatively or critically than Robert Beckford, who teaches theology at the University of Birmingham. Publishing a book almost every year his project has been to develop an increasingly comprehensive Black theology for the UK. His work is characterised by the variety of his dialogue partners.

Theology in UK universities has become a largely secular discipline. Increasingly faculties are staffed by men and women who are not ordained by any church, indeed who may have little interest in any church. Within the modern university theology has conformed to secular norms. Its methods are exercised in common with departments of literature, history and philosophy. These disciplines are its dialogue partners, not the churches. It is driven by government publishing targets rather than questions of relevance for believers or efficacy for the churches. Nor is this some recent development, merely the final outcome of a procedure recommended by a line of scholars which can be traced back through Benjamin Jowett in *Essays and Reviews*, 'Interpret the Scripture like any other book', John Toland 'nor is there any different rule to be followed in the Interpretation of Scripture from what is common to all other books', back to G.E. Lessing himself 'read the Bible just as you read Livy'.[68] This approach was already condemned by Karl Barth in the Preface to the second edition (1921) of his *Epistle to the Romans*.

> I have nothing whatever to say against historical criticism. I recognize it, and once more state quite definitely, that it is both necessary and justified. My complaint is that recent commentators confine themselves to an interpretation of the text which seems to me to be no commentary at all, but merely the first step towards a commentary.[69]

The first characteristic of the work of Robert Beckford is that it takes that next step. He is familiar with both biblical criticism and the history of doctrine, but he seeks to use these resources to develop a contextual theology which takes account of the experience of the black community and addresses their situation. With no diminution of academic integrity nevertheless his dialogue partner is the Black church: 'the experiences of Black people in Britain become our primary text'.[70] But even this text is subject to critical appraisal. Beckford is highly critical of the anti-intellectualism found in many black ministries. 'The major disadvantage of prioritising experience at the beginning of the theological task is that without the mediating benefit of tradition and reason it can lead to dangerous, destructive and errant theological interpretations.'[71] (Womanists from the previous chapter might ponder this observation.)

A second feature of the work of Robert Beckford, already hinted at, is the level of his critical evaluation. He is well connected with black churches, community projects, religious traditions, activists, artists and musicians. He is insightful in identifying their strengths and what they can or might contribute to the black community and to his project of Black theology. But in virtually every case he ends with a nuanced criticism of their continuing assumptions, practices, attitudes or behaviour which fall short of the ideal. In previous chapters we have noted the sacrilising of blacks within Black theology, a reluctance to criticise. Not so with Beckford. He is well aware of the weaknesses found in the black community, including chauvinism towards women, lack of affirmation of the disabled, homophobia towards the non-heterosexual. But with refreshing honesty (for me, reminiscent of Albert Cleage himself) Beckford is speaking in love: it is broken and it needs fixing. This criticism in love is seen in his consistent observations about the Black church itself. This is his dialogue partner and he criticises because he cares. He offers a new Black theology, credible and empowering. The theology they have is essentially colonial, frequently irrelevant, on occasion unworthy. Are they attentive to his criticism? Are they wearied by his constant cajoling? I suspect they manage to ignore it, or dismiss it as 'academic' (a term of abuse). But all credit to him, Robert Beckford is still there in the worshipping community, raising his voice. Few academic theologians see this as their vocation today.

Another feature of Beckford's work is that he presents Black theology as a political theology and it is on this basis that he frequently criticises the Black church. As we have seen, the first generation of Caribbean immigrants assumed that they would be in the UK for a limited number of years only. They therefore endured racial attitudes together with discrimination in housing and employment without feeling any responsibility for addressing these issues. Their religion was therefore restricted to their individual lives and the immediate family and community relations. It did not project them into the community at large. Robert Beckford's parents came from Jamaica and he grew up in the UK. His generation therefore identifies 'the failure of the majority of Black Churches to address political issues past and present'.[72] Britain is their home and they have the right to expect to live without the discrimination or harassment which seemed to be accepted by the older generation and certainly was not addressed by the churches. Berdyaev famously said, 'If I go hungry it is a physical evil; if others go hungry it is a moral evil.' We might add, 'and if some go hungry and others do not, it is a political evil'. Beckford acknowledges that the older generation helped their neighbours when in need, but he says that 'Many Black Christians fail to make the distinction between social welfare and social justice.'[73] They do not distinguish between the moral and the political. They do not ask what systems and practices of injustice make gestures of social welfare necessary. Thus he has yet to hear a sermon in a black church addressing the political issues which affect the lives of the black community. Nor is he likely to when pastors are preaching from a theology which focuses on personal piety and sexual morality. In the Black church in the UK 'we have not yet developed explicit political theologies that unequivocally engage with the social policies and economic strategies that stalk Black communities'.[74] Thirty years ago some of us were involved in a movement to identify the 'spiritual dimensions to political struggle'.[75] The spiritual without the political is a retreat, unworthy of faith, but politics without the spiritual is just management, which develops into bureaucracy and threatens to become tyranny. I see something of this dialectic in the work of Robert Beckford. He wishes to convince the Black church that Christians must take responsibility as Christians for political realities. Whatever affects the lives of the black community must be addressed by Christians. At the same time Beckford lives on the streets. He sees the harm and hurt of black youth. He would like to demonstrate to them that the Black church is concerned for their lives and is lending its considerable weight to changing their situation. One of the central concerns of his first book was 'to show that Black culture contains a prophetic and spiritual dimension'.[76]

As indicated above, a further feature of Robert Beckford's work is not his scathing criticism of those with whom he disagrees, but his nuanced criticism of those whom he first praises. It is a constant feature and those who read his books recognise the pattern. Does he praise this writer for her insights, then be prepared at the end of his exposition for a devastating critique. Does he admire some initiative on the streets, then be assured that his positive assessment will end with identifying some weakness. Even so, it must all be seen in the context of his passion for the cause, the changing of the Black church and the service of the whole black community. It is very different from that destructive criticism so much a feature of academic life as people try to build their reputations on the ruins of others'. Beckford is fulsome in his praise of Valentina Alexander's 'Breaking Every Fetter: to what extent has the Black led church in Britain developed a theology of liberation?' This PhD dissertation from the University of Warwick is available on microfilm, but it is awkward to read the text and the endnotes at the same time. Unfortunately it has never been published. Books on the theology of peoples at the ends of the earth are published constantly in the UK: why is there so little interest in a home grown theology of an indigenous community? Elsewhere Beckford acknowledges that in his experience 'unwitting, institutionalized racism is also at work in England's theological colleges and universities'.[77] Alexander's dissertation was written in the Department of Caribbean Studies and the models of liberation which she examines come from North and South America and an 'Emancipatory Theology of the Caribbean'. Has the Black church in the UK developed a comparable theology through which to break the fetters of oppression in this country? She refers to conferences held under the auspices of the African Caribbean Evangelical Alliance, the work of the New Testament Church of God, black feminists including Sonia Hicks, Kate Coleman and Yvonne Hall and theologians such as Ronald Nathan and Robert Beckford himself. She acknowledges the development of a liberation spirituality which has decolonised theology and raised awareness about the need to confront oppression, but there is something missing.

The most interesting categories developed by Alexander are passive radicalism and active radicalism. There is radicalism in parts of the black church, but it is essentially a response to forces of oppression. It is passive radicalism, a theology for survival. What is needed is a more proactive stance, one which employs a more sophisticated social analysis of the roots of oppression. This active radicalism depends on a theology which is prophetic. As noted, Beckford is fulsome in his praise of the project of Valentina Alexander but it requires to be supplemented in two respects. The first is that it is too dependent on theologies from elsewhere. Although she advocates contextualism in theory her work does not allow a distinctively Black British theology to emerge. The second criticism is that Alexander's own position does not illustrate the critical theology she describes. 'Any meaningful Black British political theology must take active radicalism seriously but provide it with a holistic theology to replace the vague liberational spirituality Alexander describes.'[78] Beckford uses Alexander's terminology to evaluate otherwise promising developments. The Mile End New Testament Church, in the East End of London, displays a broader understanding of ministry, addressing for instance the marginalisation of women. It moves towards radicalism, but of the passive kind. The largely respectable middle-class congregation is content with an approach which is apolitical. The Ruach Ministeries in Brixton, south London for all its strengths he finally considers to be passive rather than active, failing to be prophetic. His criticism even extends to the Black Theology Support Group, instrumental in the founding of the *Journal of Black British Theology*, which Beckford describes as 'the most advanced Black theological centre in the UK context. Nowhere else do Black theologians "do theology"'.[79] As an academic group it is something of a mirror image of the Black church.

> I want to suggest that the implicit spirituality in the explicit politics of the BTSG is an inversion of the implicit politics within the explicit spirituality of Black churches. Neither approach creates a healthy relationship between spirituality and political action. This is because neither approach allows a creative and explicit spirituality of liberation.[80]

If the theologians have interpreted the world in various ways but the point is to change it, then Beckford proposes a Liberation Theological Praxis. With this he is fully armed with a rather bewildering array of concepts.

> Therefore, in terms of LTP, the BTSG offers limited liberation praxis. Whereas Mile End represented *passive active radicalism* and Ruach, *reactive active radicalism*, from my perspective the BTSG represents a *cognitive active radicalism.* That is to say, its focus is primarily intellectual radicalism. However, intellectual development by itself is only limited challenge. I argue that *cognitive active radicalism* is synonymous with the survival tradition in Black faith. Survival nurtures full-blown liberation from oppression, similarly, *cognitive active radicalism* nurtures full *active radicalism.* Hence, in many ways the BTSG has not moved beyond the limitations of passive radicalism within the Black Church. Instead it has reconfigured the weaknesses of passive radicalism in academic clothes.[81]

There is no denying the incisiveness of Beckford's criticisms, but there is a danger of final isolation. This may be inevitable since I believe he is a world class black theologian who lacks theological dialogue partners in the relatively small Caribbean community in the UK. Indeed he seems to acknowledge just that when discussing his project of Dread Pentecostal Theology. 'The current Black academia does not have the capacity to meet the demands of DPT.'[82] We might mention, for example, Emmanuel Lartey (then teaching in Birmingham) who offers a list of ten characteristics of Black British theology and a seven point agenda. However, they are purely formal lists with little content. Some of the points are aspirational. If Beckford's purpose is 'to show that Black culture contains a prophetic and spiritual dimension' it is not surprising that his dialogue partners include artists and musicians.

Freud once wrote of 'the omnipotence of thought' in Christianity. We might speak more specifically of the tyranny of the word, not the Word made flesh but precisely its opposite – the word of what Nietzsche called 'theoretical man'. Since most Christians throughout the world have been, perhaps still are, illiterate, more attention should be paid to aesthetics rather than epistemology. No doubt, but that is not Robert Beckford's point. When in 1606 Caravaggio completed *The Death of the Virgin* the Camelite monks, who had commissioned the painting, rejected it. They did not do so on aesthetic grounds but because of the powerful and challenging statement it made about the mother of Jesus. Original art is more than aesthetics. Robert Beckford therefore enters into dialogue with black artists. They have something to say about the black community, frequently a prophetic word that the Black church does not know and cannot speak. As we have seen sexuality is an issue in black culture, not only because of male chauvinism but also because of white stereotyping of black men – and black women. But the Black church cannot address the issue. Beckford turns to the work of Robert Lentz, specifically to 'Lion of Juday' in which Jesus is depicted as a Masai warrior. 'The squatting position of the Christ means his genitalia are visible underneath his robes. In other words, the icon depicts Jesus as a Black warrior and a Black sexual being.'[83] Sexuality and oppression by sexuality are immediately drawn into a black theology of liberation. 'A Black socio-political sexual wholeness, which comes from seeing Jesus as a sexual being, can reclaim sexuality by ensuring that it is a fundamental aspect of God-given human life.'[84] Sexuality becomes more than the sexual act and becomes a central element in human identity and relationship. This is the 'prophetic and spiritual dimension' of black culture which Beckford seeks to explore. Another dialogue is with Faisal Abdullah, a Muslim artist whose paintings include figures who disrupt the white male dominance in biblical images. Beckford discusses the figures represented in *The Last Supper I* and *II*, *Da Resurrection* and *The Struggle is Ordained.* In *The Last Supper I* black men at the table are dressed in white robes, heads covered. The young women sit modestly, their heads veiled. They look towards the men (who ignore them) and listen attentively to them. In the *Last Supper II* the young black men and women wear fashionable contemporary clothes. The young men sit and stand, staring at the viewer. The young black women are independent of the men, with the same steady gaze. Much as Beckford appreciates these paintings, we should not expect him to be uncritical. Abdullah's work is still male oriented and this is one of the negative aspects of black culture that Beckford wishes to overcome. In fact it is only in the Muslim painting that the women are portrayed as dependent. In the contemporary, secular painting the young women are confident and independent. However, in *Last Supper II* Beckford is right to draw attention to the prominent place given to a young man holding a gun proudly, visibly. It is a matter of pride, a symbol of status and an implied threat. Guns used to be part of the poster art of the 1960s in a time of armed liberation struggles. But in London and Birmingham black men with guns do not symbolise freedom from white oppression. They are the hallmark of drugs, destruction and death. We see here a feature of the best of Black theology, its refusal to sacrilise the worst in black culture. The Black church can learn from artists, but it can also have a word to speak to a secular culture which glamorises the gun and those above the law. We have been here before. We saw Black Power in the USA opposing state violence with its own counter-violence. We saw that Black theology in the USA could not risk its street cred by criticising this violence. And we saw Black theology in South Africa trying to address the abuse of power without falling under the spell of power. Black theology in the USA could not bring love and justice together, except sequentially. Robert Beckford addresses this important issue with sensitivity and creativity.

It is not surprising that there is rage in the black community, a rage which expresses an intolerable frustration at its own impotence, a rage which becomes destructive when it finds some satisfaction in the sight of young men with guns who have no respect for the law. Beckford can learn from the street, but he is courageous enough to address a word to the street. This is the subject of *God of the Rahtid: redeeming rage*. How as a Christian is it possible to begin with rage and so redeem it that it 'becomes a constructive force in our lives'.[85] English is spoken on the islands of the Caribbean with a distinctive rhythm and accent. It is a form of English and as we shall see later its variations can be deliberately adopted to be destabilising and disruptive: departing from the rules of language of the colonial masters can make a political point. Beckford is writing about the God of Wrath, but that English phrase does not describe his subject. Instead he uses the Jamaican word *rahtid*, God of the Rahtid. It is not difficult to hear in the cadence of the Caribbean that it is derived from wrath, but it enables him to make a connection with black experience not conveyed by the English term. In neither case is he speaking simply about anger. It is not the anger of God who has stubbed his toe while walking in the garden in the cool of the day. It is not the anger of black people because Brian Lara refuses to give up the captaincy of the West Indies cricket team. Rudolf Otto in his classic study of the holy took as one of his prime examples the wrath of God. Wrath is not simply a moral concept, far less an affect. It embraces the whole gamut of the *mysterium, tremendum et fascinans*. It includes power, threat, presence, attraction yet danger. It is the original meaning of 'awesome', something which chills the blood. The wrath of God is powerful, but effective, it is discriminating but not chiding, it is intolerant but constructive. Above all it is righteous. Is there any way by which black rage can associate with the divine rage, transcend the corrosive destructiveness of anger and be thereby redeemed? In 1993 the black teenager Stephen Lawrence was murdered in London. A number of young white men are widely believed to have carried out the attack, for purely racial reasons. The police were criticised for their investigation of the case and failure to secure a successful prosecution. Indeed the Macpherson Report of 1999 accused the police of 'institutionalised racism'. Not surprisingly this has caused rage and outrage in the black community. The rage is likely to fuel retaliatory and indiscriminate violence and further alienate the entire community from the institutions of British society. This alienation is already present by what Beckford terms 'pernicious exclusion'. The black community could not turn to the police for a resolution of their rage. But Beckford suggests the churches offered little help. Were the white churches not also characterised by 'institutionalised racism'? And were the black churches not paralysed by 'internalised pernicious exclusion'?[86] The black rage was entirely justified, but would its outcome be positive or negative? 'In such cases our principled anger must have an outlet. To ensure that this righteous anger or vengeance is used to its best effects, it must be redemptive.'[87] We have seen all this before. James Cone would not hear of love before justice was established. Blacks were being asked to love their enemies while their enemies continued their lives and privileges. And in South Africa the Truth and Reconciliation Commission was content to call for forgiveness without justice. Beckford is addressing an issue with reference to the UK, but an issue which recurs throughout the world. Hegel asked how the slave could redeem the master. Beckford asks how the oppressed can redeem the oppressor. How can the sufferer achieve 'a redemptive vengeance as part of a Black Christian spirituality'[88] such that evil is returned with good and the outcome is the salvation not only of the sufferer but of the perpetrator. Righteous rage is justified: God in His wrath takes the side of the oppressed. But 'forgiveness is not a substitute for justice'.[89]

> Righteous rage demands a broader analysis and a response to injustice which seeks to do more than redress or compensate. Instead righteous rage seeks to build a new order that makes injustices less likely. This kind of rage can be distinguished from unrighteous rage, which is geared towards petty revenge, as the 'eye for an eye, tooth for a tooth' became.[90]

To make rage righteous requires 'both spiritual renewal and socio-political transformation'.[91] Beckford distinguishes between two types of reconciliation.

> Weak reconciliation is resolution without justice. It pays no attention to the past and focuses on the future. Therefore, past injustices are not corrected. Also, weak reconciliation makes no demands from the victimiser; instead it is the victim who has to cover most ground by forgiving the most and receiving the least. In contrast, strong reconciliation views justice as an integral component of reconciliation.[92]

The process of exchange must not leave the situation as before. If the oppressed repents of revenge and moves towards forgiveness, this creates the circumstances in which the oppressor can repent. Reconciliation is the new beginning for both victim and victimiser. And if this sounds rather idealistic the victim is not naïve. The new circumstances include social analysis and a clear grasp of the situation. They open a path to new relationships and the reform of institutions which previously made oppression both possible and acceptable. In 1999 Beckford visited Jamaica to do a TV documentary. As is his way he was fulsome in his praise of churches which preserved African elements, but critical of their lack of commitment to political transformation. He took the opportunity to visit the plantation from which his name is taken and discovered that a namesake, Robert Beckford, in 1831 was one of the leaders of a movement of civil disobedience. Like militant blacks in the USA he had been tempted to change his name, to reject the plantation name and all its associations. However, he was able to keep the name, not now the name of the slave owner, but the name which was redeemed by a Christian slave.

As we have seen, in the absence of dialogue within the churches, Beckford has found creative dialogue partners among artists. This is even more true within the spectrum of black music. It is a fruitful area and he is at present writing a book on this subject. 'What I want to suggest is that the origins of hip-hop provide us with a Black cultural creativity, central to redemptive vengeance.'[93] He traces it from its origins in the south Bronx in the 1960s. This was the beginning of the postmodern period, a time of de-industrialisation in economic relations and deconstruction in cultural associations. In response African-Americans, Caribbean migrants and Hispanic youth developed new forms of music, dance and art to create alternative identities for themselves and a whole generation. An oppressive situation was redeemed by the oppressed. Easier said than done.

> To redeem a situation requires ingenuity and intelligence. Ingenuity provides resourcefulness necessary for addressing situations of rage, inequality and oppression. Likewise, creativity enables marginalised people to find ways to turn around or stir up so as to redeem the current situation.[94]

He refers specifically to the Jamaican born 'Kool DJ Herc', whose popularity amongst black youth sprang from his use of the technology to deconstruct, through breaks, and reconstruct. However, Beckford is particularly interested in the social and political grounding of the movement. He traces the career of Afrika Bambaataa who in 1975 formed the 'Zulu Nation'. 'The aims of the Zulu Nation were to add consciousness and social critique to hip-hop.'[95] The break, which in music combines past and present in a new sound, suggests to hip-hoppers the possibility of combining traditional relations and a new identity in life. Beckford traces the sequence into rap in which the technology is used to create rupture and new possibilities. However, he would not be Robert Beckford if he were content with fulsome praise. There is much in the break tradition that he values: it can be socially committed and prophetic in a non-directive way. If it is true that 'to redeem a situation requires ingenuity and intelligence', these qualities are not always present.

Redemption does not happen automatically. Rap is not inherently redemptive and much of it is anti-redemptive. This is particularly true of gangsta rap which Beckford characterises as the stance of the black male outlaw who is machismo, gun-toting, violent, misogynistic and entirely lacking in hopefulness. In all this there is a powerful word from the street, but there must on occasion be a word to the street. That is why it is a dialogue and not a legitimation.

Having said that, Beckford does not simply give up on black youths who go to prison. Without being patronising he visits prison to speak to them about their lives. He came from their background: there but for the grace of God. The career criminals are another matter, but he has a film and discussion programme to raise the consciousness of those who through misfortune or racial difficulties find themselves in prison, but who are open to being redeemed. He is not now as they are and would like to be to them what Gramsci called an 'organic intellectual': compare the work of Cornel West. Out of genuine compassion he visits those in prison: compare the commission of Jesus. This concern for dysfunctional black youths is seen in his latest book, *God and Gangs: an urban toolkit for those who won't be sold out, bought out or scared out.* He praises (without the usual criticism) the exemplary work of the Street Pastors in London, for their holistic response in mounting 'a direct presence on the streets blighted by crime'.[96] It is here that he comes closest to the kind of legitimation that we found in James Cone.

> Those involved in gun crime and gang violence are on one level internalising and living out postcolonial oppression. From this perspective a black youth holding and using a gun is not an expression of power or an outlaw mentality but an example of the postcolonial system winning the battle to control black people.[97]

This is one of the most craven statements in all of Beckford's writings. The drugs and guns phenomenon among black youth is present in the Yardie culture imported from Jamaica. It is not possible to relate it to colonial oppression, which predated the phenomenon. In which case it is attributed to 'postcolonial oppression'. Not only does this scenario lack credibility, it is perhaps the only example of Beckford resorting to sacrilising of the black community.

We come now to the most complex of Beckford's dialogue partners. This dialogue involves three different elements, Rastafarianism, Bob Marley and the concept of Dread – which sounds like the title of a novel by J.K. Rowling. Beckford says little by way of explanation about Rastafarianism and so we should begin with a brief introduction. Rastafarianism is a complex phenomenon, combining political protest, eclectic religion and popular culture. Politically it is inspired by Marcus Garvey, whom we have already met, whose UNIA movement was motivated by his desire to address the injustice and racism suffered by poor blacks in the Caribbean. In religion, Garvey declared his faith in the God of Ethiopia. These two themes came together when Ras Tafari defeated the pro-Turkish Lij Yasu in 1916 and in 1930 was crowned Emperor Haile Selassie. He was deposed when Italy invaded in 1936 but reinstated when the British defeated the Italians in 1941. As Emperor Haile

Selassie he was regarded as a divine figure, a messiah come to liberate Africa and defeat the colonial powers. The religious and political were further mixed when colonial powers were identified as Babylon. Babylon is that culture which oppresses Jamaica economically, subverts local African traditions and undermines self-esteem and identity among black people. Rastafarianism is therefore a political movement, rebelling against colonialism (Babylon), a religious movement, combining biblical reference with the primal element of the earthforce (Jah), a counter-culture expressed in the valuing of the holy herb (ganja) and the fierce rejection of western cultural values (dreadlocks). Its most potent weapon in the struggle for the hearts and minds has been reggae, the first revolutionary movement in history to be carried on through music, its roving ambassador being Bob Marley.[98]

With this cursory introduction to the movement it is not difficult to see why Beckford is enthusiastic about Rastafarianism. It is the Caribbean's first liberation theology and can provide 'a theo-political catalyst for Christians in the UK'.[99]

> Rastafari represents the first attempt to construct a liberation theology in African Caribbean history. For African Caribbean people it is an important resource, because there is no other contemporary African Caribbean religious tradition in Britain that embraces Black identity, politics and struggle.[100]

Indeed 'Christafari' are a witness to the fact that 'Rastafarian Christianity is now being articulated in a variety of locations.'[101] Reggae is therefore 'an important theological resource for a critical reflection on Black Christianity'.[102] In particular the lyrics of Bob Marley form a canon of 'theological literature' expressing the aspirations of oppressed people. Beckford sums up Marley's analysis of the psychological brain-washing and mental slavery carried out upon blacks. 'It was a systematic dehumanisation based on aesthetics (you are ugly), cognition (you are stupid) and esteem (you are worthless).'[103] Not that this is going to be hagiography. We know better than to think that Beckford will be uncritical in his reception of Marley's work. There are religious objections. Marley, and here we might recall Edward Blyden, did not believe that black people could achieve their full humanity within Christianity. They should turn to Rastafarianism. While there is much in that tradition which Beckford finds attractive at a political and cultural level, he rejects Rastafarianism as a religion. Obviously he rejects the divinity of Haile Selassie, not least with the death of the emperor. Seeing Ras Tafari as coming from the tree of Jesse is unlikely speculation. Rastafarianism is still very dependent on the Christian Bible, especially as it was received in the Caribbean. But there are other criticisms. Marley presupposes 'an idealised and romanticised view of African history'.[104] So what is new here? This criticism stems from Beckford's postmodern and therefore anti-essentialist view of Afrocentrism. There are two issues. The first is that Afro-Caribbeans in the UK are now two diasporas removed from Africa. African origins are no longer decisive.[105] The second is his brave assertion that 'much can also be learned from exploring the grotesque in Black life'.[106] The 'idealised and romanticised view of African history' can actually undermine political mobilisation.

In addition to this criticism Beckford disapproves of Marley's personal attitude towards women which displayed a lack of respect. Robert Beckford is particularly sensitive to black male chauvinism, which should not be shrugged off with a tolerant smile which accepts the intolerable. Beckford is well aware of the black women in the UK who might be grouped under the perspective of womanist. When he reviewed their work in 1998 they were postgraduate students for the most part. Kate Coleman, for example, was pastor of a Baptist Church in London, and comments on the lack of acceptance of her leadership amongst Baptists. She makes the following point about borrowing from America.

> As Black British women we cannot simply depend upon the insights of our African-American cousins. This will require that we dispense with an essentialist concept of Black womanhood and with the idea of a monolithic Black identity and instead recognise that there are many and varied models of black womanhood.[107]

She later admitted that womanist theology is in its infancy in the UK.[108] Sadly we recall the words of Abraham in heaven, 'If they do not hear Moses and the prophets ...' If the Black church does not listen to the male theologian, what chance is there that it will attend to womanist voices? With such criticisms of Bob Marley we might wonder why Beckford is so enamoured of him. Walter Rodney, born in Guyana, was more prominent in shaping the political agenda of Rastafarianism. He eschewed the romaniticised view of Africa and adopted certain aspects of Marxist analysis to develop a form of socialism appropriate to an African-centred approach to history. But Marley's lasting contribution to black liberation from Babylonian captivity lies in the concept of Dread.

As earlier noted, there is a tradition in the Caribbean of subverting colonial rule by deconstructing the master's language. This became a feature of the Rastafarian revolt. As Ernest Cashmore explains, 'language was one of the blades used by the Rastaman to cut his links with the encompassing Babylon. It aided maximal detachment from the everyday experience of white society and encouraged insularity and the development of in-group solidarity.'[109] He goes on to say that Rastafarians used the lyrics of reggae 'to provoke social consciousness'.[110] It is not difficult to see why Robert Beckford is enthusiastic about Rastafarianism as a political theology which addresses the black struggle for liberation and identity – even though he does not find it attractive as a religion. And this is nowhere better illustrated than in the redefinition of the word 'dread'.

> Rastafarians *invert* the traditional English usage of 'dread', so that rather than meaning fear and anxiety, Dread means upliftment, freedom and empowerment. Rastafarians wore dreadlocks to symbolise the process of mental decolonisation, freedom, power and upliftment.[111]

Dread was originally used politically in Jamaica but in the UK it is applied more generally to qualify certain cultural movements, gestures, symbols or individuals in the black community. It was Søren Kierkegaard who introduced *The Concept of Dread* into Christian theology. As with Otto's concept of *fascinans* it is not a fear of the known, but of the unknown, a reality from which we should flee but one to which we are also drawn. It is a confrontation in which freedom but also identity are at stake. Rasta Dread retains something of this dialectic, except that there is an inversion of values: that which was feared is now embraced, that which was admired is now despised. It is Beckford's intention to appropriate Rasta Dread into Christian theology, specifically Christology. This may be surprising, since it is Black Pentecostalism that offers the best hope of a political theology on Beckford's view and he sees 'dread pneumatology' as the resource which enables the socio-political work to take place.[112]

> Black Christology must underpin the dual task of resisting systems of White supremacy, as well as developing a political and social structure which is capable of challenging the domestic, neo-colonial situation faced by Black British people. I suggest we begin by calling Jesus Dread. Naming Jesus Dread uses the power of Black-talk in the Black Church, where language is used symbolically as a form of empowerment.[113]

However, as ever Beckford is not short of a word of criticism. Much has been said about Dread in relation to the psychology of black people, the struggle to expel whites from their minds, cultural resistance and the formation of a truly African-Caribbean identity. This internal movement has been well developed. Beckford's criticism, like his criticism of the Black church, is that 'the socio-political outworking of dread has been primarily "weak"'.[114] There is also the non-sacrilising theme that it has not led to an 'internal critique of its own inadequacies'.[115] Male chauvinism is again identified. Nevertheless the concept has great potential. What are the hallmarks of a Dread Christ?

> A Dread Christ equips Black folk to face and destroy all structures of oppression – being Dread, for the Black Church, is to engage in the struggle for Black freedom. Furthermore, to say that Christ is Dread is to unveil a Christ of Black upliftment, Black empowerment and Black progress. Similarly, a Dread Christ tells Black British people that the Jesus of history is with them as they protest, fight, boycott, celebrate and progress. In short, a Dread Christ is a Black Christ participating in Black lives and Black struggles. In the context of Britain, a Dread Christ is the focus of our socio-political struggle and the source of joy for our resurrected lives.[116]

The conclusion is that the Dread Christ is therefore the basis of a Black liberation theology. I find this not only predictable, but disappointing. Beckford can even describe the concept of Dread as 'in some sense passé' and claims that it is necessary to go beyond it. But in describing 'the hallmarks of a Dread Christ' does he go beyond Dread, does he even come close to appropriating the full implications of Dread? Or is the whole exotic display of Rasta Dread not laid like a seamless robe over the already delineated figure of the Black Christ? The hallmarks of the Black Christ are those we have already met in James Cone and Albert Cleage. But the dimension of Dread is strangely absent. The agenda for the Black Christ is the north American agenda during the civil rights movement. It entirely omits the specific, particular and peculiar contribution of the Caribbean. The Black Christ of the USA is essentially a White Christ with a black skin, leading his Chosen People into American democracy as full citizens, relying on the American constitution and asking only that the Bill of Rights be fairly applied. But this is not Dread. It has lost the dialectic, the inversion. This religious option was well known to Bob Marley when he died in 1981 – and it was not Dread. The development of a Dread theology is an exciting prospect, but it requires 'ingenuity and intelligence'. Robert Beckford is not lacking in either, but at this moment he has taken a short cut, he has reverted to a previous paradigm.

Beckford may have begun with American Black Theology, but he has quickly moved beyond its narrow race analysis. He is a contextual theologian and increasingly writes about the UK appropriation of African-Caribbean culture, especially in music and religion. It is disappointing that he has decided that Dread is passé since, from a theological perspective, it was not only original but had great potential. But that is the cost of being contextual: culture changes. But his fundamental objectives have not: a critical engagement of culture and religion, the word from the street and the Word to the street, continues. This can be seen in a further book, which was not available when the first edition of this book was published. In *Jesus Dub: theology, music and social change* Beckford returns to further develop themes found in his previous book, *God and the Gangs*.

Dub emerged in Jamaica in the 1950s with the importation of black American music. With too few musicians for live performances, sound systems were developed. The music was not simply reproduced but, dubbed, remixed by sound engineers. At the same time the DJs were also dubbing words to give them a new meaning. The clash of sounds was accompanied by the confrontation of realities, 'the explicit politicisation of sound'.[117] Beckford once again deals with a dialectical relationship, now the relationship of the dance hall to the church hall. It is dialectical, because it is not a matter of jazzing up church music. Church music has had a considerable influence on the popular music of the African-Caribbean community, well illustrated in an extended interview between Beckford and the DJ and scholar William (Lez) Henry. Just as important, prophetic preaching has had an influence on the words of some DJs: not all, for there is also 'slackness', the advocacy of negative themes of sexual predatory behaviour, violence, chauvinism, selfish gratification.

Dub in this sense makes the familiar track strange but also provides the occasion for a hermeneutics of suspicion towards the familiar in society. It is the socio-political possibilities which interest Beckford. In dubbing, the DJ can raise the consciousness of the audience about themselves, the circumstances of their lives, their experiences of the justice system, discrimination in employment – raise their consciousness but also challenge them to respond. The DJ acts as 'an organic intellectual'. There is an element of idealism, even idealisation here, not least because of Beckford's criticism of black preachers for avoiding such a role. But this is part of the project, to challenge the church to perform in practice – in praxis – what it has the potential to do. He wishes to see the critique of hegemony, currently practised by the organic intellectuals, paralleled by the critique of ideology that should be the mark of the prophetic church. Dubbing should provoke the church to its true role. 'I believe that listening to music as encoded political language introduces a "hermeneutic of sound" – that is, a particular way of listening and interpreting what is being heard.'[118] The dub is in the music and the words. 'In short, dub is a three-part process of *deconstruction* guided by the *emancipation ethic* to produce a dub or a *new praxis*.'[119]

It is now clear why dub is of interest to Beckford as a Christian theologian of the UK African-Caribbean tradition. He sees a parallel between some DJs and some prophetic preachers, between true worship, disrupted by the presence of the Spirit, and the experience of dub. His project is not to garnish the church hall with popular sounds but something much more ambitious, 'to *dub* Jesus and to find new ways of hearing the message of the Gospel.'[120] There is potential here, but also the danger of absurdity and unworthiness. The comedian Billy Connolly has derided those who wish to make the traditional message of the gospel attractive to modern people by associating Jesus with some contemporary movement to which youth especially are attracted.

Vicar's son:	And was Jesus an Arsenal supporter, Daddy?
Vicar:	Yes, in a sense he was.
Connolly:	(Expletive deleted).

It would be anachronistic to say that Jesus was a dub DJ. The more substantial issue for Beckford is this: did Jesus perform a disruption and remix of the familiar in such a way that it is not inappropriate to describe it as dub? That is the project. Did Jesus dub such that those who read or hear his message are emancipated by it and have their lives transformed? Was Jesus a dub artist? At the most trivial and unworthy level the answer is, 'Yes, in a sense he was.' At the most serious level the test is whether his words redeem.

Beckford could make a preliminary case at the level of communication. Those who experience disruption and transformation in the dance hall might be surprised to find a similar experience in the church hall (if the music, which comes from the same roots, is joined to prophetic proclamation). His best examples are drawn from the Gospel of John, which in contrast to the traditional narratives of the Synoptic Gospels, represents a remix, a re-reading, a dubbing of the life of Jesus to produce a new perspective on Jesus and the believer. But the dubbing continues in the incidents of the gospel. In chapter 4 Jesus deconstructs the life of the Samaritan woman at the well, confronting her with her present reality but emancipating her for a new reality. In chapter 8 Beckford sees Jesus acting like a DJ in the temple. There is a sound clash with the religious authorities over the meaning of the Law on adultery. 'He offers a dub version of the law and reworks it so that its core elements are restructured.'[121] There are many other examples which Beckford could have used to support his presentation of Jesus, not only in the Gospel of John. The Gospel of Matthew uses the language of the old order as the medium for presenting the new. In chapter 12 a minor incident of the disciples plucking ears of grain on the Sabbath becomes the occasion for a complete deconstruction of the theology of the temple, an emancipation which discloses the mercy of God. And in Mark the same incident launches the critique of the ideology of the Sabbath with its condemnation and control of the poor by the elite: 'the Sabbath was made for man' dubs the whole system of organised religion. It is a devastating dismantling of the reifications which seek to limit the love of God. To these examples could be added most of the parables of Jesus, which typically remix the familiar by introducing a surprise element and ending with an unsettling question. 'What should the householder do?' That is, 'What would you do?' Beckford makes an interesting and ingenious case for presenting Jesus as a dub artist. Many who read this will remain unconvinced – but perhaps they have never been to a dance hall. This, after all, is contextual theology. Those who trace their roots through the Caribbean to Africa may find the Platonic Christ of European contextual theology completely bizarre.

Beckford's project goes beyond an *apologia* to the denizens of the dance hall. Once again it is more ambitious. It applies the paradigm of Jesus dub to two important issues in contemporary, global Christianity – pneumatology and the prosperity gospel. Pneumatology is of special interest to Beckford who stands in the Pentecostal tradition. But is this the Holiness tradition, which values the gifts of healing, prophesy and tongues – gifts for the individual? Paul warns against a too-private focus on the Spirit. 'If I speak in the tongues of men and of angels, but have not love, I am a noisy gong or a clanging cymbal.'[122] But it is Jesus himself who dubs the Spirit. In his first sermon he reads from a familiar text:

> The Spirit of the Lord is upon me, because he has anointed me to preach good news to the poor. He has sent me to proclaim release to the captives and recovery of sight to the blind, to set at liberty those who are oppressed, to proclaim the acceptable year of the Lord.[123]

The familiar text is remixed. 'Today this scripture is fulfilled in your hearing.' This is the challenge to the Pentecostal churches: is the Spirit manifest only in ecstatic experiences or also in the well-being of the community? This encourages Beckford to return to issues of racism, poverty, agism, sexism, homophobia. 'The experience of the Spirit is never separate from the quest for justice.'[124]

This leads, finally to Beckford's criticism of the Word of Faith movement and the prosperity gospel. We shall come this is in a moment, but it may be that he has missed the opportunity to apply dub in a very different way. The Gospel of Health and Wealth originated with Kenneth Hagin of Tulsa, Oklahoma who in 1934, while diagnosed terminally ill, re-read Mark 11:24, 'Therefore I tell you, whatever you ask in prayer, believe that you receive it, and you will.' In Beckford's terms he dubbed the text: Christians should not receive gifts from God and then believe. No, they should believe they already have them and then they will receive. Hagin experienced this for both health and wealth and says of God, 'He wants His children to eat the best, He wants them to wear the best clothing, He wants them to drive the best cars, and He wants them to have the best of everything.'[125] In Beckford's terms would Hagin not be an example of a 'slackness' DJ, dubbing the gospel text to advocate utter selfishness and crass materialism?

For Beckford, Jesus dubs such selfishness and indifference to others in the Feeding of the Multitude. In this too Beckford might have made his case more forcefully. It is not just the prosperity gospel which is dubbed by Jesus, but the economy of the Pharisees. The teaching of Jesus also dubs the economics of the global market, the ideology of neo-liberalism. Contextual theology is a risky business: contexts change. It also requires 'ingenuity and intelligence' to discern new outbreaks of the Spirit in the contemporary world. It will be interesting to see how Robert Beckford's project develops. He is the major contributor to Black Theology in the UK – although it may be that this title, like Dread before it, is itself passé. To continue with the name 'Black' Theology might suggest too close a link to the American race model. This contextual theology is African-Caribbean theology – in the UK.

We noted in Chapter 3 that Black Theology in South Africa was not dependent on American Black Theology. It arose from the Black Consciousness movement to produce a contextual theology appropriate to the experience of black and coloured communities in South African. The result was a Black Theology which went beyond secular or purely political analyses, to make its own contribution to the future of the country. One of the disappointing features of books and articles on Black Theology in the USA has been the tendency to repeat secular analyses, perhaps from the social sciences, as if exposing racism was itself Black Theology. Thus a Womanist theologian will ask rhetorically, 'What do I mean by Black Theology? It is when I see black women discriminated against simply because of their race. That is Black Theology. It is when I see black children attending inferior schools. That is Black Theology.' Of course these are important social, even moral issues – but they are not Black Theology. Some religious or spiritual insights must be added to contribute to the analysis. Without this readers are misled. They buy books entitled 'Black Theology' but all they get are the analyses that have already appeared in the literature of the social sciences. What makes the work of Robert Beckford refreshing, exciting and hopeful is that to the social and cultural analyses, to the politically conscious art or music there is something added, some religious or spiritual element. It is this that makes his work genuinely Black Theology – or Theology of Dread. And what makes other books and articles on the subject disappointing is that they lack this dimension. Authors claiming to be writing Black Theology make no contribution to the subject whatsoever. They repeat worn out clichés from the social sciences or inappropriate mantras from the USA. I have been criticised in my account of Black Theology in the UK for concentrating so much attention on the work of Robert Beckford and for failing to pay enough attention to others writing on this subject. I make no apology for concentrating on his work: it is world class and there is absolutely no one else in the UK writing with this level of sophistication. As for not paying attention to other writers, the situation is actually worse than that. I have paid attention to them, but decided that they do not merit inclusion. It is not that they are not in the same class of Beckford, it is that they make no contribution to Black Theology at all.

I have not previously dealt with these other writers for this reason and I think it is not fruitful to spend time criticising their work. But since I have been challenged to include them, let me briefly indicate why I originally omitted them. One of the most recent collections is *Postcolonial Black British Theology* edited by Michael N. Jagessar and Anthony G. Reddie.[126] The book begins with a reference to Black British theology, but fails to address the subject: this is also true of specific articles. Thus David Isiorho begins with reference to 'a Black Anglican theology of liberation' (p. 62), but that is the last we hear of it. His article is on defining 'Englishness', before going on to deal with racism-awareness, a subject on which he has lectured to a Church of England diocese. Delroy A. Reid-Salmon promises to construct a theology of (black) identity. His PhD was on diasporic studies and so that is what we get instead. It is not Black theology, indeed it is not very good diasporic studies, failing as it does to take account of some current analyses of the dialectical dynamics of religion and diasporic transactions. Caroline Redfearn, a minister of the Metropolitan Community Church, advocates an 'inclusive' Black theology. Her article is a work-in-progress report from her PhD research. Unfortunately it concentrates on the history of sexual behaviour and oppression in the eighteenth and nineteenth centuries. It tells us nothing about how homophobia is being addressed in the Black majority churches today in, say, Birmingham. The selection of contributors, mainly young and inexperienced, tells us something about the shallow pool from which they are chosen. But the same features recur in the contributions by the editors, who are much more experienced. Anthony Reddie proposes an 'interactive methodology' for Black theology. He provides a detailed account of how three groups of young people responded to his invitation that they participate in the construction of 'an imaginary barn dance'. Michael Jagessar advocates a 'spinning theology', without considering why the British people, White and Black, are hostile to the idea of spin. He has in mind the Caribbean paradigm of Anancy, the figure of the trickster, present in a variety of cultures throughout the world. Although he claims this element is found in the Bible he gives us no examples and no indication of how it could lead to a renewed Black theology. The most revealing comment in the book is a quotation from David Muir's unpublished dissertation claiming that 'Black Theology is relatively underdeveloped in Britain among [Black majority churches].' Far from undermining this claim, the present collection confirms it.

Anthony Reddie is frequently referred to in this type of literature, especially his book *Nobodies to Somebodies: a practial theology for education and liberation.*[127] Its subject is education and Reddie is well informed on this subject, with references almost entirely to American sources. I mention it here because of the claim that 'The two major areas that contribute to this work are the disciplines of Black and Womanist theology and transformative education.'[128] If there are influences from Black and Womanist theologies they are not appropriated for the British context. One of the few examples of a black reading of the Bible is the treatment of the conversion of the Ethiopian eunuch (Acts 8:26–40). This is approached not through the universalising of the gospel envisaged by the original writer, but through the perspective of American race analysis, forcing the narrative inappropriately into the rather dated binary polarities of white/black, rich/poor. Or again there is the double parable about inviting guests to a wedding, which Reddie interprets in terms of racial exclusion. In reality the first deals with spirituality and self-promotion, a subject frequently chosen by black preachers. The second is about social exclusion on economic grounds, but then in spite of his reference to Freire, the element of class is omitted from the book, as in American Black Theology.

Two books frequently cited as contributing to Black Theology are *A Time to Speak* and *A Time to Act: Kairos* both edited by Paul Grant and Raj Patel.[129] The two volumes, taken together form incoherent collections of short articles, some consisting of random thoughts of two to four pages. For the most part they provide anecdotal material about racial discrimination suffered by black people in the UK. As such there is no reason for these articles to be discussed in this book. However, the editorial of *A Time to Speak* claims that the book is 'the first self-conscious attempt to map out a Black Theology for Britain' (p. 1). None of the articles makes the slightest contribution to Black Theology and that is why the books are not discussed. By comparison, a writer who might have been able to contribute is Robinson A. Milwood. Much of his work is a blow-by-blow account of the problems he has experienced in his frenetic and successful ministry in the Stoke Newington area of London. *Suspension: a testimony of faith, suffering and perseverance* is a rather Victorian-sounding testimony 'of one man's struggle against many years of attacks by foes from all walks of life, but especially that of the Local Authority and the Methodist Church in the UK.'[130] A more promising work is his *Liberation and Mission: a black experience*.[131] Indeed this is his project: 'liberation and mission is impossible and ineffective without the black experience collectively.'[132] Christians should have 'a profound social and political consciousness and conviction'.[133] The project seems even more promising as he recounts how he has taught Religious Studies, Old Testament, New Testament, Liberation Theology and Pastoral Studies at several institutions including Tottenham College of Technology, Birkbeck College/University of London and Greenwich University. Unfortunately for our purposes, no comprehensive statement of Black Theology emerges. 'I have also resisted intellectually to avoid the presentation of my academic theological postulations and biblical liberation reflections.'[134] We shall never know.

For anyone seeking a British Black Theology, the most disappointing experience is to read through a journal dedicated to this subject, namely *Black Theology*, which began life in 1998 as *Black Theology in Britain: a journal of Contextual Theology* and was re-launched in 2002 as *Black Theology: an international journal*. It is encouraging to see several articles on British Womanist Theology, but disappointingly they lack content, beyond distancing themselves from the American model. As noted earlier, Kate Coleman writes on 'Black Theology and Black Liberation: a womanist perspective':

> As Black British women we cannot simply depend upon the insights of our African-American cousins. This will require that we dispense with an essentialised concept of Black womanhood and with the idea of a monolithic identity and instead reconise that there are many and varied models of Black womanhood.[135]

That tells them, but it does not tell us how a British womanist perspective differs in content from the American. In a later article, 'Black Women in Theology' she reviews American womanist theology, but admits that the subject is in its infancy in Britain.[136] Marjorie Lewis contributes an article on 'Diaspora Dialogue: womanist theology in engagement with aspects of the Black British and Jamaican experience'. She draws a parallel between Alice Walker's womanist and Nanny, that 'icon and prototype' of strong Jamaican women, 'our only national heroine'.[137] As an expression of resistance and contempt Nanny showed her ass to the attacking Red Coats:

> This tradition of vulgar display of the female body invites Jamaican women to re-examine the aesthetics and moral conventions of the inherited European norms, and to embrace the Black woman's rights to have control over and celebrate her body sexually.[138]

Whether black British Christian women would welcome the right to follow the example of this 'icon and prototype' or not, the article makes no contribution at all to Black Theology. Maxine Eudalee Howell-Baker writes on the theme 'Towards a Womanist Pneumatological Pedagogy: an investigation into the development and implementation of a theological pedagogy by and for the marginalized'.[139] She begins by recounting her own educational life history. It may be an imposition on the reader, but it seems to be what the author means by 'Womanist Pneumatological Pedagogy'. It makes no contribution to Black Theology. Chigor Chike writes on 'Black Theology in Britain – One Decade On', i.e. on from the Sheffield conference of 1993.[140] The article begins with literature on slavery in the UK and ends with a review of Black Theology, turning to sociological observations about life in this country, but without itself making any contribution to Black Theology. Michael Jagessar and Stephen Burns write on 'Liturgical Studies and Christian Worship: the postcolonial challenge'.[141] It contains surprisingly little about acts of worship, apart from the Ecumenical Service for the Women's World Day of Prayer. This leads to a rather trivial discussion of religious language concerning light and darkness. Postcolonial criticism problematises language, but in fact language such as 'king', 'lord', 'supplication' is part of a wider problem of continued feudal images rather than colonial perspectives. The article breaks no new ground for Black Theology.

The lack of substance in these works is the more disappointing in view of the magisterial two-volume work of Roswith Gerloff, *A Plea for British Black Theologies*, published as early as 1992, but reflecting exhaustive research undertaken during the previous decade.[142] The subtitle is 'The Black Church Movement in Britain and its transatlantic cultural and theological interaction with special reference to the Pentecostal Oneness (Apostolic) and Sabbatarian Movements'. The second study was completed first, and as a blow-by-blow account of divisions in the Seventh Day

Adventist Church over race could well have been omitted. The later case study, of the Oneness (Apostolic) Pentecostal Church, is more varied and interesting, ending as it does with a challenge. Personal commitment and detailed research combine to produce an immense and impressive work. Not surprisingly it is possible in the midst of this dissertation to lose sight of its thesis. What is the plea? There are two elements. The first is a plea to academic theologians to recognise this development within the UK. Christians looked for a revival, but did not recognise it when it came because it was black. In the providence of God something new and authentic has happened in the UK. Gerloff claims that this phenomenon in its African and Caribbean, especially Pentecostal, forms has much to contribute to biblical exegesis, the reinterpretation of ancient doctrinal formulations and to praxiology. Following her mentor in Birmingham, Walter Hollenweger, she declares it inconceivable that this dialogue should not take place. But of course it has not taken place, nor will it. Academic theology, which has resisted incorporating the insights of feminist theology and the moral and spiritual dimensions of liberation theology, has had no trouble in ignoring the African-Caribbean Church and the unruly presence of the Holy Spirit. Gerloff's plea for recognition and response has gone unheeded, giving credibility to the claims we have already encountered that western theology is incorrigibly racist. Western theology has become a secular academic discipline devoid of devotion and well able to reduce the manifestations of the Spirit to a metaphysical controversy.

But when all that is said in criticism of the White community, both academic and ecclesial, there is a second element in Gerloff's dissertation. It is a challenge to the Black community to produce theologies which can be worthy and powerful dialogue partners. Nor should they be simply mirror images of White theology. Gerloff, in dealing with Oneness (Apostolic) Pentecostalism, points to its biblical reinterpretations. 'It is, in fact, trying to recreate the "Holy Book" in the light of "Holy experience". In this sense, it is not primarily a dogmatic but a racial and cultural issue, however, precisely because of this, it is no less theology.'[143] The last thing White academic theology needs is a Black theology which repeats its own assumptions and values. It is the great contribution of Robert Beckford that he has produced a Black theology to challenge White theology. The fact that he has had so little response is no criticism of his work. Those who could ignore Daly, Gutiérrez and Cone from the Americas, have no difficulty in ignoring Beckford, writing of the UK. With this one exception, the examples of Black theology in the UK we have examined have singularly failed to produce worthy and powerful dialogue partners. Sadly the Black Church has failed to take up the plea of Roswith Gerloff.

There is then only one major black theologian in the UK, Robert Beckford, but there is another very significant figure – Joe Aldred. In their professions, constituencies and theologies they stand in great contrast and yet a dialogue between the two would be most fruitful. Joe Aldred is a bishop in the Church of God of Prophecy and has been active in ecumenical and inter-racial organisations at both local and national levels. He has edited several collections but his main work is *Respect: Understanding Caribbean British Christianity*, which is his PhD dissertation from the University of

Sheffield.[144] This work had not been published when the first edition of my own work went to press. It is an important book and I am glad to be able to include it in this new edition. Aldred's work has a very different feel to it from that of Beckford. Although, as we have seen, Beckford is an active member of his church, his constituency is the black community, especially black youth who may live their lives apart from the churches. His subject is black culture: the word *from* the street to the churches and the Word of God *to* the street. To that extent the subject of *Respect* is more narrowly focused: British-Caribbean Christianity in its 'ethno-religious experience'.[145] At the outset therefore Joe Aldred is distancing himself from most of the American writers we have discussed. In contrast to Cone and his acolytes, Aldred's subject is not to be described as 'the black experience'. 'I use the term "ethnicity" in preference to "race" in an effort to convey my understanding that the latter is an unhelpful and divisive, largely Western, terminology.'[146] We shall return to this very important point in Chapter 6 below, but we have already noted that for Claire Alexander the identities of her young black men were determined by culture rather than race. For Aldred ethnicity should not imply colour: the majority population are also ethnic in their own context. This in turn introduces the following claim which may well be contentious, but one which Aldred makes with absolute confidence.

We have already discussed the three main contextual theologies. Latin American Liberation Theology has taken as its subject those for whom poverty and oppression are the defining experiences of life. Feminist Theology has chosen as its subject those who experience oppression through gender discrimination. Black and Womanist Theologies in the USA have focused on those who are oppressed on grounds of race. Aldred boldly distances himself from this paradigm. His subject, the existence of British-Caribbean Christians, 'is certainly not one that is defined exclusively, or overwhelmingly, in terms of their experience of and response to oppression. Rather, oppression is but one of their experiences, and it is not *the* one that defines them.'[147] A too-ready use of the phrase 'Black liberation' arises from an uncritical transposition of a concept from the USA to the UK. Aldred's position is also a contextual theology, based on visits to many congregations, worship services, meetings and conferences in the UK – and the people he is in touch with do not define themselves as victims. They do not see themselves as in need of liberation from oppression. Nor does he find the term 'African-Caribbean' useful, suggesting as it does a parallel with 'African-American'. There is no homogeneous African identity for all Caribbean people, but beyond that the British element must be included. Those of British-Caribbean descent are now at two removed from Africa and their experience cannot be described under such categories as neo-slavery or neo-colonialism.[148] Aldred therefore takes the bold step of insisting that there must be a British-Caribbean Theology, made in Britain, without undue borrowing from the American situation which is significantly different for historical, social, economic and legal reasons. To that contextual theology we shall turn in a moment, but there is a further related issue which Aldred feels must be clarified.

Many British-Caribbean Christians worship separately from the majority

Christian community and it is frequently said and assumed that this is because they were rejected for racial reasons when they or their parents came to the UK. Aldred offers a different interpretation. Those who arrived from the Caribbean were already members of Christian denominations. Some of these were not present in the UK and this led to the creation of house churches and later to the obtaining of appropriate buildings. In other cases immigrants found that church buildings had closed in the inner city areas in which they lived. With new energy and commitment old churches were reopened or new premises acquired. There has been some debate as to whether these congregations should be called 'Black-led churches' or 'Black majority churches', but Aldred sees little difference between the terms. In both cases race or ethnicity is taken to be the most important factor in determining their identity. It is to this that Aldred objects. For the members themselves, their identity lies in the denomination: they should be shown the courtesy of being referred to by the name they give themselves. Such churches are not Black in principle, but only in their membership.[149] This issue had been raised by Roswith Gerloff in *A Plea for British Black Theologies*, and informs Beckford's criticism of Malcolm Calley. 'Far from providing compensation, our worship experience was simultaneously a negotiation, engagement and overcoming of the social and cultural limitations place on Black life outside of the church.'[150]

The treatment of these various issues so far points in a surprising, intriguing – and, to some, unacceptable – direction. It seems that Aldred has little sympathy for the phrase 'Black Theology'. Symptomatic of this is the case of the journal *Black Theology*. Although involved in the establishment of the journal, Aldred points to its failure to attract a significant readership from within the British-Caribbean community. One reason of course is that most people are turned off by the title 'Theology'. But Aldred makes a more important point concerning this community: 'they do not associate their faith with "Black". For them, their faith is a denominational faith with Jesus at the head of their church'.[151] They will buy literature from their denomination on religious subjects, but are not attracted to anything entitled 'Black'. The title of the journal was changed in 2002 and he goes on to make the gnomic suggestion that 'it may be that in time we will need to modify the title again, even if the contents remain similarly focused.'[152] Presumably that would mean replacing the phrase 'Black Theology' altogether. This is hardly surprising since Aldred has already criticised the undue emphasis on race, colour and the whole oppression/liberation paradigm of Black Theology in the USA. He has in reality prepared us for this from the outset. His constituency is not a Black British community but the British-Caribbean Christian community. His theology, when it finally appears, is not a 'British Black Theology'. Race, colour and ethnicity have a place, but are firmly put in their place. When he turns to an evaluation of the work of Robert Beckford there is a certain ambiguity as he acknowledges him to be 'the central figure in contemporary Black British theology'.[153] Aldred identifies Beckford as the leading contributor to a movement over which he has grave reservations.

By this time the reader can anticipate Aldred's criticism of Beckford's position.

'Beckford therefore locks his philosophy exclusively with an oppression/liberation model, and advocates "a political theology for the Black church in Britain" as the only remedy.'[154] As we have seen, Aldred disputes that the experience of oppression – present though it is – deserves the central place given to it in the liberation paradigm. He has sympathy with a review of Robert Beckford's work by Paul Grant:

> One of the ironies of Robert's work is that it seems a little caught out of time. For all the post-modern cleverness that Robert uses to shape his arguments and make his points, Robert is most definitely a child of the 1970s.[155]

In the final two chapters of this book we shall return to this question of the relationship of Black Theology (born of the 1960s) to Black Theology today in a postmodern context. Aldred's own criticism is more radical, questioning as it does the usefulness of the term 'Black theology', modern or postmodern. His final criticism of Beckford arises from his reading of *God of the Rahtid: redeeming rage*. As we saw earlier, the rage is caused by racially motivated actions and even more so by racially motivated inaction. This is another form of the experience of oppression. Its existence is acknowledged by Aldred, but not its centrality or constant presence:

> By presenting wrath as yet another aspect of Caribbean British Christian life that needs liberation or redemption, Beckford demonstrates the intractable nature of the oppression/liberation dialectic. In effect, this is a self-perpetuating philosophy that has the potential to have Blacks perpetually beholden to White benevolence, or, dependent upon their eventual overthrow.[156]

Yes, British-Caribbean Christians should be more politically involved and they are well justified in expressing righteous anger at certain events but for Aldred, while these are important elements in their experience, it would be a distortion to give them a central and definitive place. 'A less polemical, more multi-faceted and holistic analysis of what the context of Caribbean British Christianity consists of, and therefore what tools are necessary to make progress, is needed.'[157]

As indicated above, I believe that Robert Beckford and Bishop Joe Aldred are the two most interesting and creative writers in this field and that a dialogue between them could be very instructive and constructive. In the meantime two observations might be made. The first concerns contexts and constituencies. Beckford writes in critical dialogue with the Church, but from outside, from the street. It may well be that many of his constituents experience more oppression and more anger than those within the churches. Beckford is attempting to develop a theology which would make sense of their experience and address their problems. He claims that the theology inherited by the black church and its preachers is inadequate for this task. Evidence for this can be found in a collection published by Joe Aldred, *Preaching with Power: sermons by Black preachers*. On closer inspection the sermons deal with none of the familiar themes of Black theology. They could have been preached by White Pentecostalists. They are mainly about individual salvation and entirely omit the dimension of the black community. It may be that by restricting his constituency to the black churches Aldred has eliminated the voice of protest from out with the churches (or, as a bishop, has stilled some voices of criticism within) and has re-enforced a theology which is unwilling or unable to address the issues raised and is content to repeat the theology of another time and place.[158]

In addition to constituencies, there is a second observation. Our discussion of Beckford's works has revealed a development. He may have begun with American Black Theology, but he has moved on from there. Yes, from time to time he repeats the old rhetoric of Black Liberation Theology, but increasingly he has concentrated on the appropriation of the African-Caribbean culture in the UK. This was seen in his Theology of Dread, which has great potential, expressly arising from the Caribbean spiritual tradition, with the potential to energise worship and meaningfully reinterpret traditional doctrines such as redemption. It is unfortunate that Aldred chooses not to mention this. It is also seen most recently in his *Jesus Dub*. Aldred is justified in criticising the old paradigm of oppression when it is given central place, but this is no longer fundamental to Beckford's developing position. Beckford and Aldred are the two most theologically creative figures in this field in the UK. If anything there is a certain convergence in their positions. Both are focusing on the British-Caribbean experience rather than the black experience. For neither of them is the term 'Black theology' useful in their projects. We can only hope that there is a sustained dialogue between them. Aldred could reflect on the significance of Beckford's more recent work. Beckford in turn has already expressed his admiration for Aldred's work, *Respect*, which he finds to be a good example of counter-ideology, 'promoting alternative identities full of Christian hope, optimism and potential.'[159] It is significant that Beckford, departing from his normal practice, does not follow this up with a criticism of Aldred. Significant, too, that he does not respond to Aldred's rather sharp criticism of his earlier position. We can only hope.

Aldred's work is bold, perceptive and even courageous: he rejects some of what I have been calling the 'mantras' of Black theology. He is seeking a biblically based alternative. The faithful of his constituency do not recognise themselves in the paradigm of the Exodus. It is too negative, too reactive. They have arrived at a new destination and are creating their new lives; more Promised Land than flight from Egypt. 'Exodus or liberation from oppression then has been set aside as an overarching or paradigmatic theme and in its place comes a paradigm of "Incarnation". This represents a theology of realized liberty rather than one in search of it.'[160] They are not longing for freedom: thankfully they have achieved that. 'They are not held prisoner by their past, neither do they labour under the burden of inferiority, or a lack of identity.'[161] As we shall see in the next chapter, much Black Theology in the USA still repeats the rhetoric of the freedom struggle of the 1960s. For Aldred, the Caribbean people of the UK have moved beyond that stage. Now they are ready to incarnate their Christian faith and responsibility. What they need is the opportunity and this requires respect. It is tempting to return to our earlier discussion of contextual theologies and to say that on this analysis Aldred's constituents experience the oppression of disrespect. They need to be liberated from a lack of respect, respect from others and even lack of self-respect.

Contextual theologies offer a perspective from which some aspects of traditional theology can be reinterpreted creatively. We can think of Gustavo Gutiérrez's reworking of the doctrine of salvation from the perspective of liberation or the example we have discussed of Robert Beckford's reworking of rage and redemption. But for the most part the terminology 'Theology of …' offers a perspective rather than a complete system. So it is with Aldred's own position, which he calls the 'Theology of Respect'. He offers some examples. There is respect for one's elders. There is the mutual greeting of young black men: 'Respect!' This does not look promising as the foundation of a new theology, but there is something here to consider. Etymology is sometimes suggestive and I think this offers a more fruitful line of development. The 'looking again', which is implied in 're-spect' requires a change of mind, similar to conversion. It is a re-vision of first impressions. The first look may be superficial, guided by assumptions and stereotypes: the man scarcely noticed is 'only a foreigner', the passer-by is 'only an elderly woman'. But something happens to make us look again, causes a revision, a seeing with new eyes. We are now aware of the figure not as an instance of a type, on the margins of our lives, but as a person of uniqueness, significance and worth. This can also be a reflexive process, as people become convinced of their self-worth. I doubt if there is sufficient potential in a Theology of Respect to produce a reinterpretation of doctrine, but it has a contextual importance for Aldred's constituents. As an experience of conversion it has potential in social, political, moral and religious life. It also has the merit of biblical antecedents.

Notes

1 Kalbir Shukra, *The Changing Patterns of Black Politics in Britain*, Pluto Press, 1998, p. 60.

2 Peter Fryer, *Staying Power: the history of black people in Britain*, Pluto Press, 1984; James Walvin, *Black and White: the Negro in English society 1555–1945*, Allen Lane, 1973.

3 *De Generis Humani Varietate Nativa*, reproduced in Michael Banton, *Ethnic and Racial Consciousness*, Longman, 1997 (1988), p. 55.

4 Shukra, *The Changing Patterns of Black Politics*, pp. 31–2.

5 Claire Alexander, *The Art of Being Black: the creation of Black British youth identities*, Clarendon Press, Oxford, 1996, p. 40.

6 Ibid., p. 59.

7 Beverley Bryan, Stella Dadzie and Suzanne Scafe, *The Heart of the Race: black women's lives in Britain*, Virago Press, 1985, p. 227.

8 Patricia R. Pessar (ed.) *Caribbean Circuits: new directions in the study of Caribbean migration*, Center for Migration Studies, New York, 1997, p. 3. This volume is mainly concerned with the Caribbean–USA circuit in which the Dominican Republic corresponds to Jamaica. See in that volume Lourdes Bueno, 'Dominican Women's Experiences of Return Migration: the life stories of five women' and Luis Eduardo Guarnizo, 'Going Home: class, gender and household transformation among Dominican return migrants'.

9 Danièle Joly, *Blacks and Britannity*, Ashgate, 2001, p. 42.

10 Alexander, *The Art of Being Black*, p. 45.

11 Paul Gilroy, *There Ain't No Black in the Union Jack*, Routledge, 1995 (1987), p. 46, a reference to the UK flag.

[12] Trevor Carter, *Shattering Illusions: West Indians in British politics*, Lawrence & Wishart, 1986, p. 17.

[13] Quoted in Shukra, *The Changing Patterns of Black Politics*, p. 56.

[14] Ibid., p. 73.

[15] Quoted ibid., p. 74.

[16] Ibid., p. 110.

[17] Carter, *Shattering Illusions*, p. 140, unattributed source.

[18] Ibid., p. 43.

[19] Quoted in Alexander, *The Art of Being Black*, p. 93.

[20] Carter, *Shattering Illusions*, p. 62; also Cedric Robinson, *Black Marxism*, Zed Books, 1983.

[21] Ibid., p. 116.

[22] Ibid., p. 115, unattributed interview.

[23] Mary Chamberlain, *Narratives of Exile and Return*, Macmillan Caribbean, 1997, p. 2.

[24] Andrew Pilkington, *Racial Disadvantage and Ethnic Diversity in Britain*, Palgrave Macmillan, 2003, p. 212.

[25] Quoted in John Solomos, *Race and Racism in Contemporary Britain*, Macmillan, 1989, p. 55.

[26] Quoted in Pilkington, *Racial Disadvantage*, p. 222.

[27] Solomos, *Race and Racism*, p. 141.

[28] Quoted in Pilkington, *Racial Disadvantage*, p. 244.

[29] Ibid., p. 244.

[30] 'The Offence of the West Indian: political leadership and the communal option' in Pnina Werbner and Muhammad Anwar (eds) *Black and Ethnic Leadership in Britain: the cultural dimensions of political action*, Routledge, 1991, p. 316.

[31] Pilkington, *Racial Disadvantage*, p. 119.

[32] Alexander, *The Art of Being Black*, p. 7.

[33] Martin Baker, quoted in ibid., p. 4.

[34] Ibid., p. 5.

[35] Ibid., p. 18.

[36] Pilkington, *Racial Disadvantage*, p. 206.

[37] Ibid., p. 125.

[38] Shukra, *The Changing Patterns of Black Politics*, p. 35.

[39] Pilkington, *Racial Disadvantage*, p. 168.

[40] Chamberlain, *Narratives of Exile and Return*, p. 3.

[41] Sharon Daye, *Middle-Class Blacks in Britain: a racial fraction of a class group or a class fraction of a racial group?*, Macmillan, 1994, p. 253; my emphasis.

[42] Ibid., p. 283.

[43] Ibid., p. 287.

[44] Bryan, Dadzie and Scafe, *The Heart of the Race*, p. 173.

[45] Ibid., p. 174.

[46] Ibid.

[47] Ibid., p. 175.

[48] Hazel V. Carby, quoting Achola Pala in 'White Women Listen! Black feminism and the boundaries of sisterhood' in Centre for Contemporary Cultural Studies, *The Empire Strikes Back: race and racism in 70s Britain*, Hutchinson, 1988 (1982), p. 227.

[49] Bryan, Dadzie and Scafe, *The Heart of the Race*, p. 144.

[50] Quoted ibid., p. 147.

[51] Carby, 'White Women Listen!', p. 217.

[52] Ibid., p. 214.

[53] Quoted in Alexander, *The Art of Being Black*, p. 157.

[54] Ibid., p. 163.

[55] Ibid., p. 166.

[56] Ibid., p. 176.
[57] Ibid., p. 172.
[58] Ibid., p. 174.
[59] Quoted in Winston James and Clive Harris (eds) *Inside Babylon: the Caribbean diaspora in Britain*, Verso, 1993, p. 163.
[60] Ibid., p. 163; my emphasis.
[61] In Heidi Safia Mirza (ed.) *Black British Feminism: a reader*, Routledge, 1997, p. 280.
[62] Ibid., p. 281.
[63] Ibid., p. 283.
[64] Ibid., p. 293.
[65] Ibid.
[66] Ibid., p. 294.
[67] Martin Baumann, 'A Diachronic View of Diaspora, the Significance of Religion and Hindu Trinidadians' in Waltraud Kokot, Khachig Tölölyan and Carolin Alfonso (eds) *Diaspora, Identity and Religion: new directions in theory and research*, Routledge, 2004, pp. 171–2.
[68] For references, see Ieuan Ellis, *Seven Against Christ: a study of 'Essays and Reviews'*, E.J. Brill, Leiden, 1980.
[69] Karl Barth, *The Epistle to the Romans*, trans. Hoskyns, Oxford University Press, 1933, p. 6.
[70] Robert Beckford, *Jesus is Dread: Black theology and Black culture in Britain*, Darton, Longman and Todd, 1998, p. 147.
[71] Robert Beckford, *God and the Gangs: an urban toolkit for those who won't be sold out, bought out or scared out*, Darton, Longman and Todd, 2004, p. 31.
[72] Beckford, *Jesus is Dread*, p. 2.
[73] Ibid., p. 13.
[74] Robert Beckford, *God of the Rahtid: redeeming rage*, Darton, Longman and Todd, 2001, p. 1.
[75] Alistair Kee, *Seeds of Liberation*, SCM Press, 1973.
[76] Beckford, *Jesus is Dread*, p. 17.
[77] Robert Beckford, *Dread and Pentecostal: a political theology for the Black Church in Britain*, SPCK, 2000, p. 27.
[78] Ibid., p. 47.
[79] Ibid., p. 152.
[80] Ibid., p. 154.
[81] Ibid., p. 155.
[82] Ibid., p. 214.
[83] Beckford, *Jesus is Dread*, p. 75.
[84] Ibid., p. 77.
[85] Beckford, *God of the Rahtid*, p. viii.
[86] Ibid., p. 24.
[87] Ibid., p. 27.
[88] Ibid., p. 38.
[89] Ibid., p. 63.
[90] Ibid., p. 45.
[91] Ibid., p. 40.
[92] Ibid., p. 46.
[93] Ibid., p. 101.
[94] Ibid.
[95] Ibid., p. 104.
[96] Beckford, *God and the Gangs*, p. 118.
[97] Ibid., p. 50.
[98] See Ennis Barrington Edmonds, *Rastafari: from outcasts to culture bearers*, Oxford University Press, 2003.

[99] Beckford, *Dread and Pentecostal*, pp. 118, 161.

[100] Ibid., p. 160.

[101] Ibid., p. 216.

[102] Beckford, *Jesus is Dread*, p. 116.

[103] Beckford, *God and the Gangs*, p. 45.

[104] Beckford, *Jesus is Dread*, p. 123.

[105] Beckford, *Dread and Pentecostal*, p. 13.

[106] Ibid., p. 136. Beckford takes this term from Victor Anderson, whose work will be discussed in Chapter 6.

[107] Kate Coleman, 'Black Theology and Black Liberation: a womanist perspective', *Black Theology in Britain: a journal of Contextual Praxis,* Issue 2 (1999), p. 68.

[108] Kate Coleman, 'Black Women in Theology', *Black Theology*, Issue 3 (1999).

[109] Ernest Cashmore, quoted in Barrington Edmonds, *Rastafari*, p. 62.

[110] Cashmore, quoted in ibid., p. 108.

[111] Beckford, *Jesus is Dread*, p. 144.

[112] Beckford, *Dread and Pentecostal*, p. 189.

[113] Beckford, *Jesus is Dread*, pp. 145–6.

[114] Beckford, *Dread and Pentecostal*, p. 163.

[115] Ibid., p. 164.

[116] Beckford, *Jesus is Dread*, pp. 146–7.

[117] Robert Beckford, *Jesus Dub: theology, music and social change*, Routledge, 2006, p. 27.

[118] Ibid., p. 26.

[119] Ibid., p. 96.

[120] Ibid., p.2.

[121] Ibid., p.99.

[122] 1 Cor. 13.1

[123] Luke: 4:18–19

[124] Beckford, *Jesus Dub*, p. 127.

[125] Quoted in D.R. McConnell, *A Different Gospel: a historical and biblical analysis of the modern faith movement*, Hendrickson Publishers, Peabody, MA, 1988, p. 175.

[126] Michael N. Jagessar and Anthony G. Reddie (eds) *Postcolonial Black British Theology,* Epworth, 2007. Some of these comments are taken from my review of the book for *The Expository Times.*

[127] Anthony G. Reddie, *Nobodies to Somebodies: a practial theology for education and liberation,* Epworth Press, 2003.

[128] Ibid., p. 3.

[129] Paul Grant and Raj Patel (eds) *A Time to Speak*, Racial Justice Black Theology Working Group, Birmingham, 1990. *A Time to Act*; Birmingham, Black and Third World Working Group, 1992.

[130] Robinson A. Milwood, *Suspension: a testimony of faith, suffering and perseverance*, Stoke Newington Mission, 2002, Foreword.

[131] Milwood, Robinson A. *Liberation and Mission: a black experience*, African Caribbean Education Resource, London, 1997.

[132] Ibid., p. 91.

[133] Ibid., p. 95.

[134] Ibid., p. 103.

[135] *Black Theology in Britain,* Issue 1, 1998, p. 68.

[136] *Black Theology in Britain*, Issue 3, 1999.

[137] Marjorie Lewis, 'Diaspora Dialogue: womanist theology in engagement with aspects of the Black British and Jamaican experience', *Black Theology*, 2.2, 2004, p. 100.

[138] Ibid., p. 105.

[139] 'Towards a Womanist Pneumatological Pedagogy: an investigation into the development and implementation of a theological pedagogy by and for the marginalized', *Black Theology*, 3.1, 2005.

[140] *Black Theology,* vol. 4.2, 2006.

[141] 'Liturgical Studies and Christian Worship: the postcolonial challenge'. *Black Theology*, 5.1, 2007.

[142] Roswith Gerloff, *A Plea for British Black Theologies*, Peter Lang, Frankfurt, 2 vols, 1992.

[143] Ibid., p. 264.

[144] *Respect: Understanding Caribbean British Christianity*; Epworth, 2005 *Preaching with Power: Sermons by Black Pastors*; Cassell, London: 1998 *Sisters with Power* Continuum Books, London, 2000; *Praying with Power* Continuum Books, London, 2000.

[145] Ibid., p. 3.

[146] Ibid., p. 15.

[147] Ibid., pp. 24–5.

[148] Ibid.

[149] Ibid., p. 88.

[150] Gerloff, *British Black Theologies*, vol 1, p. 38 Beckford, *Jesus Dub*, pp. 43–44, criticising Calley; Malcolm, *God's People: West Indian Pentecostal Sects in England*, Oxford University Press, 1965.

[151] Aldred, *Respect,* pp. 152–3

[152] Ibid.

[153] Ibid., p. 28

[154] Ibid., p. 160.

[155] Ibid.

[156] Ibid., pp. 160–61

[157] Ibid.

[158] The variety of practice on this point is brought out by contrasting it with the account offered by Gerloff *British Black Theologies*, vol. 1, pp. 260–62 when she deals with 'Self-help and community development'.

[159] Beckford, *Jesus Dub*, p. 58.

[160] Aldred, *Respect*, p. 164.

[161] Ibid., p. 181

CHAPTER 6

Gender, Race and Class: the Closed Circle of Black Theology

Race and Reification

We have spent most of our time examining the *rise* of Black theology. It was a phenomenon of its time and that time was the very end of the period of modernity. (In fact Foucault's works of the 1960s were published *before* Black theology appeared.) It shared the presuppositions of that era, including the possibility of truth, an appeal to a moral consensus, the sources of identity, the formation of the self, the aspiration to freedom and what Hayek would call a 'constructivist' view of social reality. But that era has gone and it is for this reason that Black theology now looks like a survival. It is time to face reality and acknowledge its *demise.* Twenty years after the end of the Second World War the occasional Japanese soldier would be found on a Pacific island. No one had told him that the war was over. In the case of Black theology the war was not concluded, the struggle moved on. The old strategies do not address the new conflict. As we have seen, although Black theology in South Africa stalled, it had reached the point where it was no longer about race. It was poised to become a political theology of power. In the UK it is poised to become a political theology of Dread. But in America, because it avoids the issue of class, it cannot become a political theology. It is unable to respond to the new reality. Two examples illustrate the point, gender and race.

One of the constant, self-congratulatory mantras of American Black and womanist theologies is that they deal with oppression on the basis of gender, race and class. As we have seen the reality is that they steadfastly refuse to deal with class at all. But at least they deal with gender and race. Well, yes and no. These theologies deal with gender and race, but according to the discourse of modernity. The issue of gender is raised for womanist theology because of its dialogue with feminist theology. (Let us set aside for the moment the question of whether shouting abuse over a fence constitutes dialogue.) But what happens to womanist theology if the category of gender is problematized?

Radical movements are never radical enough: it is notoriously difficult to begin at the beginning. At least in the first attempt it is impossible to avoid continuing with the presuppositions and assumptions of those from whom the radicals wish to dissociate themselves. An example of this can be found in Nietzsche's essay 'On Truth and Falsity in Their Extramoral Sense': 'truths are illusions of which one has forgotten that they are illusions; worn-out metaphors which have become powerless to affect the sense; coins with their images effaced and now no longer of account as coins but merely as metal.'[1] There is no truth of the world, independent of us, merely patterns of meaning and value which we have projected onto the world, 'so that it is we who thereby make the impression on ourselves'.[2] Nietzsche thereby prepared the way for the deconstruction of modernity under the category of 'genealogy'. It is this thought that is pursued by the postmodern writer Michel Foucault. There are no inner truths waiting to be discovered. Everything is the result of human activity, often masked. What are referred to as truths are constructs effected by power, which suit the interests of those exercising power. Foucault is here uncovering a Nietzschean reversal, his project is

> To substitute for the enigmatic treasure of 'things' anterior discourse, the regular formation of objects that emerge only in discourse. To define these objects without reference to the ground, the foundation of things.[3]

What is identified as a *cause* from which certain *effects* flow is in fact itself an effect of the political sources which have (surreptitiously) caused it. The long-term significance of this farewell to innocence is that we must now adopt an attitude of suspicion towards anything which is represented to us as neutral and natural.

Judith Butler's anti-foundationalism applies this perspective to the claim that gender is a category of origins, part of the natural, biological world. She concludes *Gender Trouble* with this programmatic: she intends her book to bring about 'the denaturalization of gender as such'.[4] Historically the question 'What is woman?' cannot be asked until there is an answer to the prior question, 'What is man?' But feminists have assumed that they can take as their subject an existing entity called woman, as if women were not already constructed with respect to the male world. 'The feminist subject turns out to be discursively constituted by the very political system that is supposed to facilitate its emancipation.'[5] She therefore proposes 'a *feminist genealogy* of the category of women'.[6] Political systems and juridical powers claim to represent certain natural foundations of society. In reality they actually produce these foundations. This analysis is parallel to the theory of ideology, by which socially constructed institutions, such as the state, represent themselves as part of a natural order of things. The question is whether gender is part of the natural order of things, from which identity is formed, with implications for behaviour and relationships. Or is it itself a construct, produced by centres of power and interest in the political world? Is gender an ontological category from which secondary and accidental features flow. Or to the contrary, is gender a performative, 'constituting the identity it is purported to be'.[7] This is Butler's famous theory of performativity. 'There is no gender identity behind the expressions of gender; that identity is performatively constituted by the very "expressions" that are said to be its results.'[8] Gender is not the cause of these expressions, but their reification. But the process is disguised to conceal its own genealogy. To illustrate, male interests can be served by identifying a foundational 'maternal instinct', which might well be 'a culturally constructed desire which is interpreted through a naturalistic vocabulary'.[9] The law requires conformity to its own notion of 'nature'. At this point Butler follows Foucault on deviance.

> S/he is 'outside' the law, but the law maintains this 'outside' within itself. In effect, s/he embodies the law, not as an entitled subject, but as an enacted testimony to the law's uncanny capacity to produce only those rebellions that it can guarantee will – out of fidelity – defeat themselves and those subjects who, utterly subject, have no choice but to reiterate the law of their genesis.[10]

It does not matter that the law of gender is not part of the natural world: gender construction means that individuals know how to play their part, even in emancipatory protest. Nor can sex be established as a purely natural category. The language of biology is already infiltrated by cultural assumptions: 'the category of "sex" is itself a *gendered* category, fully politically invested, naturalized but not natural.'[11] Butler writes with sophistication and discernment but the whole book might be seen as a series of examples of the distinction between the expressive and the performative: gender, sex and even the body itself. 'The sex/gender distinction and the category of sex itself appear to presuppose a genderization of "the body" that pre-exists the acquisition of its sexed significance.'[12] But of course by this time we know what is coming: the inscription of the body as of the male or female sex is a social or in some cases a political act. The body no less than sex, is already gendered.

Finally, all this is relevant to the feminist movement and therefore to womanism. Feminism is not in control of its own subject and is liable to incorporate assumptions which are antipathetic to its declared aims.

> The feminist 'we' is always and only a phantasmatic construction, one that has its purposes, but which denies the internal complexity and indeterminacy of the term and constitutes itself only through the exclusion of some part of the constituency that it simultaneously seeks to represent.[13]

As an emancipatory movement feminism has naively bought into a system of reifications guaranteed to frustrate its best intentions. 'The internal paradox of this foundationalism is that it presumes, fixes and constrains the very "subjects" that it hopes to represent and liberate.'[14] Womanism claims to be in critical dialogue with feminism, but neither movement is aware of their common problem. Womanist theology claims to be addressing the issue of gender: the work has not yet begun. It is still functioning within the discourse of modernity which will ensure its failure.

We began by noting that American Black and womanist theologies claim to respond to oppression and discrimination based on gender, race and class. We have just examined the implications of this claim with respect to gender, in the light of the work of Judith Butler. Inevitably we must now ask whether and to what extent it is possible and useful to apply Butler's theory of genealogy, not to gender but to race. Indeed we might feel emboldened to attempt this in view of the fact that at several points Butler mentions gender and race at the same time. She is critical of 'the totalizing gestures of feminism' which mimic the oppressor by identifying a singular enemy. '"Colonizing gestures" relate also to race and class.'[15] Applying

Butler's distinction between the expressive and the performative, we can formulate the following proposition:

Colour is to gender
as
race is to sex.

Black is not an ontological category. Being black is not part of the natural order of things. Being black is not a foundational state of affairs from which certain heuristic or accidental features flow. Associated characteristics of appearance, gesture or behaviour are not expressive of being black. To the contrary they are reifications of a social construct. These associated features are performative. Being black does not determine the features: the features define being black.

There are two questions raised here. The first is, if being black is not a natural state but a social and political construct, who is responsible for the construction? Certainly not black people. It is white people who have defined the essence of being black. And behind this essentialism they have postulated a foundational, neutral condition. On this view being black is natural and from it certain features are manifest. But of course we know that this is not the case. The reality is quite the opposite. The features predate the reification: the features in their performativity create the 'natural' state. The content of being black, the features that it is claimed are determined are not constructed by whim or whimsy but according to the political interests of those who hold and exercise power. Those responsible for the construct are mainly white, although on occasion the construct could suit the interests of some blacks who are in positions of power. It has proved notoriously difficult for black writers to define what they mean by the category. This is because it is a received term, already formed elsewhere. It is possible to assert other meanings, but not without contradiction.

The second question raised by the construction of the category black concerns normativity. If being black were a natural state then it would be self-defining, but it is not. In the feminist context we saw that the question 'What is woman?' is dependent on an answer to the prior question, 'What is man?' If it is white people who construct the category 'black', then the question, 'What is black?' cannot be answered without reference to the prior question 'What is white?' Except that *that* question is not asked. Men ask the question, 'What is woman?' because woman is the Other. They do not ask the question 'What is man?' because that is the given. The difficulty in defining being black is not just that it is a social construct, effected by whites, but that initially the definition of black is not-white. The difficulty is compounded by the situation that whites refuse to provide the definition by which not-white would begin to make sense.

This calls into question the usefulness of the term 'black' in Black theology. We saw that Alice Walker discovered that to describe herself as black in Cuba was a 'perverted categorization'. It was obviously not part of the natural world as far as the school children to whom she spoke were concerned. I do not presume to know what was in the mind of Alice Walker at that moment. I can imagine that someone in her situation might well experience a moment of illumination. It might become clear that all her life she had been duped. She had been describing herself according to a category constructed by her enemy. In describing herself to others as 'black' she had adopted a self-reference which was not her description of herself, but a description of her by others. Nor was the category 'black' a natural or neutral term, but a political and social construct which expressed not her reality but the view of her held by those who had never met her In the context of performativity 'black' does indeed seem a perverted category and the use of the term by blacks would seem to be a form of perversion or self-abuse. It is difficult to imagine how the interests of white oppressors could be better served than by blacks accepting this politically motivated and socially constructed term.

More briefly, if sex is already gendered, race is already coloured. Race is not a natural phenomenon. It is not the foundation from which accidental features flow. It does not express certain characteristics. To the contrary, politically selected features through performativity create the content of what is taken to be race. When I first travelled to the USA to begin my graduate studies many years ago I found myself unable to answer the immigration question on race. I was blond, blue eyed and fair skinned. I could be described as 'white' but that was a colour, not a race. Some of my contemporaries answered 'human race'. I am sure this angered officials but intuitively it was not an inappropriate response. Sex is not a biological category: it is a juridical term found to be convenient in recommending and then enforcing certain relationships and activities. It is does not describe a natural phenomenon but is a construct that serves social and especially economic interests. Can we say the same about race? It is not a biological category: it is a juridical term found to be convenient in recommending and then enforcing certain relationships and activities. It is does not describe a natural phenomenon but is a construct that serves social and especially economic interests. We might think of the example of South Africa during the period of apartheid.[16] But let us not be so naive as to think that racism departed this world in 1989 or that it is peculiar to white people.[17] We could say, paradoxically, that race has nothing to do with race. It has everything to do with the political interests of those who construct negative images of social groups they seek to oppress and use to their advantage. When I lived in southern Africa Japanese businessmen were treated as 'honorary whites' because of their economic importance. In the postmodern world sex is no longer a useful term for categorising people. We might well be suspicious of anyone who declared themselves to be absolutely and unconditionally heterosexual. Why are they so strident about it? But is race any more useful? Strolling along the Copacabana on a Sunday afternoon when the carriageway of the Avenida Atlantica is closed to traffic, thousands of people mingle freely. Race seems an irrelevant category. In Chapter 4 Alice Walker found that in Cuba, race was a 'perverted categorization'. In Chapter 5 Martin Barker described it as a 'pseudo-biological' category and Bishop Joe Aldred described race as 'an unhelpful and divisive, largely Western, terminology.' Cantwell Smith proposed that the term 'religion' was an imposed category, used to describe people's faith and traditions in spite of them: we should dispense with it.[18] Is it not time to dispense with the category of race: it is one of the master's tools.

Earlier in this discussion we stated that 'Black is not an ontological category.' It will be recalled that in Chapter 2 Cone asserted that blackness *is* 'an ontological category'. Our rejection of this claim recalls the work of Victor Anderson in *Beyond Ontological Blackness: an essay in African American religious and cultural criticism.* We have developed our position in a trajectory from Nietzsche, through Foucault and Butler. Anderson proceeds along a different trajectory but draws parallel conclusions. We are claiming that black *is not* an ontological category: Anderson claims that it *should not* be, but in fact has become so. Using the distinction between the expressive and the performative we have been claiming that features which are taken to express race are, to the contrary, reifications which in fact constitute race. The parallels can be seen as Anderson sets out the objectives of his book.

> The disclosure of the ways that race is reified – i.e., treated as if it objectively exists independent of historically contingent factors and subjective intentions – in the writings of history and contemporary African American cultural and religious thinkers is the first theme of the book. Throughout this book, I describe this tendency toward racial reification as ontological blackness. Ontological blackness is a covering term that connotes categorical, essentialist and representational languages depicting black life and experience.[19]

He is writing to expose the process by which blackness is made ontological. His project is to propose a path by which ontological blackness is transcended. We have maintained that in this context black cannot be defined until white is defined, since black is constructed out of being not-white. For Anderson, 'ontological blackness signifies the blackness that whiteness created'.[20] Ontological blackness does not begin with black consciousness but racial consciousness, a consciousness of unresolved binary dialectics: slavery and freedom, negro and citizen, insider and outsider, black and white, struggle and survival. 'However such binary polarities admit no possibility of transcendence or mediation.'[21] Ontological blackness therefore prevents the development of 'a new cultural politics of black identity that meaningfully relates to the conditions of postmodern North American life'.[22] On this reading Black theology lies within the discourse of modernity. It undermines the unlikely claim by James Evans that 'the most obvious and significant religious response to the postmodernist mood, especially within the United States, is African-American Christianity'.[23]

As we earlier noted, it is notoriously difficult for radical movements to be radical enough: the new self which they construct is still determined by their oppositional stance in relation to those who previously defined them, who still exercise power by holding up a mirror. We saw this in discussing the womanist revolt, quoting Marx.

> The traditions of all the dead generations weigh like a nightmare on the brain of the living. And just when they seem engaged in revolutionising themselves and things, in creating something that has never yet existed, precisely in such periods

> of revolutionary crisis they anxiously conjure up the spirits of the past to their service and borrow from them names, battle-cries and costumes in order to present the new scene of world history in this time-honoured disguise.

In this chapter we quoted Butler, following Foucault on the defiance of deviance. According to Anderson even black critical thinkers have shown their dependence on the white European cultural philosophy they aspired to oppose. 'Pressing beyond ontological blackness requires African American religious critics to subvert every racial discourse, including their own, that would bind black subjectivity to the totality of racial identity.'[24]

The particular relevance of Anderson's criticism is that he maintains that Black theology is determined by ontological blackness. It is a theology of the 1970s and is defined by the paradigmatic binaries of conflict and suffering, of oppression and survival. And its chief architect is James H. Cone. 'In the matrix of black existence and white racism, Cone explicates the meaning of ontological blackness in terms of an emergent collective black revolutionary consciousness.'[25] For Anderson, Cone's project is beset with problems from the outset. 'Black theology appeared to posit within itself a revolutionary consciousness that looked more like the mirror of white racism and less like an expression of the evangelical gospel that characterized most black churches.'[26] As we saw in Chapter 2, Cone, in attempting to distance himself from white sources, turned to black sources, but without any critical distance between them and Christian faith. 'Because Cone collapses metaphysics into ontology, blackness is reified into a totality or a unity of black experience.'[27] Ironically or is it tragically, 'while black theology justifies itself as radically oppositional to whiteness, it nevertheless requires whiteness, white racism, and white theology for its self-disclosure of its new black being and its legitimacy'.[28]

More briefly, it is no surprise that Anderson claims womanist theology is also bound by ontological blackness. 'It proposes the privilege of self-definition. Yet ontological blackness binds the discourse almost exclusively and exceptionally to suffering and resistance.'[29] There are two further ironies here. First, womanist theology has made a great deal of separating itself from Black theology, which it claims is not only man made, but male oriented, intent on serving male interests. But just as Black theology is dependent on the white theology it purports to criticise, so, according to Anderson, 'the womanist theologian has become, it seems, the mirror of black masculinity: strong and rebellious, surviving and resisting, heroic and epochal'.[30] Second, womanist theology repeatedly claims to have overcome binarism, which it identifies as one of the evils of white Eurpean thought. Yet, according to Anderson, it inherits all the 'unresolved binary dialectics' of ontological blackness.

Gender, race and class. If Black and womanist theologies have been unable to mount a critical account of gender and race, how have they coped with class?

Black theology was originally concerned only with race, with oppression caused by racial discrimination. Later it was to become involved in a trialogue with feminist theology and Latin American liberation theology. The three became known as liberation theologies and challenged each other to add further perspectives to their original analyses. From that time Black theology has repeated as a mantra that it is holistic, dealing with oppression on the basis of race, gender and class. But as far as the USA is concerned, neither Black theology nor womanist theology has ever addressed the subject of class. It would be somehow unAmerican. This in turn raises the question just what is it that they claimed to have learned from Latin American Liberation theology. The name 'liberation theology' arose in the 1960s at a time when there were Marxist inspired revolutionary movements throughout Latin America. The Cuban revolution of 1959 was to be the paradigm. If it is permitted to draw but one line dividing society, then theology must be on the side of the poor and oppressed, must be on the side of the revolution, must be a liberation movement. Of course the liberation theologians were motivated by their Christian faith, but historically that faith had been used to legitimise and sacrilise every kind of tyrannical dictatorship and repressive regime in history. Their Christian faith had been influenced, clarified, by an engagement with Marxism. Gustavo Gutiérrez is regarded as the father figure of liberation theology and he claimed that those active in the struggle for the liberation of the oppressed 'are more or less inspired by Marxism'.[31] He was later to claim that,

> Contemporary theology does in fact find itself in direct and fruitful confrontation with Marxism, and it is to a large extent due to Marxism's influence that theological thought, searching for its own sources, has begun to reflect on the meaning of the transformation of this world and the action of man in history.[32]

These Christian theologians, Catholic and Protestant, were not Marxists, but without the fruitful dialogue there would have been no liberation theology. They were men (at that time) of good will, but that did not provide them with the theoretical tools necessary to understand social processes. This, according to José Miguez, was the contribution of Marxist analysis. 'At this point, the dynamics of the historical process, both in its objective conditions and its theoretical development, have led them, through the failure of several remedial and reformist alternatives, to discover the unsubstitutable relevance of Marxism.'[33] In its mantra Black theology claims to have learned from Latin American liberation theology that it is necessary to deal with the issue of class. In reality it simply avoids the issue. The reason is that it has deliberately avoided 'a fruitful confrontation with Marxism' and has failed to discover 'the unsubstitutable relevance of Marxism'. Albert Cleage mentions the issue only in passing, giving two reasons for ignoring Marxism. The first is that Marx did not write about racial oppression: the European countries which formed the model for his analysis did not contain significant numbers of black people. The second is that the blacks in America are a minority within a white country. He acknowledges that in other circumstances unnamed – his pan-Africanism does not extend to considering examples in Africa – communism or socialism might apply. He considers that poor whites still see their future with rich whites, not poor blacks. Class conflict does not apply. 'Marxism does not suit the American condition.'[34] Thus he insists on restricting consideration of oppression only to race. And only to the black race, although Marx as a Jew living in Prussia had personal experience of racism. He omits Marx's critique of capitalism as a source of human alienation.

The case of James Cone was different. The year after *Black Theology and Black Power* appeared he published *A Black Theology of Liberation*. It was not the first book in which the title outstrips the content. He had not yet met the liberation theologians and while Marx is mentioned briefly on two pages, Rudolf Bultmann is discussed in detail on 13 pages, the same Bultmann who, while the fires of racism burned all around him in Germany in 1941, could write of the challenge to religion of the rational, secular modern world. Three years later Cone was in touch with the liberation theologians and became aware that they regarded Marxist analysis as 'fruitful' and of 'unsubstitutable relevance'. In *For My People: Black theology and the Black church* he turns to the subject of 'Black Christians and Marxism'. This comes at the very end of the book where it can have no relevance to the main topics already covered. In his brief treatment of Marx he concentrates on 'the opium of the people', an early criticism which does not deal with economic issues, but eventually he gets to the point. 'The challenge of Marxism emerges out of Marx's critique of religion, but the necessity of Marxism arises out of his critique of capitalism.'[35] It may be 'a necessary tool for analyzing capitalism'[36] but Cone gives absolutely no indication as to why capitalism should be analysed, what might just be wrong with it or how it might oppress the lives of black people. This is all the more surprising because Cone claims that his 'interpretation of Marxism has been influenced by my colleague Cornel West'.[37] I doubt that West was impressed to read that.

Cornel West is a black Baptist, 'a Chekhovian Christian' with an intense interest in Black theology. A widely read philosopher of religion and a sensitive and sophisticated culture critic, West does not consider himself to be a theologian. However, his work is potentially one of the most valuable critical resources available to Black theology. His Marxist analysis of class and his criticism of capitalism have been almost entirely ignored: that is the tragedy. Yet Black theologians frequently insist that such analysis and criticism are necessary: that is the farce. West does not accept historical materialism, especially if it undervalues human culture as a locus of agency. Nor does he admire actually existing communist regimes, though he seems to have former East European examples in mind rather than African or Latin American examples. Even so, he views the dialogue with Marxism in the same kind of terms as the Latin American sources already quoted, 'fruitful' and of 'unsubstitutable relevance'. 'My general social analytical perspective – deeply neo-Gramscian in spirit – is more influenced by the Marxist tradition than by any other secular tradition.' In several places he repeats his judgement 'that the Marxist tradition is indispensable yet inadequate'.[38] What Marx said of Feuerbach, West now says of Marx.

> The Marxist model, despite its shortcomings, is more part of the 'solution' than part of the problem for black intellectuals. This is so because Marxism is the brook of fire – purgatory – of our postmodern times. Black intellectuals must pass through it, come to terms with it and creatively respond to it if black

> intellectual activity is to reach any recognizable level of sophistication and refinement.[39]

By restricting their criticism to racial discrimination, black intellectuals focus on the symptoms of a sickness within American society, but fail to relate these to the dynamics of capitalism, to the disparity of power, the maldistribution of wealth, oppressive relations of production and economic insecurity. 'The more black theologians disregard or overlook Marxist social criticism, the farther they distance themselves from the fundamental determinants of black oppression and any effective strategy to alleviate it.'[40] By restricting their concern to racial matters they have failed to understand the relationship between capitalism and imperialism abroad. West is well aware of the suspicion of international communism amongst black Americans, but that is not the most fruitful form of the dialogue he is advocating between progressive Marxism and prophetic black Christianity. He is calling for 'the will, vision and imagination to *Afro-Americanize* socialist thought and practice'.[41] Dwight Hopkins is recognised as one of the leaders of the second generation of Black theologians. He has at least attempted to address this issue. In *Introducing Black Theology of Liberation* he begins to introduce a new subject, the black poor. There is a need for 'a social analysis that will help poor black folk see the connection between global monopoloy capital and its control of the U.S. domestic economy'.[42] It was left to the second wave, especially Cornell West, to identify the black poor as the working class. 'If the political and cultural wings of the first generation did not define the poor specifically as working people, then black theology would simply be another form of a bourgeois, capitalist ideology.'[43] We find here an echo from Chapter 3 where Lebamang Sebidi described race analysis as 'bourgeois – and somehow reactionary'. There are two issues here. The first requires Black theology to move on from race analysis to class analysis. As we shall see, to the last, Cone and now Hopkins decline to take this step. The second issue is that class analysis is a Marxist concept. The poor have always been with us, the poor of the countryside who could normally, even with difficulty, find something to eat. Marx was concerned with a new poor, a new class appearing for the first time in history. They were actually produced by capitalism and the transition from the country to the city. This new working class was always at risk of destitution. Whether Black theology is prepared to understand the plight of the black urban poor through a Marxist critique of American capitalism remains to be seen. In *Heart and Head: black theology – past, present and future* Hopkins insists that Black theology must be a Black theology of liberation. He chides those second generation Black theologians who have omitted 'liberation', indeed 'have jettisoned not just the liberation of the poor but the very category of black theology'.[44] Hopkins seems to be reaching out to the liberation theology of Latin America when he takes over the signature concept of 'the preferential option for the poor'. Yet even here he takes fright and is content to speak of 'a spiritual calling' and 'spiritual possessions'.[45] He can even devote seven pages to an exposition of the work of Gutiérrez, without mentioning the 'fruitful confrontation with Marxism' or 'the unsubstitutable relevance of Marxism'. Sadly, at the end his radicalism is of the utopian type of socialism which Marx so much despised. 'Poverty will disappear when the poor share in the abundance of wealth and break the current global monopolization of the earth's resources, thereby bringing democracy into economics.'[46] There is no analysis, no policy. It is a vision: he has a dream.

American Black and Womanist theologies may deal badly with issues of gender and race, as we have already seen. They resolutely refuse to deal with class altogether. Curious. It is not that they consider it to be irrelevant. To the contrary, in their mantras of 'race, gender and class' they never cease to proclaim the necessity of dealing with class. It is not that they are unaware of its importance. As we have just noted, the formidable Cornel West sees the issue of Marxist analysis as a criterion of academic seriousness. 'Black intellectuals must pass through it, come to terms with it and creatively respond to it if black intellectual activity is to reach any recognizable level of sophistication and refinement.' They resolutely refuse to deal with the issue, although as West goes on to point out, avoiding it means failing the black poor. 'The more black theologians disregard and overlook Marxist social criticism, the farther they distance themselves from the fundamental determinants of black oppression and any effective strategy to alleviate it.' A utopian dream is no substitute for social analysis: this was the message of Liberation Theology. In the face of these facts it is curious that American Black and Womanist theologies avoid the issue of class. They resolutely refuse to deal with class altogether. But why *resolutely*? The answer, as ever, lies in the question. Other liberation theologies do not avoid class analysis: Latin American, South African, Caribbean, British. American Black and Womanist theologies avoid class analysis because they are American, because their concept of liberation is restricted to full entry into American society. It does not permit any fundamental economic criticism of America, at home or abroad.

Consider these two examples. The first concerns two European thinkers, Karl Marx and Sigmund Freud. By the early twentieth century the works of Marx were out of print in all European languages (some had never been printed at all). They existed in Russian translations, in the hands of the Moscow Publishing House. In the 1950s a new critical edition of the whole corpus of Marx's German works was undertaken. What was published, volume by volume, came as a shock, a revelation to European academic, intellectual and cultural life. The emerging philosophy of Marx had nothing to do with Leninism or Stalinism – indeed it provided a powerful critique of these systems. It was clearly possible to be a Marxist, but not a communist. Marxist analysis was immediately applied to all aspects of western societies – to philosophy and religion, to art and literary criticism, to education, politics and the institutions of the state. Through the theory of ideology, individuals were seen to be manipulated by the covert actions of economic and political power. Both wealth and poverty were created and sustained by these forces. The poor were to be defended, not blamed. Marxist analysis was widely adopted and creatively applied – in Europe, but not in America. America also required critical social analysis but turned instead to Freud, who died in 1939 and whose works were taken to America by German-speaking immigrants. The two outcomes were very different. For Marx, the problems of individuals arise from oppressive forces within society. For Freud the problems of individuals come from within themselves. For Marx the solution is social change. For Freud the solution is for the individual to become adjusted to existing society. With the embargo on Marx in the USA some attempted to force Freud into substituting for Marx. Marx had offered a completely new account of human history and just as his works were appearing again in Europe, Norman O. Brown was attempting to break out of 'the catastrophe of so-called neo-Freudianism' to reshape psychoanalysis into 'a wider theory of human nature, culture and history'.[47] It seems to be a matter of taste. But no, the preference of Freud over Marx was itself ideological. The forces and interests within American society which benefited from economic liberalism preferred an analysis which blamed the individual and exonerated the powerful. American Black and Womanist theologies, in refusing to make use of Marxist class analysis, have succumbed to an ideology which steers them away from addressing the fundamental causes of black oppression. They resolutely refuse to be so un-American as to consider issues of economic class, or a critique of capitalism – avoiding the fact that millions of blacks are also Americans and deserve to be defended against that other America which oppresses the poor at home and abroad.

Consider a second example, the argument of Benjamin DeMott in a book subtitled *Why Americans Can't Think Straight About Class*. As we saw in Chapter 4 above, Katie Cannon discussed this book while contriving to avoid its central thesis. In the twentieth century America had the reputation of being counter-revolutionary, as in the case of Cuba – although covertly formenting anti-democratic revolutions, for example in Chile and Nicaragua. This may seem strange for a country founded on a revolution. However, the revolution of 1776 was a bourgeois revolution, initiated by landowners and entrepreneurs. It is a feature of revolutions that the new ruling class generalises its own interests as if they were the interests of the whole society. No one consulted the slaves or the poor whites, many of whom were also slaves. Women were not consulted. The assertion in the Declaration of Independence that 'all men are equal' led to the idea that the USA was an egalitarian, classless society. Benjamin DeMott has declared this 'icon of classlessness' to be a myth, concluding that 'America as a classless society is, finally, a deceit [which] causes fearful moral and social damage.'[48] Class differences exist, but since they are denied they have to be masked by various modes of evasion or fantasy. In the myth, children are not limited by the socio-economic circumstances of their parents. Thus, aspirants to high office claim humble origins: the American dream. Different chances are attributed to life choices, not class origins: rags to riches. In this meritocracy all belong to the middle class, 'the imperial middle'. Obstacles are of an individual, moral nature, rather than inherent in the class structure. 'Pressed to perceive the imperial middle's norms as all-inclusive, they [the very poor] concur in the proposition that their own marginality and non-participation result from personal faults, moral and intellectual.'[49] As in the Freudian analysis, the fault lies in the character of the poor rather than the character of capitalist society. The myth of the imperial middle is reinforced through popular stereotypes. In TV series class differences are undermined and people are shown to be basically the same. People whose lives appear to contradict the myth through social superiority are in the end brought down low, while those thought to be of a lower class turn out to have the same values as the imperial middle: the constant plot of Colombo. Social distance is unreal. The president is filmed wearing jeans down on the ranch. The rich once knew the experiences of the poor. 'Be all you can', 'Be whatever you wish': 'life (in the imperial middle) is an omni orgy.'[50]

The myth of classlessness is also found in newspapers. 'There are but two discourses, one of superiority, the other inferiority; the former places readers not as a social class, but as persons of moral and mental distinction; the latter places outsiders not as members of a class but as people mentally and/or morally deficient.'[51] The implications for our study are that blacks must face up to the truth that no one can change their situation apart from themselves. According to the myth blacks have failed society: society has not failed them. There is a lack of reflexivity: the imperial middle feel no need to consider their faults and their part in the oppression of others. The imperial middle see no value in what is different from themselves. But by the law of ideology, the poor also believe in the myth which acts against them and are prepared to accept its judgement. The fault lies within them as individuals and no blame attaches to society.

The myth of course has implications for public policy. Myths do not solve social problems: they provide a guarantee to those who do not suffer from the problems that the issues will not be successfully addressed.

> It means that social problems resulting in significant inequalities are metamorphosed into incidents in a grand struggle between good and evil – a struggle represented by 'realists' as lying beyond government intervention. It means an endless succession of program failures is blamed on 'bureaucracy' instead of upon obscurantist, legislatively consecrated definitions of problems with which bureaucracy is obliged to work.[52]

The myth now directing social policy leads inevitably to 'state-administered class injustice.'[53] DeMott illustrates this from the disproportionate number of poor and black men who were drafted to Vietnam: their families did not know how to gain exemption for them. We might update this by reference to a speech given by John Kerry, former presidential candidate, in November 2006 in which he told school kids in California they should concentrate on their education – or they would get Iraq.

The myth is also given religious legitimation, one of the things religion does particularly well. We might supplement DeMott by reference to David Chilton and the prosperity gospel. 'The Bible shows that poverty will be abolished through godly productivity and rising real wealth. The biblical answer is not, as the saying goes, to redistribute the pie, but to make a bigger pie.' Or the supply side theology of Rich DeVos. 'The free-enterprise system has outperformed, outproduced any other in the world ... It is a gift of God to us, and we should understand it, embrace it and believe in it.'[54] Black Theology is more likely to affirm these views than contest them, since it also lies under the sway of the myth of the classless society. It resolutely refuses to entertain class analysis because of its unquestioned commitment to the myth of the American dream. DeMott concludes:

> The language that needs desperately to be spoken – the only language in which the interconnectedness of bad schools, bad housing, bad nutrition, and horrific family life can be grasped, and strong but hidden joint interests can be defined – is the indispensable language of class, and that language is proscribed.[55]

DeMott does not deal with race. His list of issues, all describing the experience of poor black people, can only be dealt with under class analysis. But that language is proscribed by those who benefit from the myth. American Black and Womanist theologies may deal badly with gender analysis and race analysis, but they are resolute in their avoidance of class analysis, the only means of addressing the conditions which oppress poor black people in the USA today.

The Ideology of Retrieval

Gender, race and class were the original features of the three liberation theologies. They in turn were made possible because of three forms of critical consciousness, but all of them depended on the development of historical consciousness, the most important feature of modernity which appeared in Europe in the eighteenth century. It has proved to be absolutely fundamental to the way in which academic disciplines proceed, especially in the Humanities and Social Sciences. 'For King Midas, legend says, everything he touched turned to gold. For modern man everything, the whole of reality, turns to history.'[56] Such is the all-pervasiveness of historical consciousness, according to Gerhard Ebeling, that we feel that we cannot understand any phenomenon until we have traced its historical development. Not surprisingly American books on Black theology frequently include chapters on the history of capture, the middle passage, slavery, emancipation, segregation and the civil rights movement. Womanist books frequently rehearse the biographies of black slave women. Nothing could be more natural. But as we saw at the beginning of this chapter we must be suspicious of anything which is advocated because it is 'natural'. The historical route is not the only way of understanding contemporary phenomena. Indeed to insist that they must be related to historical origins is itself an ideological position which deserves to be questioned. We can offer two alternative methods for understanding social movements.

In the same decade which saw the rise of the three liberation theologies, the 1960s, Michel Foucault was proposing an alternative understanding of social phenomena, the 'archaeology of knowledge'. Although he admitted that the term was not entirely appropriate he was clear on the perspective adopted. The archaeology of knowledge 'suspends the theme that succession is an absolute: a primary indissociable sequence to which discourse is subjected by the law of its finitude'.[57] He rejects any 'total history'.

> Questioned at this archaeological level, the field of modern *episteme* is not ordered in accordance with the ideal of a perfect mathematicization, nor does it unfold, on the basis of a formal purity, a long, descending sequence of knowledge progressively more burdened with empiricity. The domain of the modern *episteme* should be represented rather as a volume of space open in three dimensions.[58]

It is customary to treat social phenomena in isolation from each other, attributing them to a historical sequence. His alternative was to understand them by relating them to other social phenomena of the same period. Thus when clinical medicine was established at the end of the eighteenth century it was contemporary with 'a number of political events, economic phenomena, and institutional changes'.[59] Archaeology of knowledge 'wishes to show not how political practice has determined the meaning and form of medical discourse, but how and in what form it takes part in its conditions of emergence, insertion, and functioning'.[60] Let me give a specific example from Edinburgh, the historic city in which I live. In the eighteenth century, three luminaries of the Scottish Enlightenment lived within a mile of each other: Adam Smith in the Cannongate, Adam Ferguson in the Sciennes and David Hume in the New Town. They were the creators of the new economics, the new anthropology and the new critical philosophy. These developments cannot be understood discretely, but only within 'a volume of space open in three dimensions'.

The relevance of this approach to Black theology is obvious enough. Did Black theology arise in 1969 because of a historical sequence which can be traced back to the export of captives from West Africa in the seventeenth century? Clearly not. A more promising approach is to ask why it was that three liberation theologies arose at precisely the same time, theologies which had nothing in common in their historical trajectories. These theologies appeared within months of May 1968, when intellectual unrest swept through European and American universities. The 1960s was a decade in which traditional relations of oppression, coercion, exteriority, together with discourses of authority, were all called into question. This cultural milieu encouraged the quest for liberation in all human life: liberation in sexual behaviour and gender assignation, in post-colonial relations and racial stereotypes, in social stratification and the privilege of inheritance. There is no mystery about the appearance of theologies of liberation in this context. It would have been a disgraceful dereliction if they had *not* appeared. If we adopt the perspective of the archaeology of knowledge then we can understand the origins of liberation theologies, but we are also prepared for an inevitable consequence. If the cultural milieu turns against liberation, then these three theologies will die. Just as the historicism of trajectories does not explain why all three appeared within months of each other, so it cannot explain why they all foundered at the same time. It is not so easy to be precise about the date on which these theologies ended since, as noted, the post mortem literature continues, for reasons of economic survival, professional esteem and personal identity. But regardless of what purposes they now serve, they are no longer liberation movements.

In addition to the archaeology of knowledge, concerned mainly with discourse formation, another alternative perspective is provided by Marxist analysis which uncovers the relationship between culture and economic formations. History is frequently comprehended in relation to ideas. The periodicity of modern Europe is encapsulated in such concepts as the Renaissance, Reformation, Enlightenment, Romanticism. This was most profoundly entertained by Hegel in his presentation of world history as the history of freedom. World history is the progressive incarnation of the Spirit and he can conclude that, for example, 'the State is the Divine Idea as it exists on Earth'.[61] This idealist view of history might appeal to philosophers reflecting from positions of security, but lacks credibility for individuals, communities and societies whose energies are turned towards survival. Marx continued to follow Hegel (and Christianity) in assuming historical progression, but turned the process on its head. History can be represented not by a series of ideas which become incarnate but by a sequence of material formations which have social consequences. Hegel presented world history as running from east to west. So in the Preface to *A Contribution to the Critique of Political Economy* Marx sketches a progression of epochs, each characterised by a different mode of production, running from China to Europe and America. Primitive communalism gives way to slavery (as a mode of production). Slavery gives way to feudalism. Most importantly feudalism is overtaken by capitalism.[62] But individual social phenomena are not understood in relation to this long sequence but rather in relation to the mode of production of that particular epoch.

> In the social production of their existence, men inevitably enter into definite relations, which are independent of their will, namely relations of production appropriate to a given stage in the development of their material forces of production. The totality of these relations of production constitutes the economic structure of society, the real foundation on which arises a legal and political superstructure and to which correspond definite forms of social consciousness. The mode of production of material life conditions the general process of social, political and intellectual life.[63]

The mode of production of each society provides the new base upon which new institutions arise and new forms of consciousness and intellectual life appear. The new mode of production revolutionises society and increases individual freedom. Thus democracy in the modern world does not arise from a decision to revive the ideas of Pericles from the Athens of the fifth century BCE. No, democracy arises from the capitalist revolution. For idealism, democracy creates freedom: for historical materialism capitalism creates democracy. (That is why democracy cannot be imposed on African countries which have not been revolutionised by capitalism. At the time of writing it remains to be seen whether it can be imposed on Iraq.) The new economic base revolutionises the institutions of society, a society now governed by the new entrepreneurial class who for the sake of their economic activity require an extension of personal freedom. The corollary of historical materialism is that no significant changes in the superstructure of society (legal, marital, religious, leisure, aesthetic) can take place without a change in the base. Alternatively, changes in the superstructure are inevitable when there is a change in the mode of production.

It will now be clear why a Marxist reading of the situation provides a second alternative to historicism. New theologies, especially theologies of liberation, will arise if, and only if, there is a change in the mode of production. Conversely if there is a change in the mode of production new theologies will certainly appear. But this is precisely the claim of postmodern analysis. Precisely in the decade of the 1960s there was a transformation in the mode of production in western countries. One way of describing this change is to describe it as post-Fordist. The previous era had begun in 1914 when Henry Ford opened his automated car-assembly plant at Dearborn, Michigan. For David Harvey, the intention was not simply to devise a new mode of mass production, but thereby to create 'a total way of life'.[64] (Ironically Henry Ford assumed here what Marx had described: it takes a change in the mode of production to substantially change the social life.) The close of the Fordist era of production marked the end of industrial regimes which required the rigidities of fixed capital investment, rationalisation of process, mass production, piece work, continuous assembly, long-term employment, routinisation of skills, inflexibility of design, continuity of market and the dehumanisation of labour. That phase of capitalism described as industrialisation came to an end and the next successive and progressive phase, technology, began. It is not difficult to see why this change in the mode of production would lead to aspirations to freedom in social relations. The Fordist industrial model was coercive and repressive. The new mode of production required human creativity and subjective freedom at an economic level, but it had immediate consequences for societal and individual relations. Like the archaeology of knowledge, historical materialism provides an explanation of why three liberation theologies with different historical trajectories arose at the same time. And like the archaeology of knowledge historical materialism prepares us for the death of these three theologies, except that it can be much more specific in its account of the date of their sad demise.

The year 1989 saw the release of Nelson Mandela. It also marked the end of Black theology in South Africa, at least when it identified the problem as a race problem. But the same year saw the fall of the Berlin Wall. This marked the end of the cold war. Up till that point the world had been divided between the camps of the two superpowers – with some countries such as India attempting to remain outside: hence the concept of the third world. The end of the cold war saw the virtual end of the second world: the break up of the USSR and the eventual entry of former Warsaw Pact countries into the European Union. The concept of the third world is now an economic rather than an ideological category and includes most countries outside the USA, the EU and a few selected Asian countries, notably Japan. The end of the cold war brought about a change in American foreign policy. Previously it seemed as if it would count as an ally any dictatorship, regardless of its human rights record, so long as it was anti-communist. After 1989 the criteria changed. Its foreign policy was economic rather than political, the marketisation of the world. Now it looked favourably on any country which was prepared to accept neo-liberal economic policies and open up its market to the USA. The exporting of neoliberalism has meant such a revolutionary change that global capitalism must now be regarded as a new mode of production. It has led not to the extension of freedom so much as the concentration of freedom in fewer hands. Previous phases of capitalism (following Weber, but also Adam Smith himself) have seen the necessary association of production and morality. It was in this context that Hayek could promote freedom as a moral issue. Liberation theologies thrived in such a utopian period. However, global capitalism is marked by consumption rather than production and by aesthetics rather than ethics. It is for this reason that the moral basis of the call for liberation has collapsed. The three liberation theologies have lost their way: they have come to the end of their natural term. However, this has not prevented Black theology and womanist theology from conducting business as usual, *adversus post-modernitatem.*

Much is made of the fact that there is now a second generation of Black theologians, graduate students of those of the first generation, now installed in university positions. One of the main features of this second wave is the return to sources. We have already noted this with regard to womanist theology: the previously unheard voices of slave women, biographies of foremothers. Amidst the accounts of great cruelty and heartbreak there is also an element of hagiography. All their ducks are swans and there is a reluctance to enter any note of critical evaluation. This has been noted by Cornel West, when he observes that 'the reactionary essays (some of which appeared in *Readers' Digest*) and Republican Party allegiance of the most renowned African-American woman of letters, Zora Neale Hurston, are often overlooked by her contemporary feminist womanist followers'.[65] There is no end of material. There are the 41 volumes of interviews with ex-slaves in *The Slave Narrative Collection: a composite autobiography*. There are over 100 autobiographical accounts by former slaves who ran away, purchased their freedom or were manumitted in *The Slave Narrative: its place in American history.* There is also the collection of documents entitled *Slave Testimony: two centuries of letters, speeches, interviews and autobiographies*.[66] However, the question of method still remains. A historical review of this material could be interesting as a study in social history. It is tempting for the next generation of Black theologians to focus attention on particular historical figures who have been so far 'neglected'. But the pristine condition of this material does not equate to originality in writing Black theology.

What could be more natural than seeking to understand the present by reference to the past? All of this seems quite natural, but we have already warned about social constructs which are represented as natural. This is one of the most powerful ideologically charged procedures of modern times. The irony is that Black theology, in purporting to escape the encompassing grasp of the European intellectual and cultural tradition, has only embraced it more completely. The idea that the present is determined by the past, even an alternative past, cannot suit the purposes of a constructivist movement. The owl of Minerva cannot be its guide. The unwitting acceptance of European historicism is tragedy: its conscious adoption in the name of post-colonialism is farce. Of course historical knowledge is valuable, but what are its values and to whom is it valuable? Those who seek to write history normally seek to rewrite it. There are two motives.

The first motive is to preserve the present, the status quo. The reference to history serves the interests of those whose privileges derive from the past. Take the example of male privilege in the Roman Catholic Church. How is this privilege to be maintained in face of the modern consensus on equity and fairness between the sexes? Ideologies do not come straight out and assert interest. To the contrary they proclaim their innocence. Thus celibate male theologians in effect say 'Of course we should like women to be ordained (dear), but what can we do? There is no example of it in history.' The answer should be, 'Today we know better.' But instead of that feminists have fallen into the historicist trap. They have tried to demonstrate such leadership in the tradition. This plays directly into the hands of their enemies. They have signed up to the very premises on which the ideology is based. Judith Butler points to this danger. 'The feminist recourse to an imaginary past needs to be cautious not to promote a politically problematic reification of women's experience in the course of debunking the self-reifying claims of masculinist power.'[67] We have argued earlier for a parallel between 'gender trouble' and 'race trouble'. By focusing on historical sources Black and womanist theology have bought into the very method characteristic of European scholarship of the last 250 years.

The second motive for rewriting history is to contest the present, the status quo. This is what feminists have attempted, and this is now a feature of the second wave of Black theology. Is this return to the sources a purely historical attempt to present the foremothers, such as Zora Neale Hurston, warts and all? Far from it. And is this retrieval of aspects of slave life and religion a purely historical attempt to recreate the ancestors? Certainly not. Will Coleman has written an introduction to a book edited by Dwight Hopkins and George Cummings, *Cut Loose Your Stammering Tongue: black theology in slave narratives*, in which he identifies the perspective as 'historical trajectory' and 'the turn to indigenous African American sources'.[68] Hopkins has contributed an article to the book entitled 'Slave Theology in the "Invisible Church"' in which he presents a contrast between the Christianity of the slave owners and that of the slaves, in terms of beliefs and worship. 'Out of these illegal and hidden religious practices, the "Invisible Institution", black Christianity and black theology arose.'[69] However, in this selective and imaginative reconstruction of slave religion, 'bush arbor theology' comes to look very much like Black theology: God liberates slaves and Jesus liberates captives. On the larger scale white Christianity is contrasted with African traditional religion. But these 'remains' make traditional religion look very Christian. Ironically traditional African beliefs are presented through concepts that reflect Greek metaphysics rather than biblical theology. Hopkins purports to discover that slave religion is the source of Black theology, that is Black theology is an expression of slave religion. In Butler's terminology the reverse would be the case. Through performativity certain features of Black theology are reified to become slave religion. Slave religion is not a historical source of Black theology: certain selected elements of the past which correspond to the black present become the ingredients for a social construct. The intention is not to tell us about the past, but to legitimise the present and to adorn it with the authority of the ancestors. The past is therefore redescribed to confirm the present. Amazingly the God of the slaves is exactly like the God of Black theology and, amazingly, the slaves had the same revolutionary consciousness as Black theologians. This is a further example of ontological blackness, and Victor Anderson is scathing in his criticism of 'the hermeneutics of return'. It is significant that he takes this phrase from Edward Said's *Culture and Imperialism.* He is especially critical of the approach of Dwight Hopkins in *Shoes that Fit Our Feet: sources for a constructive black theology*, which he considers guilty of 'committing a performative contradiction'.[70] For Anderson the slave narratives constitute a 'protoblack liberation theology'. 'Hopkins's hermeneutics of narrative return ends up justifying the black theology project by a vicious circularity of reasoning that renders the legitimacy of slave religion coterminous with black theology and the legitimacy of black liberation theology coterminous with slave religion.'[71] Are we being provided with an objective account of traditional African religions? Consider this incident. In 2001 the limbless, headless torso of a baby boy was found in the river Thames, in London. Through a patient and prolonged forensic investigation, using DNA evidence, the boy was traced back to the Benin province in Nigeria. Dozens of children go missing every year in this area, taken for ritual sacrifice. The boy had been imported into the UK for the use of Nigerians as a religious commodity. I suspect that this would qualify as an aspect of what Anderson calls 'the grotesque'.[72] Anyone with a real historical interest in African traditional religion would have to deal with such practices. Did the Christian missionaries after all do some good in Africa? But more than that, how can African-Americans who profess a love for Africa take some moral responsibility not for Africa of the past, but for African children today, at this very moment?

The historicist approach is deeply flawed, not least when it selects and censors historical sources to suit its own ideological purposes. In this respect the Bible is a historical source for Black theology and is used for various purposes. One of the leading black biblical scholars is Cain Hope Felder. In *Troubling Biblical Waters*[73] he raises our expectations, especially with the sub-title *Race, class and family.* The works of Eurocentric scholars have apparently been 'calm'. (How calm were the works of, for example, Reimarus who did not dare publish his epoch breaking study till after his death; Strauss who being accused of reducing the Bible to 'rubble' was not allowed to occupy his chair in Zürich; Barth whose commentary on Romans fell like a bomb into the playground of the theologians who supported the German Reich; Byers Naude with his critique of the religious legitimation of apartheid.) But of course Felder turns out to be a sheep in wolf's clothing. Far from troubling the waters his work is a sea of tranquillity. One of the most superficial contributions to early feminism was 'women in the Bible'. So now we are offered a list of 'black people in the Old Testament' and 'black people in the New Testament'. Good examples of anachronism. There is also the attempt to link New Testament people to Africa, meaning Egypt and Ethiopia. Good examples of essentialism. At the time of writing this present book we can see in the massacres and genocide being carried out in Sudan by the Arab militias against the African tribal population that such essentialisms are inappropriate. In discussing the Bible and justice Felder reproduces the arguments and references from Eurocentric scholarship. In dealing with class we are treated to a sermon on Galatians 3: 28, while in The Letter of James economic analysis is reduced to social class and the issue of how people dress in church. The discussion of Paul's view of women is entirely dependent on white feminist scholarship. In Felder's edited book *Stony the Road We Trod* he reports the view of black scholars that, 'What passes for normative hermeneutics is in fact white, male, Eurocentrichermeneutics.'[74] More essentialism. One of the most important issues being discussed at the moment amongst Euro-American scholars is the deconstruction of the historical critical method. Black scholars have simply accepted this method as if it were 'natural'. Once this is accepted nothing 'troubling' will arise. Even more disappointing is the collection edited by Randall C. Bailey, *Yet With a Steady Beat: contemporary U.S. Afrocentric biblical interpretation*. Published by the prestigious Society of Biblical Literature it reads as a demonstration by black scholars that they should be admitted as full members of the Euro-American guild. The studies are driven by the normal SBL agenda, not black perspectives or values. Thus Brad Ronnell Braxton discusses 'The Role of Ethnicity in the Social Location of 1 Corinthians 7.17–24'.[75] Circumcision is reduced to an ethnic issue. Why was it chosen at all to illustrate an Afrocentric perspective, in view of the fact that it was irrelevant to women and slaves? There is no mention of the fact that Paul immediately goes on to demonstrate his quietism about slavery. No account is taken of the work of Dolores Williams on circumcision and the covenant.

Whether biblical specialists or not, most Black theologians assume that the Bible provides a historical basis for their positions. We end this discussion with a final example which goes beyond selection and settles for historical error. It was briefly alluded to in the Introduction above. One of the truisms of Black theology of liberation is that God frees slaves, a claim so obvious and unexceptionable that it need be supported by only passing references to the Exodus and the first sermon of Jesus. Yet there is no historical basis to this mantra. It is ironic that theologians who insist on calling themselves 'contextual' fail to see that these references are highly contextual and historically specific. Consider the Exodus. The reason for the Exodus was the Conquest. The Hebrews were liberated not because God liberates slaves but so that they could enter the Promised Land. In Deuteronomy 7 God describes the brutal genocide and ethnic cleansing by which they will take possession of the land. The Exodus-Conquest is certainly not a paradigm for Christians seeking liberation from oppression. Exodus is contextual and cannot be used as an argument against slavery. In the Book of Exodus, in the chapter immediately following the setting out of the Ten Commandments the institution of slavery is not only assumed to continue, God's detailed regulations for the treatment of slaves, including Hebrew slaves, are set out. It would be better to argue against slavery on moral grounds than by such questionable appeals to the Bible. But with this we are drawn back into historical trajectories. Has God always been a God who releases captives? Clearly not. Or again, the first sermon of Jesus is a quotation from Isaiah 61. 'He has sent me to proclaim release to the captives' (Luke 4: 18). The prophet is promising that the Jews, who were taken as captives to Babylon, would be released and the ruins of Zion rebuilt. This is a reference to events of the sixth century BCE. This is highly contextual: the Jews were soon conquered by three further empires. Jesus himself became a captive a few months after preaching this sermon. Such quotations cannot be the basis of strategies of liberation today. Slavery is not an issue in the Bible. What did Paul say on the subject? Very little. What did Jesus say about slavery? Nothing at all. And that is the most significant fact of all. When writing to the church in Rome Paul commends the empire.

> Let every person be subject to the governing authorities. For there is no authority except from God, and those that exist have been instituted by God. Therefore he who resists the authorities resists what God had appointed, and those who resist will incur judgement. (Rom. 13: 1–2)

But reflect for a moment: the mode of production of the Roman empire was slavery. The empire in that form could not have existed without slavery. It was not a practice that could have been set aside, but rather the very basis of society. It was not a moral issue but an economic necessity. By his religious legitimation of the Roman empire Paul is associating God with slavery. It was a Roman tribune, stationed in the Antonia castle in Jerusalem, who saved Paul's life from the wrath of the Jews. Paul even knew his name, Claudius Lysias. (Good morning Claud, always good to see you. Children well?) It was his Roman citizenship which saved him from being scourged – the fate of slaves, as of Jesus (Acts 22: 25) Slavery was not an issue for Jesus. Paul, more aware of it, could present an *apologia pro imperium*,a legitimation of an empire based on slavery. God is not represented in the Bible as one who releases slaves. But the same is true for examples outside the Bible. The enslavement of Africans by Africans was a social institution long before it became a commercial enterprise. Indeed it still exists to this day, notably in West Africa, where it continues without any protest from African-Americans who claim ancestry in the region. Nor was there any divine intervention for over one million Europeans taken captive in North Africa in the eighteenth-century slave trade (an example of slavery which I have not seen mentioned in Black theology).[76] The God of all mankind clearly does not intervene to release captives. Black theology represents God as a God who releases Christian slaves in the USA. Emancipation took place in 1863, after 250 years. Without a hint of irreverence we might consider that a reasonable response amongst slaves might be not 'Praise the Lord!' but 'What kept you?' No, the representation of God as a God who releases captives, has no basis in history. James Cone in his first book on Black theology quotes the Great Emancipator.

> My paramount object in this struggle is to save the Union, and is not either to save or to destroy slavery. If I could save the Union without freeing any slaves, I would do it; and if I could save it by freeing some and leaving others alone, I would also do that.[77]

It is ironic that Marx, who was a great admirer of Abraham Lincoln, should consider the 'pro-slavery rebellion' (as he routinely referred to the Civil War) to be a moral issue. It was in fact an economic issue and would have confirmed his historical materialism, the view that the great social events of history are brought about by changes in the mode of production. In a country rapidly moving into industrialisation slavery was no longer an efficient way of organising the required workforce. Black theology misrepresents the historical trajectories of slavery and emancipation. The representation of God as a God who releases captives emerges in the 1960s as a response to the cultural and economic features of that decade already discussed. The fact is that today, in a very different situation, this representation of God is tired, over used and lacking in credibility. It is time to move on to discover a more appropriate representation. What must be said about God in a time of globalisation, when American blacks are now full citizens of a country which is intent on the economic domination of the world? What is to be said by blacks who are now complicit in the economic enslavement of women and children in Africa? Hopkins identifies the problem, but completely fails to address it. Just as he mentions the work of Delores Williams, but learns nothing from her critical account of Hagar the slave woman, so he mentions the work of Cornel West, but learns nothing about the mechanism of capitalism. He mentions Victor Anderson, but far from responding to him, actually provides an example of ontological blackness. To the end he is still presenting Black theology as 'the struggle against powers of slavery and for powers of liberation'.[78] The struggle is to be pursued through boycotts, sit-ins and mass demonstrations. Thus the context, message and strategies of the 1970s are replicated, with no concession to the new context 30 years later.

Notes

1 Friedrich Nietzsche, 'On Truth and Falsity in Their Extramoral Sense' in *Philosophical Writings*, ed. Reinhold Grimm and Caroline Molina y Vedia, Continuum, 1995, p. 92.

2 Ibid., p. 96.

3 Michel Foucault, *The Archaeology of Knowledge*, Routledge, 2002 (1969), pp. 52–3.

4 Judith Butler, *Gender Trouble: feminism and the subversion of identity*, Routledge, 1999 (1990), p. 190.

5 Ibid., p. 4.

6 Ibid., p. 9.

7 Ibid., p. 33.

8 Ibid.

9 Ibid., p. 116.

10 Ibid., p. 135.

11 Ibid., p. 143.

[12] Ibid., p. 164.

[13] Ibid., p. 181.

[14] Ibid., p. 189.

[15] Ibid., p. 19.

[16] Richard E. van der Ross, 'Foreword' in Jon Michael Spencer, *The New Colored People: the mixed-race movement in America*, New York University Press, 1997. Classification by race cannot serve the interests of minorities.

[17] 'The negativity of blackness is not a tradition peculiar to the West'. Robert E. Hood, *Begrimed and Black: Christian traditions on black and blackness*, Fortress Press, Minneapolis, 1994, p. 17.

[18] Wilfred Cantwell Smith, *The Meaning and End of Religion*, SPCK, 1978 (1962), p. 56.

[19] Victor Anderson, *Beyond Ontological Blackness: an essay in African American religious and cultural criticism*, Continuum, New York, 1999 (1995), p. 12.

[20] Ibid., p. 13.

[21] Ibid., p. 14.

[22] Ibid., p. 15.

[23] James Evans, 'African-American Christianity and the Postmodern Condition', *Journal of the American Academy of Religion*, LVIII.2, (Summer 1990), p. 216.

[24] Anderson, *Beyond Ontological Blackness*, p. 85.

[25] Ibid., p. 87.

[26] Ibid., p. 90.

[27] Ibid., p. 91.

[28] Ibid. James Cone occasionally addresses issues raised by Anderson. 'How do blacks avoid racial essentialism, talking and acting as if biology alone defines truth?' James H. Cone, 'Theology's Great Sin: silence in the face of White Supremacy', *Black Theology: an international journal*, 2.2 (July 2004), p. 145. But here his dialogue partner is not Anderson, but Reinhold Niebuhr's *The Nature and Destiny of Man*, being the Gifford Lectures delivered in Edinburgh in 1939.

[29] Anderson, *Beyond Ontological Blackness*, p. 111.

[30] Ibid., p. 112.

[31] Gustavo Gutiérrez, 'The Meaning of Development: notes on a theology of liberation' in *In Search of a Theology of Development*, SODEPAX, Geneva, n.d., p. 138.

[32] Gustavo Gutiérrez, *A Theology of Liberation*, Orbis, Maryknoll, NY, 1973, p. 9.

[33] José Miguez Bonino, *Christians and Marxists: the mutual challenge of revolution,* Hodder & Stoughton, 1976, p. 19.

[34] Cleage, *Black Christian Nationalism*, p. 158.

[35] James H. Cone, *For My People: Black theology and the Black church*, Orbis, Maryknoll, NY, 1984, p. 184.

[36] Ibid., p. 187.

[37] Ibid., p. 255.

[38] Cornel West, *Keeping Faith: philosophy and race in America*, Routledge, 1993, p. 133.

[39] Cornel West, *The Cornel West Reader*, Basic Civitas Books, 1999, pp. 310–11.

[40] Cornel West, *Prophesy Deliverance: an Afro-American revolutionary Christianity*, Westminster Press, Philadelphia, Pa., 1982, p. 115.

[41] Cornel West, *Prophetic Fragments*, William B. Eerdmans, Grand Rapids, Mich., 1988, p. 48.

[42] Dwight N. Hopkins, *Introducing Black Theology of Liberation*, Orbis, Maryknoll, NY, 1999, p. 46.

[43] Ibid., p. 188.

[44] Dwight N. Hopkins, *Heart and Head: black theology – past, present and future*, Palgrave, New York, 2002, p. 162.

[45] Ibid., p. 54.

[46] Ibid., p. 179.

[47] Norman O. Brown, *Life Against Death: the psychoanalytical meaning of history*, Sphere Books

Ltd., 1968 (original 1959), p. 12.

[48] Benjamin DeMott, *The Imperial Middle: why americans can't think straight about class*, Yale University Press, New Haven, 1992 (original 1990), p.12.

[49] Ibid.,

[50] Ibid., p. 92.

[51] Ibid., p. 111.

[52] Ibid., p. 173.

[53] Ibid., p. 174.

[54] Both quoted in Michael Lienesch, *Redeeming America: piety and politics in the New Christian Right*, University of North Carolina Press, 1993, chap. 3.

[55] DeMott op. cit., p. 190.

[56] Gerhard Ebeling, *Word and Faith*, Fortress Press, Philadelphia, 1963, p. 363.

[57] Foucault, *The Archaeology of Knowledge*, p. 186.

[58] Michel Foucault, *The Order of Things: an archaeology of the human sciences*, Routledge, 2002 (1966), p. 378.

[59] Foucault, *The Archaeology of Knowledge*, p. 180.

[60] Ibid., p. 181.

[61] G.W.G. Hegel, *The Philosophy of History*, Willey Book Co., New York, 1900, p. 39.

[62] Marx/Engels, *Collected Works*, 29.263.

[63] Ibid., p. 262.

[64] David Harvey, *The Condition of Post-Modernity*, Blackwell, 1990, p. 135.

[65] Cornel West, *Race Matters*, Beacon Press, Boston, 1993, p. 49.

[66] George P. Rawick (ed.) *The Slave Narrative Collection: a composite autobiography*, Greenwood Publishing Co., Westport, Conn., 1972, 1977, 1979; Marion Wilson Starling, *The Slave Narrative: its place in American history*, Howard University Press, Washington, DC, 1988; John W. Blassingame, *Slave Testimony: two centuries of letters, speeches, interviews and autobiographies*, Louisiana State University Press, Baton Rouge, 1977.

[67] Butler, *Gender Trouble*, p. 46.

[68] Dwight N. Hopkins and George C.L. Cummings (eds) *Cut Loose Your Stammering Tongue: black theology in slave narratives*, Westminster John Knox Press, Louisville, Ky., 2003 (1991).

[69] Ibid., p. 1.

[70] Anderson, *Ontological Blackness*, p. 97. Dwight N. Hopkins, *Shoes that Fit Our Feet: sources for a constructive black theology*, Orbis Books, Maryknoll, NY, 1993.

[71] Anderson, *Ontological Blackness*, p. 98.

[72] Ibid., p. 132. See also Victor Anderson, *Divine Grotesquery*, Continuum, 2002.

[73] Cain Hope Felder, *Troubling Biblical Waters: race, class and family*, Orbis Books, Maryknoll, NY, 1989.

[74] Cain Hope Felder (ed.) *Stony the Road We Trod: African American biblical interpretation*, Fortress Press, Minneapolis, 1991, p. 6.

[75] Randall C. Bailey (ed.) *Yet With a Steady Beat: contemporary U.S. Afrocentric biblical interpretation*, Society of Biblical Literature, Atlanta, Ga., 2003.

[76] Giles Milton, *White Gold: the extraordinary story of Thomas Pellow and North Africa's one million European slaves*, Hodder, 2004.

[77] Quoted in Cone, *Black Theology and Black Power*, p. 10.

[78] Hopkins, *Introducing Black Theology of Liberation*, p. 195.

Conclusion: an Obituary

A Radical Race Critique

Freud wrote three books about religion: two on the past and the present; the third was *The Future of an Illusion*. For Freud religion was not a mistake, an error, but something much more significant. What then is the nature and function of an illusion? In *The Naked and the Dead* Norman Mailer described a platoon of American soldiers on a small island in the Pacific theatre of the Second World War. We are not spared the detail of the appalling conditions in which they lived under constant enemy attack. The only thing which kept them sane was the belief that back home there was normal life, their families, their wives and sweethearts. It was the captain's unpleasant duty to tell one of the solders that news had come in by radio that the man's wife had died. So alienated were the infantrymen from the war that they automatically disbelieved anything the officers told them. The soldier therefore believed that the captain was lying, that his wife was still alive. In confirmation of this his wife's letters continued to arrive for some weeks afterwards. He suffered the illusion that life continued. It was not a mistake: his confident belief was sustained by the necessity of that belief for his own identity. The point of this harrowing tale? What if in the oppressive conditions of contemporary academic life, where publication is less about the dissemination of truth than the survival of the author; what if in the alien environment of the modern university which is now run by experts recruited because of their skills in managing fast-food outlets; what if in the *bellum omnium contra omnes*, the conflict of colleagues now transformed into competitors in the cut-throat struggle for a dwindling number of tenured posts; what if in these circumstances a message arrived by email 'Black theology is dead'? How would academics react, those working in this field? Would they analyse the message in a rational and objective way, as befits those who have been well-trained in critical evaluation? Or would they cry, 'Spam!' Would they consider the evidence with an open mind or would they throw a brick through the monitor screen – the modern equivalent of shooting the messenger? Would they laugh, a slightly nervous laugh, perhaps too quick or too loud, and point to the pile of books on the table, books on Black theology waiting to be reviewed? How can Black theology be dead! The continuing flood of books on the subject proves that the message is wrong. Exactly the evidence on which the soldier refuted the message from the captain. If the soldier had paid attention to the date of the letters he would have been better placed to recognise the truth about his wife. Yes, books and articles continue to produce Black theology, or rather they continue to *reproduce* it. They are already dated. The presence of rigor mortis can be detected. Black theology is dead. The denial of this fact is not due to a simple mistake: it stems from an illusion. A mistake is a situation which is easily cleared up: an illusion is a condition which needs to be acknowledged before it can be treated.

How can Black theology be dead: it is in the university calendar of courses to be taught this year? How can Black theology be dead: was there not a conference in 1998 to celebrate the thirtieth anniversary of the publication of James Cone's epoch-making work *Black Theology and Black Power*? On closer inspection we might well ask whether that conference provided evidence against the claim that Black theology is dead – or rather *substantiated* the claim. The inevitable book which arose from the conference, *Black Faith and Public Talk: critical essays on James H. Cone's Black Theology and Black Power* was intended to demonstrate how formative the book had been (retrospect) and how it was still the springboard to further developments (prospect). It may well be both, but that is not the substance of the essays published. For the most part they follow a familiar pattern. (1) Many of the essays simply ignore *Black Theology and Black Power*, indeed in some cases the illustrious author seems not to be acquainted with it. (2) Many of the essays have been previously published 'in another form'. They ignore the work of James Cone in favour of the author's favourite research topic. (3) Some of the previously published essays add a few paragraphs to give the appearance that they are deeply indebted to Cone's work. (4) 1989 marked the twentieth anniversary of the consultation on 'Theology and Devlopment' held in Cartigny, Switzerland at which Gustavo Gutiérrez delivered his first paper on liberation theology. To mark his achievement a collection was published, *The Future of Liberation Theology: essays in honor of Gustavo Gutiérrez.*[1] Of the 50 contributions there is only one critical engagement. And without *critical* engagement how can there be a future? I wish to draw a parallel with the thirtieth anniversary collection *Black Faith and Public Talk: critical essays on James H. Cone's Black Theology and Black Power.* Of the 20 contributions I could not detect one that was creatively critical. Victor Anderson was not among the contributors, nor was his criticism of Black theology or James Cone discussed. For reasons of racial solidarity Black theologians have been reluctant to criticise each other: they might give ammunition to their enemies. This attitude may well be a further illustration of what Anderson calls ontological blackness. In this volume there was no critical evaluation. Cone deserved better. The exception to all of these features is the essay by Cornel West. With characteristic erudition and insight he underlines the original significance of *Black Theology and Black Power.* But even he, in deference to his friend and former colleague, is restrained in his criticism. If this book is evidence that Black theology is alive and well, it is time to order the flowers.

My sympathies, however, lie with James Cone, for two reasons. In Chapter 2 I set out my criticisms of his theology. Notwithstanding these, however, I began teaching and recommending his work from the time it was first published and continued to do that throughout my teaching career. I also expressed my view that he should have apologised for nothing. He was a man of his time when others did not know what time it was. He is to be praised for his achievement. Others can come later and be more balanced: without him they would have had nothing to say. One of the criticisms levelled against Cone is that his early work was too Barthian. This seems to me to be a rather precious criticism, when set against his subject, the life and death of black people in the USA. Perhaps Cone should have followed Barth the man, *der Kämpfer*, the fighter, more closely than the theologian. Barth was criticised because his early work was too one-sided and unbalanced. Looking back he knew that too, but refused to apologise: his book had created a new situation, which was more than could be said for his critics.

> Well roared lion! There is nothing absolutely false in these bold words. I still think that I was right ten times over against those who then passed judgement on them and resisted them. Those who can still hear what was said then, cannot but admit it was necessary to speak in this way.[2]

Well roared lion! *Black Theology and Black Power* is such an epochal work and it is a matter of regret that those attending the conference and contributing to the subsequent book did not say this loudly and clearly, did not *celebrate* this unique book. Even so, all that refers to the past, to the rise of Black theology: it is no defence against its demise.

But my sympathies lie with James Cone for a second reason. The book concludes with an essay by Cone, but which Cone? As if to show that he has learned from womanists, he begins by telling us his story: Cone the new black man. He goes on to recall the frustration and oppression: the original Cone, the angriest Black theologian in America. However, the essay ends rather poignantly. He is aware of the new directions in Black theology, the full spectrum of the second wave. He can even allude to the criticism about blackness. He can approve, except that there is one fundamental respect in which they are flawed. 'But what troubles me about all these new theological constructs is the absence of a truly radical race critique.'[3] Since the conference presupposed the unique contribution that Cone has made to the founding and development of Black theology it is no small thing that he considers that Black theology has lost its way. Or rather instead of keeping to the way, the new practitioners have gone off in every which way but that one way.

As we saw in the last chapter some have disappeared into historical studies. But the return to sources lacks a clear method: it is less about the past than about the selective affirmation and legitimation of the present. And 'the hermeneutics of return' (Anderson) has not freed itself from the Euro-American scholarship it purports to reject. There has also been a movement into cultural studies. But there is less to this than meets the eye. *Changing Conversations*, edited by Dwight Hopkins and Sheila Davaney, promises to deal with 'religious reflections and cultural analysis', but it does not fulfil its promise. Karen Baker-Fletcher in 'Passing on the Spark: a womanist perspective on theology and culture' simply substitutes 'culture' for 'experience' and goes on to repeat the familiar themes of womanist theology. Similarly Dwight Hopkins in 'Theological Method and Cultural Studies: slave religious culture as a heuristic' combines the two. 'This essay uses the culture of enslaved African Americans' religious experience to explore how theological method can learn from cultural studies.'[4] Although Baker-Fletcher quotes Harvard psychologist Robert Coles with approval when he claims that 'people from different cultures can learn something about the diverse potential of Spirit in humankind from each other'[5] there is in fact no intention of relating to other cultures. There is only the determination to set out black culture as if it could stand alone. This unwillingness to interact with other cultures is a feature of *The Ties that Bind: African American and Hispanic American/Latino/a theology in dialogue*, edited by Pinn and Valentin. The structure of the book is that in each chapter a Black theologian writes a position paper, to which a Hispanic theologian responds, followed by a paper by the Hispanic theologian, to which the Black theologian responds. But in the event there is no dialogue. Nothing is learned. Hispanic theology is exposed as a very limited and superficial movement[6] incapable of enriching Black theology. At the same time Black theology does not expect or attempt to learn from this partner. There are no 'ties that bind'. Inevitably the most incisive contribution to the project is the essay by Victor Anderson. He raises questions about the assumptions underlying the thesis of 'ties that bind'. Race was the focus which united the black community in the 1960s and 1970s.

> However, on the dawn of the twenty-first century it is not very clear whether racial discourse can garner such agreement among the theologians. What is clear is that the fragility of black liberation theology in the United States is being tested by a class differential that is nonreducible to the racial categories of white over black.[7]

There might indeed be grounds for dialogue and even concerted action between black and Hispanic communities if they focused on their common experience of economic oppression. Reinforcing the point made above, Anderson is also critical of the continued dependence of Black theology on the Euro-American method with respect to historical sources. 'Unfortunately, too many African American religious thinkers have not transcended the Western epistemic paradigm preoccupied with ocular clarity and transparency in theological method.'[8]

The cultural studies, as we have seen, avoid the economic issue. This is made clear in an essay by Kasimu Baker-Fletcher, a response to the Million Man March which took place in Washington, DC on 16 October 1995. The essay, 'Xodus or X-scape' is included in a book which he edited on *Black Religion After the Million Man March: voices on the future*. 'The call for an XODUS represents a new generation of thinking about the ways in which the take-charge, no-nonsense rhetorical fire of Malcolm X can be brought together with the militant multicultural envisioning power of Martin Luther King Jr. to galvanize our liberation hopes.'[9] Significantly this call is for 'a renewed sense of cultural, psychological and spiritual revival'. It is 'psycho-spiritual *liberation*' and certainly not 'overtly political or economic'.[10] In this collection of responses to the Million Man March, the most original – and dramatic – is that by Victor Anderson, 'Abominations of a Million Men: reflection on a silent minority'. Largely because of the rhetoric of Louis

Farrakhan (preaching for two and a half hours!) the occasion was marked by 'a conversionist ideology that accents sectarian emphasis on repentance, separation, sanctification, and a summons toward the moral transformation of one's racial self-consciousness'.[11] In his earlier work, which we have discussed, Anderson dealt with 'the cult of black masculinity'. Its essentialism is reinforced on the day: 'a million Man, One Black Man',[12] and that essentialised black man is heterosexual. Homosexuality in this sacred context is regarded as an abomination. For Anderson the real abomination is that no gay or lesbian person addressed the crowd, there was no affirmation of black homosexual love, no love of the neighbour who is gay.[13] Perhaps the most astonishing feature of the Million Man March was the 'Pledge'. Of the nine pledges which each man was called upon to take, two refer to the economy, but recalling Marcus Garvey's programme of a black economy: black owned businesses, houses, hospitals, factories, newspapers, radio and television. Six of the nine are concerned with personal behaviour. I was not present on the day – neither were most of the contributors to Baker-Fletcher's book – but I suspect the Pledge must have been taken with mixed feelings by many. There is a familiar trick question: 'Have you stopped beating your wife yet?' Answer yes, and you confess to beating your wife. Answer no, and you confess to still doing it. Some men present that day must have felt the same ambiguity as they pledged themselves never to raise a knife or a gun against a member of their family (except in self-defence); pledged themselves never to strike or abuse their wives; pledged themselves never to sexually abuse little children; pledged themselves never to use the 'B' word against any woman; pledged themselves not to use drugs. If the Pledge is astonishing, so is the lack of any prophetic dimension in the responses of the Black theologians. It is not difficult to see why Cone is disappointed. 'But what troubles me about all these new theological constructs is the absence of a truly radical race critique.'

Cone himself led the way into a theological reflection on the music of black religion with *The Spirituals and the Blues.*[14] The field was defined by *Black Sacred Music: a journal of theomusicology.*[15] A good example is *Protest and Praise: sacred music of black religion* in which Jon Michael Spencer defines theomusicology as 'musicology as a theologically informed discipline'.[16] Although it has the potential to be prophetic, or at least to draw attention to protest elements in contemporary music, it too is drawn into historical sources. David Emmanuel Goatley in 'Godforsakenness in African American Spirituals' draws attention to an early study undertaken in the nineteenth century. 'In his 1894 thesis for Yale School of Divinity, Henry Hugh Proctor offered what is perhaps the first theological analysis of black spirituals by a credentialed African American scholar.'[17] There has been a long and distinguished tradition in American universities of the study of religion(s). In deference to the separation of church and state universities set up departments of Religion, as distinct from Theology. One of the growth areas of the second generation of Black theology has been towards Black Religious Studies.[18] One of the leading scholars in this field is Anthony B. Pinn, one of the editors of the dialogue collection we have already considered, *The Ties that Bind*. He has also, and significantly, edited *By These Hands: a documentary of African American humanism.* His first monograph was *Varieties of African American Religious Experience*. A more recent study is *Terror and Triumph: the nature of black religion.*[19] It is a well informed and readable series of studies on subjects from the conditions of slavery to the aesthetics of the black churches. It is clearly not Black theology. As if to stress the point he discusses the social function of Black theology in five pages. Pinn sees a third wave of Black theology as scholars of religion move 'to include religious traditions such as vodoo and santería that are seldom discussed by theologians'.[20] He is also critical of the claim by Hopkins to engage with non-Christian religious sources, when 'his conversation always comes back to the place of the sacred, liberation, and spirituality within the familiar Black Church'.[21] Another example of the failure to engage with other cultures. Pinn's own contribution to *Black Religion After the Million Man March* is a study of the Spike Lee film *Get on the Bus* in which 12 black men drive to the March.[22]

Finally, running through several of these developments in Black theology has been the influence of Afrocentrism, arising from the work of M.K. Asante in *Afrocentricity*.[23] This can be seen in works including Cheryl Sanders's *Living the Intersection: womanism and Afrocentrism in theology*[24] and those already discussed by Felder, *Stony the Road We Trod* and *Troubling Biblical Waters*. But does this Afrocentrism contribute to Black theology or is it an exotic construction for those who have nothing to say on this subject? Cornel West calls the whole movement gallant but misguided. 'It is misguided because – out of fear of cultural hybridization and through silence on the issue of class, retrograde views on black women, gay men, and lesbians, and a reluctance to link race to the common good – it reinforces the narrow discussions about race.'[25] The lifestyle of the middle class that affects to this position militates against 'the development of high quality political and intellectual leaders'.[26] He therefore comes to the conclusion that 'rhetoric becomes a substitute for analysis, stimulatory rapping a replacement for serious reading, and uncreative publications an expression of existential catharsis. Much, though not all, of Afrocentric thought fits this bill.'[27]

There is no end apparently to the diversity of research of this second generation, but is it Black theology at all? Or is it cultural studies, ethnography, even therapy? The first generation formulated the concept of Black theology at considerable risk to themselves, academic risk and in some cases physical risk. The second generation of Black theologians have the luxury of being able to spread their wings, without the danger of having them clipped. Cone relates the loss of 'radical race critique' to the new circumstances of black scholars. 'When whites opened the door to receive a token number of us into the academy, church, and society, the radical edge of our race critique was quickly dropped as we enjoyed our new-found privileges.'[28] Does Cone include himself in this dismal scenario? It is a long way from Bearden, Arkansas to Knox Hall. 'But what troubles me about all these new theological constructs is the absence of a truly radical race critique.' It is not difficult to see why

Cone does not recognise these developments as Black theology. But for our purposes the more important point is that Cone has reaffirmed that ontological blackness which stops the clock in the 1970s. It essentialises black experience according to the liberation discourse of modernity. He is not the first contextual theologian who fails to acknowledge when the context changes.

Unmet Needs

Black Faith and Public Talk: critical essays on James H. Cone's Black Theology and Black Power is a disappointing collection, therefore, in two respects. It does not properly engage with the achievement of Cone's original book. But it ends with Cone reaffirming the centrality of race, even as he pays lip service to the broader agenda. There is, however, one essay which makes reading the whole book worthwhile. It is by Gayraud Wilmore, one of the most creative thinkers and committed activists of the first generation of Black theology. He describes the tentativeness and confusion of the special project of the Theological Commission of the National Committee of Negro Churchmen in 1967 and the transformation effected by Cone's book the following year. They changed their name: they now saw clearly the way ahead. *Black Theology and Black Power* was supposed to be the subject of the conference and collection: Wilmore cannot praise it enough. Then, and only then can he venture to raise a question, a question that can only be asked not by an enemy but by a friend, not by an implacable critic but by an indefatigable supporter. If you have no stomach for this, look away now.

> The unspoken question hovering over this conference on the thirtieth anniversary of the publication of Cone's seminal work is whether or not black theology ought not to be pronounced dead at the Divinity School of the University of Chicago [where the conference took place] and given a decent burial back at Union Theological Seminary in New York City [where James Cone teaches] and at the Interdenominational Theological Center (ITC) in Atlanta [from which Wilmore had recently retired] where it was first acclaimed.[29]

Naturally he answers his own question in the negative. Or rather he says that the protagonists are not ready to agree that Black theology is dead: not Cone, not Hopkins, not the new president of ITC. Is it of any significance that he does not actually include himself amongst those who continue to defend Black theology? No matter: of more significance is the fact that the question can be asked, that the question makes sense, that it is neither inappropriate nor absurd. Of course those present acclaimed Black theology and its future (their careers require it). At the conference they re-enforced each others assumptions.

> But let us lay aside our rose-colored glasses for the moment. What indeed is the future of this way of doing theology in the United States? Is there any hope that the ideas that *Black Theology and Black Power* introduced to the church, the academy, and the public in 1969 have enough staying power, in this vastly

> different ideological and socio-economic climate in both the black and the white communities, to carry over beyond the turn of the century and give renewed impetus and meaning to the struggle for human liberation?[30]

Wilmore is seeking to change the angle of vision, to focus on the true subject, to acknowledge that the context has radically changed. The question is not really whether Black theology is dead or not: what does that matter in the great scheme of things (apart from paying the mortgage). He is attempting to turn the question around. The real issue concerns 'the struggle for human liberation'. The secondary question is whether that struggle can be continued, or best continued by Black theology. And if the answer to that question is negative, then Black theology is either dead, or deserves to be laid to rest. But how can such questions be addressed? Indeed Wilmore claims that many people who respect Black theology have serious questions about the future. For some it is already too late: he would like to think it is not, not quite. Ten years previously he had already set out some reasons why Black theology had failed to fulfil its potential. Now he formulates three 'unmet needs'. It may or may not be the case that Black theology can meet them: it has not done so up till now.

1. There needs to be a mass movement, comparable to Garveyism, or Dr King's non-violent campaign or even the Million Man March of October 1995. Black theology has never been able to grasp the imagination or stir the loyalty of the mass of people. Its academic exponents are more of a guild than a think-tank for activists. They are middle class and securely distant from the mass of people. But Wilmore's view of unmet needs cannot be summed up under the category of race: they are at the intersection of the political and the economic, the spiritual and the civic.

> Today comparable issues to the ones black religious leaders of the past were embroiled in are hunger, homelessness in the wealthiest nation in the world, the discouraging number of poor black women and children in a time of unprecedented prosperity, the so-far unsuccessful attempt to dismantle the Civil Rights acts of the 1960s, the disproportionate and demonstrably unjust incarceration of young black men, the infestation of black neighbourhoods with guns and crack cocaine, whose source and distribution system seem beyond our control, the unequal treatment of blacks by the police and the courts, the reduction of black voting power by Congressional redistricting, the shameful condition of our public schools, the proliferation of white supremacy hate groups, and the current attack on both affirmative action and the idea that welfare is a necessary safety net for many deserving and unfortunate poor people.[31]

And if this agenda seems familiar, it has still not been addressed. Wilmore continues, 'It is precisely these so-called "secular" issues that black theology promised to deal with in the 1960s but has not effectively addressed in the 1990s.'

2. The second unmet need concerns the need 'to "blackenize" Christian education materials'. 'Black theology cannot hope to become public discourse among ordinary people until larger numbers of African American Christians have been immersed in what black theology, at its best, teaches'.[32]

3. The third unmet need is 'the reality of the black world outside the United States'.[33] In addition to the Caribbean and black Latin American churches, he directs attention to the African diasporas in Europe and the UK. Wilmore sees Africa itself as a rich source of spiritual and humanising powers. (In this he seems to have resumed the rose-coloured glasses so far as the brutalities and atrocities presently characteristic of many independent African states are concerned.) But he is also concerned about Africa as 'the new target of American capitalism and racism'.[34] Once again we have a reference to American capitalism without the merest hint of why it is a danger to the rest of the world or the extent to which American blacks are complicit in the havoc it is dealing on black women and children in Africa.

These are the issues, the unmet needs. Wilmore's energy is undiminished in identifying them and seeking to address them. He seems less confident that Black theology has the ability, the personnel or the will to do so. But the issues have to be addressed, 'even if one does not use the term "black theology"' in doing so'.[35] The overall tone and effect of the essay is to attempt to divert attention from Black theology, in its inadequacies, back to the issues. In a context other than a conference of Black theologians it would be easier to say that Black theology is dead and its life-support system is diverting attention and resources from the real life crisis of the black community in America and beyond. Is this so surprising? We noted earlier that liberation theologies arise at the same time and decline at the same time. Let me illustrate with regard to Latin America. There is a parallel. As Cornel West has noted, 'beneath this intense intellectual ferment and heated political discourse lurks a hidden truth. *The high moment of liberation theology has passed.*'[36]

In 1998, the year of the Cone conference, there was a conference held in Birmingham, England. One of the speakers was Jon Sobrino, of the first generation of Latin American liberation theologians. I was asked to respond to his lecture. He acknowledged that during the period in which liberation theology had proclaimed God's option for the poor, the poor had become steadily, dramatically poorer. In my response to his lecture I raised this issue with him, referring first of all to Marx's XIth Thesis on Feuerbach: 'The philosophers have only interpreted the world in various ways, the point however is to change it.'[37] To what extent had liberation theology simply provided an interpretation of the poverty of the poor, without actually changing the situation.[38] Marx praised religion as the one voice raised on behalf of the poor living in the worst conditions of European industrialisation. Religion is the 'heart of heartless conditions, the soul of a soulless society'.[39] But this praise quickly turned to criticism. Marx's criticism is that religion made the intolerable tolerable. It provided an interpretation of these intolerable conditions by relating them to the grand narrative of the Providence of God. Theology therefore stole from the mind of the poor the capacity to imagine a better future, stole from the heart the will to bring it about. Liberation theology has not ended the poverty of the poor: how could it? But that does not mean that it has been ineffectual. No, it has had a particular effect. It has given poverty a meaning, it has given the poor a value in virtue of their poverty. It is worth drawing a parallel with Black theology. In an article written 30 years after Black theology first appeared James Cone acknowledged: 'Black suffering is getting worse, not better, and we are more confused than ever about the reasons for it.'[40] There are two issues here. Black theology has not ended the poverty of the ghettos: how could it? But that does not mean that it has been ineffectual. It has provided a racial interpretation of the conditions of black poverty and has provided a theological meaning and value for blackness. But there is a second issue. 'Black suffering is getting worse, not better, *and we are more confused than ever about the reasons for it.*' It is time to turn to the more fundamental issue – the economic reasons for the increase in black poverty. And can it really be true that a man as intelligent and observant as James Hal Cone is more confused than ever about the reasons for it. It is 20 years since Cone first visited South Africa, where, as we have seen, it was made clear that the issue even there and even then was not race but power. It seems that African-American Black theology is determined not to learn from Black theology in South Africa. Closer to home he could have learned from the civil rights activist Bayard Rustin who, according to David Garrow argued that 'the Movement had to turn from a singular focus on race, and confront the basic issues of wealth and poverty in America, but his voice had largely been drowned out'.[41] Is there any excuse for being 'more confused than ever about the reasons for it'? An increasing number of black Americans have a slice of the American pie and an increasing number have gone down the prosperity gospel route. As Chicago pastor Jeremiah Wright observes: 'A growing number of black congregations live on this theological boulevard. They have erected mansions there and have no desire to move to another location.'[42] As we have seen, in spite of the mantra of 'race, gender, class', Black theology has steadfastly refused to address the economic basis of black poverty.

Pastor Wright implies that Black theology has had no influence whatsoever on 'a growing number of black congregations'. Does this imply that it once did? Not according to Emilie Townes, a colleague of James Cone at Union Theological Seminary, New York, as she identifies 'a major flaw' in Black theology.

> Black theology has not had a sustained and integrated impact on the black church in all its manifestations. Though I suspect that the reasons for this are complex, let me point to what I believe to be the major reason: folks refuse to give up whatever privilege they have to help craft a better day for the African American Christian church and the black societies of the United States. We are caught in whirlpools of individualistic narcississm. Even though black theology is largely ignored by the majority of adherents and practitioners of dominant academic discourse, it appears that this weary state of affairs is even more so in the majority of black Christian churches. I do not hear, witness, or see a groundswell of calls for liberation from most black churches. I do not hear calls for living the dream and making a way out of no way. What troubles me about this is that we have little biblical or theological anchor in this. It is as though we in the academy and we in the church are ships passing in the night and we are not even looking for one another. Our continued arrogance and hoarding of our meagre privileges

> must stop, or we need to find another name for ourselves because we have ceased to be Christian.[43]

But is the problem that no one in the academy or the Black church is listening to Black and womanist theology? Not so. Some people in the academy are reading Black theology and some in the Black church are listening, though to judge from Pastor Wright's article, they are not getting much from it. So what is the problem? Blame academics and pastors. There is, however, another possible response. When politicians lose an election, when voters reject their overtures in droves, how do they respond? Do they conclude that there must be something wrong with the message? No, they declare that next time they must explain their message more clearly. The lack of enthusiasm amongst voters is because they did not understand the message. Really? Or did they understand it all too well. Emilie Townes, in a confusingly mixed metaphor, identifies too little 'biblical or theological anchor' in these ships that pass in the night. She identifies 'narcissism', 'arrogance' and even a 'need to find another name for ourselves'. But what if the narcissism and arrogance belonged to the exponents of Black theology. What if the need were to find a new theological agenda which connected with people in todays conditions? And following Gayraud Wilmore we might find that such a theology need no longer be described as Black theology. And following West, it should certainly drop 'the meretricious and flamboyant term "liberation"'.[44] There is the arrogance of Black theology, repeating year after year the same essentialisms and stereotypes which are frankly embarrassingly naive in academic circles. There is the need for a proper analysis of the worsening situation of black poverty, a little more humility in view of the fact that 'we are more confused than ever about the reasons for it'.

Why is this of concern to a white European male? Because the forces of oppression and exploitation are increasingly taking control of the world through the processes of global capitalism. They cannot be successfully opposed simply by progressive Europeans. It requires an alliance of men and women of goodwill throughout the world. In this black Americans could play a vital part, if they read the new context and move their agenda forward.

Notes

1 Marc H. Ellis and Otto Maduro, *The Future of Liberation Theology: essays in honor of Gustavo Gutiérrez*, Orbis Books, Maryknoll, NY, 1989.

2 Karl Barth, *Church Dogmatics*, vol. II, Part I, p. 635.

3 James H. Cone, 'Looking Back and Going Forward: black theology as public theology' in Dwight N. Hopkins (ed.) *Black Faith and Public Talk: critical essays on James H. Cone's Black Theology and Black Power*, Orbis Books, Maryknoll, NY, 1999, p. 256.

4 Dwight N. Hopkins and Sheila Greeve Davaney, *Changing Conversations: religious reflection and cultural analysis*, Routledge, 1996, p. 163.

5 Ibid., p. 160.

[6] Luis G. Pedraja, *Teología: an introduction to Hispanic theology*, Abingdon Press, Nashville, 2003; Miguel De La Torre and Edwin David Aponte, *Introducing Latino/a Theologies*, Orbis Books, Maryknoll, NY, 2001.

[7] Victor Anderson, '"We see through glass darkly": black narrative theology and the opacity of African American religious thought' in Anthony B. Pinn and Benjamin Valentin (eds) *The Ties that Bind: African American and Hispanic American/Latino/a theology in dialogue*, Continuum, 2001, p. 80.

[8] Ibid., p. 91.

[9] Garth Kasimu Baker-Fletcher, *Black Religion After the Million Man March: voices on the future*, Orbis Books, Maryknoll, NY, 1999 (1998), p. 27.

[10] Ibid., p. 28. See also these themes in Garth Baker-Fletcher, *Xodus: an African American male journey*, Fortress Press, Minneapolis, 1996.

[11] Baker-Fletcher, *Black Religion After the Million Man March*, p. 19.

[12] Ibid., p. 21.

[13] See also Horace Griffin, 'Their Own Received Them Not: African American lesbian and gays in black churches', *Theology and Sexuality*, No. 12 (March 2000).

[14] James H. Cone, *The Spirituals and the Blues*, Seabury Press, New York, 1972.

[15] The journal *Black Sacred Music: a journal of theomusicology* is published by Duke University Press, Durham, NC.

[16] Jon Michael Spencer, *Protest and Praise: sacred music of black religion*, Fortress Press, Minneapolis, 1990, p. viii. See also his *Sing a New Song: liberating black hymnody*, Fortress Press, Minneapolis, 1994.

[17] In Hopkins and Cummings, *Cut Loose Your Stammering Tongue*, pp. 135–6.

[18] See, for example, Anthony B. Pinn, *Varieties of African American Religious Experience*, Fortress Press, Minneapolis, 1998; Albert J. Raboteau, *A Fire in the Bones: reflections on African-American religious history*, Beacon, Boston, 1995; Gayraud S. Wilmore (ed.) *African American Religious Studies: an interdisciplinary anthology*, Duke University Press, Durham, NC, 1989; related studies such as Ennis Barrington Edmonds, *Rastafari: from outcasts to culture bearers*, Oxford University Press, 2003 and Yvonne Chireau and Nathaniel Deutsch (eds) *Black Zion: African American religious encounters with Judaism*, Oxford University Press, 2000.

[19] Anthony B. Pinn, *By These Hands: a documentary of African American humanism*, New York University Press, 2001; *Varieties of African American Religious Experience*, Fortress Press, Minneapolis, 1998; *Terror and Triumph: the nature of black religion*, Fortress Press, Minneapolis, 2003.

[20] Anthony B. Pinn, '1969–99 Reflections on the maturation of Black theology', *Reviews in Religion and Theology* (1999/1), p. 23.

[21] Anthony B. Pinn, 'Black Theology Then and Now: a second generation assessment', *Reviews in Religion and Theology* (2002/5), p. 405.

[22] Anthony B. Pinn, 'Keep on Keepin' On: reflections on "Get on the Bus" and the language of movement' in Baker-Fletcher, *Black Religion After the Million Man March*.

[23] M.K. Asante, *Afrocentricity*, Africa World Press, Trenton, NJ, 1988; see also S. Howe, *Afrocentrism: mythical pasts and imagined homes*, Verso, 1998.

[24] Cheryl Sanders (ed.) *Living the Intersection: womanism and Afrocentrism in theology*, Fortess Press, Minneapolis, 1995. Delores Williams has contributed a chapter to this book, 'Afrocentrism and Male–Female Relations in Church and Society', in which she describes Asante's work as 'women-exclusive' and 'thoroughly sexist' (pp. 45, 50). She also claims that Asante 'romanticizes African heritage' by ignoring the fact that women were oppressed by men in African societies before the intervention of colonialism (p. 52).

[25] West, *Race Matters*, p. 36.

[26] Ibid., p. 36.

[27] Ibid., p. 43.

[28] Hopkins, *Black Faith and Public Talk*, p. 255.

[29] Gayraud S. Wilmore, 'Black Theology at the Turn of the Century: some unmet needs and challenges' in Hopkins, *Black Faith and Public Talk*, p. 236.

[30] Ibid.

[31] Ibid., p. 239.

[32] Ibid., p. 240.

[33] Ibid., p. 241.

[34] Ibid., p. 242.

[35] Ibid., p. 237.

[36] West, *Reader*, p. 394.

[37] Marx/Engels, *Collected Works*, 5.5.

[38] Alistair Kee, 'The Conservatism of Liberation Theology: four questions for Jon Sobrino', *Political Theology*, Issue 3 (November 2000), pp. 30–43.

[39] I have preferred the translation given by T.B. Bottomore, *Karl Marx: early writings*, C.A. Watts, 1963, p. 44.

[40] James H. Cone, 'Calling the Oppressors to Account: God and black suffering' in Linda E. Thomas (ed.) *Living Stones in the Household of God: the legacy and future of Black Theology*, Fortress Press, Minneapolis, 2004, p. 10.

[41] David Garrow, *Martin Luther King: challenging America at its core*, Democratic Socialists of America, 1983, p. 28, quoted by Robert Michael Franklin, 'An Ethic of Hope: the moral thought of Martin Luther King, Jr.', *Union Seminary Quarterly Review*, 11.4 (1986), p. 44.

[42] Jeremiah Wright, 'Doing Black Theology in the Black Church' in Thomas, *Living Stones in the Household of God*, p. 15.

[43] Emilie Townes, 'On Keeping Faith with the Center' in Thomas, *Living Stones in the Household of God*, pp. 200–201.

[44] West, *Prophesy Deliverance*, p. 112.

Bibliography

Aldred, Joe, *Respect: Understanding Caribbean British Christianity*, Epworth, 2005.

——— *Preaching with Power: Sermons by Black pastors*, Cassell, London, 1998.

——— *Sisters with Power*, Continuum Books, London, 2000.

——— *Praying with Power*, Continuum Books, London, 2000.

Alexander, Claire, *The Art of Being Black: the creation of Black British youth identities*, Clarendon Press, Oxford, 1996.

Anderson, Victor, *Beyond Ontological Blackness: an essay in African American religious and cultural criticism*, Continuum, New York, 1999 (1995).

——— *Divine Grotesquery*, Continuum, 2002.

——— '"We see through glass darkly": black narrative theology and the opacity of African American religious thought' in Anthony B. Pinn and Benjamin Valentin (eds) *The Ties that Bind: African American and Hispanic American/Latino/a theology in dialogue*, Continuum, 2001.

Andolsen, Barbara Hilkert, *Daughters of Jefferson, Daughters of Bootblacks*, Mercer University Press, Macon, Ga., 1986.

——— 'Roundtable: racism in the women's movement', *Journal of Feminist Studies in Religion*, 4.1 (1988).

Asante, M.K., *Afrocentricity*, Africa World Press, New Jersey, 1988.

Bailey, Randall C. (ed.) *Yet With a Steady Beat: contemporary U.S. Afrocentric biblical interpretation*, Society of Biblical Literature, Atlanta, Ga., 2003.

Baker-Fletcher, Garth [Kasimu], *Xodus: an African American male journey*, Fortress Press, Minneapolis, 1996.

——— *Black Religion After the Million Man March: voices on the future*, Orbis Books, Maryknoll, NY, 1999 (1998).

Banton, Michael, *Ethnic and Racial Consciousness*, Longman, 1997 (1988).

Barrington Edmonds, Ennis, *Rastafari: from outcasts to culture bearers*, Oxford University Press, 2003.

Barth, Karl, *The Epistle to the Romans*, trans. Hoskyns, Oxford University Press, 1933.

——— *Church Dogmatics*, vol. II, Part I, T. & T. Clark, Edinburgh, 1957. Baumann, Martin, 'A Diachronic View of Diaspora, the Significance of Religion and Hindu Trinidadians' in Waltraud Kokot, Khachig Tölölyan and Carolin Alfonso (eds) *Diaspora, Identity and Religion: new directions in theory and research*, Routledge, 2004.

Beckford, Robert, *Jesus is Dread: Black theology and Black culture in Britain*, Darton, Longman and Todd, 1998.

——— *Dread and Pentecostal: a political theology for the Black Church in Britain*, SPCK, 2000.

——— *God of the Rahtid: redeeming rage*, Darton, Longman & Todd, 2001.

——— *God and the Gangs: an urban toolkit for those who won't be sold out, bought out or scared out*, Darton, Longman & Todd, 2004.

——— *Jesus Dub: Theology, Music and Social Change*, Routledge, 2006.

Biko, Steve, *I Write What I Like*, The Bowerdean Press, 1978.

Blassingame, John W., *Slave Testimony: two centuries of letters, speeches, interviews and autobiographies*, Louisiana State University Press, Baton Rouge, 1977.

Blyden, Edward W., *Christianity, Islam and the Negro Race*, Edinburgh University Press, 1967 (1887).

Boesak, Allan, *Coming in Out of the Wilderness: a comparative interpretation of the ethics of Martin Luther King and Malcolm X*, Kamper Cahier No. 28, Kampen, 1976.

——— *Farewell to Innocence: a socio-ethical study on Black Theology and Black Power*, 1976, published as *Black Theology Black Power*, Mowbrays, 1978.

——— *Black and Reformed: apartheid, liberation and the Calvinist tradition*,ed. Leonard Sweetman, Orbis Books, Maryknoll, NY, 1986 (1984).

Bonino, José Miguez, *Christians and Marxists: the mutual challenge of revolution*, Hodder & Stoughton, 1976.

Bottomore, T.B. (ed.) *Karl Marx: early writings*, C.A. Watts, 1963.

Brandon, S.G.F., *Jesus and the Zealots: a study of the political factor in primitive Christianity*, Manchester University Press, 1967.

Brown, Norman O., *Life Against Death: the psychoanalytical meaning of history*, Sphere Books Ltd., 1968 (original 1959).

Bryan, Beverley, Dadzie, Stella and Scafe, Suzanne, *The Heart of the Race: black women's lives in Britain*, Virago Press, 1985.

Bueno, Lourdes, 'Dominican Women's Experiences of Return Migration: the life stories of five women' in Patricia R. Pessar (ed.) *Caribbean Circuits: new directions in the study of Caribbean migration*, Center for Migration Studies, New York, 1997.

Butler, Judith, *Gender Trouble: feminism and the subversion of identity*, Routledge, 1999 (1990).

Calley, Malcolm, *God's People: West Indian Pentecostal sects in England*, Oxford University Press, 1965.

Cannon, Katie G., *Black Womanist Ethics*, Scholars Press, Atlanta, Ga., 1988.

——— 'Womanist Perspectival Discourse and Canon Formation', *Journal of Feminist Studies in Religion*, 9.1 (1993).

——— *Katie's Canon: womanism and the soul of the black community*, Continuum, New York, 1995.

——— 'Unearthing Ethical Treasure: the intrusive markers of social class', *Union Theological Seminary Quarterly Review*, 53.3–4 (1999).

Cantwell Smith, Wilfred, *The Meaning and End of Religion*, SPCK, 1978 (1962).

Carby, Hazel V., 'White Woman Listen! Black feminism and the boundaries of sisterhood' in CCCS, *The Empire Strikes Back: race and racism in 70s Britain*, Hutchinson, 1982.

Carmichael, Stokely and Hamilton, Charles V., *Black Power: the politics of liberation in America*, Penguin Books, 1969 (1967).

Carter, Trevor, *Shattering Illusions: West Indians in British politics*, Lawrence & Wishart, 1986.

Caute, David, *Fanon,* Fontana, 1970.

Centre for Contemporary Cultural Studies (CCCS), *The Empire Strikes Back: race and racism in 70s Britain*, Hutchinson, 1982.

Césaire, Aimé, *Return to My Native Land,* Penguin Books, 1970 (1956).

Chamberlain, Mary, *Narratives of Exile and Return*, Macmillan Caribbean, 1997.

Chike, Chigor 'Black Theology in Britain – One Decade On', *Black Theology*, 4.2, 2006.

Chireau, Yvonne and Deutsch, Nathaniel (eds) *Black Zion: African American religious encounters with Judaism*, Oxford University Press, 2000.

Clarke, John Henrik (ed.) *Marcus Garvey and the Vision of Africa*, Random House, New York, 1974. Cleage, Albert, *The Black Messiah*, Sheed & Ward, 1968.

——— *Black Christian Nationalism*, William Morrow & Co., New York, 1972. Coleman, Kate, 'Black Women in Theology', *Black Theology*, Issue 3 (1999).

——— 'Black Theology and Black Liberation: a womanist perspective', *Black Theology in Britain: a journal of Contextual Praxis*, Issue 2 (1999).

Cone, James H., *Black Theology and Black Power*, Seabury Press, New York, 1969.

——— *A Black Theology of Liberation*, Orbis Books, Maryknoll, NY, 1986 (1970).

——— *The Spirituals and the Blues*, Seabury Press, New York, 1972.

——— *For My People: Black theology and the Black church*, Orbis Books, Maryknoll, NY, 1984.

——— 'Looking Back and Going Forward: black theology as public theology' in Dwight N. Hopkins (ed.) *Black Faith and Public Talk: critical essays on James H. Cone's Black Theology and Black Power*, Orbis Books, Maryknoll, NY, 1999.

——— 'Calling the Oppressors to Account: God and black suffering' in Linda E. Thomas (ed.) *Living Stones in the Household of God: the legacy and future of Black Theology*, Fortress Press, Minneapolis, 2004.

——— 'Theology's Great Sin: silence in the face of White Supremacy', *Black Theology: an international journal*, 2.2 (July 2004).

Copeland, Shawn, 'Wading through Many Sorrows' in Emilie M. Townes (ed.) *A Troubling in My Soul: womanist perspectives on evil and suffering*, Orbis Books, Maryknoll, NY, 1996 (1993).

Cox, Oliver C., *Caste, Class and Race*, Doubleday, Garden City, NY, 1948.

Culpepper, Emily Erwin, 'New Tools for Theology: writings by women of color', *Journal of Feminist Studies in Religion*, 4.2 (1988).

Daye, Sharon, *Middle-Class Blacks in Britain: a racial fraction of a class group or a class fraction of a racial group?*, Macmillan, 1994.

De La Torre, Miguel and Aponte, Edwin David, *Introducing Latino/a Theologies*, Orbis Books, Maryknoll, NY, 2001.

de Beauvoir, Simone, *The Second Sex*, trans. and ed. H.M. Pashley, Penguin Books, 1983.

De Generis Humani Varietate Nativa, reproduced in Michael Banton, *Ethnic and Racial Consciousness*, Longman, 1997 (1988).

de Klerk, W.A., *The Puritans in Africa: a history of Afrikanerdom*, Penguin Books, 1976.

DeMott, Benjamin, *The Imperial Middle Way: why Americans can't think straight about class*, Yale University Press, New Haven, 1992 (original 1990).

Douglas, Kelly Brown, *The Black Christ*, Orbis Books, Maryknoll, NY, 1998 (1994).

——— *Sexuality and the Black Church: a womanist perpsective*, Orbis Books, Maryknoll, NY, 1999.

Du Bois, W.E.B., *The Souls of Black Folk*, Dover Publications, New York, 1944 (1903).

Ebeling, Gerhard, *Word and Faith*, Fortress Press, Philadelphia, 1963.

Ellis, Ieuan, *Seven Against Christ: a study of 'Essays and Reviews'*, E.J. Brill, Leiden, 1980.

Ellis, Marc H. and Maduro, Otto, *The Future of Liberation Theology: essays in honor of Gustavo Gutiérrez*, Orbis Books, Maryknoll, NY, 1989.

Essien-Udom, E.U., 'Introduction' in Amy Jacques Garvey, *Philosophy and Opinions of Marcus Garvey* (2nd edn), Frank Cass & Co., 1967 (1923).

Evans, James, 'African-American Christianity and the Postmodern Condition', *Journal of the American Academy of Religion*, LVIII.2 (Summer 1990).

Fanon, Franz, *Black Skin/White Masks*, Paladin, 1970 (1952).

——— *A Dying Colonialism*, Penguin Books, 1970 (1959).

——— *The Wretched of the Earth*, Penguin Books, 1967 (1961).

——— *Toward the African Revolution*, Penguin Books, 1970 (1964).

Felder, Cain Hope, *Troubling Biblical Waters: race, class and family*, Orbis Books, Maryknoll, NY, 1989.

——— (ed.) *Stony the Road We Trod: African American biblical interpretation*, Fortress Press, Minneapolis, 1991.

Foucault, Michel, *The Order of Things: an archaeology of the human sciences*, Routledge, 2002 (1966).

——— *The Archaeology of Knowledge*, Routledge, 2002 (1969).

Franklin, Robert Michael, 'An Ethic of Hope: the moral thought of Martin Luther King, Jr.', *Union Seminary Quarterly Review*, 11.4 (1986).

Friedan, Betty, *The Feminine Mystique*, Penguin Books, 1971.

Fryer, Peter, *Staying Power: the history of black people in Britain*, Pluto Press, 1984.

Garrow, David, *Martin Luther King: challenging America at its core*, Democratic Socialists of America, 1983.

Garvey, Amy Jacques, *The Philosophy and Opinions of Marcus Garvey*, Frank Cass & Co., 1967 (1923).

Gerloff, Roswith, *A Plea for British Black Theologies*, Peter Lang, Frankfurt, 2 volumes, 1992.

Gifford, Paul, *Christianity and Politics in Doe's Liberia*, Cambridge University Press, 1993.

Gilroy, Paul, *There Ain't No Black in the Union Jack*, Routledge, 1995 (1987).

Goba, Bonganjalo, 'The Black Consciousness Movement: its impact on black theology' in Itumeleng J. Mosala and Buti Tlhagale (eds) *The Unquestionable Right to be Free: essays in black theology*, Skotaville Publishers, Johannesburg, 1986.

Grant, Jacquelyn, *White Women's Christ and Black Women's Jesus: feminist Christology and womanist response*, Scholars Press, Atlanta, Ga., 1989.

Grant, Paul and Patel, Raj (eds.) *A Time to Speak*, Racial Justice Black Theology Working Group, Birmingham, 1990.

——— *A Time to Act*, Black and Third World Working Group, Birmingham, 1992.

Gregory of Nyssa, *On the Divinity of the Father and the Son*, PG 46, 557 C.

Griffin, Horace, 'Their Own Received Them Not: African American lesbian and gays in black churches', *Theology and Sexuality*, No. 12 (March 2000).

Guarnizo, Luis Eduardo, 'Going Home: class, gender and household transformation among Dominican return migrants' in Patricia R. Pessar (ed.) *Caribbean Circuits: new directions in the study of Caribbean migration*, Center for Migration Studies, New York, 1997.

Guevara, Che, *The Complete Bolivian Diaries*, Allen & Unwin, 1968.

Gutiérrez, Gustavo, 'The Meaning of Development: notes on a theology of liberation', *In Search of a Theology of Development*, SODEPAX, Geneva, n.d.

——— *A Theology of Liberation*, Orbis, Maryknoll, NY, 1973.

Harvey, David, *The Condition of Post-Modernity*, Blackwell, 1990.

Hayes, Diana, *And Still We Rise: an introduction to black liberation theology*, Paulist Press, New York, 1996.

Hegel, G.W.F., *Logic*, Oxford University Press, 1975 (1812–16).

——— *The Philosophy of History*, Willey Book Co., New York, 1900.

Hood, Robert E., *Begrimed and Black: Christian traditions on black and blackness*, Fortress Press, Minneapolis, 1994.

hooks, bell (Gloria Watkins) *Ain't I a Woman: black women and feminism*, Pluto Press, 1982.

——— *Feminist Theory: from margin to center*, South End Press, Boston, 1984.

——— *Talking Back: thinking feminist, thinking black*, South End Press, Boston, 1989.

——— *Where We Stand: Class Matters*, Routledge, 2000.

Hopkins, Dwight N., *Shoes that Fit Our Feet: sources for a constructive black theology*, Orbis Books, Maryknoll, NY, 1993.

——— *Introducing Black Theology of Liberation*, Orbis, Maryknoll, NY, 1999.

——— *Heart and Head: black theology – past, present and future*, Palgrave, New York, 2002.

——— and Maimela, Simon S. (eds) *We Are One Voice*, Skotaville, Braamfontein, SA, 1989.

——— and Cummings, George C.L. (eds) *Cut Loose Your Stammering Tongue: black theology in slave narratives*, Westminster John Knox Press, Louisville, Ky., 2003 (1991).

——— and Davaney, Sheila Greeve, *Changing Conversations: religious reflection and cultural analysis*, Routledge, 1996.

Howe, S., *Afrocentrism: mythical pasts and imagined homes*, Verso, 1998.

Howell-Baker, Maxine Eudalee, 'Towards a Womanist Pneumatological Pedagogy: an investigation into the development and implementation of a theological pedagogy by and for the marginalized', *Black Theology*, 3.1, 2005.

Hymans, Jacques Louis, *Léopold Sédar Senghor: an intellectual biography*, Edinburgh University Press, 1971.

Irigaray, Luce, 'Equal to Whom?' in Graham Ward (ed.) *The Postmodern God: a theological reader*, Blackwell, 1997.

Isiorho, David 'Black Theology, Englishness and the Church of England', in Jagessar and Reddie (eds) *Postcolonial Black British Theology*, Epworth, 2007.

Jagessar, Michael and Burns, Stephen 'Liturgical Studies and Christian Worship: the postcolonial challenge', *Black Theology*, 5.1, 2007.

Jagessar, Michael N. and Reddie, Anthony G. (eds), *Postcolonial Black British Theology*, Epworth, 2007.

James, Winston and Harris, Clive (eds) *Inside Babylon: the Caribbean diaspora in Britain*, Verso, 1993. Joly, Danièle, *Blacks and Britannity*, Ashgate, 2001.

Kokot, Waltraud, Tölölyan, Khachig and Alfonso, Carolin (eds) *Diaspora, Identity and Religion: new directions in theory and research*, Routledge, 2004.

Kee, Alistair, *Seeds of Liberation*, SCM Press, 1973.

——— *Marx and the Failure of Liberation Theology*, SCM Press, 1991.

——— 'The Conservatism of Liberation Theology: four questions for Jon Sobrino', *Political Theology*, Issue 3 (November 2000).

King Jr., Martin Luther, *Where do We Go from Here: chaos or community*, Harper & Row, 1967.

Lapping, Brian, *Apartheid: a history*, Grafton Books, 1986.

Lewis, Marjorie, 'Diaspora Dialogue: womanist theology in engagement with aspects of the Black British and Jamaican experience', *Black Theology*, 2.2, 2004, p. 100.

Lienesch, Michael, *Redeeming America: piety and politics in the New Christian Right*, University of North Carolina Press, 1993, chap. 3.

Lorde, Audre, *Sister Outsider: essays and speeches*, The Cross Press, Trumansburg, NY, 1984.

Lynch, Hollis R. (ed.) *Selected Letters of Edward Wilmot Blyden*, KTO Press, New York, 1978.

——— (ed.) *Black Spokesman: selected published writings of Edward Wilmot Blyden*, Frank Cass & Co., 1971.

Magida, Arthur J., *Prophet of Rage: a life of Louis Farrakhan and his nation*, Basic Books, New York, 1996.

Maimela, Simon S. and Hopkins, Dwight N. (eds) *We Are One Voice*, Skotaville, Braamfontein, SA, 1989.

Malcolm X, *The Autobiography of Malcolm X, with the assistance of Alex Haley*, Penguin Books, 1968 (1965).

Mandela, Nelson, *The Struggle is My Life*, International Defence and Aid Fund for Southern Africa, 1978.

Marcuse, Herbart, *One Dimensional Man*, Sphere Books, 1970.

Markovitz, Irving Leonard, *Léopold Sédar Senghor and the Politics of Negritude*, Heinemann, 1969.

Marx, Karl and Engels, Frederick, *Collected Works*, Lawrence & Wishart, 1973–.

——— 'The Critique of Hegel's Philosophy of Right: introduction' in *Karl Marx: early writings*, trans. and ed. T.B. Bottomore, C.A. Watts & Co., 1963.

McConnell, D.R., *A Different Gospel: a historical and biblical analysis of the modern faith movement*, Hendrickson Publishers, Peabody, MA, 1988.

Mercadante, Linda, 'Roundtable: racism in the women's movement', *Journal of Feminist Studies in Religion*, 4.1 (1988).

Milton, Giles, *White Gold: the extraordinary story of Thomas Pellow and North Africa's one million European slaves*, Hodder, 2004.

Milwood, Robinson A., *Suspension: a testimony of faith, suffering and perseverance*, Stoke Newington Mission, 2002.

——— *Liberation and Mission: a black experience*, London: African Caribbean Education Resource, 1997.

Mirza, Heidi Safia (ed.) *Black British Feminism: a reader*, Routledge, 1997.

Mitchem, Stephanie, *Introducing Womanist Theology*, Orbis Books, Maryknoll, NY, 2002.

Mofokeng, Takatso, 'Black Theological Perspectives, Past and Present' in Simon S. Maimela and Dwight N. Hopkins (eds) *We Are One Voice*, Skotaville, Braamfontein, SA, 1989.

Moltmann-Wendel, E., *Humanity in God*, SCM Press, 1983.

Moore, Basil (ed.) *Black Theology: the South African voice*, C. Hurst & Co., 1973.

Mosala, Itumeleng J., *Biblical Hermeneutics and Black Theology in South Africa*, William B. Eerdmans Publishing Co., Grand Rapids, Mich., 1989.

——— and Tlhagale, Buti (eds) *The Unquestionable Right to be Free: essays in black theology*, Skotaville Publishers, Johannesburg, 1986.

Motlhabi, Mokgethi, 'Black Theology and Authority' in Basil Moore (ed.) *Black Theology: the South African Voice*, C. Hurst & Co., 1973.

——— 'The Historical Origins of Black Theology' in Itumeleng J. Mosala and Buti Tlhagale (eds) *The Unquestionable Right to be Free: essays in black theology*, Skotaville Publishers, Johannesburg, 1986.

Ngubane, J.B., 'Theological Roots of the African Independent Church and their Challenge to Black Theology' in Itumeleng J. Mosala and Buti Tlhagale (eds) *The Unquestionable Right to be Free: essays in black theology*, Skotaville Publishers, Johannesburg, 1986.

Nietzsche, Friedrich, 'On Truth and Falsity in Their Extramoral Sense', *Philosophical Writings*, ed. Reinhold Grimm and Caroline Molina y Vedia, Continuum, 1995.

Pagels, Elaine, *The Gnostic Gospels*, Penguin Books, 1986.

Pedraja, Luis G., *Teología: an introduction to Hispanic theology*, Abingdon Press, Nashville, 2003.

Pessar, Patricia R. (ed.) *Caribbean Circuits: new directions in the study of Caribbean migration*, Center for Migration Studies, New York, 1997.

Pilkington, Andrew, 'The Offence of the West Indian: political leadership and the communal option' in Pnina Werbner and Muhammad Anwar (eds) *Black and Ethnic Leadership in Britain: the cultural dimensions of political action*, Routledge, 1991.

——— *Racial Disadvantage and Ethnic Diversity in Britain*, Palgrave Macmillan, 2003.

Pinn, Anthony B., *Varieties of African American Religious Experience*, Fortress Press, Minneapolis, 1998.

——— '1969–99 Reflections on the maturation of Black theology', *Reviews in Religion and Theology* (1999/1), p. 23.

——— (ed.) *By These Hands: a documentary history of African American humanism*, New York University Press, 2001.

——— 'Black Theology Then and Now: a second generation assessment', *Reviews in Religion and Theology* (2002/5).

——— *Terror and Triumph: the nature of black religion*, Fortress Press, Minneapolis, 2003.

——— 'Keep on Keepin' On: reflections on "Get on the Bus" and the language of movement' in Garth Baker-Fletcher, *Black Religion After the Million Man March: voices on the future*, Orbis Books, Maryknoll, NY, 1999 (1998).

——— and Valentin, Benjamin (eds) *The Ties that Bind: African American and Hispanic American/Latino/a theology in dialogue*, Continuum, 2001.

Pro Veritate, 'An Open Letter Concerning Nationalism, National Socialism and Christianity', *Pro Veritae* Supplement (July 1971).

Raboteau, Albert J., *A Fire in the Bones: reflections on African-American religious history*, Beacon, Boston, 1995.

Rawick, George P. (ed.) *The Slave Narrative Collection: a composite autobiography*, Greenwood Publishing Co., Westport, Conn., 1972, 1977, 1979.

Reddie, Anthony G., *Nobodies to Somebodies: a practial theology for education and liberation*, Epworth Press, 2003.

Redfearn, Caroline, 'The Nature of Homophobia in the Black Church', in Michael N. Jagessar and Anthony G. Reddie (eds) *Postcolonial Black British Theology*, Epworth Press, 2007.

Reid-Salmon, Delroy A. 'Out of Every Tribe and Nation: the making of the Caribbean Diasporan Church' in Michael N. Jagessar and Anthony G. Reddie (eds) *Postcolonial Black British Theology*, Epworth Press, 2007.

Riggs, Marcia Y., 'A Clarion Call to Awake! Arise! Act!' in Emilie M. Townes (ed.) *A Troubling in my Soul: womanist perspectives on evil and suffering*, Orbis Books, Maryknoll, NY, 1996 (1993).

Roberts, J. Deotis, *Liberation and Reconciliation: a black theology*, Westminster Press, Philadelphia, Pa., 1971.

——— *A Black Political Theology*, Westminster Press, Philadelphia, Pa., 1974.

——— *The Roots of a Black Future: family and church*, Westminster Press, Philadelphia, Pa., 1980.

——— *Black Theology Today: liberation and contextualization*, Edwin Mellon Press, New York, 1983.

——— *Black Theology in Dialogue*, Westminster Press, Philadelphia, Pa., 1987.

Robinson, J.M. (ed.) 'The Gospel of Philip', *The Nag Hammadi Library in English*, E.J. Brill,1984.

Ruether, Rosemary Radford, 'A White Feminist Response to Black and Womanist Theologies' in Linda E. Thomas (ed.) *Living Stones in the Household of God: the legacy and future of Black Theology*, Fortress Press, Minneapolis, 2004.

Sanders, Cheryl, 'Roundtable: Christian ethics and theology in womanist perspective', *Journal of Feminist Studies in Religion*, 5.2 (1989).

——— (ed.) *Living the Intersection: womanism and Afrocentrism in theology*, Fortress Press, Minneapolis, 1995.

Sartre, Jean-Paul, 'Preface' to Franz Fanon, *The Wretched of the Earth*, Penguin Books, 1967 (1961).

Schnier, Mariam, *Feminism: the essential historical writings, edited with an introduction and commentaries*, Vintage Books, New York, 1972.

Sebidi, Lebamang, 'The Dynamics of the Black Struggle and its Implications for Black Theology' in Itumeleng J. Mosala and Buti Tlhagale (eds) *The Unquestionable Right to be Free: essays in black theology*, Skotaville Publishers, Johannesburg, 1986.

Senghor, Léopold, *African Socialism: a report on the constitutive congress of the Party of African Federation*, American Society of African Culture, New York, 1959.

——— 'Remarks on Negritude', *Conference of African Literature in French*, University of Dakar, 1963.

——— 'Edward Wilmot Blyden, Precursor of Negritude', Foreword to Hollis R. Lynch (ed.) *Selected Letters of Edward Wilmot Blyden*, KTO Press, New York, 1978.

Shukra, Kalbir, *The Changing Patterns of Black Politics in Britain*, Pluto Press, 1998.

Singh, Robert, *The Farrakhan Phenomenon: race, reaction and the paranoid style in American politics*, Georgetown University Press, Washington, DC, 1997.

Smith, Adam, *The Theory of Moral Sentiments*, Clarendon Press, Oxford, 1976 (1759).
Solomos, John, *Race and Racism in Contemporary Britain*, Macmillan, 1989.
Spencer, Jon Michael, *Protest and Praise: sacred music of black religion*, Fortress Press, Minneapolis, 1990.
——— *Sing a New Song: liberating black hymnody*, Fortress Press, Minneapolis, 1994.
——— *The New Colored People: the mixed-race movement in America*,New York University Press, 1997.
Spleth, Janice, *Léopold Sédar Senghor*, Twayne Publishers, Boston, 1985.
Starling, Marion Wilson, *The Slave Narrative: its place in American history*, Howard University Press, Washington, DC, 1988.
Thomas, Linda E. (ed.) *Living Stones in the Household of God: the legacy and future of Black Theology*, Fortress Press, Minneapolis, 2004.
Townes, Emilie M. (ed.) *A Troubling in my Soul: womanist perspectives on evil and suffering*, Orbis Books, Maryknoll, NY, 1996 (1993).
——— *Womanist Justice, Womanist Hope*, Scholars Press, Atlanta, Ga., 1993.
——— 'On Keeping Faith with the Center' in Linda E. Thomas (ed.) *Living Stones in the Household of God: the legacy and future of Black Theology*, Fortress Press, Minneapolis, 2004.
Vaillant, Janet G., *Black, French and African: a life of Léopold Senghor*, Harvard University Press, Cambridge, Mass., 1990.
van der Ross, Richard E., 'Foreword' in Jon Michael Spencer, *The New Colored People: the mixed-race movement in America*, New York University Press, 1997.
Vincent, Theodore G., *Black Power and the Garvey Movement*, The Ramparts Press, New York, 1975.
Walker, Alice, *The Color Purple*, The Women's Press, London, 1983.
——— *The Complete Stories*, The Women's Press, London, 1994.
——— *In Search of Our Mothers' Gardens*, The Women's Press, London, 1994.
——— *Anything We Love Can Be Saved: a writer's activism*, The Women's Press, London, 1997.
——— 'The Only Reason you Wanting to go to Heaven is that you have been Driven out of your Mind' in Anthony B. Pinn (ed.) *By These Hands: a documentary history of African American humanism*, New York University Press, 2001.
Walvin, James, *Black and White: the Negro in English society 1555–1945*, Allen Lane, 1973.
Ward, Graham (ed.) *The Postmodern God: a theological reader*, Blackwell, 1997.
Werbner, Pnina and Anwar, Muhammad (eds) *Black and Ethnic Leadership in Britain: the cultural dimensions of political action*, Routledge, 1991.
West, Cornel, *Prophesy Deliverance: an Afro-American revolutionary Christianity*, Westminster Press, Philadelphia, Pa., 1982.
——— *Prophetic Fragments*, William B. Eerdmans, Grand Rapids, Mich., 1988.
——— *Keeping Faith: philosophy and race in America*, Routledge, 1993.
——— *Race Matters*, Beacon Press, Boston, 1993.

——— *The Cornel West Reader*, Basic Civitas Books, 1999.

West, Traci C., *Wounds of the Spirit: black women, violence and resistance ethics*, New York University Press, 1999.

White, John, *Black Leadership in America 1895–1968*, Longman, 1985.

Williams, Delores, 'Lesbian and Feminist Theology', *Journal of Feminist Studies in Religion*, 2.2 (1986).

——— *Sisters in the Wilderness: the challenge of womanist God-talk*, Orbis Books, Maryknoll, NY, 1994 (1993).

——— 'Womanist/Feminist Dialogue: problems and possibilities' *Journal of Feminist Studies in Religion*, 9.1–2 (1993).

——— 'Afrocentrism and Male–Female Relations in Church and Society' in Cheryl Sanders (ed.) *Living the Intersection: womanism and Afrocentrism in theology*, Fortress Press, Minneapolis, 1995.

Wilmore, Gayraud S., *Black Religion and Black Radicalism*, Doubleday & Co., New York, 1972.

——— (ed.) *African American Religious Studies: an interdisciplinary anthology*, Duke University Press, Durham, NC, 1989.

——— 'Black Theology at the Turn of the Century: some unmet needs and challenges' in Dwight N. Hopkins (ed.) *Black Faith and Public Talk: critical essays on James H. Cone's Black Theology and Black Power*, Orbis Books, Maryknoll, NY, 1999.

Wright, Jeremiah, 'Doing Black Theology in the Black Church' in Linda E. Thomas (ed.) *Living Stones in the Household of God: the legacy and future of Black Theology*, Fortress Press, Minneapolis, 2004.

Woods, Donald, *Biko*, Paddington Press, 1978.

Name Index

Subject Index

Biblical References